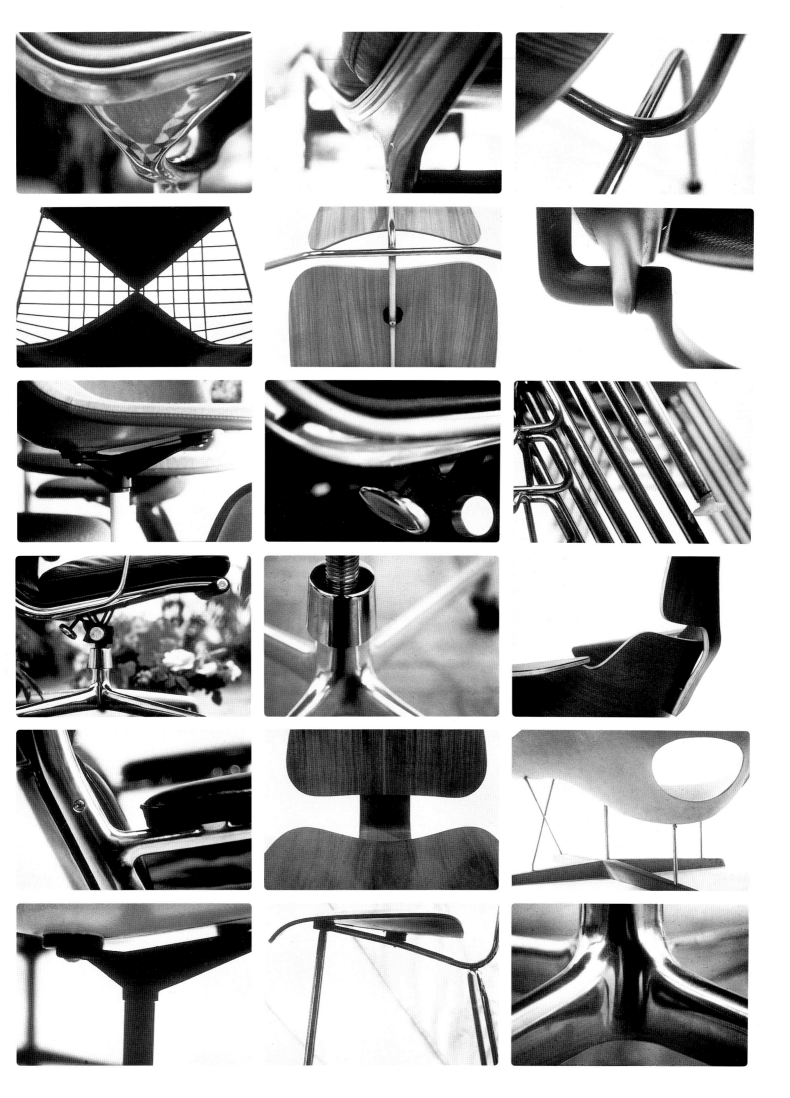

Eames design

The Work of the Office of Charles and Ray Eames

John Neuhart   Marilyn Neuhart   Ray Eames

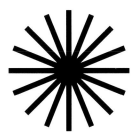

Abrams, New York

Editor: Charles Miers
Designers: John Neuhart and Marilyn Neuhart

All photographs, drawings, and illustrations are the property of the estate of Ray Eames or of John and Marilyn Neuhart

Frontispiece: Charles and Ray Eames in October 1976. This photograph was used in the title panel for the exhibition Connections: The Work of Charles and Ray Eames (Wright Art Gallery, University of California, Los Angeles, California; December 6, 1976–February 7, 1977)

Pages 1 and 452: details of furniture designed by the Eames Office, 1944–1978

Library of Congress Cataloging-in-Publication Data

Neuhart, John.
Eames design: the work of the office of Charles and Ray Eames by John and Marilyn Neuhart with Ray Eames.
p. cm.
Bibliography: p.453
ISBN 978-0-8109-0879-6
1. Eames Office. 2. Design—United States—History—20th century. I. Eames, Charles . II. Eames, Ray. III. Neuhart, Marilyn. IV. Title.
NK1535.E25N48   1989
745.4 4922—dc19   89–169
                                              CIP

Copyright © 1989 John Neuhart, Marilyn Neuhart, and the Estate of Ray Eames

Published in 1989 by Abrams, an imprint of ABRAMS. All rights reserved. No portion of this book may be reproduced, stored in a retrieval system, or transmitted in any form or by any means, mechanical, electronic, photocopying, recording, or otherwise, without written permission from the publisher.

Printed and bound in China
20 19 18 17 16 15 14 13 12 11 10

Abrams books are available at special discounts when purchased in quantity for premiums and promotions as well as fundraising or educational use. Special editions can also be created to specification. For details, contact specialsales@abramsbooks.com or the address below.

115 West 18th Street
New York, NY 10011
www.abramsbooks.com

901 Washington Boulevard, Venice, California, site of the Molded Plywood Division of Evans Products and the Eames Office

Office street number

Reception area

Contents

	Introduction	8
	What Is Design?	13
	Charles and Ray Eames	16
1941	Experimental Molded Plywood Chair Seats	26
1941–1942	Molded Wood Experiments, Molded Plywood Splint and Litter	28
	Arts & Architecture Magazine Covers	30
1943	Leg Splint Production	32
	Plywood Litter and Arm Splint	35
	Architectural Forum Magazine City Plan	36
	Arts & Architecture Magazine Covers	38
	Molded Plywood Experiments	40
	Molded Plywood Aircraft Parts	42
	Plywood Glider	43
1944	*Arts & Architecture* Magazine Covers	44
	Arts & Architecture Magazine Industrial Housing	46
1945	*Arts & Architecture* Magazine Case Study Houses #8 and #9 Announcement	48
	Slide Show: *Lecture I*	50
	Experimental Chairs	52
	Children's Furniture	54
	Molded Plywood Animals	56
	Molded Plywood Chair	58
	Molded Plywood Tables	62
1946	Plywood Lounge Chair	64
	Case Goods	66
	Exhibition: *New Furniture Designed by Charles Eames*	68
	Herman Miller Furniture	72
	Radio Enclosures	76
	Plywood Folding Screen	78
	Plywood Table Production	80
1947	Folding Tables	81
	"Jefferson National Expansion Memorial" Competition	84
	Fabric Designs and *Arts & Architecture* Magazine Covers	86
1948	Herman Miller Furniture Company Graphics	88
	Circus Photography	90
	The Museum of Modern Art "International Competition for Low Cost Furniture Design"	96
1949	Herman Miller Furniture Company Showroom	102
	Arts & Architecture Case Study House #8	106
	Arts & Architecture Case Study House #9	122
	An Exhibition for Modern Living	124
1950	Eames Storage Units	126
	Good Design Exhibition Program	130
	Carson Pirie Scott Windows	132
	Herman Miller Furniture Company Graphics	133
	Film: *Traveling Boy*	134
	The Billy Wilder House	136
	Plastic Armchair	138
	Plastic Side Chair	142
	Toy Masks	144
	Herman Miller Furniture Company Showroom	146
	Low Table Wire (or Rod) Base	148
1951	Elliptical Table Rod Base (ETR)	149
	Wire Mesh Chair	150
	Wire Sofa	154
	Kwikset House	155
	The Toy	156
	Herman Miller Furniture Company Graphics	158
	Macy 4-Room Display	160
1952	The Little Toy	161
	Film: *Blacktop*	162
	Film: *Parade*	164
	Philip Dunne Office	166
	Herman Miller Furniture Company Showroom	167
	House of Cards	168
1953	A Rough Sketch for a Sample Lesson for a Hypothetical Course	176
	Film: *Bread*	178
	Herman Miller Furniture Company Graphics	179
	Giant House of Cards	180
	Film: *A Communications Primer*	182
	Hang-It-All	184
	Berkeley Course	185
	Slide Shows: *Railroad, Seascape, Townscape*	186
1954	Sears Compact Storage	188
	Max De Pree House	189
	Sofa Compact	190
	Film: *S-73*	192
	Stadium Seating	193
	Herman Miller Furniture Company Graphics	194
1955	Stacking Chair	196
	Film: *House*	198
	Film: *Textiles and Ornamental Arts of India*	200

Graphics room

Layout area

Central work area

	Film: *Two Baroque Churches in Germany* 202	
	Slide Show: *Konditorei* 203	
	The Coloring Toy 204	
1956	Lounge Chair 206	
	Film: *Lounge Chair* 208	
	Stephens Speaker 209	
1957	Film Montage: *The Spirit of St. Louis* 210	
	Film: *Stars of Jazz* 211	
	Film: *Day of the Dead* 212	
	Film: *Toccata for Toy Trains* 214	
	Griffith Park Railroad 218	
	Alcoa Solar Do-Nothing Machine 220	
	Film: *The Information Machine* 222	
1958	Aluminum Group Furniture 226	
	Film: *Herman Miller at the Brussels World's Fair* 230	
	Film: *The Expanding Airport* 231	
	India Report 232	
	Film: *De Gaulle Sketch* 234	
1959	Revell Toy House 235	
	Film: *Kaleidoscope Shop* 236	
	Film: *Time & Life International Lobby* 237	
	Film: *Glimpses of the U.S.A.* 238	
	Herman Miller Furniture Company Showroom 242	
1960	Film: *"The Fabulous Fifties"* 244	
	Time & Life Building Lobbies 246	
	Time-Life Chair and Stool 248	
	Film: *Kaleidoscope Jazz Chair* 250	
	Film: *Introduction to Feedback* 251	
1961	La Fonda Chair 252	
	Exhibition: *Mathematica: A World of Numbers and Beyond* 254	
	Film: *Mathematica Peep Shows* 260	
	Herman Miller Furniture Company Showroom 262	
	Eames Contract Storage 264	
	Film: *ECS* 266	
	Slide Show: *Tivoli* 267	
1962	Film: *The Good Years* 268	
	Film: *The House of Science* 270	
	Tandem Sling Seating 274	
	Film: *Before the Fair* 276	
	Films: *IBM Fair Presentation #1 and #2* 277	
1963	Herman Miller, Inc., Showroom 278	
	Tandem Shell Seating 280	
1964	School Seating 281
	3473 Sofa 282
	IBM Corporation Pavilion for the New York World's Fair 284
	Film: *The House of Science* 292
	Segmented Base Tables 293
1965	Exhibition: *Nehru: His Life and His India* 294
	Film: *Westinghouse in Alphabetical Order* 300
	Film: *The Smithsonian Institution* 301
	Film: *Computer Day at Midvale* 302
	Film: *Sherlock Holmes and the Singular Case of the Plural Green Mustache* 303
	Film: *IBM at the Fair* 304
1966	Film: *View from the People Wall* 306
	Smithsonian Carousel 308
	Film: *The Leading Edge* 309
	Timeline: "Men of Modern Mathematics" 310
	Herman Miller, Inc., Showroom 312
	National Aquarium Proposal 314
1967	Film: *National Fisheries Center and Aquarium* 318
	Slide Show: *G.E.M.* 319
	Film: *The Scheutz Machine* 320
	Slide Show: *Herman Miller International* 321
	Timeline: *A Pictorial History of Herman Miller, Inc.* 322
	Slide Show: *Picasso* 324
1968	Film: *A Computer Glossary* 325
	Film: *Babbage's Calculating Machine* 326
	Intermediate Desk Chair 327
	Proposal and Film: *IBM Museum* 328
	Exhibition: *Photography & the City* 330
	Film: *The Lick Observatory* 334
	Washington Presentation Center 335
	Film: *Powers of Ten: A Rough Sketch* 336
	Chaise 338
1969	Booklet: National Fisheries Center and Aquarium 340
	Soft Pad Group 342
	Film: *Image of the City* 344
	Exhibition: *What Is Design?* 345
	Film: *Tops* 346
1970	Film: *Soft Pad* 348
	Film: *The Fiberglass Chairs* 349
	Film: *A Small Hydromedusan: Polyorchis Haplus* ..350
	Film: *The Black Ships* 351
	Computer House of Cards 352

Film building

Furniture development area

Tool shop

	Drafting Chair	354
	Charles Eliot Norton Lectures	355
	Charles Eliot Norton *Lecture #1*	356
	Charles Eliot Norton *Lecture #2*	357
1971	Charles Eliot Norton *Lecture #3*	358
	Charles Eliot Norton *Lecture #4*	359
	Charles Eliot Norton *Lecture #5*	360
	Charles Eliot Norton *Lecture #6*	362
	Two-Piece Plastic Chair and Two-Piece Secretarial Chair	363
	Exhibition: *A Computer Perspective*	364
	Film: *Computer Landscape*	370
	Loose Cushion Armchair	371
	Film: *Clown Face*	372
1972	Film: *Computer Perspective*	374
	Film: *Sumo Wrestler*	375
	Exhibition: *Wallace J. Eckert: Celestial Mechanic*	376
	Exhibition: *Fibonacci: Growth and Form*	378
	Film: *Cable: The Immediate Future*	380
	Film: *Alpha*	381
	Film: *Banana Leaf*	382
	Film: *SX-70*	383
	Exhibition: *Copernicus*	384
	Film: *Design Q&A*	388
1973	Film: *Exponents: A Study in Generalization*	389
	Film: *Franklin and Jefferson*	390
	Book: *A Computer Perspective*	392
	Exhibition: *Movable Feasts and Changing Calendars*	394
	Film: *Two Laws of Algebra: Distributive and Associative*	398
	Film: *Copernicus*	399
	Exhibition: *On the Shoulders of Giants*	400
	Exhibition: *Isaac Newton*	404
1974	Film: *Newton's Method*	408
	Film: *Kepler's Laws*	409
	Newton Cards	410
	Film: *Callot*	411
	Exhibition: *Philosophical Gardens*	412
1975	Film: Metropolitan Overview	414
	Exhibition: *The World of Franklin and Jefferson*	416
1976	Book: *The World of Franklin and Jefferson*	426
	Film: *The World of Franklin and Jefferson (Paris Opening)*	427
	Film: *The World of Franklin and Jefferson*	428
	Film: *Atlas*	430
	Book and Exhibition: *Images of Early America*	431
	Film: *Something About Photography*	434
	Slide Show: *Tall Ships*	435
	Film: *The Look of America*	436
1977	Film: *Daumier: Paris and the Spectator*	437
	IBM 590 Corporate Exhibit Center Proposal	438
	Film: *Powers of Ten*	440
	Film: *Polavision*	442
1978	Film: *Sonar One-Step*	443
	Film: *Art Game*	444
	Film: *Merlin and the Time Mobile*	445
	German *Mathematica* Timeline	446
	Film: *Cézanne—The Late Work*	448
	Film: *Degas in the Metropolitan*	449
1979	Film: *A Report on the IBM Exhibition Center*	450
1984	Leather and Teak Sofa	451
	Bibliography	453
	Photography Credits	456

Introduction

Charles Eames. For us, the name is synonymous with the word "designer." He is the measure of the definition, and his work the standard against which the work of other designers (and our own) is gauged.

From Charles we learned about the process of solving problems by structuring the information to be conveyed. We learned that no detail is too insignificant to be overlooked, and we learned that quality in everything is what counts. We learned the difference between being forced to make compromises and the necessity to recognize constraints. We learned that the *process* of arriving at an end result is what is really important and that work should be completely and totally involving and all-consuming; that there is no separation between work and the rest of life.

Our first face-to-face contact with Charles and the Eames Office was in 1952. We were students in the art department at UCLA, working our way through school and not at all certain what path to choose—teaching, graphic design, industrial design, or "art." Charles appeared one evening at Long Beach City College (at the invitation of Norma Matlin and Pedro Miller, two of our former instructors at the college who were familiar with Charles's work) with a rough cut of the film *A Communications Primer*. He showed the film and talked about other projects in the Eames Office and about a lot of things that were incomprehensible to us—Depression children from poor families, struggling to get through school and get that all-important first job and "security." Here was someone doing precisely what he wanted to do, apparently happily living and working in an atmosphere designed and orchestrated according to his own dictates. And he worked with his wife— an occurrence that we had seldom, if ever, encountered. We all had copies of the summer 1950 issue of *Portfolio* magazine (a short-lived quarterly on the arts published by Zebra Press), and it became a kind of Bible. The pure color and the joyful expression of form of the furniture, the toys, the kites, and the Eames House were like bolts from the sky and ever after influenced our work as students and as designers. Coming from a "serviceable" world of brown frieze sofas, we felt liberated and suddenly privileged with a vision of another existence.

Charles was one of the most *self*-centered persons we have known. He knew what was important to him, he knew what interested him, and he felt that if he worked only on problems that interested him deeply, the solutions to those problems would probably interest other people. When the staff of the office increased dramatically in the early 1960s, never again to decrease to the eight or ten people of the 1950s, he worried about keeping it busy on projects of real interest and not occupying it with commissions accepted merely to keep salaries paid.

For Charles, the business of life was to integrate the parts into a meaningful whole. He distrusted specialists whose interests were so narrowly focused as to make them blind to the connections between science and art, hand and machine, work and play. "Take your pleasures seriously," was an admonition seriously tendered on many occasions, to students and professionals alike. In many ways, Charles was first and foremost a teacher. His interest in the continuities between experiences and relationships was the theme of many lectures and talks given to audiences in many disciplines. The subjects he chose to work on included everything from toys to the history of science and mathematics, and he did not fit into any mold established by any designer before him. Always tenacious on the subject of quality in all things, he became evangelical about it in the last few years of his life.

The Eames Office appeared to run on democratic principles but was in fact a kind of monarchy. All projects began and ended with Charles. Except on rare occasions, and at luncheon meetings (where no business was discussed), only Charles met with clients. After the early years when he was called "Charlie" by his coworkers, Charles maintained a distance from the staff, and the few key people, who in most cases had been with Charles for several years, were given the responsibility of the day-to-day communication with office personnel and of letting people go. When it came time for an employee to leave the office, no matter how long the association, Charles was always away on business. There were no "associate" designers and no daily staff meetings other than discussions (probably at your desk or work table) about the progress of your work. Charles had his own code, a code that often had to be deciphered for new employees by old hands who had learned the nuances of Eames language and behavior. His comments to staff members about a project were often deliberately vague and ambiguous to avoid giving the impression that it was safe to stop thinking about a problem because it was finally solved. Charles left no protégés to carry on the work of the office; Charles *was* the office and it essentially died with him.

Money, as such, did not seem to concern Charles. Most of what was made on one project was plowed back into the next one. He would say that he had learned to live on virtually nothing during the Depression and that he knew he could always do it again, if necessary. His high standards of quality frequently led him to invest his own money in a project in order to see it through. Many of the most memorable Eames projects, among them several films, were initially and often totally funded by the Eameses themselves.

Charles had good clients, and he always had a good staff—a remarkable group of hardworking, intelligent, caring, and capable individuals (of whom a few key persons are mentioned in the text for each project) who truly gave their all for him. These people worked long hours and often through

Left and right: Charles's desk and office

the night (especially in the early years). His standards for the staff were straight out of the Puritan ethic: no radio playing, no socializing, no whistling or gum chewing (you couldn't possibly be thinking about your work if you were doing either). Working in the Eames Office has been called "a delicious agony." The projects were absorbing and challenging, demanding, and often exhausting. You couldn't wait to get to the office in the morning, and you were always expected to give more than you thought you had. You were often asked to perform some task outside the realm of the expertise for which you were hired, whether it was graphic design, photography, furniture design, or architectural planning, to test your flexibility and your ability to transfer your problem-solving capabilities to new areas.

People extended themselves for Charles because the work was always interesting and because they felt the depth of Charles's own commitment. Charles seldom if ever thanked or praised anyone; he felt deeply that people knew if they were doing a good job, and if they weren't, they knew that too. And, if they weren't truly interested and performing at peak levels they didn't last. Pay was always on the lower end of the design scale. Credit, especially in the early years, was rarely given to staff members. Any rewards, Charles felt, were intrinsic to the process of working through the problem and arriving at solutions that would have extended meaning beyond the confines of the office staff. Fitting into this mold wasn't easy for a lot of people, and they left after a few days or weeks. But those who stayed remember their years in the Eames Office as turning points in their lives.

Many of the people who worked for Charles gave immensely of their own talents in innovative and intelligent ways. (The office staff is listed just above the horizontal rule on each of the book's project pages.) Don Albinson (a former Cranbrook student), who joined the office in January 1946 and left in 1959, is a remarkably intelligent designer with a great knowledge of and sensitivity to materials and industrial processes. Many of the technical and design innovations in Eames furniture produced in that period were the result of his understanding of production processes and engineering. Charles Kratka started at the Eames Office in 1948 and was responsible for much of the graphic design until he left in 1954, ultimately to begin his own office. Graphic designer Deborah Sussman came to the Eames Office in 1953 from the Institute of Design in Chicago to work for a summer and stayed until 1957. She returned on several occasions to work on projects, until she opened her own office. Glen Fleck worked for Charles from 1961 to 1973, bringing to the office a unique ability to visualize complicated concepts and to transfer them to the film medium. He, too, has his own design practice. Gordon Ashby, Robert Staples, Richard Donges, Peter Pearce, John Neuhart, and many others left the office to begin their own practices and offices, to teach and to work in

much the same areas as the Eameses. The dozens of technical assistants, part-time specialists, and free-lance staff were all important in making the Eames work as good as it is and in contributing their special talents and abilities.

Charles liked to say that his clients were all located east of the Mississippi River and that he and Ray moved to California to devote themselves to their work and to get away from the pressures of life in an urban setting. Although Charles was approached by many potential clients, he actually worked for relatively few, most of whom remained with him for many years—especially Herman Miller, Inc., the IBM Corporation, and the federal government. Charles was particular about choosing clients whose objectives and motives he was in agreement with, and he was not cynical about them, as designers can be. These clients were extremely supportive and regularly provided funding for Eames projects that were not of obvious immediate advantage to them. Although clients usually brought to the office fixed notions about what they thought they wanted, Charles more often than not redefined the project and expanded its scope.

Charles was also fortunate in having, from his earliest years, dedicated and earnest supporters who believed in him, brought him work, supported projects, and championed his efforts. Eliel and Eero Saarinen, Eliot Noyes, John Entenza, Howard Meyers (of *Architectural Forum* magazine), Edgar Kaufmann, Jr., and many individuals at the IBM Corporation were good, loyal, and staunch Eames friends.

Writing about the early years in the Eames Office requires delving into ancient history—a simpler, clearer, and more idealistic time that feels farther away than the actual number of years that have passed. The earnestness and single-minded dedication (exemplified by the Eameses and a host of other designers and architects working in the period immediately after the war) to the ideal of building a better society and better lives after the long wartime years was premised on the foundation that designers could be instrumental in changing our environments in positive and fulfilling ways. The wholehearted belief that if people had the right information they would make the right decisions and choices was the cornerstone of many designers' work in the postwar period. Anything was possible, "good design" was going to save us, and we would have not only a chicken in every pot and a car in every garage, but good pots to put chickens in and cars and houses that were honestly and beautifully made (and honestly priced) to reflect the mass-production techniques that were necessary to provide these things for the numbers of people who expected to have them. Utility was the guiding principle and the key to the new aesthetic.

In today's design climate it is difficult to recall a past in which functionalism was the key to design expression, when utility was the ultimate determinant of form, and when beauty was defined as a by-product of rational decisions that

Left and right: Ray's desk and a wall in her room

reflected the relationship of one to the other. Charles continued to believe in the importance of honest and direct expression of form, whether the product was furniture, film, or exhibition. He didn't change his mind about his objectives as he got older and other rationale became uppermost in design circles. Although projects changed in emphasis and the office moved away from furniture as a full-time occupation to projects in which the transmission of information was the most important factor, the inherent goal remained the same. Charles never became cynical about human intelligence and the ability to make the right choices if the right information was made available.

Charles once said that the hand of the designer should not be in evidence in a well-designed product—that good design should be anonymous. The opposite is true of his own work—from Eames chairs to Eames exhibitions and films the name is always a part of the expression. The questions are often asked: How will Charles be remembered and what will be his enduring achievements? The furniture, although but one aspect of the Eames work, most readily comes to mind. Arthur Drexler, in the catalog for the 1973 Museum of Modern Art exhibition of Eames furniture, wrote: "The most original American furniture designer since Duncan Phyfe, Charles Eames has contributed at least three of the major chair designs of this century. He has also given a personal and pervasive image to the idea of lightness and mobility. His work has influenced furniture design in virtually every country, and his mastery of advanced technology has set new standards of both design and production."

Charles was a loner; he was part of no school or movement, and his work cannot be comfortably categorized. He was committed to redefining the present by using the best ingredients from the past and the present, and by reminding people that they must not forget the best of what they have already learned. As Paul Schrader noted in his Spring 1970 article in *Film Quarterly*: "[Charles] is architect, inventor, designer, craftsman, scientist, film-maker, professor. Yet, in all his diversity Eames is one creator, and his creation is not a series of separate achievements, but a unified aesthetic with many branch like manifestations...Eames remains greater than the sum of all his parts."

Ray Eames. She was unique—a wonderful blend of Victorian and contemporary sensibilities. People always ask what part Ray played in the workings of the Eames Office. Charles, the Eames House, and the Eames Office were the most important things in her life, and she protected Charles's interests and her perception of the legacy of the Eames Office with undying loyalty and fierce tenacity.

Ray was in large part responsible for the Eames "look." Her extraordinary eye for form and color, which never deserted her, often made the difference between good, very good, and "Eames." Though the Eames work set many of the visual standards in the worlds of furniture, film, and graphic design in the 1940s, 1950s, and 1960s, the Eames "look" did not follow the prescribed stylistic dictates of stripped-down modernism. The Eameses made their own rules that were based on extracting as much visual richness as possible out of an experience or an idea and integrating that richness into the project—be it furniture, exhibition design, graphics, toys, or film. This visual richness was not *decoration*, or icing on the cake, but part of the cake, which developed organically out of the ingredients in the mix.

Ray's perception of events was always filtered through the prism of the Eames Office and through Charles's philosophy. She had a special way of connecting apparently dissimilar events and objects, finding something in the connection that pointed to a new combination or a new direction. Although her reluctance to make decisions could make working with her frustrating, her ability to root out odd bits of information and find just the right color sample or the right shape, often made *the* difference in the final product. Ray kept every scrap of potentially useful visual reference material she came across—which she stored on her desk, the walls in her "room" in the Eames Office, and in her remarkable visual memory, which was enormous—for just the occasion when it might be needed. She was responsible for the look of the office itself, deciding what vestige of each project would remain in evidence after the major part of the residue was discarded or packed away. Once an object, a photograph, a poster, or a color swatch was in place, it remained there; she only added to the mix and never subtracted anything. She gradually built a visual panoply behind the unadorned exterior of the building on Washington Boulevard that reflected layers and layers of projects, people, and experiences.

Ray never lost her intense interest in and curiosity about the visual world. She could be counted upon to have seen and taken special notice of everything new and eventful in the world of design. She did not have much to do with the "business" of the office, nor was she included in meetings with clients, except those that were essentially social in nature. She was uncomfortable with speaking publicly and usually deferred to Charles on those occasions when she was asked to do so. (After his death she became more public and often showed films and spoke to groups.) She was not a writer, although she read with great conscientiousness the words for every project, film, and exhibition. After the first few years, she did not do layout or graphics, but she knew every image in every film and exhibition. She did not do drawings, but she knew which drawings were in the works. She always participated in the choice of color and fabric, and when she erred, she erred on the side of too much richness and too much imagery. She did not work in the darkroom, but she kept watch over every print and every slide (her favorite form of photograph). She made it her personal responsibility to protect the immense photographic record of the work of the office, accumulated over the years, which ultimately made it possible to put this book together.

After Charles died on August 21, 1978, the actual work of the office came to an end, although the IBM Corporation continued to retain Ray as a consultant. (She also consulted on an exhibition produced for the Federal Reserve building in San Francisco.) Ray kept the Eames Office open (with a staff of up to ten people) to catalog the immense amount of material that had accumulated in the building since 1943 and to ready the correspondence, drawings, records, and photographic files for transfer to the Library of Congress, to which they had been promised. (IBM, wishing to honor Charles after his death, had made a grant to the library to establish the Charles Eames Collection.) For the ten years between Charles's death and her own on August 21, 1988 (ten years to the day after Charles's), Ray supervised the counting and labeling of photographs, the disposition of furniture prototypes and production models and countless items of film, camera, and shop equipment. Because she could not bear to part with anything from the great productive working years in the office, the process was never-ending and was not yet resolved at her death. She also continued to open the Eames House to students, architects, and designers on countless occasions.

We began work on this book in the fall of 1982. In early 1982 Ray was approached by Susan Grode, representing Harry N. Abrams, Inc., to do a book about the Eames Office. She in turn asked us to participate and we agreed. It seemed a reasonable enough task; John had worked full-time for the office for four years and had returned on several occasions in subsequent years as a free-lance designer. We had designed and produced an exhibition on the work of the Eames Office in 1976 (with grants from the National Endowment and from the UCLA Art Council) entitled *Connections: The Work of Charles and Ray Eames*, and in 1980 we completed an inventory for the IBM Corporation of all materials in the Eames Office that were related to IBM projects—photographs, original drawings, and production records. We knew the Eames Office photo filing system backward and forward and had been in and out of the office for thirty years.

We agreed collectively that we would do a complete catalog of the Eameses' work from the start of their lives in California in 1941 to 1978, the year of Charles's death. We also agreed that we would do a definitive, factual record of the work only and not attempt a critical assessment of either the work or Charles's place in the history of design. Such a book would allow us to include major projects alongside minor ones, successes alongside failures, proposals alongside uncompleted work—a year-by-year chronology of the work of the Eames Office.

After we completed the initial layout in our office, a long and agonizing process began—a struggle to keep the original objectives for the book on track and reviewing with Ray each word and each image on each page to ensure that just the right photograph had been chosen and just the right words had been written. Ray reviewed our text and layouts several times; each time they were given new emphasis. We understood that the production of the book represented the last project for Ray and the culmination of a long career and that it was an emotional process for her. Her final notations were finished shortly before her death; she left us with several admonitions about the book that we have very carefully taken into account.

To corroborate facts and dates we interviewed as many key people from the office as we could find. The text was sent to each person to correct errors or to add information. These valuable additions and corrections were incorporated into the text.

The book in its final form lays out the Eames work in a linear year-by-year progression. Each project page is dated; the completion date appears at the top of the text. Judgments on placement of projects in relation to other projects were made on the basis of completion dates and the first public appearance of the furniture, film, or exhibition. Though projects appear in the book one after another, often several projects were in process at the same time and their completion dates overlapped. Herman Miller, Inc., dates (in most cases a marketing date) were used for the furniture. Most of the pages have been organized into two parts—the bottom two-thirds of each project page is devoted to descriptions of projects of the office. The band at the top of each page tells another story about that project—the people and events that were part of it—employees, family, consultants, advisers, and clients—and visual anecdotes of an active design office involved in a multiplicity of projects. A record of many of the awards given Charles, Ray, and the office is also included, as well as lectures, articles, and exhibitions by and about the office. We have also included staff lists (from the Eames Office records) that include both short-term and long-term employees for each year and pictures (when they could be found) of many staff members at work.

The images in the book come mainly from the Eames Office itself. Their exhaustive photographic records on almost every aspect of the day-to-day operations, from 1941 to 1978—projects, meetings, special events, and people—provide a unique opportunity for any chronicler of events; memories need not be relied upon solely. Accurate recollections are more easily made when a visual record can be seen. On the other hand, with such a wealth of material to draw upon, it was often difficult to make a judgment about what to include and what to leave out. We also needed to add a substantial number of images to represent work that had not been recorded at the Eames Office. (Photo credits appear at the back of the book.)

Many people participated in the production of this book. Richard Donges was supportive throughout the long process, and the staff of Neuhart Donges Neuhart—Patrick Fitzgerald, Marla Berns, Danny Brauer, Karen Reeser, Rowan Moore, Lucinda Leach, Jeffrey Darnall, Suzanne Donges, Shirley Padilla, and Eva Pryciak—helped immeasurably with the organization, research, design, writing, layout, and pasteup. Patrick Fitzgerald deserves special thanks for his help in producing computer text and in computer coding the text for the typographer and for his friendship and moral support. Our sons, Andrew and Benjamin, were helpful throughout. Andrew assisted in the photography of furniture, slide shows, graphics, and films whose documentation was incomplete and Ben helped in keeping track of the thousands of pictures in the files which were used to compile the book. They were also cheerleaders when the going was slow.

Several members of Ray's staff deserve special thanks. Mary Marks Bernier, who worked for the Library of Congress and for Ray cataloging the Eames materials, provided invaluable help in dating images and events. We reviewed over fifty thousand black-and-white contact prints and thirty thousand color slides with the help of Eames office staff members Robert Dean, Amy Molina, Andrew Ramsay, Hilaire Atlee, and Heather White. James Franklin and Luciano Perna printed additional photographs from Eames Office files and Garrett White and Matthew Hinerfeld assisted Ray in compiling her additions to the text. Merilyn Cuttrell and Emily Mayeda were stalwarts, helpful throughout the long process. Sam Passalacqua, a longtime Eames staff member, deserves special thanks for his invaluable assistance in retrieving archive materials.

Former Eames Office staff members and associates, from the early years on, gave generously of their time and participation in assembling the material for this book. Norman Bruns, Marion Overby Conners, Don Albinson, Jill Mitchell, Johnnie Johnson, Harlan Moore, Charles Kratka, Frederick Usher, Deborah Sussman, Parke Meek, Dale Bauer, Gordon Ashby, Robert Staples, Peter Pearce, Pamela Hedley, Richard Donges, Boyce Nemec, Barbara Charles, Glen Fleck, Jehane Burns, Jeannine Oppewall, Hap Johnson, Alex Funke, James Hoekema, Rolf Fehlbaum, and Billy Wilder participated willingly in interviews, verifying dates of events and projects and reading the final text for errors and omissions, as did Hugh De Pree and Max DePree from Herman Miller, Inc., and Michael Sullivan from the IBM Corporation. Robert Blaich (formerly with Herman Miller) added events and dates also. Edward S. Evans, Jr., an associate of the Eameses from Evans Products was extremely helpful in verifying dates and events from the mid-1940s as was Sol Fingerhut of Century Plastics. Elaine Sewell Jones provided us with copies of *Arts & Architecture* magazines. Linda Folland, archivist at Herman Miller, Inc., provided us with accurate dates and information for furniture and events related to Herman Miller. C. Ford Peatross, curator of Architecture, Design, and Engineering at the Library of Congress, assisted us in providing continued access to Eames Office photos after Ray's death. Jackie Dooley and Mary Goss, also of the Library of Congress were also helpful in verifying Eames dates. Charles's daughter, Lucia, and her husband, Aristides Demetrios, wholeheartedly supported the book.

Ray's childhood friends, Mrs. William Kleinsorg, Mrs. Andrew Simpson III, and Mrs. Howard Reese were extremely generous in sharing with us their childhood and school experiences. Barney Reese was untiring in her efforts to provide us with pictures and information.

Finally, the staff of our publisher, Harry N. Abrams, deserves gold medals for patience and fortitude. Our editor, Charles Miers, helped immeasurably in clarifying the text and in providing critical guidance through to the last stages of production.

John Neuhart
Marilyn Neuhart
June 1989

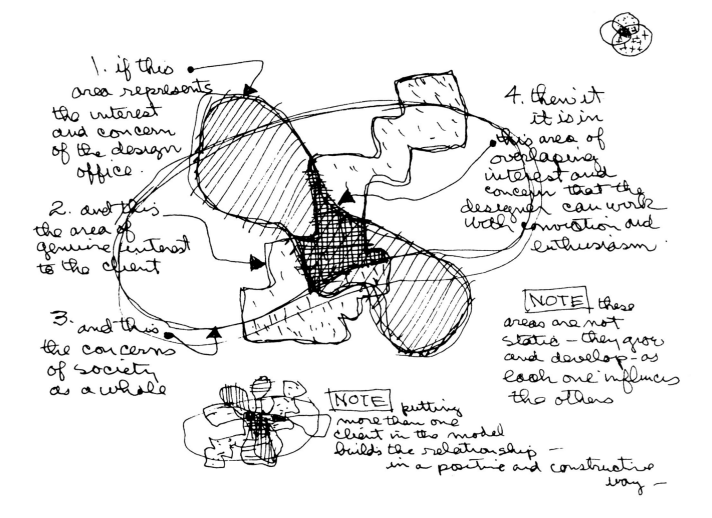

A diagram of the design process drawn by Charles

A photograph of Charles taken in 1972 by Paul Bruhwiler

What Is Design?

The following statement by Charles is an expression of his approach to the design process. These words, the accompanying diagram (p. 13), and his answers to the questions (pp. 14–15) are an explanation of the Eames philosophy and background material for this record of the work of the Eames Office.

In a statement sent to Madame L. Amic for the catalog of the exhibition *What Is Design?* (p. 345), Charles wrote:

> In the exhibit, we are trying to show something about a decision that the designer must make when he starts to work for a client. We have found it a very helpful strategy to restrict our own work to subjects that are of genuine and immediate interest to us—and are of equal interest to the client. If we were to work on things or in ways that we knew were not of legitimate concern to both of us, we probably would not be serving our clients, or ourselves, very well. Throughout the work for the various clients, the unifying force is this common interest, plus a preoccupation with structure which comes from looking at all problems as architectural ones. The enclosed diagram also includes a critical and changing area that represents the concerns of society as a whole. None of these areas is static. As client and designer get to know each other, they influence each other. As society's needs become more apparent, both client and designer expand their own personal concerns to meet these needs.

The following questions were asked by Madame Amic and answered by Charles. The questions and answers were the conceptual basis of the exhibition *What is Design?* An edited and slightly changed version of the questions was used as the basis of the 1972 film *Design Q & A* (p. 388).

Q. What is your definition of "design?"
A. A plan for arranging elements in such a way as to best accomplish a particular purpose.

Q. Is design an expression of art (an art form)?
A. The design is an expression of the purpose. It may (if it is good enough) later be judged as art.

Q. Is design a craft for industrial purposes?
A. No—but design may be a solution to some industrial problems.

Q. What are the boundaries of design?
A. What are the boundaries of problems?

Q. Is design a discipline that concerns itself with only one part of the environment?
A. No.

Q. Is it a method of general expression?
A. No—it is a method of action.

Q. Is design a creation of an individual?
A. No—because to be realistic one must always admit the influence of those who have gone before.

Q. ...or a creation of a group?
A. Often.

Q. Is there a design ethic?
A. There are always design constraints and these usually include an ethic.

Q. Does design imply the idea of products that are necessarily useful?
A. Yes—even though the use might be very subtle.

Q. Is it able to cooperate in the creation of works reserved solely for pleasure?
A. Who would say that pleasure is not useful?

Q. Ought form to derive from the analysis of function?
A. The great risk here is that the analysis may not be complete.

Q. Can the computer substitute for the designer?
A. Probably, in some special cases, but usually the computer is an aid to the designer.

Q. Does design imply industrial manufacture?
A. Some designs do and some do not—depending on the nature of the design and the requirements.

Q. Is design an element of industrial policy?
A. Certainly; as is any other aspect of quality, obvious or subtle, of the product. It seems that anything can be an element in policy.

Q. Ought design to care about lowering costs?
A. A product often becomes more useful if the costs are lowered without harming the quality.

Q. Does the creation of design admit constraint?
A. Design depends largely on constraints.

Q. What constraints?
A. The sum of all constraints. Here is one of the few effective keys to the design problem—the ability of the designer to recognize as many of the constraints as possible—his willingness and enthusiasm for working within these constraints—the constraints of price, of size, of strength, balance, of surface, of time, etc.; each problem has its own peculiar list.

Q. Does design obey laws?
A. Aren't constraints enough?

Q. Are there tendencies and schools in design?
A. Yes, but this is more a human frailty than an ideal.

Q. Ought the final product to bear the trademark of the designer? of the research office?
A. In some cases, one may seem appropriate. In some cases, the other, and certainly in some cases, both.

Q. What is the relation of design to the world of fashion (current trends)?
A. The objects of fashion have usually been designed with the particular constraints of fashion in mind.

Q. Is design ephemeral?
A. Some needs are ephemeral. Most designs are ephemeral.

Q. Ought it to tend towards the ephemeral or towards permanence?
A. Those needs and designs that have a more universal quality will tend toward permanence.

Q. To whom does design address itself: to the greatest number (the masses)? to the specialists or the enlightened amateur? to a privileged social class?
A. To the need.

Q. Can public action aid the advancement of design?
A. The proper public action can advance most anything.

Q. After having answered all these questions, do you feel you have been able to practice the profession of "design" under satisfactory conditions, or even optimum conditions?
A. Yes.

Q. Have you been forced to accept compromises?
A. I have never been forced to accept compromises but I have willingly accepted constraints.

Q. What do you feel is the primary condition for the practice of design and its propagation?
A. Recognition of need.

Q. What is the future of design?
(No answer)

A bouquet of Zeeland, Michigan, wildflowers used by the Eameses
on the Herman Miller, Inc., stock certificate

Charles and Ray Eames

This chronology covers events from Charles and Ray's births to their arrival in California in July 1941.

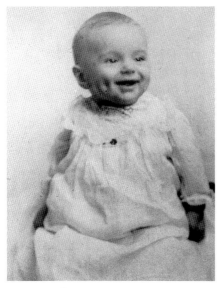

Charles, aged one year

Charles, his grandmother Lambert, and his sister, Adele

1907   Charles Ormond Eames, Jr., is born June 17 in St. Louis, Missouri. He is the second child of Marie Celine Adele Pauline Lambert Eames and Charles Ormond Eames, a Pinkerton security officer at St. Louis Union Railroad Station and an amateur photographer. (Charles's sister, Adele, was born in 1903.) The family moves to New York State, living in Buffalo and Brooklyn until 1912, when they return to St. Louis. Charles's first childhood memory is of seeing Halley's Comet.

Marie Lambert Eames

Charles Ormond Eames, Sr.

Charles (seated, middle) with his sister, Adele (standing), and their cousins

Charles and his dog, Topsy

1912   Charles enters kindergarten at David Glasgow Farragut Elementary School in North St. Louis.

Maurice, Ray, Edna, and Elizabeth Kaiser

1912 Bernice Alexandra Kaiser (called Ray-Ray; later Ray, and then legally changed to Ray Bernice Alexandra Kaiser in 1954) is born December 15 in Sacramento, California. She is the third child of Edna Mary Burr Kaiser and Alexander Kaiser. Ray's brother, Maurice, was born in 1907; her sister, Elizabeth, in 1910. Elizabeth dies within a few months of Ray's birth. Ray's father, a former jeweler, manages a Variety theater in the Bay Area and in the 1920s becomes an insurance salesman for the California State Life Company.

Ray with her father and her brother, Maurice

Edna Burr Kaiser   Alexander Kaiser

Ray, aged one year

Ray and Maurice Kaiser

1915 While on an assignment in Roanoke, Virginia, Charles's father is shot by trainrobbers and never fully recovers. He writes cloak-and-dagger stories of his experiences for *The American Weekly*.

1917 Charles begins his first job at Upton S. Cody, a printing and envelope shop, cleaning presses, sorting type, and printing and folding envelopes.

Charles at the Laclede Mill

Charles and Adele Eames

1918 Charles works for Hyke and Ebler, grocers.

Ray enters kindergarten in the winter at Sierra Elementary School in Sacramento, California.

1919 Charles's father dies. Charles and Adele live with their mother and two aunts.

1920 Charles works for Ernest Niemoller, druggist, in North St. Louis. He finds a cache of his father's old photographic materials, discovers wet-plate photography, and learns about the existence of film a year later.

1921 — In the fall Charles enters Yeatman High School in St. Louis; his neighbor and mentor Walter Kurtz gets him a job as a laborer at Laclede Steel Company, a rail rerolling mill in Venice, Illinois. He works Saturdays and Sundays during the school year and full-time in the summers, wrecking concrete forms, drawing patterns, and performing minor engineering work.

Left and right: Charles in 1924

1924 Charles is elected president of his senior class and captain of the football team. He is offered an engineering scholarship to college by the Aitkens Mill Company, which also helps him get an architecture scholarship at Washington University, St. Louis. Aitkens is hopeful that eventually Charles will help modernize the plant.

Charles's senior-class picture

Yeatman High School's 1925 senior class. Charles is fourth from the left in the front row

1925   Charles graduates in the spring from Yeatman High. He writes the school's Color Day speech, which is published in the school newspaper on March 15.

Ray enters the seventh grade at Sutter Junior High School in Sacramento, California.

Charles works at Edwin F. Guth Fixture Company, designing lighting fixtures.

In the fall Charles enters Washington University in St. Louis on an architecture scholarship. He is elected president of the freshman class. Charles works for Trueblood and Graf, Architects. His first job there is sorting the Trueblood drawings of the St. Louis Union Railroad Station.

1925– Charles continues to study architecture at Washington
1928   University and to work summers at Trueblood and Graf as a draftsman. In 1928, while at Washington University, he receives two first-place honors for his design of a bandstand and a park pavilion in the "ultra-modern" manner. He leaves the university after his sophomore year.

Charles (left) and fellow students at Washington University

1928   Ray enters the tenth grade at Sacramento High School in Sacramento, California. Art, English, history, and French are her favorite subjects.

Left: Charles at his lithography press. Right: A print by Charles of a building in St. Louis, Missouri

1927– Charles begins to learn lithography and etching and
1928   builds a pottery kiln.

1929 Charles marries Catherine Dewey Woermann, a Vassar graduate and student at Washington University. On their honeymoon, a wedding gift from Catherine's father, they visit Europe and see the work of Mies van der Rohe, Walter Gropius, Le Corbusier, and Henry van de Velde for the first time.

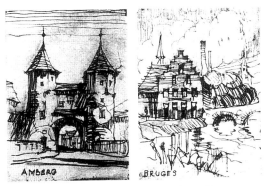

Left and right: Drawings made by Charles in Europe

Ray's father dies in San Francisco on July 5.

1930 Charles and Catherine return to St. Louis. Their daughter, Lucia Dewey Eames, is born on October 11.

Lucia Eames, aged two years, with Charles

Charles opens an architectural office—Gray and Eames—in St. Louis with Charles M. Gray, a colleague from Trueblood and Graf. They later take another partner, Walter E. Pauley, and become Gray, Eames, and Pauley. The office designs a house for Ernest O. Sweetzer, a professor in the engineering department of Washington University, in the Wydown area of St. Louis.

1931 Ray graduates from Sacramento High School in February. She is a member of the Art Club, the Big Sisters Club, and is on the decorating committee for the senior dance.

Ray's senior-class picture

The Sacramento High School Art Association. The purpose of the club was to increase knowledge of art in Sacramento. Ray is ninth from the left in the second row

The Sacramento High School Annual Football Dance Committee. Ray, the chairman of the decoration committee, is standing at left in the front row

Ray attends Sacramento Junior College in the winter semester. In the summer, to be closer to her brother Maurice, who is a cadet at West Point, Ray and her mother move to New York and rent an apartment in Manhattan. They live also for a time in Providence, Rhode Island, and summer in Gloucester, Massachusetts. In the fall of 1931 Ray enters the May Friend Bennett School in Millbrook, New York.

Ray's graduation pin from the May Friend Bennett School

Ray graduates from the May Friend Bennett School and begins studying painting with Hans Hofmann in the first year his New York school is opened. She continues to study and paint with him in New York City, Gloucester, and Provincetown, Massachusetts until 1939.

Ray in Gloucester, Massachusetts

A class portrait at the Hofmann school. Ray is seated third from the left

1933 Charles designs sets for the St. Louis Municipal Opera outdoor theater and makes stained glass windows and mosaics with Emil Frei for the Pilgrim Congregational Church in St. Louis. He also designs doors, light fixtures, and the renovation of the church spire.

Gray, Eames, and Pauley design two houses, one at 335 Bristol Place and the other at 101 Mason Avenue in Webster Grove, Missouri.

Left and right: Drawings by Ray from the Hofmann school

1934   Charles, in the depths of the Depression, with no architectural commissions forthcoming, works for the WPA in St. Louis and New Orleans measuring historical buildings. He leaves St. Louis for Mexico for eight months and spends time in San Luis Potosí and Monterrey doing odd jobs and painting.

Charles (middle) assisting in the Historic American Buildings Survey, a WPA project. The team was measuring the Jean Baptiste Valle House in Ste. Genevieve, Missouri

1935   Charles returns to St. Louis from Mexico and opens a new architectural firm—Eames and Walsh—with Robert T. Walsh, also formerly of Trueblood and Graf, designing small residences and churches. The firm designs St. Mary's Church in Helena, Arkansas (including its lighting fixtures, vestments, and vessels) and a church in Paragould, Arkansas. St. Mary's Church is published by Howard Meyer in *Architectural Forum* and is seen by Eliel Saarinen, who writes to Charles about it.

Left: St. Mary's Church in Helena, Arkansas. Right: A lighting fixture on the church

1936   Eames and Walsh design the Dinsmoor House in Webster Grove, Missouri, and begin work on a major commission, a house for John Philip and Alice Meyer (a classmate of Catherine Eames's), in Huntleigh Village. The plan includes furniture, stained glass, rug and fixture design, as well as ceramics, Carl Milles sculpture, and Loja Saarinen tapestries. Charles's designs for furniture are built by John Rausch, a St. Louis cabinetmaker. Charles confers with Eliel Saarinen on the design of the house; Saarinen thereafter becomes a major influence in Charles's architectural work.

A view of the Meyer House

Ray becomes a founding member of American Abstract Artists.

1937   Groundbreaking for the Eames and Walsh Meyer House is in January. Charles meets Eero Saarinen, who has just returned from working with Norman Bel Geddes after graduating from Yale.

Ray's paintings are shown in the first American Abstract Artists group show at the Riverside Museum in New York City.

1938   Eliel Saarinen offers Charles a fellowship to study architecture and design at the Cranbrook Academy of Art in Cranbrook, Michigan. Charles goes to Cranbrook in the fall. Among his fellow students are Florence Schust (later Knoll), Ralph Rapson, Lillian Swann Saarinen, Pipsan Saarinen (later Swanson), Charles Dusenbury, Tony Rosenthal, William Watson, Edmund Bacon, Harry Weese, Benjamin Baldwin, Jack Spaeth, Harry Bertoia, Nancy Wilkinson, Don Albinson, David Scholes, Frances Rich, Mary de Wolfe, Jean Raseman, Jill Mills, and Henry Heblein.

1939 Charles becomes an instructor of design in the Intermediate School at Cranbrook preparing students for the full Cranbrook curriculum. He and his family move into faculty housing. Lucia Eames attends the Cranbrook Day school.

Among the instructors at Cranbrook during this period are Eliel Saarinen, Loja Saarinen, Eero Saarinen, Carl Milles, Zoltan Sepeshy, Harry Bertoia, Marshall Fredericks, Maija Grotell, Wallace Mitchell, and Marianne Strengell. In December Charles and Eero design the installation of the faculty exhibition in Cranbrook Pavilion.

Charles at Cranbrook with a movie camera

Charles and Eero Saarinen

Left and right: Two views of the Cranbrook faculty exhibition

1940 Charles is made head of the Department of Industrial Design at Cranbrook and takes a part-time job in the Saarinen architectural office, working on the Kleinhans Music Hall in Buffalo, Crow Island School in Winnetka, Illinois, the Smithsonian Art Gallery competition in Washington, D.C., the Goucher College Baltimore campus plan, and a church in Columbus, Indiana. He makes the scale models and designs the basin for the Carl Milles sculpture *Meeting of the Rivers* in St. Louis.

Charles and Frances Rich, daughter of Irene Rich (film actress and radio personality), travel to California, visiting Los Angeles and the San Francisco Exposition.

An unidentified student, Frances Rich, and Charles at Cranbrook

Charles designs a studio (to be built in California) for Frances Rich. It is not constructed.

Ray's mother dies after a long illness. Ray is encouraged to study at Cranbrook by her fellow Hofmann student, Benjamin Baldwin. In September she begins auditing weaving classes at Cranbrook with instructor Marianne Strengel.

Ray in 1940

Charles and Eero collaborate on designs for The Museum of Modern Art's "Organic Design in Home Furnishings" competition organized by Eliot Noyes with Ira Hirshman and juried by Alvar Aalto, Marcel Breuer, Alfred Barr, Edward Stone, and Frank Parrish. Edgar Kaufmann, Jr., and Bloomingdale's department store are two of the sponsors. Bloomingdale's plans to market the prize-winning furniture. Ray Kaiser, Don Albinson, and Harry Bertoia work on models and entry drawings. Charles and Eero win first prize in two categories—seating for a living room and other furniture for a living room (case goods). Other entries include: armchair, conversation chair, easy chair, relaxation chair, lounging shape, sofa unit, coffee table, and end table. Two other Cranbrook students, Benjamin Baldwin and Harry Weese, win prizes for lighting fixtures and outdoor furniture. The Eames-Saarinen designs involve two new manufacturing techniques: the molding of wood into compound curvatures and cycle-welding under development by Chrysler to bond rubber to wood. A condition of the competition is that the winning designs can be manufactured and offered for sale. Haywood Wakefield Company and the Haskelite Corporation are designated to be the manufacturers of the side chair and The Red Lion Table Co. the producers of the storage cabinets. However, the outbreak of war intervenes and the furniture is not produced.

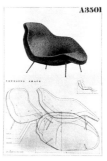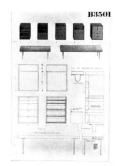

Top left and right; above left and center: Specification panels submitted to the competition. Above right: Cover of the exhibition catalog

1941   Charles and Catherine Woermann Eames are divorced in May. Charles and Ray marry on June 20, 1941, in Chicago, Illinois, at the home of Ray's friend and classmate Helen Donnolly. Ray's gold wedding ring is designed and made by Harry Bertoia. Charles and Ray drive to California where they plan to make their home, arriving in July.

Left: Ray on her wedding day. Right: Charles and Ray in the Santa Monica Mountains shortly after their arrival in California

The Museum of Modern Art publishes an account of the furniture design competition, *Organic Furniture Exhibition*. Handmade samples of the furniture are produced for The Museum of Modern Art exhibition. The developmental work on the organic furniture will be the basis of Charles's work in molded plywood furniture and wartime products through most of the 1940s.

Furniture designed by Eero Saarinen and Charles for the "Organic Design" competition at The Museum of Modern Art

July 5: Charles and Ray arrive in Los Angeles.

With the help of John Entenza, editor and publisher of *California Arts & Architecture* magazine (later renamed *Arts & Architecture*), Charles and Ray rent an apartment in a new building designed by Richard Neutra on Strathmore Avenue in Westwood. An extra bedroom is turned into a laboratory for their wood-molding experiments, and the kitchen and bathroom are used for photographic processing.

The exterior of the Eameses' Strathmore Avenue apartment

Fall: Charles begins work as an architect in the art department at Metro-Goldwyn-Mayer Studios in Culver City. The department is directed by Cedric Gibbons. Charles works on sets for movies, including *Johnny Eager* (1941), *I Married an Angel* (1942), *Random Harvest* (1942), and *Mrs. Miniver* (1942).

September: The exhibition *Organic Design in Home Furnishings Competition* (p. 25) opens at The Museum of Modern Art in New York City, featuring the first-prize designs by Eero Saarinen and Charles. Charles and Ray remain in California to work, and they miss the exhibition.

September: An article by Charles, "Design Today," appears in *California Arts & Architecture* magazine. In it, he discusses the role of the designer in the modern world. It is illustrated with examples of work by students from Charles's Cranbrook class: namely, Don Albinson, Jill Mills, and Nancy Wilcox.

December: "Organic Design," an article by Charles that expounds on his and Eero Saarinen's approach to the "Organic Design" competition, is published in *California Arts & Architecture* magazine.

1941

Experimental Molded Plywood Chair Seats

Shortly after their arrival in Los Angeles, the Eameses began to experiment in their apartment with molded, compound-curved plywood chair seats, continuing the work Charles had begun with Eero Saarinen at Cranbrook for the 1940 Museum of Modern Art "Organic Design in Home Furnishings" competition (p. 25).

After a series of experiments, the Eameses made a prototype chair seat produced by a laborious method of gluing together and heat bonding thin plies of wood. Charles built a device for molding plywood, which the Eameses named the "Kazam! machine," by using hinged two-by-four-inch pieces of lumber that he bolted together to withstand the high pressures necessary for forming the wood. The plies, coated with glue and sandwiched together (alternating the wood grain), were placed against a plaster form located at the base of the machine. An inflatable membrane, enclosed in the wooden "magic box," covered the layers of wood. After the device was securely bolted together, the membrane was inflated with a bicycle pump to keep the wood plies pressed against the plaster form. During the four-to-six-hour molding process, heating elements embedded in the plaster form dried the glue. Air was pumped into the membrane regularly to maintain the required level of pressure. Once the glue had set, the pressure was released and the formed seat was removed from the mold: "Ala Kazam!—like magic." The edges were trimmed with a handsaw to the desired finished shape and hand-sanded in the apartment shop.

The apartment experiments on the prototype seat established the basic technique for molding plywood into compound curves and were the nucleus of all further developments in the plywood-molding process. From the outset, the goal was to devise a system for mass-producing high-quality, low-cost furniture. Many designers had experimented with plywood molding in the post-World War I period, but the method developed by Charles yielded plywood bent in more than one direction, forming three-dimensional compound curves in a single molding operation that could be duplicated on an assembly line. Interrupted but also aided by the work on wartime plywood products and by the development of synthetic materials and new technologies, the molding experiments slowly evolved from the one-piece chair into a chair made of two separate but related forms that expressed the "organic," curvilinear quality sought after by Saarinen and Charles in the 1940 competition. Not upholstered and unadorned, the chairs were pure expressions of the molding process.

The closed "Kazam! machine" with the pump and gauge in the locked, molding position

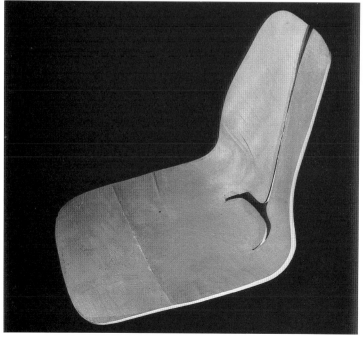

Above: A one-piece chair seat molded in the "Kazam! machine." Opposite: The open "Kazam! machine" showing the heating elements embedded in the plaster mold

At MGM, Charles works with art directors Randall Duell, Lyle Wheeler, Vincente Minnelli, George Davis, and Gabriel Scanamillo. He meets writer Laurence Bachmann, set designer Griswald Raetze, and set and costume designers Margaret Harris and Elizabeth Montgomery.

Charles and Ray on the balcony of their Strathmore Avenue apartment

1941–1942

Molded Wood Experiments: Splint and Litter

An early compound curve sculpture made in the armature on the right, which permitted more complex molding and the use of varying thicknesses of plywood

Charles and Ray continued to refine their wood-molding procedure in late 1941 and 1942 and produced their first molded plywood sculpture to test the possibility of introducing additional and varying layers of wood and more complex curves into the molding process.

In December 1941 an acquaintance from St. Louis, Wendell G. Scott, a medical doctor, visited the Eameses in their Westwood apartment and was shown their wood-molding experiments. Scott told them about problems the military was experiencing with a metal leg splint used in the field. The metal splint did not sufficiently secure an injured leg, causing loss of circulation and gangrene in the limb or death from shock following further injury to the exposed and unprotected heel. Scott suggested adapting the plywood molding process to the production of splints and body litters that would hold, immobilize, and support injured limbs safely and in relative comfort. Made of plywood, such devices would satisfy the wartime need for lightweight and compact splints that were resilient and easy to use, nest, carry, clean, and reuse.

Charles and Ray immediately began developing a molded plywood splint, working at night and on weekends in their apartment. Although the forming process differed somewhat from the method they used to make the chair seats, the goal was the same: to design a prototype that could be mass-produced.

To make the splint, a plaster mold was first taken of Charles's leg, an uncomfortable and painful process (the heat of the curing plaster and the pressure of the wooden blocks supporting the leg caused burns and bruises). A positive leg mold cast from the original mold was then shaped into a symmetrical form designed to represent

The revised leg splint and unmolded splint veneers with the mold, rubber straps, and finished splints

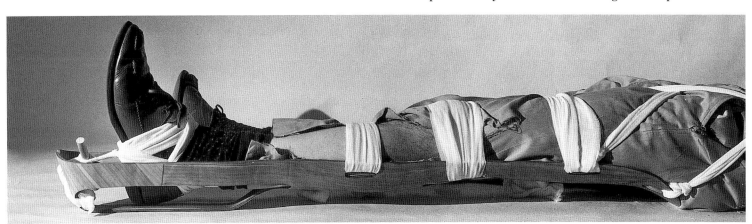

A revised splint showing limbs secured by bandages wrapped through slots

28

Staff: 1942
10946 Santa Monica Boulevard
Gregory Ain
Margaret Harris
Griswald Raetze

Right: A photograph of the setup and rigging of the Ringling Brothers' Barnum & Bailey Circus taken by Charles while observing the dawn arrival of the circus with MGM circus buffs.

right or left legs. Several shaped wood plies were coated with glue and placed in successive layers over the leg mold. The number of plies layered on each section of the splint depended on the amount of support the leg needed at each point. The wood was strapped with wide bands of rubber to hold the veneers in place and gradually compressed by heat and pressure into the desired form. At the end of the four-to-five-hour molding process, the crudely bonded splint was removed from the mold and trimmed and slotted by hand.

Charles and Ray drove to San Diego in early 1942 to show their first splint to the U.S. Navy. After determining that the molded, slotted splint needed additional heel protection, the Eameses returned to Los Angeles to make the necessary revisions. Charles, along with John Entenza, publisher of *Arts & Architecture* magazine, went back to San Diego in the early summer of 1942 with the revised splint. The navy accepted the modified prototype, and the Eameses began designing the equipment needed for mass production.

Charles and Ray were assisted in their effort by John Entenza, who provided them with financial support. (Entenza had great faith in Charles's talent and the two shared the belief that designers and architects have a responsibility to provide solutions to human problems.) Charles left MGM to work full-time on the splint in the summer of 1942, joined by architect Gregory Ain and two associates from MGM, Margaret Harris and architect Griswald Raetze. They rented a shop space at 10946 Santa Monica Boulevard in West Los Angeles, a small room with drafting tables (but no telephones), and a covered side yard that allowed them to work outside. The group immediately began developing production tooling and searching for a glue that would set faster than the glue used in the splint prototype. In November 1942 the navy placed its first order for 5,000 splints, and the group formed a company and development laboratory, Plyformed Wood Company, to manufacture the splint and produce other molded plywood products.

While the splint was readied for mass production, the group also developed a molded plywood body litter. The need to support the lower spine of an injured person was the primary consideration in determining the shape of the litter: the first version was curved along its sides and bottom to conform to the shape of a body, and the ends were elongated to provide gripping handles. In the process of refining the litter design, it became apparent that the basic shape had to be simplified to provide better support for a wider range of body sizes. The work on the litter was interrupted by the need to increase splint production, and the prototype was eventually completed only after the group moved to a new factory site (p. 35).

Above: Steps in molding the litter

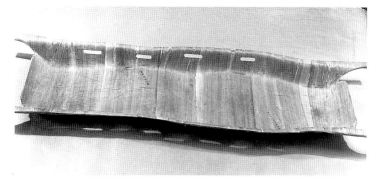

The early litter prototype

Charles lying in the early litter prototype

29

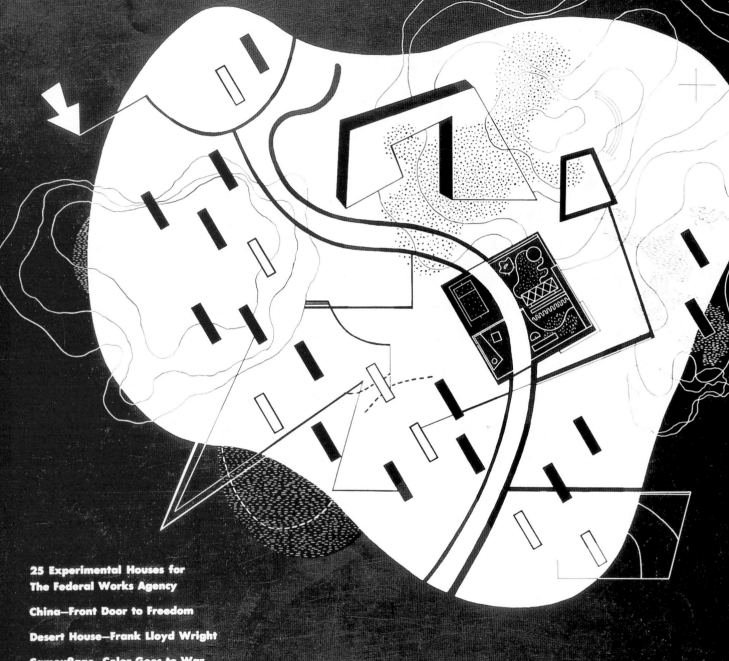

The April 1942 cover designed by Ray

February: Charles becomes a member of the editorial advisory board of *Arts & Architecture* magazine. Two months later he becomes an editorial associate (a position he holds through 1952) and Ray becomes a member of the advisory board.

Staff: 1942
10946 Santa Monica Boulevard
Gregory Ain
Margaret Harris
Griswald Raetze

February 1942 cover of *Arts & Architecture* showing the new format designed by Alvin Lustig

A wood veneer construction made by eleven-year-old Lucia Eames and photographed by Charles for the October *Arts & Architecture* magazine

Interior views of the Eames apartment showing Charles's off-the-shelf "pipe" furniture and a mobile he made out of piano wires

1942

Arts & Architecture Magazine Covers

In 1942 Ray designed six covers for the California magazine *Arts & Architecture*, which was owned, edited, and published by John Entenza. Entenza purchased the magazine in 1938 and revamped its format and content to reflect contemporary trends in architecture, design, music, and the arts. The cover designs were of primary importance in Entenza's campaign, capturing the flavor of the periodical's new directions and priorities in architecture and planning. The title typography of the magazine and some of its covers were designed by Alvin Lustig, a leading Los Angeles graphic designer and teacher whose interests encompassed both design and architecture. During the 1940s Herbert Matter, Charles Kratka, Fred Usher, and John Follis also designed covers for the magazine.

The 1942 covers, designed by Ray while the Plyformed Wood Company was in the midst of the work on the plywood splint, were completed under the pressure of last-minute deadlines and were sometimes executed in a matter of hours. Inspiration for them came from the contents of the particular issue, from photographs taken by Charles, and from the work going on in the office. Assistance on production and on the technical details for the covers often came from friends and associates. Mathematical formulas for the drawings used on the November issue's cover, for example, were provided by Ray's friend the physicist F. Hamilton Wright (who subsequently was called on as an adviser to the film *Communications Primer*; pp. 182–183). Ray's 1943 covers and those of subsequent years reflect the influence of the Spanish painter Joan Miró and her years of study with Hans Hofmann. Charles's drawings and photographs were incorporated into many of the layouts.

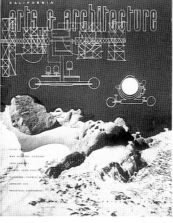

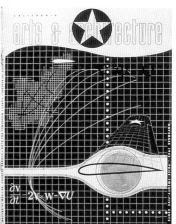

Covers designed by Ray for the May, September, October, November, and December 1942 issues

September: The *U.S. Naval Medical Bulletin* publishes "A New Emergency Transport Splint of Plyformed Wood," by Wendell G. Scott, M.D., and Charles. The article announces the development of the Eames splint.

Staff: 1943
555 Rose Avenue
901 Washington Boulevard
1122 Washington Boulevard
Gregory Ain
Dutch Aldritch
Harry Bertoia
Frances Bishop
Norman Bruns
Georgia Cunningham
William Cunningham
Milton Driggs
Ida Francesca
William Francis
Little Gus
Margaret Harris
Frances Hartwell
Fred Hartwell
Gus Holstrom
Herbert Matter
John Moon
Marion Overby
Griswald Raetze
Harry Soderbloom
Jack Spidell
Martin Ward

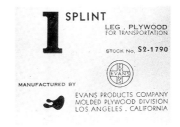

Molded Plywood Division's packing label for the splint, designed by Ray

Charles in the Eameses' 1941 (assembly-line) Ford in front of the Strathmore Avenue apartment

1943

Leg Splint Production

After the U.S. Navy placed its first order for the new splints (pp. 28–29), Plyformed Wood Company moved from Santa Monica Boulevard to larger premises at 555 Rose Avenue in Venice, California. Additional assistants were hired from the immediate Venice and Santa Monica neighborhoods and were given on-the-job training while they produced the splints. The Eameses remembered this production group as an extended family of hardworking, caring individuals dedicated to the project. The designer and photographer Herbert Matter and the designer and sculptor Harry Bertoia joined the group in September 1943.

From the outset, payment from the navy for finished splints lagged far behind orders, causing serious cash-flow problems. In May 1943 Charles began talks in Detroit with Colonel Edward S. Evans, head of Evans Products Company, a Detroit-based manufacturer of industrial equipment and a major supplier of lumber products and devices. Evans, the owner of vast forests of Douglas fir and cedar in the Pacific Northwest, was intrigued by the idea of finding new products to manufacture out of plywood—particularly if this meant new uses for Douglas fir veneer—and in October 1943 he bought the rights to produce and distribute Plyformed Wood Company's splints. His payments retroactively covered salaries, materials, and operating expenses incurred after July 1, 1943, an infusion of funds that kept the company solvent. Plyformed Wood Company thereupon became the Molded Plywood Division, a West Coast subsidiary of Evans Products Company. Evans Products took over splint production at the Rose Avenue plant while the Molded Plywood Division continued to develop the body litter and to experiment with other plywood products. The patents for the splint and the molded plywood products developed later were applied for and held by Evans.

Charles's role in the new subsidiary was that of director of operations. His official title was "Director of Research and Development." He was the contact with the parent Evans Products Company and the one to whom all communication was directed. The original members of the Plyformed Wood Company remained with the operation.

By war's end, over 150,000 splints, with exterior veneers of mahogany and birch, had been manufactured and shipped to the navy. Evans's Douglas fir was used for the core layers of the molded wood sandwich. The traction splint performed well in field use and was judged a success; letters from the navy praised its lifesaving features.

Opposite top: Unmolded, flat splint veneers
Opposite: Finished birch and mahogany production splints

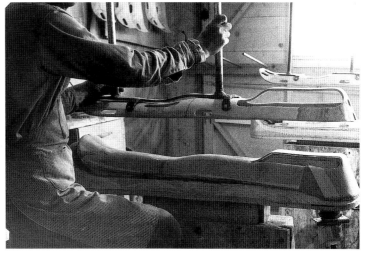

Top to bottom: Steps in the production process: routing, molding, and trimming the splints

Molded Plywood Division's design for the Evans Products Company's trademark

Molded Plywood Division's splint-production staff posing at the Rose Avenue shop to celebrate achieving the goal of manufacturing 200 splints per day

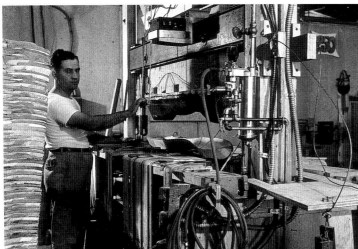

Top to bottom: Veneer gluing and splint molding with production tools

Top to bottom: Mass-produced leg splints, splint packaging, and a demonstration of the splint in use: traction is being applied to secure the broken bones and suspend the heel

Staff: 1943
555 Rose Avenue
901 Washington Boulevard
1122 Washington Boulevard
Gregory Ain
Dutch Aldritch
Harry Bertoia
Frances Bishop
Norman Bruns
Georgia Cunningham
William Cunningham
Milton Driggs
Ida Francesca
Little Gus
William Francis
Margaret Harris
Frances Hartwell
Fred Hartwell
Gus Holstrom
Herbert Matter
John Moon
Marion Overby
Griswald Raetze
Harry Soderbloom
Jack Spidell
Martin Ward

Staff member Harry Bertoia demonstrating the arm splint

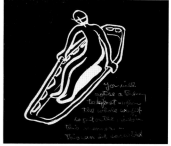

Charles's drawing of and explanation for the revised and improved litter design

1943

Plywood Litter and Arm Splint

In late 1943 the Molded Plywood Division of Evans Products rented a new plant at 901 Washington Boulevard in Venice, California. This former automobile repair shop was to be the site of the Eameses' office for the next forty-five years. Part of the original group went to 901 Washington; others remained at Rose Avenue to continue developing molding tooling and to assist in splint production.

One year after the first body litter was designed (p. 29) a second prototype of the body litter was completed at 901 Washington Boulevard using improved molding techniques. In the revised and simplified version of the litter, curvatures in the side panels, originally designed to conform to the human body, were eliminated. The bottom of the litter was now adapted to the human form by the same process that had been used in the 1940 Eames-Saarinen "organic chairs" (p. 25): a flexible blanket of wooden dowels was shifted until it conformed to the shape of the person lying on it and the optimum position was reached. The resulting shape of the blanket defined the body profile and the critical support areas. The new litter had gripping holes around its perimeter for better portability and was designed to nest easily for shipping and storage. An arm splint also was designed and developed through the prototype stage. However, neither product was mass-produced; the navy could not be convinced that either would be useful enough in field applications to warrant the cost of development and tooling.

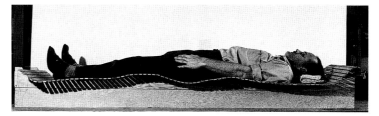

A demonstration of the flexible blanket of wooden dowels used to define the body shape

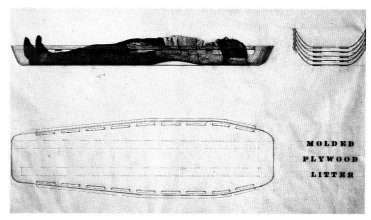

Final litter specifications

A prototype arm splint

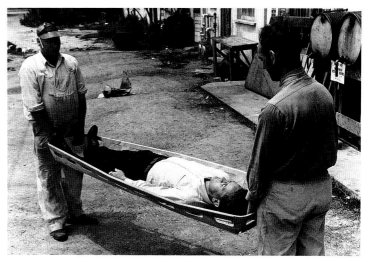

A demonstration of the ease with which the litter could be transported by using the perimeter gripping holes

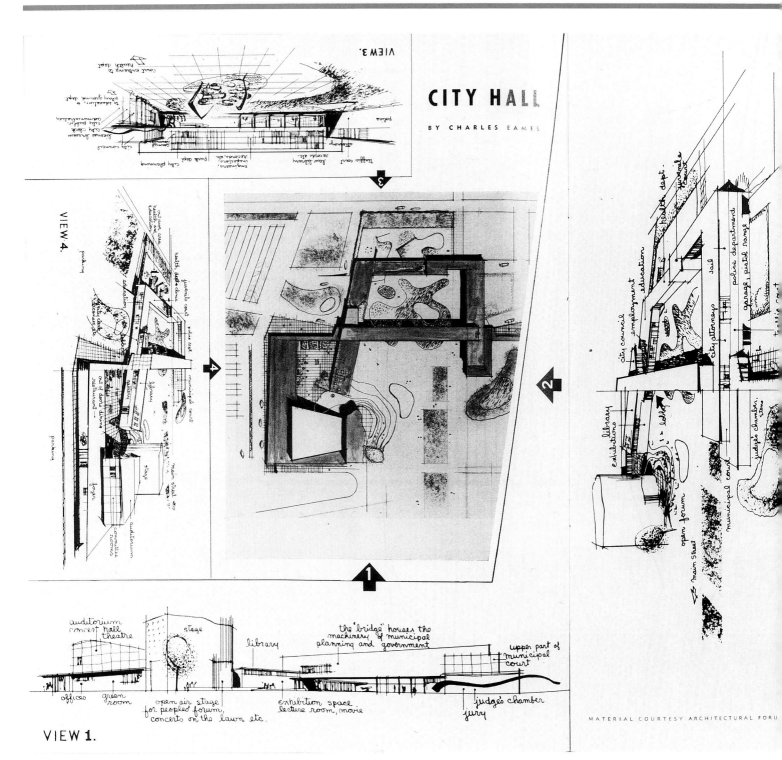

City hall layout by John Entenza and Charles; published in *Arts & Architecture*

Staff: 1943
555 Rose Avenue
901 Washington Boulevard
1122 Washington Boulevard
Gregory Ain
Dutch Aldritch
Harry Bertoia
Frances Bishop
Norman Bruns
Georgia Cunningham
William Cunningham
Milton Cunningham
Ida Francesca
Little Gus
William Francis
Margaret Harris
Frances Hartwell
Fred Hartwell
Gus Holstrom
Herbert Matter
John Moon
Marion Overby
Griswald Raetze
Harry Soderbloom
Jack Spidell
Martin Ward

April: Charles is appointed to the jury for *Arts & Architecture* magazine's competition "Designs for Postwar Living." Also on the jury are architects Gregory Ain, Richard Neutra, John Rex, and Sumner Spaulding. Eero Saarinen and Oliver Lundquist win the competition for a "pre-assembled component" row house.

Competition announcement published in the April 1943 *Arts & Architecture* magazine

1943

Architectural Forum Magazine City Plan

In early 1943 in an issue entitled "New Buildings for 194X" (the exact year in the 1940s was hypothetical), the magazine *Architectural Forum* invited architects to submit projects "to show how buildings might be improved through fuller and more imaginative use of existing resources."

John Entenza and Charles chose to develop plans for a city center. They outlined a complex in which the city hall "must be considered the heart of any community, the house of government. A building in which provision is made not only for the administration of rules and regulations, but a building which must contain facilities for the expression of the *idea* of government, which is never static and which can never be complete without the direct participation of the people who create it."

The proposal was assembled quickly to meet the deadline; it was worked out in a few days by Charles and Entenza in a loft above the splint-production factory at Rose Avenue. The plan called for all city buildings to be integrated into one complex—municipal and juvenile court offices, an auditorium, a library, a restaurant, an outdoor amphitheater, a garage, and health, education, and employment offices. The functions of city administration were physically and operationally connected to encourage citizens to work together toward achieving democratic levels of communication between the governed and the governing. In the words of the proposal: "A city government should—must—be housed as the center of a mutually cooperative enterprise in which the government talks to the people. And the people talk to the government."

The plan was published in the May 1943 issue of *Architectural Forum* and in the June 1943 issue of *Arts & Architecture*. It was the first of many "information-centering" proposals developed by the Eameses for various clients (pp. 84–85, 328–329, 414–415, 438–439), none of which was ever realized. As in many aspects of the Eameses' early work, John Entenza was an important contributor to the development of this visionary scheme. His interest in the social function of architecture and planning led him to initiate the 1943 competition "Designs for Postwar Living." In 1944 he devoted an entire issue of *Arts & Architecture* magazine to the subject of industrial housing (pp. 46–47), and in 1945 he developed the *Arts & Architecture* Case Study House program.

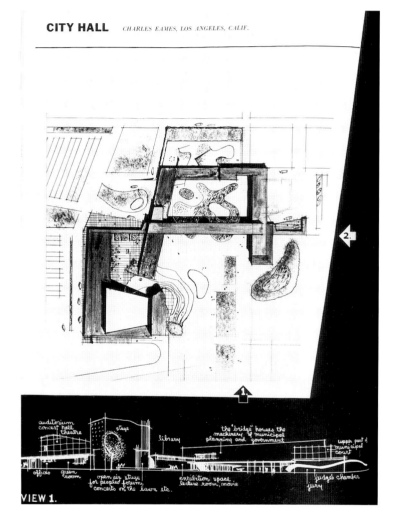

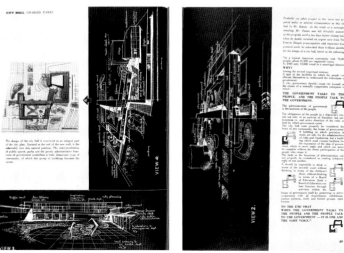

City hall layout by John Entenza and Charles; published in *Architectural Forum*

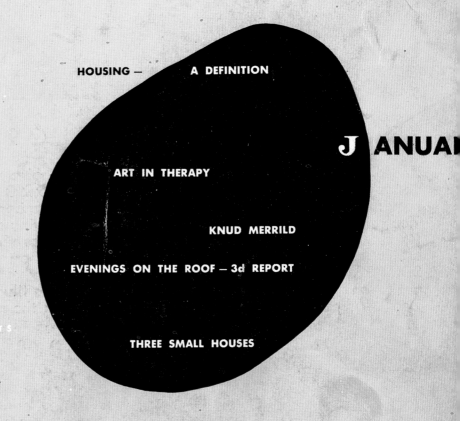

The January 1943 cover designed by Ray

Staff: 1943
555 Rose Avenue
901 Washington Boulevard
1122 Washington Boulevard
Gregory Ain
Dutch Aldrich
Harry Bertoia
Frances Bishop
Norman Bruns
Georgia Cunningham
William Cunningham
Ida Francesca
William Francis
Little Gus
Margaret Harris
Fred Hartwell
Gus Holstrom
Herbert Matter
John Moon
Marion Overby
Griswald Raetze
Harry Soderbloom
Jack Spidell
Martin Ward

A collage by Ray reproduced in the September 1943 *Arts & Architecture* magazine

A cut-paper collage by Ray

1943

Arts & Architecture Magazine Covers

In 1943 Ray designed ten covers for *Arts & Architecture* magazine. The periodical was becoming an influential force calling for the development of architectural innovations in residential design and planning to be implemented in the coming postwar period. In particular, it championed the use of industrial processes to mass-produce multiple housing units.

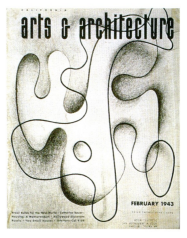

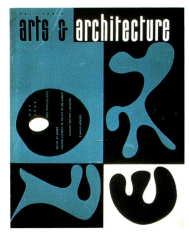
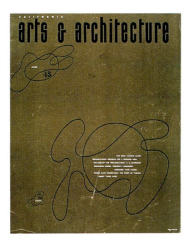

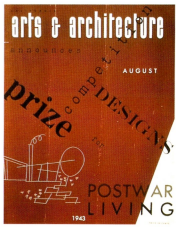

Cover designs by Ray for the February, April, May, June, July, August, September, November, and December 1943 issues

Staff: 1943
555 Rose Avenue
901 Washington Boulevard
1122 Washington Boulevard
Gregory Ain
Dutch Aldritch
Harry Bertoia
Frances Bishop
Norman Bruns
Georgia Cunningham
William Cunningham
Milton Driggs
Ida Francesca
Little Gus
William Francis
Margaret Harris
Frances Hartwell
Fred Hartwell
Gus Holstrom
Herbert Matter
John Moon
Marion Overby
Griswald Raetze
Harry Soderbloom
Jack Spidell
Martin Ward

A plywood sculpture shaped by Ray from a molded leg splint

The Molded Plywood Division's studio and design laboratory in Venice at 901 Washington Boulevard (formerly the Bay Cities Garage), where molding experiments were conducted

1943

Molded Plywood Experiments

Working by themselves as well as with the members of Plyformed Wood Company and the Molded Plywood Division of Evans Products, the Eameses experimented with plywood molding processes from 1941 to 1948. After moving to 901 Washington Boulevard in 1943—and by agreement with the Evans Products Company—the Molded Plywood Division, under Charles's direction, continued to experiment with the properties of molded plywood, while splint and aircraft-parts production (pp. 42–43) was carried on at the Rose Avenue plant and at a converted Safeway grocery store at 1122 Washington Boulevard. The emphasis on control and accuracy in the production of wartime products had a positive effect on the design and construction of later plywood products. The military commissions also meant that priority materials were made available to the group that otherwise would have been impossible for them to obtain.

The goal of the Eameses' experimentation was to arrive at a technique for mass-producing curved plywood shapes that could be used to make low-cost, high-quality furniture. Developing the capacity to apply pressure during the molding process to form compound curves without breaking the wood was the problem of greatest concern. Devices based on the principles of the original "Kazam! machine" (pp. 26–27), but more efficient and faster, were built and tested. As new wood presses were made—designed and engineered by architect Gregory Ain—steel parts were substituted for the earlier wooden ones. A major development was the introduction of a ¼-inch sheet-metal mold (instead of wood-or plaster-ribbed molds) against which the wood was formed under pressure to achieve the compound curves. This innovation made it possible to form complex shapes such as the sculpture on the left, which was made of varying layers of plies. Other experiments focused on forming plywood trusses, coils, springs, and tabs.

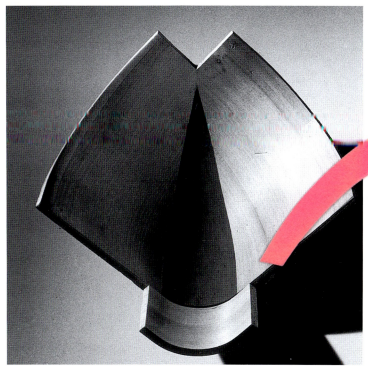

A concave form made by joining four separate pieces of molded plywood

Above: Spring and coil forms made of molded plywood. Opposite: Molded plywood sculpture (26½ x 37¾") made by Charles and Ray with wood of varying thicknesses and curvatures

Plywood strips molded into compound curves

The *Design for Use* exhibition at The Museum of Modern Art in New York City includes molded plywood splints, a litter, vertical stabilizers, and experimental plywood forms developed by the Molded Plywood Division. The exhibition focuses on relationships among function, technology, and form as exemplified in some products of the machine age.

Staff: 1943
555 Rose Avenue
901 Washington Boulevard
1122 Washington Boulevard
Gregory Ain
Dutch Aldritch
Harry Bertoia
Frances Bishop
Norman Bruns
Georgia Cunningham
William Cunningham
Milton Driggs
Ida Francesca
William Francis
Little Gus
Margaret Harris
Fred Hartwell
Gus Holstrom
Herbert Matter
John Moon
Marion Overby
Griswald Raetze
Harry Soderbloom
Jack Spidell
Martin Ward

Installation of the *Design for Use* exhibition showing Eames pieces

Chair seats for Sears, Roebuck and Company produced by the Molded Plywood Division

Christmas card from the Eameses' friends Lee Krasner and Jackson Pollock

1943

Molded Plywood Aircraft Parts

In late 1942, in the Rose Avenue shop, Plyformed Wood Company had developed molded plywood aircraft parts for Vultee Aircraft and other aircraft manufacturers. The products included horizontal and vertical stabilizers, wheel doors, boom sections, trim-tab hinges, pilot seats, gas tanks, hinges, and structural angles. In 1943, at Rose Avenue and 1122 Washington Boulevard, the Molded Plywood Division produced molded plywood vertical and horizontal stabilizers for the Vultee BT15 Trainer. This required larger and more complex versions of the "Kazam!" molding machine (pp. 26–27), and tooling had to be made in the shop to prescribed aircraft specifications. A tremendous amount of pressure was needed to form the large plywood sections, and precise control over such factors as humidity and curing times was imperative. The manufacture of the aircraft parts in general led to more sophisticated processes of molding plywood into compound curves. A plywood pilot's seat, with the parachute serving as a cushion in the molded plywood shell, was developed through the prototype stage, as was a plywood gas tank. Neither was manufactured.

Although the original contacts with the aircraft industry were initiated and developed by John Entenza, contracts in late 1943 and 1944 were brought to the Molded Plywood Division by the parent Evans Products Company, which acted as an agent for its West Coast subsidiary.

Molded plywood pilot seat

The Vultee BT15 Trainer

Griswald Raetze and assistants arranging a plywood sheet for the tail section in a molding machine

The large "Kazam!" molding machine used for molding tail sections

Molded plywood stabilizers after molding and trimming

Molded Plywood Division experiments with a plywood product for Evans Products designed to improve upon and replace the cedar separators used in automobile batteries.

Right: Molded Plywood Division staff members Norman Bruns, William Francis, Marion Overby, Harry Bertoia, Charles, Ray, and Gregory Ain posing with a blister for a glider's nose section

A landscape of freestanding molded plywood fuselage sections photographed by Herbert Matter

Staff: 1943
555 Rose Avenue
901 Washington Boulevard
1122 Washington Boulevard
Gregory Ain
Dutch Aldrich
Harry Bertoia
Frances Bishop
Norman Bruns
Georgia Cunningham
William Cunningham
Milton Driggs
Ida Francesca
William Francis
Little Gus
Margaret Harris
Frances Hartwell
Fred Hartwell
Gus Holstrom
Herbert Matter
John Moon
Marion Overby
Griswald Raetze
Harry Soderbloom
Jack Spidell
Martin Ward

1943

Plywood Glider

In 1943 the glider designer Hawley Bowlus of Airborne Transport, Inc., a subsidiary of General American Transportation Corporation, designed an experimental glider, the CG-16 "Flying Flatcar," to be used for transporting military equipment and personnel. One prototype was built, and the Molded Plywood Division of Evans Products was contracted to produce "blisters" (compound-curved body units that formed part of the nose section) and other fuselage elements out of molded plywood. Plywood parts were designed to replace components made of unobtainable metals.

Constructing a one-piece wooden section as large as the blister (which was eleven feet long, seven feet wide, and twenty inches deep) was regarded as a nearly impossible task. New steel molding machines and other production tools were produced that required intricate engineering and a period of trial and error before production could begin. A mold for forming the plywood sheets to the prescribed length and curvature was developed using a technique devised for other, smaller plywood shapes. The first pieces were to be delivered two months after the order was placed; Molded Plywood Division worked day and night to meet the deadline. The office later learned that others had tried for more than six months but had failed to produce the nose sections. Because a tremendous amount of electricity was required to produce enough heat for curing the lengths of wood, special arrangements had to be made for using the utility during off-peak hours. The 1122 Washington Boulevard space was rented specifically for this work.

The company produced one set of two curved blisters—"ship sets"—for the nose section and other elements for the glider. The cargo ship, designed to hold two jeeps, was flown and tested. However, production was discontinued after an in-flight mishap caused the cargo to shift forward suddenly, killing the pilot and a passenger.

The use of lightweight molded plywood for aircraft, pioneered by the English in their development of the Mosquito and Wellington bombers, was later replaced by the use of aluminum as the major structural material for all aircraft. Although the large-scale aircraft work was of relatively short duration, the Molded Plywood Division gained invaluable skills and experience in producing the large pieces of molded plywood.

Molding form for the plywood blister

The CG-16 glider in tow

The blister being formed in the mold. Considerable heat and pressure were required

Glider production with the blisters in place

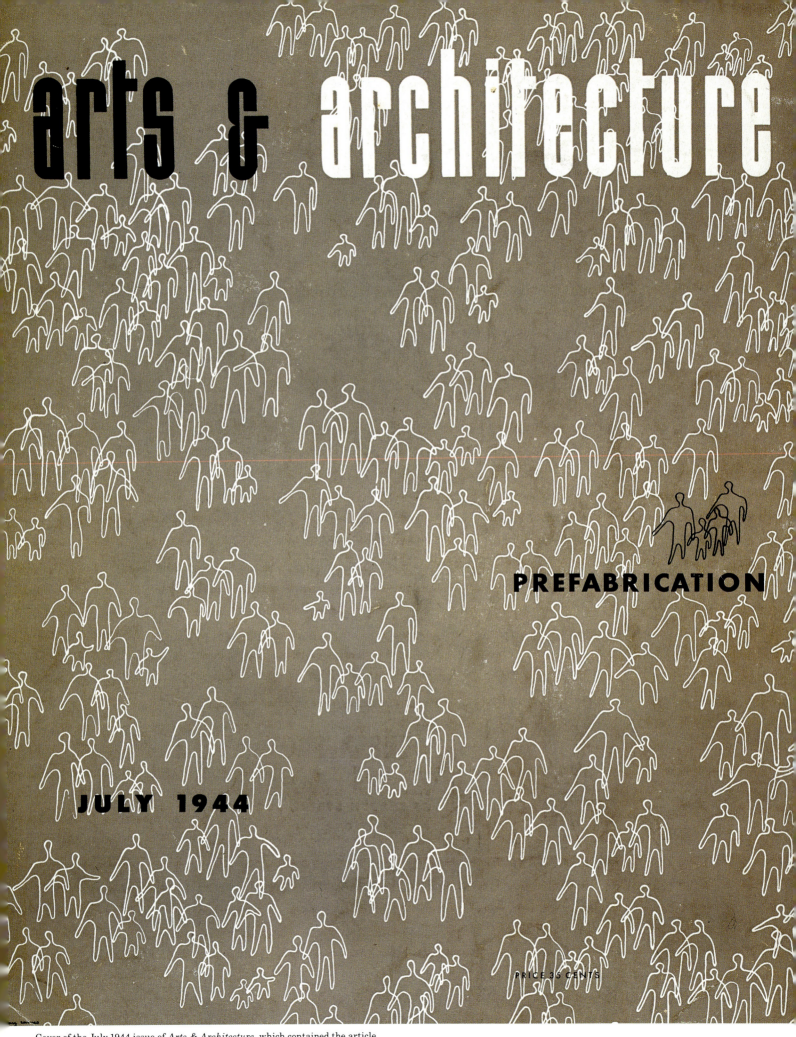

Cover of the July 1944 issue of *Arts & Architecture*, which contained the article "Industrial Housing" by John Entenza and Charles

Staff: 1944
555 Rose Avenue
901 Washington Boulevard
1122 Washington Boulevard
Gregory Ain
Dutch Aldrich
Harry Bertoia
Frances Bishop
Norman Bruns
Georgia Cunningham
William Cunningham
Milton Driggs
Ida Francesca
William Francis
Little Gus
Gus Holstrom
Herbert Matter
John Moon
Marion Overby
Griswald Raetze
Jack Soderbloom
Harry Spidell
Martin Ward

Right: *Composition with Yellow*, a painting by Ray that was included in the third group show of contemporary art at the Los Angeles Museum and published in the October 1944 issue of *Arts & Architecture* magazine

Charles and Ray posing for their 1944 Christmas card with a sculpture they carved from a plywood splint

1944

Arts & Architecture Magazine Covers

In 1944 Ray designed eight covers for *Arts & Architecture* magazine with the assistance of Charles and staff members. Her designs from that year reflect the magazine's continuing interest in the capabilities of mass production, prefabrication, and industrial technology to offer solutions for design and architecture problems. The ongoing interest in these issues, which was inspired by the technological advances made by wartime industries, led to the magazine's Case Study House program, announced by John Entenza in January 1945 (pp. 48–49).

After 1944 Ray did not design a cover for *Arts & Architecture* until March 1947 (pp. 86–87). In the intervening years, Herbert Matter was increasingly involved in producing cover and editorial graphics and photography for the magazine. Matter, a Swiss designer and photographer, already had a substantial reputation in Europe before he joined the Molded Plywood Division in 1943. He also provided much of the photographic documentation of the early work done by the Molded Plywood Division in the three years he was with the company.

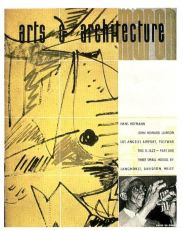

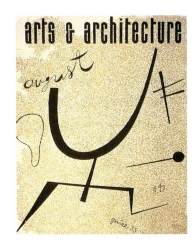
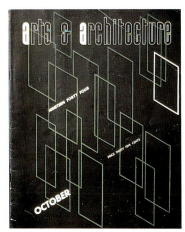
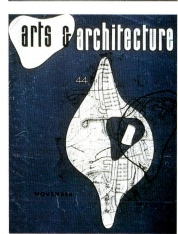

Covers designed by Ray for the January, February, March, April, August, October, and November 1944 issues of *Arts & Architecture*

45

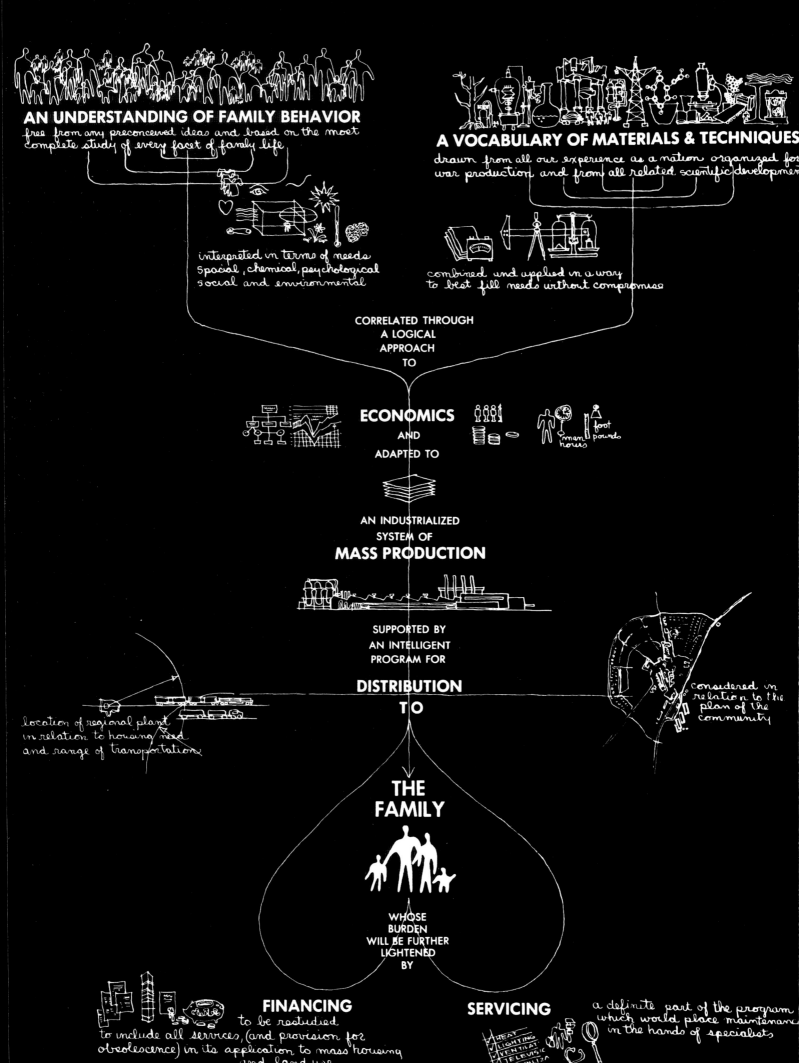

October: "Artists in Industry," an article about the Eameses' work, is published in *Fortune* magazine.

Staff: 1944
555 Rose Avenue
901 Washington Boulevard
1122 Washington Boulevard
Gregory Ain
Dutch Aldritch
Harry Bertoia
Frances Bishop
Norman Bruns
Georgia Cunningham
William Cunningham
Ida Francesca
Milton Driggs
Little Gus
William Francis
Gus Holstrom
Herbert Matter
John Moon
Marion Overby
Griswald Raetze
Harry Soderbloom
Jack Spidell
Martin Ward

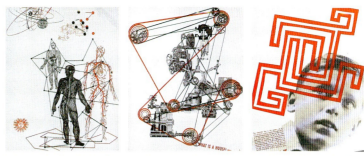

Left to right: Two Herbert Matter collages created for the article "Industrial Housing" and an advertisement he designed for Evans Products Company. All three were reproduced in the July 1944 issue of *Arts & Architecture*

1944

Arts & Architecture Magazine Industrial Housing

The July 1944 issue of *Arts & Architecture* was devoted to the prefabrication, mass production, and industrialization of residential construction. The issue, assembled by John Entenza, Herbert Matter, and Charles and Ray, contained an article by Charles and Entenza entitled "What Is a House?" Responding to a projected housing shortage problem in the postwar period, the authors explored the possibilities of using industrial technologies originally developed to meet wartime needs: "We are concerned with the house as a basic instrument for living within our own time; the house as a solution of human need for shelter that is structurally contemporary; the house that above all takes advantage of the best engineering techniques of our highly industrialized civilization."

The specific housing solution advocated was industrialized prefabrication, a solution that could utilize mass-production techniques developed during the war. Assisted by the best research, techniques, and materials available in the postwar period, architects developing prefabricated houses could incorporate the work of sociologists, scientists, economists, and industrial engineers to develop "good family living machines."

The issue and the article included numerous quotations about the relationship of technology to human problems drawn from the writings of Buckminster Fuller, whose work and philosophy Charles admired, as well as additional quotations by Eero Saarinen and Norman Bruns, an electronics engineer and the Molded Plywood Division staff member responsible for developing the diathermal heating elements for the plywood-molding process. Drawings and charts by Charles and Ray and photographs, montages, and layouts by Herbert Matter illustrated the text.

The article advocated approaching the impending housing shortage with the same urgency and energy that was employed in meeting wartime challenges. It reflected the general optimism of planners and designers that the postwar world would bring with it qualitative changes in the way people live and think about their environments and inspire a willingness to make innovative uses of the new technologies developed in wartime.

Opposite: Charles's drawing for the leading page of the article, diagraming its contents

Charles's illustration of the activities that new housing should be designed to accommodate

A page from the published article

47

CASE STUDY HOUSES 8 AND 9

BY CHARLES EAMES AND EERO SAARINEN, ARCHITECTS

This is ground in meadow and hill, protected on all sides from intrusive developments free of the usual surrounding clutter, safe from urban clatter; not, however, removed from the necessary conveniences and the reassurances of city living.

Two houses for people of different occupations but parallel interests. Both, however, determinedly agreed on the necessity of privacy, or the right to choose privacy from one another and anyone else.

While these houses are not to be considered as solutions of typical living problems; through meeting specific and rather special needs, some contribution to the need of the typical might be developed. The whole solution proceeds from an attempt to use space in direct relation to the personal and professional needs of the individuals revolving around and within the living units inasmuch as the greater part of work or preparation for work will originate here. These houses must function as an integral part of the living pattern of the occupants and will therefore be completely "used" in a very full and real sense. "House" in these cases means center of productive activities.

 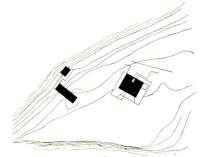 

For a married couple both occupied professionally with mechanical experiment and graphic presentation. Work and recreation are involved in general activities: Day and night, work and play, concentration, relaxation with friend and foe, all intermingled personally and professionally with mutual interest. Basically apartment dwellers, there is a conscious effort made to be free of complications relating to maintenance. The house must make no insistent demands for itself, but rather aid as background for life in work. This house—in its free relation the ground, the trees, the sea—with constant proximity to the whole vast order of nature acts as re-orientor and "shock absorber" and should provide the needed relaxations from the daily complications arising within problems.

In this house activities will be of a more general nature to be shared with more people and more things. It will also be used as a returning place for relaxation and recreation through reading and music and work—a place of reviving and refilling, a place to be alone for preparation of work, and with matters and concerns of personal choosing. A place for the kind of relaxed privacy necessary for the development and preparataion of ideas to be continued in professional work centers. The occupant will need space used elastically where many or few people can be accommodated within the areas appropriate to such needs. Intimate conversation, groups in discussion, the use of a projection machine for amusement and education, and facilities for self-indulgent hobbies, i.e., cooking and the entertainment of very close friends.

 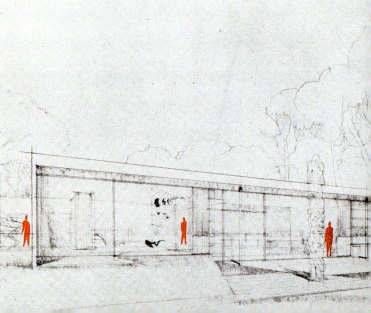

February: Charles serves on the jury for *Arts & Architecture* magazine's second "Small House" competition, organized to encourage the use of new approaches and technologies in the design of residential architecture.

Staff: 1945
555 Rose Avenue
901 Washington Boulevard
1122 Washington Boulevard
Gregory Ain
Dutch Aldrich
Harry Bertoia
Frances Bishop
Norman Bruns
Georgia Cunningham
William Cunningham
Ida Francesca
Little Gus
Gus Holstrom
Herbert Matter
John Moon
Marion Overby
Griswald Raetze
Jack Spidell
Harry Soderbloom
Ben Urmston
Martin Ward

John Entenza, editor and publisher of *Arts & Architecture* magazine

Charles, Ray, and John Entenza at the site of Case Study houses #8 and #9

Right: The cover of the issue of *Arts & Architecture*, designed by Herbert Matter, that contained the announcement of the Case Study House program

1945

Arts & Architecture Magazine Case Study Houses #8 and #9

The Case Study House program was announced in the January 1945 issue of *Arts & Architecture* magazine. The original objective of the project was to design and construct eight houses, each "fulfilling the specifications of a special living problem in the Southern California area." Eight nationally recognized architects or architectural teams (Eero Saarinen and Charles, J. R. Davidson, Richard Neutra, Spaulding and Rex, Wurster and Bernardi, Ralph Rapson, Whitney Smith, and Thornton Abell) were asked to participate. Each house had a specific budget determined by the magazine, which itself acted as the client.

The magazine's editor and publisher, John Entenza, directed the program. He believed that the combination of changes in living standards and the use of new technologies generated by the war would have a lasting impact on the way architects and designers approached their work in the postwar era. The Case Study House program was initiated to explore new attitudes, give them physical form, and provide guidelines for the future. As Entenza wrote: "We hope it will be understood and accepted as a sincere attempt not merely to preview but to assist in giving some direction to the creative thinking on housing being done by good architects and good manufacturers whose joint objective is good housing."

Beginning with the February 1945 issue of the magazine, each architect or team presented plans, specifications for materials, and a design rationale for a house. Case Study House #8 was designed by Charles and Eero Saarinen to be the Eames residence (pp. 106–121). The program was extended beyond the original eight; House #9 was designed by Charles and Saarinen for Entenza (pp. 122–123). Both houses were described in the December 1945 issue of the magazine. According to the architects, the houses were intended as "centers of productive activity" for their respective occupants, providing both working and recreational environments.

The first houses, when completed, landscaped, and furnished, were opened to the public for a six-week period. The program continued through 1966: thirty-four houses were proposed, of which twenty-three were executed. The campaign had a lasting impact on residential architecture, reaching beyond the boundaries of Southern California to influence architects and designers worldwide.

Opposite: Page from the December 1945 *Arts & Architecture* magazine announcing Case Study houses #8 and #9

Charles and Ray with their first Case Study House model, which they called the "Bridge House"

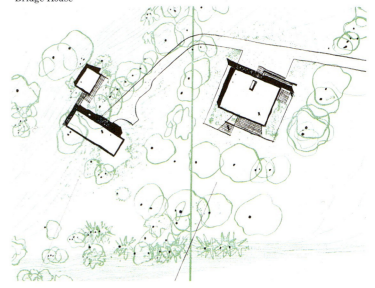

Plot plan for houses #8 and #9

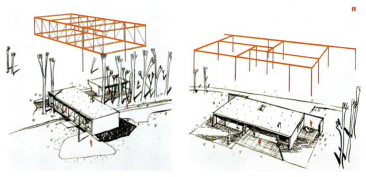

Left and right: Structural plans for houses #8 and #9

Staff: 1945
555 Rose Avenue
901 Washington Boulevard
1122 Washington Boulevard
Gregory Ain
Dutch Aldritch
Harry Bertoia
Frances Bishop
Norman Bruns
Georgia Cunningham
William Cunningham
Ida Driggs
Little Gus
Gus Holstrom
Herbert Matter
John Moon
Marion Overby
Griswald Raetze
Harry Soderbloom
Jack Spidell
Ben Urmston
Martin Ward

Charles in 1945 outside the building at 901 Washington Boulevard

1945

Slide Show: *Lecture I*

Lecture I was the first of many "fast-cut" slide shows designed by the Eameses to communicate concepts and present new projects. Photography, an important tool for Charles ever since he discovered his father's camera equipment as a child, became increasingly important to him as a medium for communicating information. The showing of sequential images in quick progression (eventually two or three slides were projected simultaneously side by side) in conjunction with a project presentation, lecture, or informal talk became a standard Eames approach. (In this volume, slide presentations that have remained in the slide-show form are presented as separate projects; slides that were later transferred to motion-picture film are designated only as films.)

Lecture I, as it was later referred to by the Eameses, was first given to an audience at the California Institute of Technology in Pasadena. Charles used a single projector to show the thirty to forty slides. The subject of the talk was the relationship between design and the structure of the natural and man-made worlds. His slides included bits of found objects—including insect wings, a feather, human skin, a flattened daisy—placed between two glass plates for projection. He also showed slides of toys, details of paintings, letterforms, tools, machines, landscapes, natural forms, and buildings in various stages of completion and disintegration, which he had photographed with a 35mm Leica camera. *Lecture I* was given on many occasions to public groups, office visitors, students, and clients, modified each time in order to address the particular occasion and to include images of new interest. Charles's Norton lectures at Harvard in 1970–1971 (pp. 355–362) were the high point in the evolution of the Eames slide show and of his treatment of the subject itself.

The 35mm camera, a more mobile tool than the view camera that Charles had used since childhood, allowed him to shoot color close-ups quickly and easily. Later, when he began using an Exacta 35mm camera with a single-lens-reflex system, which allowed him to see exactly what he was shooting, he could capture even closer and more accurate details of objects. These close-up images played a significant part in the Eameses' work and were important to them as a way of looking at the world and demonstrating the richness of everyday life and the connections between apparently dissimilar phenomena.

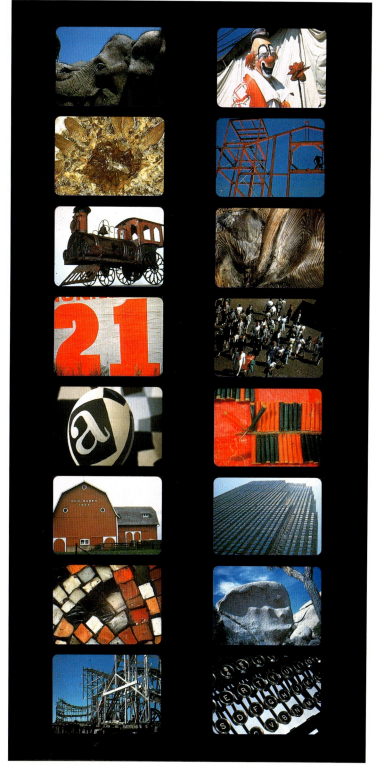

Opposite: Two slides from *Lecture 1*: detail of a drop of water on a leaf; silhouette of an oil-pumping rig

A sequence of images (reading top to bottom left, top to bottom right) from the single-screen slide show *Lecture I*

Four molded plywood tilt-back rocking chairs with metal legs

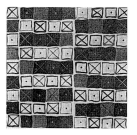

A textile design by Ray entitled *Crosspatch*, which was published in the July 1945 issue of *Arts & Architecture* magazine

1945

Experimental Chairs

As orders for war-related plywood products declined in anticipation of war's end, the Molded Plywood Division applied the knowledge and expertise gained from working on war projects to chairs and other furniture with renewed intensity. The long period of experimentation and germination, supported by the company's wartime work, culminated in a number of prototypes that could be adapted to assembly-line production. Concepts were worked up into full-scale models in both wood and metal in order to resolve technical and aesthetic problems. Several two-part prototypes were built with compound curves in the seats and back sections. Many types of leg solutions were tried in model form and in full size, including three- and four-legged wood and metal versions, T-sections, and rockers. Some chair legs incorporated an axial movement with a back-to-front tilt.

One of the most difficult obstacles to surmount was that of connecting material to material to join one part of a chair to another. Although the use of flexible rubber disks attaching the back and seat sections to the connecting spine afforded a measure of resiliency, the method of attaching the disks to the wooden parts was a problem. Different kinds of glues and other methods were tried and discarded. Staff member Norman Bruns conducted numerous partially successful experiments with electronic cycle-welding, continuing the ideas attempted by Eero Saarinen and Charles for the "Organic Design" chairs. The problem of bonding lingered throughout the early work. Bruns, recalling the experiments, said that if there was any moisture in the wooden parts, the attempt to bond them electronically to the disks resulted in explosions and fires. Don Albinson remembers the smoke and noise issuing from Bruns's corner of the office. The connection problem was finally solved on the assembly line with a glue originally developed for use in wartime production.

Charles, in an interview in 1972, said of the early plywood work: "The idea was to do a piece of furniture that would be simple and yet comfortable. It would be a chair on which mass production would not have anything but a positive influence; it would have in its appearance the essence of the method that produced it. It would have an inherent rightness about it, and it would be produced by people working in a dignified way. That sounds a little pompous, but at the time it was a perfectly legitimate thing to strive for."

Experimental plywood chairs with different leg, spine, and support configurations

Staff: 1945
555 Rose Avenue
901 Washington Boulevard
1122 Washington Boulevard
Gregory Ain
Dutch Aldritch
Harry Bertoia
Frances Bishop
Norman Bruns
Georgia Cunningham
Milton Cunningham
William Cunningham
Ida Driggs
Ida Francesca
Little Gus
Gus Holstrom
Herbert Matter
John Moon
Marion Overby
Griswald Raetze
Harry Soderbloom
Jack Spidell
Ben Urmston
Martin Ward

1945

Children's Furniture

Several pieces of children's furniture—chairs, tables, and stools—were designed and produced using wartime tooling. The low chairs were made in two pieces: the back had an attached bracing unit, and the legs and the seat were molded from one piece of wood with a small flange in the front. A compound curve was molded into the legs, which helped to strengthen them. Stools and tables were also produced as single units, with the legs a continuation of the tops. Made of laminated birch, the furniture was produced in the wood's natural color and in a variety of bright aniline-dyed colors—red, blue, black, magenta, and yellow. A heart-shaped cutout in the back section of the chairs was intended to serve as a child's fingerhold.

A trial run of 5,000 chairs and stools was produced by the Molded Plywood Division of Evans Products. Several items were included in a press preview held by Evans Products in December 1945 in the Barclay Hotel in New York City, in a showing at The Architectural League in February 1946 (both arranged by Alfred Auerbach, a New York City marketing consultant engaged by Evans Products), and at The Museum of Modern Art in March 1946 (pp. 68–71). The pieces were sold throughout 1946 and 1947 in a few shops (Alexander and Susan Girard's shop in Grosse Point, Michigan, and Kitty Weese's shop in Chicago) that were beginning to feature work by contemporary designers. Production of the children's furniture was discontinued mainly because the collection was difficult to market; it did not fit conveniently into the usual merchandising and distribution categories of living-room, dining-room, or bedroom pieces. No additional runs were made.

Production chairs and stools

Molded plywood children's stools, chairs, and table

Nested children's chairs

Opposite: Nested stacks of the lower and upper plywood units of the child's chair

Herbert Matter's son, Alexander (Pundy), astride a molded plywood elephant

Staff: 1945
555 Rose Avenue
901 Washington Boulevard
1122 Washington Boulevard
Gregory Ain
Dutch Aldritch
Harry Bertoia
Frances Bishop
Norman Bruns
Georgia Cunningham
William Cunningham
Ida Francesca
Little Gus
Gus Holstrom
Herbert Matter
John Moon
Marion Overby
Griswald Raetze
Harry Soderbloom
Jack Spidell
Ben Urmston
Martin Ward

John Entenza and Ray wearing animal masks for an impromptu performance

1945

Molded Plywood Animals

A group of animals designed as toys or furniture for children was a playful offshoot of the molded plywood experiments. Furniture-making techniques could be adapted easily to the four-legged animal forms, and the smaller pieces allowed the Molded Plywood Division to experiment with new forms with the equipment on hand while using less of the precious wartime-controlled materials. Mass-producing the smaller forms was also simpler. The animals—frogs, seals, horses, bears, and elephants—were to be made of birch plywood; a child could sit on top of an animal or crawl underneath and move around with it on his or her back. The animals could be nested and stacked.

The frog, bear, and seal were mocked up in metal and the elephant was first tried in cardboard. Two birch prototypes of the elephant and three horses were fabricated. The elephant was included in the Barclay Hotel, The Architectural League, and The Museum of Modern Art showings in late 1945 and early 1946 (pp. 68–71). The animals were not commercially produced; an existing marketing program could not be found for them, and Evans Products was not prepared at this point to set up a furniture distribution system. It was characteristic of Charles to extend the concepts or technology of a major project to ideas that seemed to be merely tangential to the main problem. In later years, many of these lateral moves developed into projects, toys, and films that became important milestones in his work.

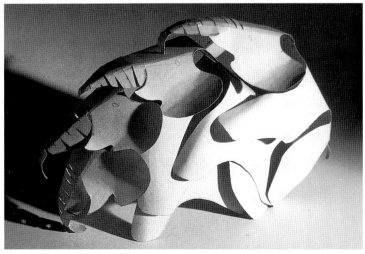

Nested cardboard mock-ups of elephants

Top: A metal mock-up of the frog and the seal. Middle: A molded plywood horse
Above: A mock-up bear in metal

57

Wood-legged dining chair (DCW)

Staff: 1945
555 Rose Avenue
901 Washington Boulevard
1122 Washington Boulevard
Gregory Ain
Dutch Aldritch
Harry Bertoia
Frances Bishop
Norman Bruns
Georgia Cunningham
William Cunningham
Ida Francesca
Little Gus
Gus Holstrom
Herbert Matter
John Moon
Marion Overby
Griswald Raetze
Harry Soderbloom
Jack Spidell
Ben Urmston
Martin Ward

The offices of the Molded Plywood Division of Evans Products Company at 901 Washington Boulevard in Venice, California

1945–1946

Plywood Chairs

In 1945, with the prospect of the war ending and materials and labor becoming more readily available for domestic purposes, plans for mass-producing plywood chairs began to crystallize. The goal was to produce an inexpensive, high-quality chair using industrial technologies developed during the war. The Molded Plywood Division of Evans Products, by now certain that its molding techniques could be adapted to the mass production of compound-curved furniture, began to build the basic tooling necessary for manufacturing the chairs in quantity. Chairs made of separate components emerged as the best candidates for mass production—the production of separate elements was easier and more economical; parts could be joined in more combinations, and if a seat or back cracked or was broken, the loss was not as dramatic as the loss of an entire chair. Of more importance, the elimination of extraneous wood needed to connect the seat with the back was a major breakthrough in terms of reducing the chair, both functionally and aesthetically, to the minimal statement that was the basis of its design and of its compatibility with mass-production requirements.

The molding process for the chairs was essentially a refinement of earlier experiments. Thin sheets of wood, roughly cut to shape, were coated with a plastic binder and placed on top of one another. The wood grain of each of the successive layers (a 5-ply thickness was judged to

Wood-legged lounge chair (LCW)

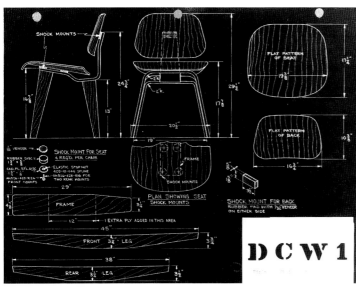

Specifications for the DCW

Back of the dining chair (DCW) showing the spine connected to the back by a single lozenge-shaped shock mount with no screws, which were added later

59

Charles and Ray posing in John Entenza's apartment with a Christmas tree made of plywood chair legs

Molded Plywood Division's staff Christmas party. A molded plywood Christmas tree is in the background

Two versions of the three-legged metal rod chair

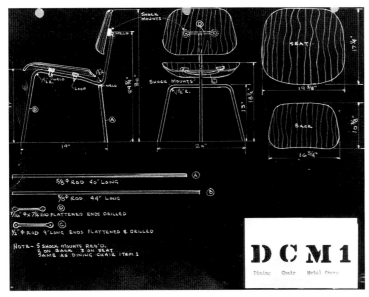
Specifications for the three-legged chair (DCM1)

be the best aesthetic and functional choice) ran counter to the one above it to increase the strength of the plywood "sandwich," which was then positioned over an inflatable neoprene and canvas air bag and beneath a metal mold filled with a synthetic heating oil. The mold used was a larger and more efficient version of the original "Kazam! machine" (pp. 26–27).

On top of the air bag was a neoprene blanket with a nichrome-wire heating element cemented in its center. Above the heating element was a canvas caul that received the precoated plywood lay-up. A plaster mold at the bottom of the machine formed the bottom half of the male/female mold. Once the wood and glue sandwich was clamped into the machine, compressed air inflated the rubber membrane, slowly (to avoid breakage) pressing the plywood into the curves of the mold. The heat from the lower pad fused the wood sheets into a single piece. While the pressure was maintained, the hot oil at the top cooked a melamine finish into the upper and lower plies of light woods. (Dark woods were sprayed with a finish.) Ten minutes were required to mold the 5-ply chair backs and seats, which were $5/16$-inch thick. The thicker legs and spine, bent in one direction only, required twenty minutes. When released from the machine, the seats and backs were trimmed on a routing template, and the legs and spine were cut on a table saw.

Lengthy experiments were conducted over a period of years in an attempt to apply the electronic cycle-welding process (first developed by the Chrysler Corporation in the 1930s), which used radio frequencies to transmit heat to a bonding agent placed between two parts, thereby bonding them together in a tough, waterproof, permanent joint. The attempts to use this technology to fuse the rubber connectors, or shock mounts, to the molded plywood chair backs, spines, and seats were only partially successful (pp. 52–53), and a satisfactory mass-production technique for connecting

Wire models of metal chair legs

Three-legged plywood chair

Prototypes of wood and metal chair legs

Staff member Norman Bruns adjusting the electronic radio-frequency bonding machine, which transmitted heat by radio waves

the parts of the chair was finally achieved on the assembly line by gluing the shock mounts to the wood pieces with a resorcinol phenolic adhesive applied with heat and pressure. The legs were then screwed to the shock-mounted spine, and the seat was attached to the legs and spine by four additional shock mounts. The shock-mount system afforded the chair backs a measure of flexibility and resiliency.

Two versions of the wood-legged chair (christened the DCW and LCW for "Dining Chair Wood" and "Lounge Chair Wood") and one version of the three-legged metal rod chair (or DCM for "Dining Chair Metal") were judged to have the most potential for production and marketing. (Charles always used basic, no-nonsense names for products and projects, and these names were later continued by the Herman Miller Furniture Company.) Although some exotic woods were tried, ash, rosewood, birch, and walnut emerged as the choices for production models, each with a "baked-on" synthetic oil finish. In addition to the natural wood finishes, chair parts were to be available in aniline-dyed black and red or covered in animal hides, leather, Naugahyde, or fabric.

Molded Plywood Division produced some chairs in the fall and early winter of 1945, and Evans Products, the parent company, began to work on the problems of marketing and distribution. The prototype chairs of both the three-legged metal and four-legged wood versions were shown at the December 1945 Barclay Hotel press and trade preview, at the February 1946 Architectural League preview, and at The Museum of Modern Art in March 1946 (pp. 68–71). After the showings, the three-legged and tilt-back chairs were reluctantly eliminated from the collection due to problems of balance and stability. Two versions of the four-metal-legged chair replaced the three-legged versions; mass-production of these (in a run of 1,000) began in Venice, California, in the summer of 1946.

Molding machine with the male/female compression molds made of Kirksite

Trimming the chair legs on a table saw

Positioning the plywood seat for final trimming

Staff: 1945
555 Rose Avenue
901 Washington Boulevard
1122 Washington Boulevard
Gregory Ain
Dutch Aldritch
Harry Bertoia
Frances Bishop
Norman Bruns
Georgia Cunningham
William Cunningham
Ida Francesca
Little Gus
Gus Holstrom
Herbert Matter
John Moon
Marion Overby
Griswald Raetze
Harry Soderbloom
Jack Spidell
Ben Urmston
Martin Ward

Right: December 4-6: A showing for the press and the furniture trade of the Molded Plywood Division's furniture held at the Barclay Hotel in New York City. The event, the first public showing of the Molded Plywood Division's plywood furniture, was sponsored by Evans Products

1945

Molded Plywood Tables

In 1945 the Molded Plywood Division used the molding process to manufacture tabletops and legs. Round coffee tables with molded tray tops and three bent, V-shaped steel rod legs or with three or four wood legs were produced to complement the plywood lounge chairs. A prototype of a rectangular, tray-topped occasional table was made with three rod legs, and a dining table with a flat, rectangular plywood top and four plyformed wood legs curved into right angles was made to be sold as a knockdown item for easy storage and shipping. Large folding tables with black laminate tops and folded steel rod legs were also produced in prototype models.

A great deal of effort was expended on resolving the functional and aesthetic problems of connecting rod legs to wooden tabletops. The three-legged wood and metal rod tables were eventually dropped as production items, and a new folding table (pp. 81–83) replaced the original version.

The design of the tables adhered to the critical objectives that defined the production of the chairs: each was to be a minimal statement of wood and hardware, mass-produced for sale at a low cost, satisfying a wide range of household needs (both indoor and outdoor) and capable of being easily stored and moved about.

Tables were included in the Barclay Hotel showing, The Architectural League preview and The Museum of Modern Art exhibition (pp. 68–71).

Rectangular knockdown table with molded plywood legs

Three-legged tray table with metal rod legs

Folding table

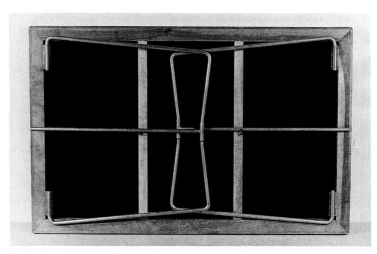

Underside of folding table

LCW and round table with three wood legs

Round coffee table with three V-shaped metal legs

Round coffee table with four wood legs

A prototype of an early tilt-back lounge chair with metal legs and spine

Staff: 1946
555 Rose Avenue
901 Washington Boulevard
1122 Washington Boulevard
Gregory Ain
Don Albinson
Milah Bernie
Harry Bertoia
Frances Bishop
Norman Bruns
Georgia Cunningham
Victor Delgado
Milton Driggs
Ida Francesca
Saul Golden
Little Gus
Gus Holstrom
Cecil James
Herbert Matter
John Moon
Marion Overby
Griswald Raetze
Harry Soderbloom
Ben Urmston

Charles and Ray in two variations of the plywood lounge chair

1946

Plywood Lounge Chair

A number of experiments were conducted in 1945 and 1946 in an effort to arrive at a comfortable plywood chair for reclining and lounging. The problem of designing a new lounge chair form had been tackled initially by Eero Saarinen and Charles in their chair designs for The Museum of Modern Art's "Organic Design in Home Furnishings" competition in 1940 (p. 25).

In the 1946 lounge-chair studies, carried on by Don Albinson (an Eames staff member and former Cranbrook student), among others, the spine connecting the seat and the back became a major structural and aesthetic element that unified the three large pieces of molded plywood. The rubber disks that connected the back, the arms, and the seat provided flexibility and resiliency and became an important part of the design solution. In one prototype, the wooden shell was supported by a metal base and the spine was a metal strap; in other versions, molded wooden legs, T-section supports, tilt-back frames, and a tubular metal base provided the leg supports.

Though never manufactured, the plywood lounge chair, also included in the three early showings of Eames furniture in New York City (pp. 68–71), was the forerunner of the Eames leather-cushioned, molded wood lounge chair produced in 1956 (pp. 206–207).

Lounge chair prototype with wood legs

Side and front views of chair backs with spine extensions

Lounge chair prototype with a low, tilt-back metal frame support developed by Don Albinson

65

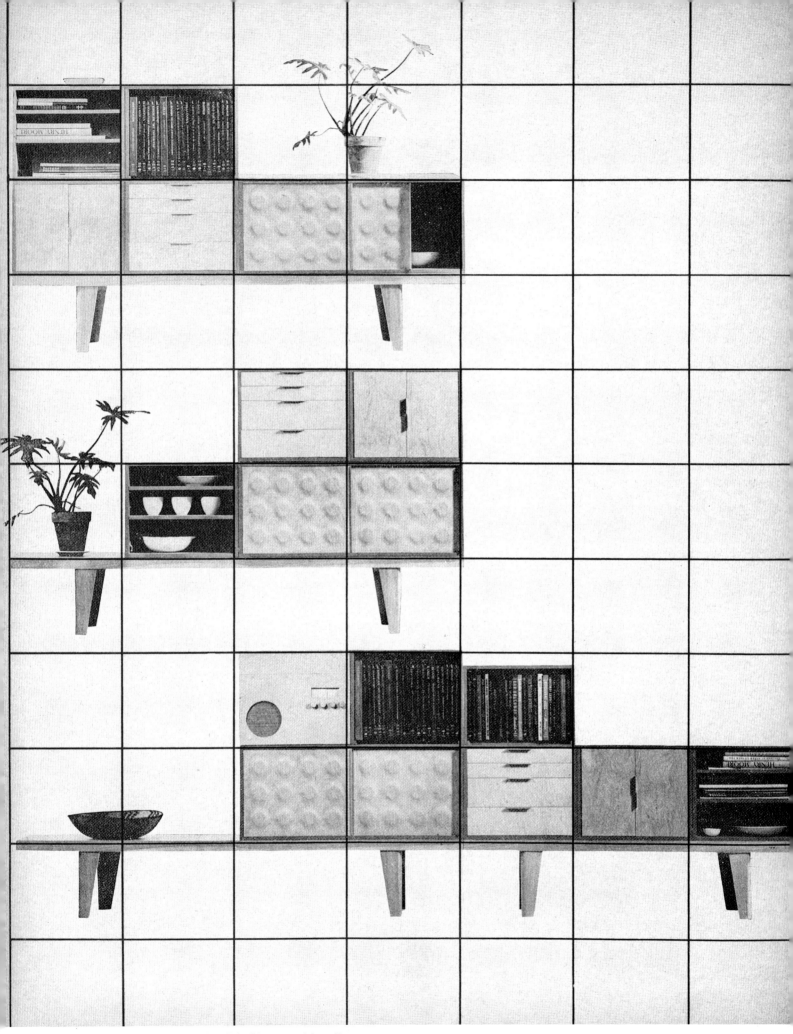

Illustration from the September 1945 *Arts & Architecture* article on Eames molded plywood furniture written by Eliot Noyes, director of the Industrial Design department at The Museum of Modern Art

February: A showing for the press and the furniture trade of the Molded Plywood Division's furniture opens at The Architectural League in New York City. The exhibition is sponsored by Evans Products.

Staff: 1946
555 Rose Avenue
901 Washington Boulevard
1122 Washington Boulevard
Gregory Ain
Don Albinson
Milah Bernie
Harry Bertoia
Frances Bishop
Norman Bruns
Georgia Cunningham
Victor Delgado
Milton Driggs
Ida Francesca
Saul Golden
Little Gus
Gus Holstrom
Cecil James
Herbert Matter
John Moon
Marion Overby
Griswald Raetze
Harry Soderbloom
Ben Urmston

Charles reclining on a Case Goods bench

Herbert Matter photographing staff colleagues Marion Overby and Ben Urmston at work

1946

Case Goods

In 1945 the Eameses and the staff of the Molded Plywood Division of Evans Products began to extend their plywood technology to the production of modular storage systems. Named "Case Goods," the system of freestanding, low cabinets was based on units Eero Saarinen and Charles had entered in the 1940 "Organic Design in Home Furnishings" competition (p. 25). The Molded Plywood Division system, completed in prototype form between late 1945 and early 1946, consisted of groupings of wooden storage cabinets placed on low benches of different lengths. The modular cabinets, available in standardized sizes, were interchangeable and allowed for various storage configurations, depending upon what was added to the standard wooden case shell: the options included versions with drawers, shelves, or radio housings. Hinged swinging or sliding doors could also be added to individual cabinets. Interchangeable front panels were produced with different exterior treatments; one variety had an embossed round "dimple" pattern designed to add strength and rigidity to the thin lamination. The inherent versatility of the system allowed customers to design furniture units to suit individual storage needs.

Prototypes of the Case Goods system were included in The Architectural League showing and the 1946 Museum of Modern Art show (pp. 68–71). The Case Goods collection was not mass-produced.

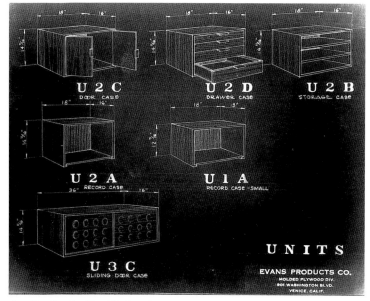
Specifications for Case Goods units

Example of Case Goods system with two benches

Staff member Ben Urmston in a room setting with Case Goods units

Example of Case Goods system with two stacked units, the maximum advisable height

Plywood furniture installed at The Museum of Modern Art

Staff: 1946
555 Rose Avenue
901 Washington Boulevard
1122 Washington Boulevard
Gregory Ain
Don Albinson
Milah Bernie
Harry Bertoia
Frances Bishop
Norman Bruns
Georgia Cunningham
Victor Delgado
Milton Driggs
Ida Francesca
Saul Golden
Little Gus
Gus Holstrom
Cecil James
Herbert Matter
John Moon
Marion Overby
Griswald Raetze
Harry Soderbloom
Ben Urmston

Entry panel to the exhibition *New Furniture Designed by Charles Eames*

1946

Exhibition: *New Furniture Designed by Charles Eames*

Fifteen examples of the Molded Plywood Division's plywood furniture were shown in a press preview held at the Barclay Hotel in New York City during the first week of December 1945. The showing was sponsored by Evans Products and arranged by Alfred Auerbach Associates to introduce Evans's entry into the consumer furniture market. Architects, designers, representatives of retail furniture companies and department stores, and the press were invited to see the chairs and tables, children's furniture, the Case Goods system, and a photographic display of the Molded Plywood Division's wartime and experimental work. It was in this setting that George Nelson, the newly appointed design director of The Herman Miller Furniture Company, first saw the plywood furniture. In February 1946 The Architectural League in New York City made space available for a three-week showing of the furniture to the trade and the press.

After the Barclay Hotel showing, Charles was invited by Eliot Noyes, director of Industrial Design at The Museum of Modern Art, to have a "one-man" furniture exhibition. (Although the museum was concerned that the show would be perceived as too "commercial," and not of museum quality, Noyes persisted and the exhibition went ahead.) Noyes first became acquainted with Charles in 1940 when he organized the "Organic Design in Home Furnishings" competition at the museum. In 1945, while Noyes was serving in the military, Serge Chermayeff and René d'Harnoncourt had included the splints and other plywood wartime products produced by the Molded Plywood Division in *Design for Use*, a traveling exhibition organized by The Museum of Modern Art. During the war Noyes also was kept abreast of the Eameses' California work. In September 1946 an article by Noyes about Charles appeared in *Arts & Architecture* magazine, praising the new plywood furniture as "a compound of aesthetic brilliance and technical inventiveness." (Molded Plywood Division staff members Gregory Ain, Griswald Raetze, Harry Bertoia, and Herbert Matter left the operation shortly after the article was published.)

The Museum of Modern Art exhibition of the new plywood furniture opened on March 13, 1946, and closed on March 31, 1946. It featured the all-plywood furniture, the upholstered side and lounge chairs, plywood and metal-legged side chairs, coffee and dining tables with wood and metal legs, the Case Goods, and the children's plywood

Two views of The Museum of Modern Art installation

The Eameses' friend Doris Knox in a tilt-back chair. The multiple-exposure photograph was taken by Herbert Matter

furniture. Other prototype chairs were also displayed, including the two versions of the three-legged wooden chair, the tilt-back chair with rod legs (pp. 52–53), and the children's plywood elephant (pp. 56–57). It was in this exhibition that the plywood "Eames Chair" (pp. 72–75) made its public debut. Some of the chairs in this exhibition had shock mounts attached to the wooden members by the electronic cycle-welding process experimented with at length by the Molded Plywood Division (pp. 52–53). Shock mounts on other chairs were bonded by various glues.

The Eames staff, with the help of the museum's staff, designed the exhibition, supplementing their previous two installations with objects, photo panels, and potted plants. The exhibition included additional graphic panels, composed of photographic images and three-dimensional pieces of molded-wood experiments and chair parts designed by Herbert Matter and produced at the Venice shop, that described the plywood-molding process and the rubber shock-mount system used to connect furniture components. Devices (also built in the Venice shop) were installed to demonstrate the strength of the new chairs. One showed the durability of the rubber shock mounts; another tested the chair's structural durability by tumbling it inside a drum. These kinetic devices produced their own audio accompaniment. Stop-motion, stroboscopic photographs taken by Herbert Matter of the latter test were also part of the show.

It was through this exhibition that George Nelson introduced D. J. De Pree and James Eppinger, president and sales manager, respectively, of the Herman Miller Furniture Company, to the Eames plywood furniture, thus beginning a long-lasting and rewarding relationship that helped to make the Herman Miller Furniture Company a leader in the field of contemporary furniture.

 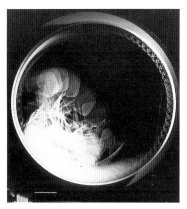

Left: The tumbling drum built to test the chair's durability. Right: Herbert Matter's stroboscopic, multiple-exposure photograph of a chair being tested

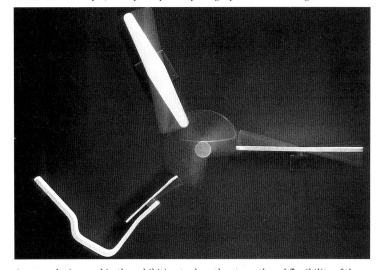

A rotary device used in the exhibition to show the strength and flexibility of the rubber shock mount

  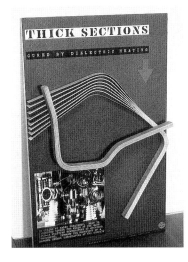 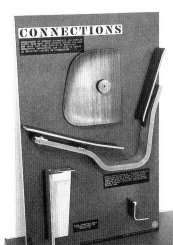

Above: Graphic panels made for the exhibition to explain chair production. Opposite: An assemblage of photographs and three-dimensional objects designed by Herbert Matter for the exhibition

Edward S. Evans, Jr., who succeeded his father, Colonel Edward S. Evans, as head of Evans Products

Edward S. Evans, Jr., and his wife, Flossie, visiting the site of the Eames Case Study House #8

Lucia Eames posing in the LCW

Underside of the DCW, showing the screw-attached assembly of legs and shock mounts

Staff: 1946
555 Rose Avenue
901 Washington Boulevard
1122 Washington Boulevard
Gregory Ain
Don Albinson
Milah Bernie
Harry Bertoia
Frances Bishop
Norman Bruns
Georgia Cunningham
Victor Delgado
Milton Driggs
Ida Francesca
Saul Golden
Little Gus
Gus Holstrom
Cecil James
Herbert Matter
John Moon
Marion Overby
Griswald Raetze
Harry Soderbloom
Ben Urmston

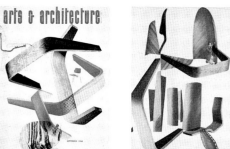 

The cover and a double-spread from the article "Charles Eames," written by Eliot Noyes and published in the September 1946 issue of *Arts and Architecture* magazine. The article and the cover were designed by Herbert Matter

1946

Herman Miller Furniture

The Barclay Hotel and Architectural League showings of the Eames plywood furniture in December 1945 and February 1946 marked the entry of Evans Products—primarily producers of aircraft, automobile, and railway equipment—into the consumer furniture market. The furniture also was shown in early January 1946 in the Chicago and Grand Rapids winter furniture marts to retail salespeople, who were enthusiastic about the new, "modern" designs. Evans Products, through Alfred Auerbach Associates, began setting up sales promotions and selecting the department and furniture stores in which the plywood collection would be launched.

The Molded Plywood Division of Evans Products in Venice started producing display chairs for showrooms, refining the production process, and working out shock-mount and manufacturing problems on the spot while Evans Products set up a marketing and distribution system. Several stores were candidates for the inaugural campaign, among them Kaufmann's in Pittsburgh and Macy's and Bloomingdale's in New York. Hans Knoll of Knoll Furniture actively campaigned to handle the collection. Earlier, Knoll had expressed interest in the marketing of the children's furniture (pp. 54–55).

On March 26, 1946, D. J. De Pree and James Eppinger of the Herman Miller Furniture Company saw the Eames furniture at The Museum of Modern Art show (pp. 68–71). Evans Products, at this point, was still not convinced that they wanted to enter the furniture market, and Eppinger, learning that the company might be interested in divesting itself of the plywood furniture operation, negotiated to take over the production and distribution of the furniture. Herman Miller's director of design, George Nelson, was eager to have the plywood pieces for Herman Miller's line, but the company found itself in a dilemma: its manufacturing facilities were already overburdened, and there was no place in the Zeeland, Michigan, plant for the plywood-molding equipment. In the course of the discussions, Evans Products decided to manufacture the furniture if a distributor could be found. Herman Miller agreed to manage this part of the program, and in June 1946 Evans Products granted Herman Miller exclusive rights to market and distribute the plywood furniture as of October 1946.

The initial plan was to show the furniture at the January 1947 furniture markets and to fill orders immediately from a warehouse stock built up in the last months of 1946. The strategy included making the

Back and front views of the DCW with screw-attached shock mounts

Back and front views of the LCW with early cycle-welded shock-mount system

Component parts of the LCM, showing the screw attachment of the lozenge shock mount

Charles with a factory production-line of finished chairs

Underside of the DCM, showing screw-attached shock mounts

furniture available first to architects and designers on a limited basis until full production could be achieved in mid-1947. The Molded Plywood Division in Venice supplied the Herman Miller sales force with sample furniture, photographs of the collection, and informational graphics.

The death in September 1945 of Colonel Edward S. Evans, president of Evans Products, had initiated a new period in the relationship with the Molded Plywood Division in Venice. The new management of Evans Products, under the leadership of Edward S. Evans, Jr., decided to sever its ties with the California subsidiary and to consolidate its operations, including the plywood molding, at a new plant in Grand Haven. The complications of producing, marketing, and shipping from the West Coast were a factor in Evans's decision.

On April 15, 1947, all manufacturing of plywood furniture in Venice ceased, and the "Kazams!" and other machinery were readied for the trip east. Some members of the Molded Plywood Division staff went to Grand Haven for two months to install the equipment, but with this transfer from California to Michigan, the staff employed by the Molded Plywood Division was out of work and everyone left the company, which was then dissolved. Charles and Ray continued to use the 901 Washington space, which eventually became known as the "Eames Office." In 1950 Herman Miller transferred some of its Eames furniture operations to the West Coast and took over most of the 901 building. In 1958 Miller moved to a larger facility in Culver City, and the Eameses occupied the entire 901 building.

The plywood furniture distribution arrangement with Herman Miller continued for two years. In 1949 Herman Miller bought the manufacturing rights for the chairs from Evans Products, and some of the former Venice staff returned to Michigan to install the machinery in Zeeland. Herman Miller has produced the metal-legged plywood chair ever since, in addition to all of the furniture subsequently designed by the Eames Office. The two wood-legged versions of the plywood chair were discontinued in 1953 and 1957. Charles officially joined Herman Miller as design consultant in 1947 on the recommendation of George Nelson, who had been acquainted with his work since The Museum of Modern Art "Organic Design in Home Furnishings" competition in 1940. The acquisition of the plywood furniture was an important turning point for Herman Miller. Through the efforts of George Nelson and the designers he contracted (Eames, Isamu Noguchi, and Alexander Girard, among others), the company gained international visibility producing contemporary furniture and fabrics.

Front views of the DCM and LCM

Back views of the DCM and LCM

Component parts of the LCM

Staff: 1946
555 Rose Avenue
901 Washington Boulevard
1122 Washington Boulevard
Gregory Ain
Don Albinson
Milah Bernie
Harry Bertoia
Frances Bishop
Norman Bruns
Georgia Cunningham
Victor Delgado
Milton Driggs
Ida Francesca
Saul Golden
Little Gus
Gus Holstrom
Cecil James
Herbert Matter
John Moon
Marion Overby
Griswald Raetze
Harry Soderbloom
Ben Urmston

Charles in his office

1946

Radio Enclosures

A line of radio enclosures was among the postwar offspring of the plywood-molding process. Working with Evans Products, the Molded Plywood Division developed techniques for mass-producing plywood enclosures in significant numbers. Cabinet forms were designed for such manufacturers as the Bendix Corporation, Emerson Radio, Farnsworth Company, Hamilton Radio Corporation, Federal Telephone & Radio Corporation, Majestic Radio, Magnavox, Stromberg Carlson Company, and Zenith Corporation. In addition to the molded cases, which were made of birch and ash, cabinet fronts were formed with a "dimpled" surface, a pattern used first in the Case Goods storage system (pp. 66–67) and later incorporated into the Eames Storage Units (pp. 126–129) for the same reason: the compound surface strengthened the panels and kept them from warping. Approximately 200,000 radio cabinets were fabricated in a wide variety of designs, first in the Rose Avenue building in Venice (through 1946) and later in the Evans Products plant in Grand Haven, Michigan (where production was transferred in early 1947). Manufacturing was discontinued after 1952.

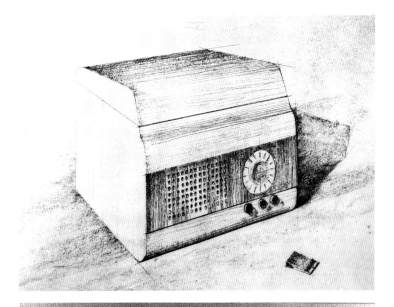

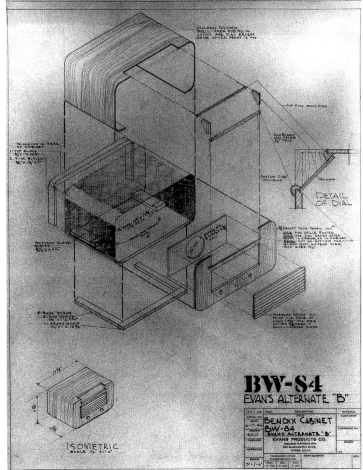

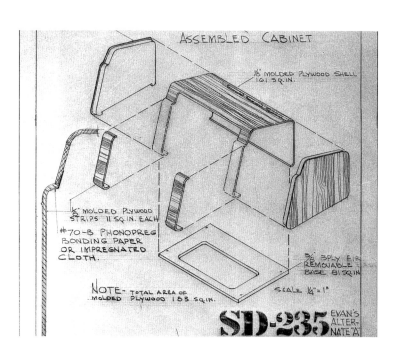

Top: Charles's pencil rendering for a radio enclosure
Above and right: Ben Urmston's specification drawings for radio enclosures

In 1946, while Charles was in Detroit at a meeting with Evans Products' management and their marketing consultant Alfred Auerbach, he saw and admired some radio enclosures designed by Alexander Girard, an architect who worked in Grosse Point, Michigan. The two met and began a lifetime friendship and professional association. In 1950 Charles recommended to George Nelson that Girard become a consulting designer for the Herman Miller Furniture Company.

Charles with a 4x5 camera on the site of Case Study houses #8 and #9

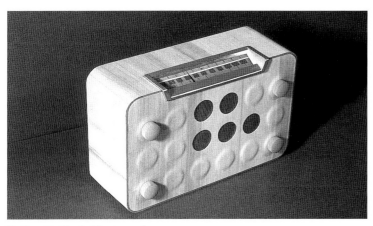

Radio with dimpled front panel

Two radio case variations

Front panels for radios

Machine operator with the wood-molding machine designed for producing radio enclosures

Stacked molded plywood enclosure frames

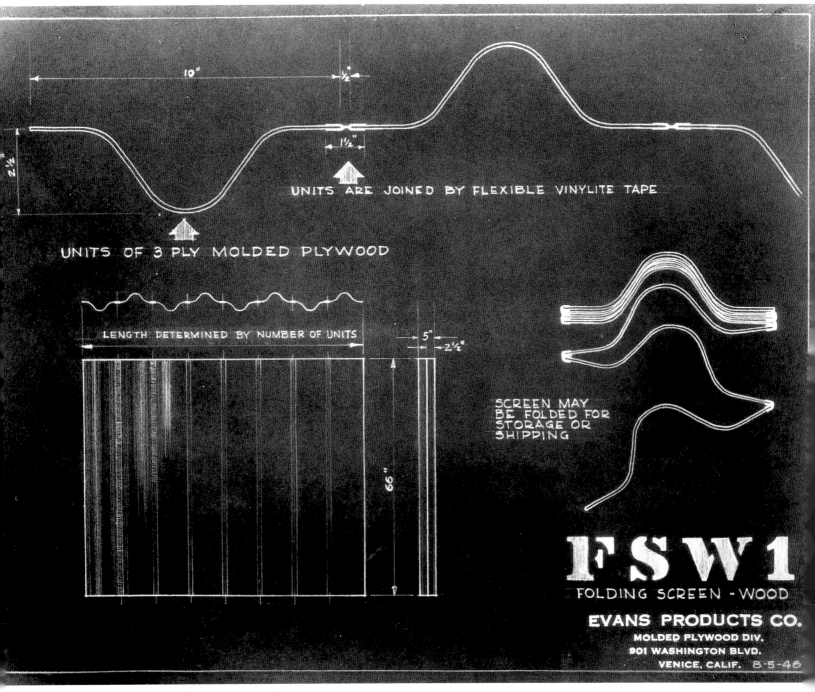

Don Albinson's drawing of the specifications for the folding screen

Staff: 1946
555 Rose Avenue
901 Washington Boulevard
1122 Washington Boulevard
Gregory Ain
Don Albinson
Milah Bernie
Harry Bertoia
Frances Bishop
Norman Bruns
Georgia Cunningham
Victor Delgado
Milton Driggs
Ida Francesca
Saul Golden
Little Gus
Gus Holstrom
Cecil James
Herbert Matter
John Moon
Marion Overby
Griswald Raetze
Harry Soderbloom
Ben Urmston

1946

Plywood Folding Screen

In one of the early molding experiments, U-shaped cross sections of plywood were produced. When the sections were lined up end to end, it was discovered that with a suitable flexible connector the units could be folded together neatly or extended to the full width of the connected pieces. In addition, they could be set up in a variety of positions and were stable enough to stand alone without additional support. In short, a folding screen that was easy to adjust and carry and relatively simple to manufacture could be mass-produced. Made of 9½-inch-wide molded plywood sections, the screen was designed and made in Venice during the early postwar period. Each plywood unit, three layers thick, was formed in a mold into a U-shaped curve with straight extensions. The first method devised for joining the plywood sections together utilized a flexible vinylite tape, a synthetic adhesive developed during the war. (Charles and his coworkers were among the first designers to fully exploit the wartime revolution in the development of new technologies, materials, and bonding substances in the design of products for the civilian market.) Two lengths of the 1½-inch hinge were fixed along the length of each side of each wooden section and joined together in the center. This solution did not stand up to rigorous folding and unfolding, however, and another method had to be found.

In the final production-line model, full-length canvas hinges glued and sandwiched into saw-slots in the plywood were used to join the units. These flexible connectors allowed the screen to be folded for shipping and storage and to be positioned in a variety of configurations, fully or partially opened.

The folding plywood screens were made of ash or birch and were available in heights of 34 and 68 inches. Each was made up of eight sections; the extended length of each screen was 80 inches. The tooling and the first units were produced at the 901 Washington Boulevard shop. Subsequently, production was transferred to the Evans Products plant in Grand Haven and then to the Herman Miller Furniture Company in Zeeland, Michigan. However, the insertion of the canvas hinge required a great deal of hand labor, which made the screen too expensive to manufacture. Production was discontinued in 1955.

Plywood screen in expanded and closed positions

Screen with round coffee table and the three-legged metal dining chair (DCM)

Staff: 1946
555 Rose Avenue
901 Washington Boulevard
1122 Washington Boulevard
Gregory Ain
Don Albinson
Milah Bernie
Harry Bertoia
Frances Bishop
Norman Bruns
Georgia Cunningham
Victor Delgado
Milton Driggs
Ida Francesca
Saul Golden
Little Gus
Gus Holstrom
Cecil James
Herbert Matter
John Moon
Marion Overby
Griswald Raetze
Harry Soderbloom
Ben Urmston

Right: 1946 Christmas card from Charles and Ray, which was sent to colleagues and friends. Charles photographed his and Ray's reflection in a Christmas ornament

1946

Plywood Table Production

Beginning in mid-1946 the designs for the round coffee table with wood legs (CTW) and the round coffee table with metal legs (CTM), included in the three New York City showings of plywood furniture, were refined and then produced commercially by the Molded Plywood Division of Evans Products Company in Venice, California. Four-legged variations in wood and metal rod of the round coffee tables were substituted for the three-legged versions. Plywood coffee tables were manufactured by the Molded Plywood Division until manufacturing operations moved from Venice to Grand Haven in April 1947 (pp. 72–75).

A knockdown dining table with molded plywood legs, also designed by the Molded Plywood Division and produced in Venice, California, was initially sold by Evans Products but discontinued after production was transferred to Grand Haven. The Herman Miller Furniture Company took over marketing and distribution in late 1946. Production and merchandising of the round tables were transferred to Evans Products in Grand Haven, Michigan, in 1947 and continued there through 1948. All table production was shifted to Herman Miller in 1949. The round tables were discontinued in 1957.

Dining table with molded plywood legs

Middle and above: Metal rod and wood base tray tables

Plywood chairs and tables with wood legs

Right: Charles and Ray "pinned" by chair bases. From the roof above the office Don Albinson photographed the Eameses lying on the sidewalk during a shooting session for a Herman Miller advertisement (p. 88)

Don Albinson's son Jon seated at the child's table

Staff: 1947
555 Rose Avenue
901 Washington Boulevard
Don Albinson
Frances Bishop
Georgia Cunningham
Milton Driggs
Charles Kratka
Marion Overby
Harry Soderbloom
Ben Urmston

1947

Folding Tables

The Eames plywood folding table shown at The Museum of Modern Art in 1946 (pp. 68–71) was replaced with another folding table whose four legs folded into a recess under the tabletop and could be fastened into place individually with a metal clip. The tabletop was made from a single piece of plywood rounded at the corners. The plywood layers were exposed and a veneer of wood added for finish. Three metal-legged versions of this table—square (card table), rectangular (dining table), and occasional or children's size—were produced at 901 Washington Boulevard by Kerkman Manufacturing (managed by Warren Kerkman, a former Evans Products staff member and a St. Louis acquaintance of Charles's) under a special agreement with the Herman Miller Furniture Company. Kerkman manufactured and shipped the tables and was the first Herman Miller subsidiary to produce Eames furniture. He took over most of the 901 Washington Boulevard space after the departure of Evans Products and brought in his own staff. In 1948 he was joined by Harlan Moore (who later became a manager of the Herman Miller, Inc., plant in Irvine, California). Charles and Ray occupied the front of the building.

Although the table was a relatively simple one to produce, Kerkman encountered major production problems in achieving a suitable finish for the table's top. He experimented at length with the difficult process of baking a smooth and even resin coating onto the plywood to make it impervious to damage from heat and staining. The undersides of the tables were coated with a resin-impregnated black paper.

Kerkman invested a considerable amount of his financial resources into the production of the table and eventually took on a partner, George Horning. He then abruptly left the operation. In 1950 Herman Miller moved into the 901 Washington Boulevard space and assumed the production of the round coffee tables and plywood folding tables, which were manufactured until 1964.

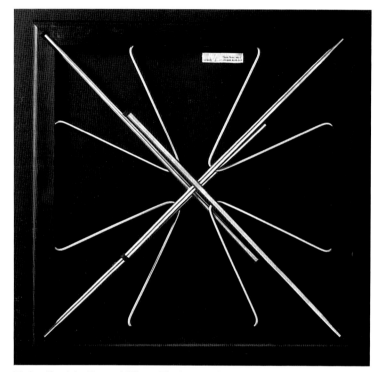

Underside of the Eames folding table showing the legs in the folded, clipped position

Small (children's), rectangular, and square Eames folding tables. Overleaf: A photographic superimposition of Charles with the plywood tables and chairs

Right: Dinner at the Girard house in Grosse Point, Michigan, with Lily and Eero Saarinen and Alexander and Susan Girard. Eero and Alexander, introduced by Charles, formed a lasting friendship and professional collaboration

A setup on the sidewalk at 901 Washington Boulevard for photographing the models for the Jefferson Memorial sculptural monuments

JEFFERSON NATIONAL EXPANSION MEMORIAL COMPETITION

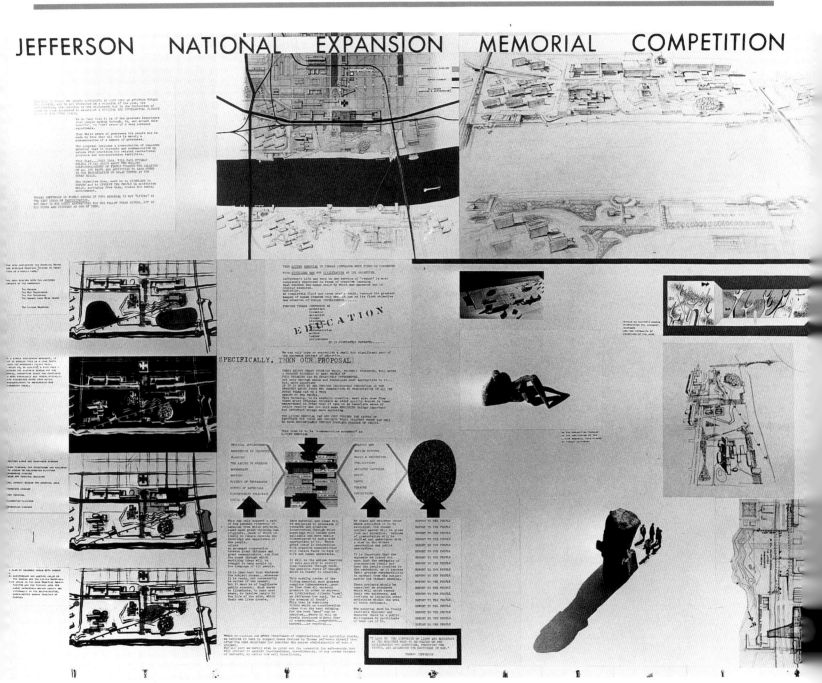

Eames proposal presentation panel submitted to the jury

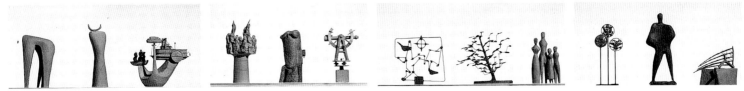

Scale models of proposed sculptures to be erected along the memorial's walkway

February 11: *Useful Objects for the Home*, an exhibition at the Akron Art Institute, includes Eames furniture.

Staff: 1947
555 Rose Avenue
901 Washington Boulevard
Don Albinson
Frances Bishop
Georgia Cunningham
Milton Driggs
Warren Kerkman
Charles Kratka
Marion Overby
Harry Soderbloom
Ben Urmston

Ray and Charles on Easter Day

Architect Gregory Ain, a former Molded Plywood Division staff member

1947

"Jefferson National Expansion Memorial" Competition

In 1947 the city of St. Louis sponsored a design competition for a memorial to Thomas Jefferson and his commitment to westward expansion. Architects and designers, including the Eameses, were invited to submit proposals. Charles and Ray's proposed monument to Thomas Jefferson's memory was an "information center": a place where education—which Jefferson believed was "the greatest weapon of human freedom"—could be encouraged and perpetuated. The objective was "to stimulate, to inform, and to involve the people in activities that, springing from them, create the social environment." Charles believed that Thomas Jefferson would be poorly served if the memorial was not "living, in the best sense of participation, not only in his great aspirations for his fellow human beings, but in his humor and richness as one of them."

The Eames plan (their first large-scale exhibition project) called for the monument to have four sections: a public park with a memorial mound and amphitheater; a new museum and existing historical structures (the old courthouse, the old cathedral, and the Manuel Lisa Rock House); a "living memorial" complex, housing a reference library, design laboratories, living and working quarters for students and researchers, and a printing plant; and a walkway (parallel to the levee and visually connecting the museum and living memorial) lined with sculptural monuments symbolizing Jeffersonian ideals and the westward movement. The elements were designed to encourage individual involvement in the process of "creative learning."

Charles and Ray produced two presentation panels of plans and elevations of the site and photographs of a model built in the office. John Entenza assisted in developing the proposal guidelines and in writing the text. The Eames Office considered its proposal an expression of an "attitude toward the problem" of creating a monument appropriate to Jefferson's place in American history and a fulfillment of his hope that we "look to the diffusion of light and education as the resource most to be relied on for ameliorating the condition, promoting the virtue, and advancing the happiness of man."

The first prize was awarded to a group of architects led by Eero Saarinen. Their proposal, a 590-foot stainless-steel parabolic arch symbolizing St. Louis as the "Gateway to the West," was completed on the banks of the Mississippi in 1965.

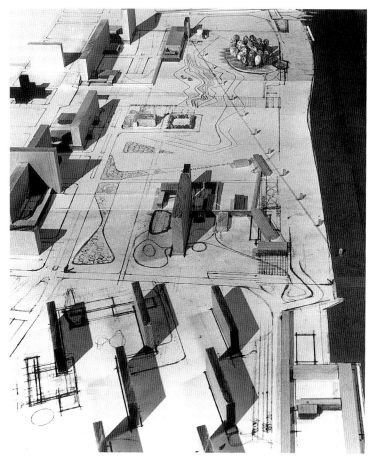

Plan of the proposed Jefferson Memorial

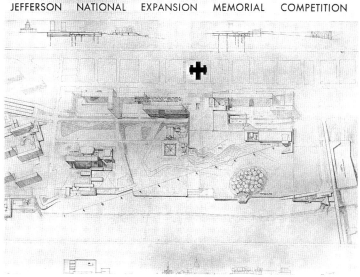

Eames proposal presentation panel

The *Good Design Is Your Business* exhibition at the Albright Art Gallery in Buffalo, New York, includes Eames furniture.

Staff: 1947
555 Rose Avenue
901 Washington Boulevard
Don Albinson
Frances Bishop
Georgia Cunningham
Milton Driggs
Charles Kratka
Marion Overby
Harry Soderbloom
Ben Urmston

D. J. De Pree (then president of Herman Miller Furniture Company) and his wife, Nellie, on a visit to the Eameses in California

Left: Herman Miller's Chicago showroom in January 1947, featuring Eames furniture for the first time. Right: A column in the showroom papered with magazine covers

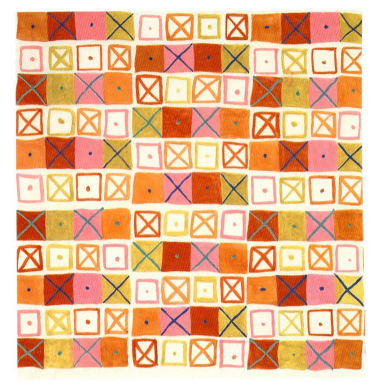

Crosspatch fabric design by Ray, 1945

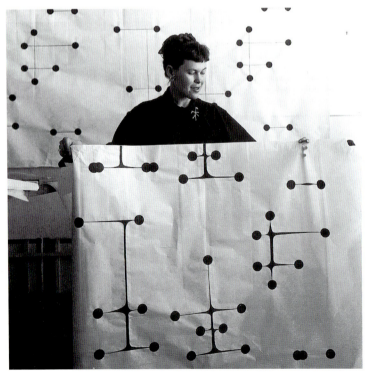

Ray working on a fabric design called *Dot Pattern*

1947

Fabric Designs and *Arts & Architecture* Magazine Covers

In 1947 textile and graphic designers were invited to submit textile designs to "The Competition for Printed Fabrics," an event sponsored by The Museum of Modern Art in New York City. Ray responded with two designs, *Crosspatch* and *Brown and Black Free Shapes on a White Ground* (also known as *Sea Things*). The latter design received an "honorable mention." The award-winning textiles were shown in an exhibition at the museum entitled *Printed Textiles for the Home*, which ran from March 11 to June 15, 1947. *Crosspatch* was produced and sold by Schiffer Prints, a division of Mil-Art Company in New York City, and later exhibited at the *Good Design Is Your Business* show in Chicago and New York City in 1950. Another of Ray's fabric designs, *Dot Pattern*, was completed but not submitted to the competition.

Ray designed the March and December 1947 covers for *Arts & Architecture*; these were the last covers she produced for the magazine. As with the covers she designed in 1943 and 1944 (pp. 38–39, 44–45), the 1947 layouts were composed of images that reflected the contents of the particular issue. Photographs and other materials used for the cover were produced by the Eames Office.

Ray was not trained as a graphic designer, but the years she spent studying under Hans Hofmann had provided her with a painterly vocabulary and visual syntax that she transferred to the design of *Arts & Architecture* covers, textiles, proposal presentation panels, and Herman Miller graphics. Ray also learned a great deal about graphic design from the Swiss designer Herbert Matter during the years he spent as a member of the Molded Plywood Division staff. His influence can be seen in her extensive use of montage—combining and superimposing images and type—in her first magazine covers (pp. 30–31, 38–39, 44–45). The 1943 cover assignments had introduced her to production requirements for specifying type and handling color separations and pasteup; help and advice could be had from Charles, Entenza, and others. In the early years in the office everyone had a hand in every project; specialists were expensive, and cooperation among the small staff was an important element in the way the office functioned. In later years, other designers in the office undertook much of the Eames graphic design and production tasks—with Ray providing critical guidance.

Through the summer and early fall of 1947 the Eameses worked alone in the front office of 901 Washington Boulevard. In the late fall the Eameses asked Don Albinson to rejoin the Venice studio (to start on the "International Competition for Low-Cost Furniture Design;" pp. 96–101). He was the first employee to return after the transfer of the plywood operation to the Evans Products factory in Grand Haven; shortly thereafter, Frances Bishop returned as office secretary, and the office became known officially as the "Eames Office."

November: Charles visits an exhibition of the work of Mies van der Rohe at The Museum of Modern Art. His photographs and comments are published in the December 1947 issue of *Arts & Architecture*. It is in this exhibition that Charles sees the Mies "Bridge House" (pp. 106–121).

A birthday card for John Entenza, publisher of *Arts & Architecture* magazine, made by Charles

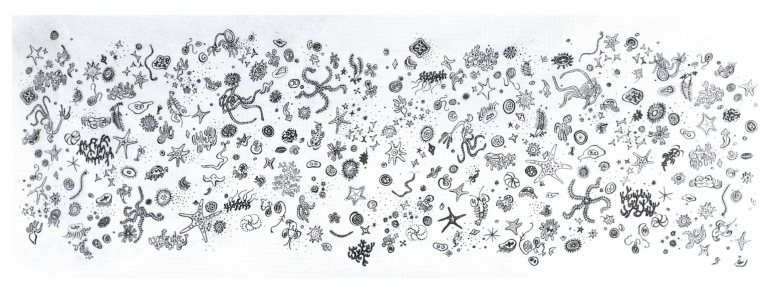

Brown and Black Free Shapes on a White Ground fabric design by Ray, 1945

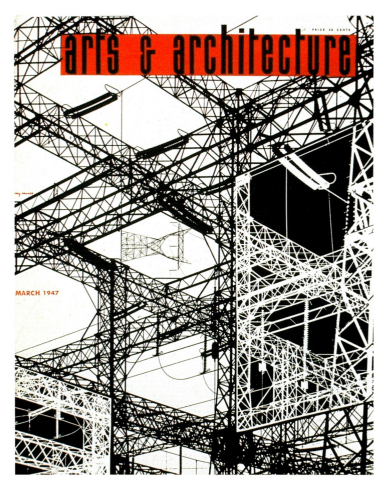

Left and right: Covers designed by Ray for March and December 1947 issues of *Arts & Architecture* magazine

Staff: 1948
901 Washington Boulevard
Kenneth Acker
Don Albinson
Frances Bishop
Jay Connor
Georgia Cunningham
Milton Driggs
Robert Jacobsen
Charles Kratka
Harlan Moore
Marion Overby
Verla Shulman
Harry Soderbloom
Ben Urmston
Frederick Usher

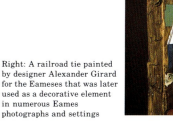

Right: A railroad tie painted by designer Alexander Girard for the Eameses that was later used as a decorative element in numerous Eames photographs and settings

1948

Herman Miller Furniture Company Graphics

As Herman Miller's marketing campaigns for the Eames plywood chairs developed, the Eames Office gradually assumed the creation of graphics and advertisements featuring their furniture (although no formal plan or contract for the work was ever drawn up). The office designed and wrote the copy with the help of Alfred Auerbach, Herman Miller's marketing consultant. The first ads, designed by Ray with Charles Kratka, featured the plywood chairs, the round-top table, the folding table with rod legs, and the folding screen. The ads were published in such trade journals as *Retailing Daily* and in consumer periodicals, including *Arts & Architecture*, *Interiors*, and *Architectural Forum*.

Herman Miller's advertising budget was small; the ads were printed in black and white or in two colors (black and "Herman Miller red") and featured images of plywood furniture photographed in the Eames Office, combined on occasion with drawings that emphasized and dramatized the organic quality of the furniture. Photographs of Eames displays in Herman Miller showrooms were also used. The informal, almost playful graphics conveyed the same energy and liveliness that was inherent in the approach to the design of the furniture itself. In addition to brochures and advertisements, the Eames Office produced other graphics for Herman Miller, including the cardboard shipping carton and the instructional guides for the assembly of knockdown furniture. The office produced Herman Miller graphics until the mid-1960s.

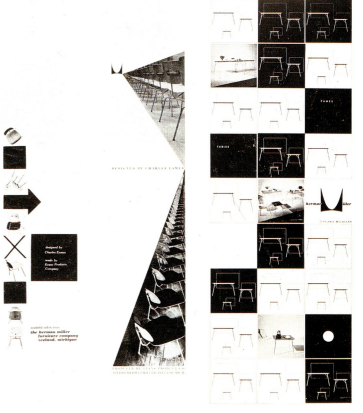

Three one-column magazine advertisements designed by the Eames Office

Above: Front and back sides of a brochure on the plywood furniture designed by the Eames Office. Opposite: Full-page magazine advertisement for Herman Miller that won a New York Art Directors Club award

Elephant enclosure tent

Charles and Ray become friends with Bill Ballantine, a writer and illustrator whose love of the circus led him to join Ringling Brothers' Barnum and Bailey Circus as a clown. Later, as head of the Clown College, he appointed Charles an honorary member of the faculty.

Staff: 1948
901 Washington Boulevard
Kenneth Acker
Don Albinson
Frances Bishop
Jay Connor
Georgia Cunningham
Milton Driggs
Robert Jacobsen
Charles Kratka
Harlan Moore
Marion Overby
Verla Shulman
Harry Soderbloom
Ben Urmston
Frederick Usher

Charles and Ray on a Triumph motorcycle that belonged to Warren Kerkman's son

1948

Circus Photography

Charles was always fascinated by the circus, perceiving the organization and operation of the tightly orchestrated ensemble of many disparate parts to be analogous to the practice of design, of art, and of science. The analogy became a central theme in his design philosophy. In a talk given before the American Academy of Arts and Sciences and in a subsequent article published in October 1974 in the *Bulletin of the American Academy of Arts and Sciences* he summed up his thoughts about the circus:

> The circus is a nomadic society which is very rich and colorful but which shows apparent license on the surface....Everything in the circus is pushing the possible beyond the limit....Yet, within this apparent freewheeling license, we find a discipline which is almost unbelievable. There is a strict hierarchy of events and an elimination of choice under stress, so that one event can automatically follow another. The layout of the circus under canvas is more like the plan of the Acropolis than anything else; it is a beautiful organic arrangement established by the boss canvas man and the lot boss....The lot boss knows exactly what his relationship is to the boss canvas man because the mutual objective and the method of accomplishing it are clear to both. In the actions of circus people waiting to rehearse or preparing to perform, there is a quality of beauty which comes from appropriateness to a given situation....The concept of "appropriateness," this "how-it-should-be-ness," has equal value in the circus, in the making of a work of art, and in science.

Charles sustained his interest in the circus throughout his life. From the 1940s to the 1970s he took hundreds of black-and-white and color photographs of circuses. In Los Angeles in 1948, using a 4x5 Linhoff camera, he photographed every aspect of the circus. The images he shot over the years were used in the *Circus* slide show (p. 356), a film entitled *Clownface* (pp. 372–373), and in other projects. The idea of the circus as an event that offered a multitude of experiences for the visitor—something for everybody, and more than could be taken in one viewing or visit—was mirrored in Charles's approach to the amount of information and visual material he included in exhibitions, films, and slide shows.

Top to bottom: Circus billboard, tent stakes, and rigging

A selection of circus images photographed by Charles over many years

A clown rehearsal between performances

Showgirl Roberta Ballantine (wife of Bill Ballantine) and clown Emmet Kelly

A clown alley dressing room

Left to right: Four circus clowns

Above: Clown Lou Jacobs. Opposite: Details of clowns' facial makeup

Top: Circus jugglers. Above: Clown Bill Ballantine in a sailor-and-mermaid costume

conversation, rest & play

Gondola, Confortable, Duchesse, Psyche, Kangaroo; are some names of the past for a type of seating that fills a difficult-to-define need of the time.

13721

THE FORM OF THIS CHAIR DOES NOT PRETEND
TO CLEARLY ANTICIPATE THE VARIETY OF NEEDS
IT IS TO FILL. THESE NEEDS ARE AS YET
INDEFINITE AND THE SOLUTION OF THE FORM
IS TO A LARGE DEGREE INTUITIVE. THE FORM
CAN ONLY SUGGEST A FREER ADAPTION OF MATERIAL
TO NEED AND STIMULATE INQUIRY INTO WHAT THESE
NEEDS MAY BE.

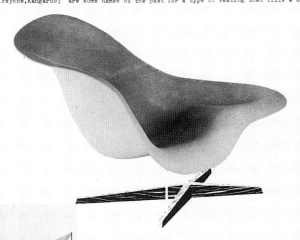

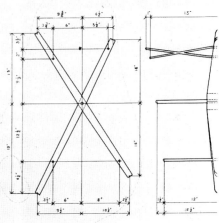

plan & elevation of base 1/8 scale

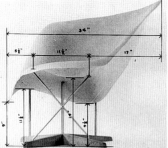

side elevation 1/8 scale

front elevation 1/4 scale

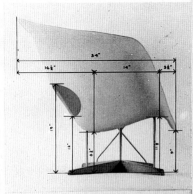

These shells can be made of low pressure
glass mat laminates with the inner surface
an integral finish in any designated color.

The tooling cost is low, and in production
the cost of the shell could be around.......$15.00

With a base of wood and stainless rod
at approximately.......$12.00

The factory price of such a chair should be.$27.00

back elevation 1/4 scale

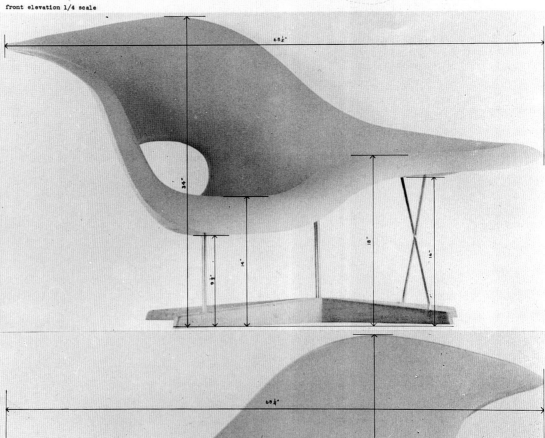

Staff: 1948
901 Washington Boulevard
Kenneth Acker
Don Albinson
Frances Bishop
Jay Connor
Georgia Cunningham
Milton Driggs
Robert Jacobsen
Charles Kratka
Harlan Moore
Marion Overby
Verla Shulman
Harry Soderbloom
Ben Urmston
Frederick Usher

Charles and Ray posing on "La Chaise"

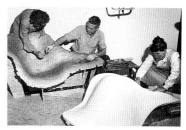
Staff members Frances Bishop and Robert Jacobsen and Ray working on the mold for "La Chaise"

1948

The Museum of Modern Art "International Competition for Low-Cost Furniture Design"

In 1948, under the direction of Edgar J. Kaufmann, Jr., The Museum of Modern Art and a group of American retailers and manufacturers organized the Museum Design Project, Inc., and sponsored the "International Competition for Low-Cost Furniture Design." The competition was motivated by the urgent need in the postwar period for low-cost housing and furnishing designs adaptable to small housing units. In the introduction to the competition's catalog René d'Harnoncourt wrote: "To serve the needs of the vast majority of people we must have furniture that is adaptable to small apartments and houses, furniture that is well-designed yet moderate in price, that is comfortable but not bulky, and that can be easily moved, stored, and cared for; in other words, mass-produced furniture that is planned and executed to fit the needs of modern living, production, and merchandising."

Designers were invited to team up with "technologists" to form "design research teams"; six teams were each given grants of five thousand dollars. The Eames Office, together with engineers from the University of California at Los Angeles under the direction of Dean L.M.K. Boelter, submitted a set of designs for low-cost seating that shared second prize in the Seating Units category with a submission by David J. Pratt. The Eames/UCLA entry stressed Charles's continuing commitment to reduce the cost of furniture by utilizing factory technologies and mass production.

The designs submitted by the Eames Office were for furniture produced from stamped aluminum or steel. In the panel text accompanying the designs, Charles wrote:

> Metal stamping is the technique synonymous with mass production in this country, yet "acceptable" furniture in this material is noticeably absent....By using forms that reflect the positive nature of the stamping technique in combination with a surface treatment that cuts down heat transfer, dampens sound, and is pleasant to the touch, we feel that it is possible to free metal furniture from the negative bias from which it has suffered.

Graphic panels with mechanical drawings, specifications, photographs, and text detailed the proposed series of low-cost solutions. Prototypes of an upright chair with steel and aluminum seats and a variety of metal and wood bases were included. A "minimum" chair, designed to test how little material and surface were needed for a seat to be

Side views of the "minimum" chair and of Dorothy Jeakins posing in it

Above: A proposal panel for "La Chaise." Opposite: A proposal panel for "La Chaise" submitted to the competition

97

L.M.K. Boelter, dean of the School of Engineering at UCLA, photographed in 1962

Charles and Ray with staff members Robert Jacobsen, Charles Kratka, Frances Bishop, Don Albinson, Jay Connor, and Fred Usher

LOW COST FURNITURE, QUALITY CONTROLLED, MASS PRODUCEABLE

The form of these chairs is not new nor is the philosophy of seating embodied in them new— but they have been designed to be produced by existing mass production methods at prices that make mass production feasible and in a manner that makes a consistent high quality possible.

   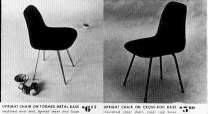  

Metal stamping is the technique synonymous with mass production in this country, yet "acceptable" furniture in this material is noticeably absent. These seating shells are designed to be fabricated in pressed metal.

By using forms that reflect the positive nature of the stamping techniques in combination with a surface treatment that cuts down heat transfer, dampens sound, and is pleasant to the touch, we feel it is possible to free metal furniture of the negative bias from which it has suffered.

For the purpose of this study each unit has been considered as having two elements — 1.) The surface or shell that receives the body.
2.) The base that holds this shell in the proper relation to the ground.

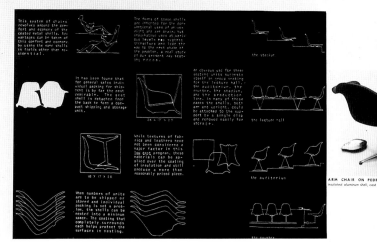

Component parts for Eames low-cost furniture

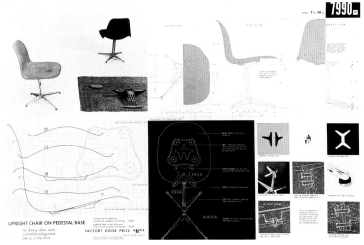

Specification panel for the upright chair on a spider pedestal base

Right: A photograph of the "Low-Cost competition" jury at The Museum of Modern Art. Front row, left to right: René d' Harnoncourt, Catherine Bauer, Luis de Florez, Mies van der Rohe. Back row, left to right: Hugh Lawson, Alfred Auerbach, Gordon Russell. Edgar Kaufmann, Jr., is standing in the rear

Left: A photograph of the winning designers in the "Low-Cost competition." Standing, left to right: Don R. Knorr, Robin Day, Clive Latimer, Professor Georg Leowald. Middle row, left to right: David Pratt, Charles Eames, Alexey Brodovitch, James Prestini. Front row, left to right: John McMorran, Jr., John O'Merrill, Jr.

comfortable, was another entry. A full-scale model of a chaise longue, nicknamed "La Chaise" (after it was made, it occurred to the Eameses that a Gaston Lachaise floating figure sculpture could just about fit in it), was made with a stressed-skin shell and a hard rubber and foam core. Both upper and lower skins were made of resin and fiberglass cloth, and the core was composed of variously sized blocks of hard rubber and styrene foam. According to the designers' cost estimates, figured as "factory-door" prices, the least expensive chair—aside from the "minimum" chair—would cost $5.80 (an upright chair with a coated steel shell and a steel rod base); the most expensive would cost $11.73 (an armchair with a coated aluminum shell and a cast aluminum pedestal).

The steel and aluminum prototype chairs were produced in the Venice shop using a drop hammer. The compression molds for the chair pieces were made of hydrocal plaster. An aluminum sheet was sandwiched in between the molds, its edges held in place by a steel-channel frame. Using a block and tackle, a 250-pound weight was hoisted four feet above the forge. When the pulley ropes were cut, the dropped weight stamped the aluminum into the mold. After about four "drops," the desired shapes were achieved. The primitive in-house stamping technique was resorted to because of difficulties in scheduling the use of hydraulic presses at the UCLA Engineering department. (People in the neighborhood reported dishes rattling in their cupboards and thought the shaking was caused by earthquakes. Local electrical power levels dropped substantially due to the overload.) The hydrocal molds were reinforced with sisal, but after three "drops" they generally broke and had to be replaced with spares. After forming, the shapes were welded together. Aluminum shells were coated with vinyl; steel ones with a neoprene "dish-drainer" coating.

Two hundred and fifty entries from the United States and nearly five hundred from European countries—in all, three thousand entries from the design teams—were submitted to the competition jury, composed of Edgar Kaufmann, Jr. (director), Alfred Auerbach, Catherine Bauer (Wurster), Luis de Florez, René d'Harnoncourt, Hugh Lawson, Ludwig Mies van der Rohe, and Gordon Russell. The exhibition, which opened in May 1950, included a molded plastic armchair (produced by Zenith Plastics in Los Angeles, working with the Herman Miller Furniture Company), alongside plaster, papier-mâché models of armchairs and metal prototypes of side chairs made for the jury. The plastic armchair was also published in the exhibition catalog.

Although it was Charles's hope that metal stamping would be an economically viable production technique, no

Top: Specification panels for the armchair on a pedestal base and the rocker Middle: Panels for the upright chair with rod legs. Above: Panels for the upright chair with wood legs

Alfred Auerbach, marketing representative for Herman Miller, during a visit to the Eames Office

Buckminster Fuller and Charles in a Fuller geodesic structure

Specification panel for the upright and "minimum" chairs

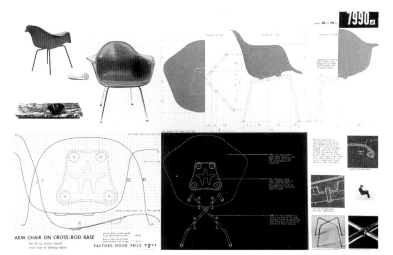

Specification panel for the armchair

LOW COST FURNITURE, QUALITY CONTROLLED, MASS PRODUCEABLE

Because realistic costing is such an important factor, two examples have been selected for complete cost breakdown.

Sample components specification sheet with cost breakdown

Charles and Fred Usher working on the side chair mold

Robert Jacobsen joining the three-piece aluminum chair

Eames chairs were ever mass-produced in this material. Instead, in 1950 Herman Miller (contracting with Zenith Plastics) began fabricating upright chairs and armchairs in molded fiberglass and polyester resin, a material that was strong and light, and in which the color was integral rather than applied. Transfer to the new medium required only minor adjustments in the design. The "minimum" chair and the "La Chaise" were never produced.

The enthusiastic response to the competition was an indication of the recognition by American and European designers of the need to create low-cost furniture for the postwar market. The Eames seating entries were both functionally and visually in keeping with the development of the Eames and Saarinen chair designs first seen in the "Organic Design" competition in 1940 and continued in the Eames plywood chairs. The armchair (pp. 138–141) and side chair (pp. 142–143), both of which have proven their serviceability, are still produced by Herman Miller and have been imitated and copied by many manufacturers.

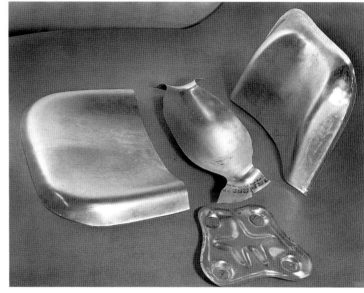
Stamped metal chair components

Don Albinson operating the drop hammer

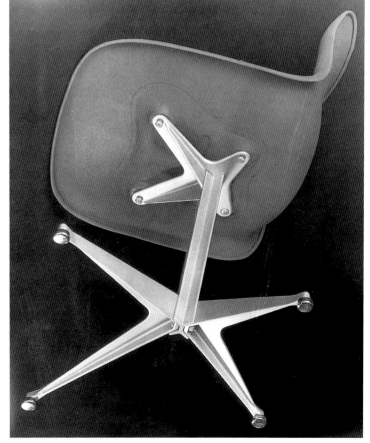
Completed metal chair prototype with cast aluminum base

Staff: 1949
901 Washington Boulevard
Kenneth Acker
Don Albinson
Frances Bishop
Jay Connor
Charles Kratka
Harlan Moore
Marion Overby
Verla Shulman
Harry Soderbloom
Frederick Usher

Staff members Verla Shulman, Ray, Don Albinson, Charles, Fred Usher, and Charles Kratka

1949

Herman Miller Furniture Company Showroom

The Herman Miller Furniture Company showroom at 8806 Beverly Boulevard in Los Angeles, the company's first on the West Coast, was designed by the Eames Office in 1948. Though it was based (in part) on Case Study House #8 (pp. 106–121) and the two bear a physical resemblance, the showroom opened in the fall of 1949, preceding the completion of the house. The Eames Office was given carte blanche to design the building after D. J. De Pree (president of Herman Miller) and Hugh De Pree approved the site and determined the building's budget and deadline for completion.

Charles's intention was to employ a "minimum of architecture," so that the structure existed only as a backdrop for the furniture. Using the lessons learned on the Case Study houses, Charles, with architect Kenneth Acker, kept the plan simple and minimized the number of connections. The interior consisted of a modular grid of seven-foot bays, into which a variety of partition panels could be installed by means of pipe-standard supports. By using this flexible system, different spaces were created to satisfy the needs of changing furniture arrangements.

The exterior of the showroom was similar in treatment to that of the Eames House. It employed an industrial steel frame; two factory sash windows were used for ventilation. Fixed panels of clear, translucent, and opaque patterned glass completed the front wall. The side walls of the showroom were brick, exposed on the exterior and painted

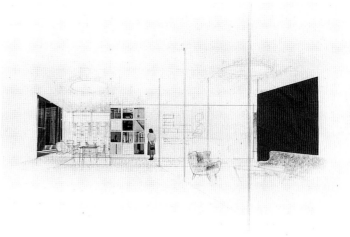

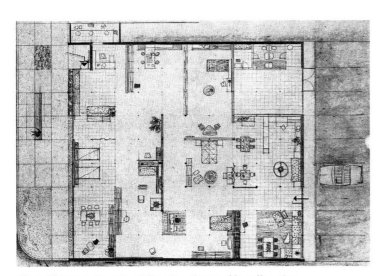

Above: Showroom floor plan delineating the movable wall sections
Opposite: Exterior views of the Herman Miller showroom

Above: Three drawings of interior elevations of the showroom

Johnny Johnson, manager of the Herman Miller Furniture Company's Los Angeles showroom, at his makeshift desk

on the interior. Three six-foot circular skylights and windows in the front facade provided natural lighting. The 5,000-square-foot showroom included a kitchen and two bathrooms. As with the Eames House, Acker, a licensed California architect, was the architect of record.

Over the next several years the Eames Office designed, fabricated, and installed many of the furniture and object settings used in the Los Angeles showroom as well as in the New York City and Chicago showrooms (pp. 146–147, 167, 242–243, 262–263, 278–279, 312–313). Opening-night parties were given to introduce new pieces and collections of furniture and movie nights were held featuring Eames films. Herman Miller occupied the showroom until 1976, when its Los Angeles offices were moved to the Pacific Design Center on Melrose Avenue.

Above: Two views of showroom interior with furniture

104

Lucia Eames posing for a Herman Miller advertisement

Herman Miller magazine advertisement

Above: Six furniture and accessory groupings, including Eames, Nelson, and Noguchi furniture

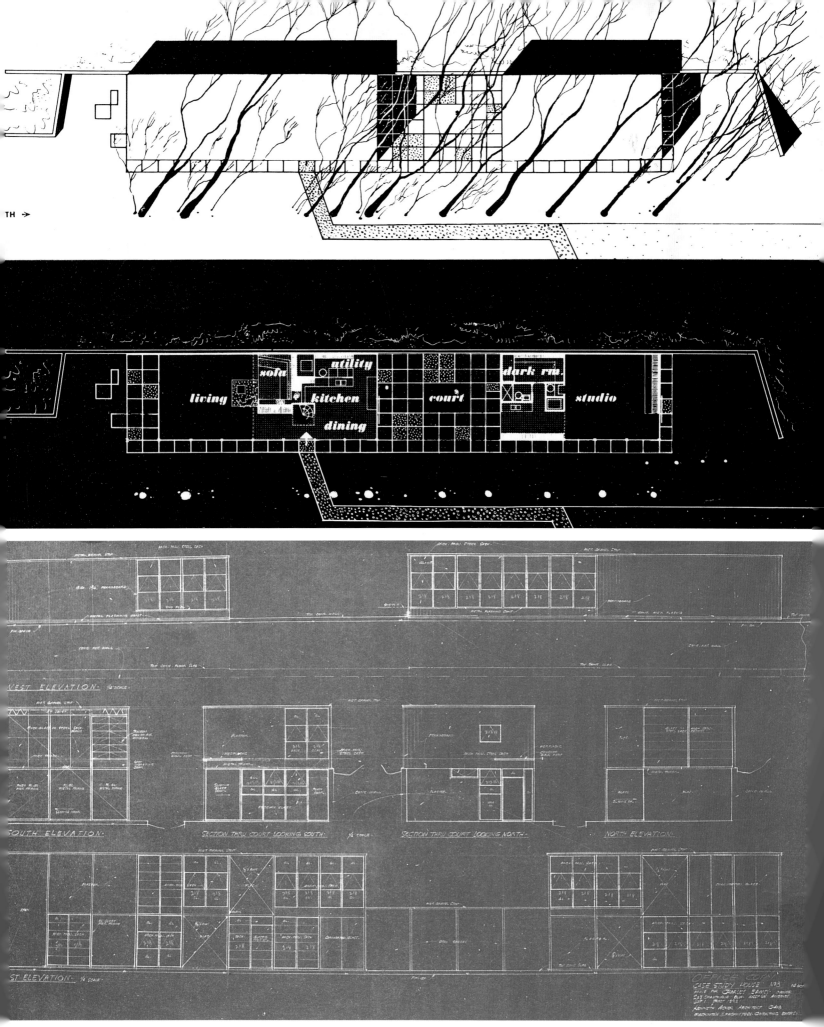

Plan view and blueprint of Eames House's steel framing sections

106

Staff: 1949
901 Washington Boulevard
Kenneth Acker
Don Albinson
Frances Bishop
Jay Connor
Charles Kratka
Harlan Moore
Marion Overby
Verla Shulman
Harry Soderbloom
Frederick Usher

Ray in the meadow at the site of Case Study House #8

Charles and Ray, 1949

1949

Arts & Architecture Case Study House #8

The Eames Office, working with Eero Saarinen, designed two houses for the Case Study House program sponsored by *Arts & Architecture* magazine (pp. 48–49). Both are situated in a meadow on top of a 150-foot cliff overlooking the Pacific Ocean. The three-acre site above the Santa Monica Canyon in the city of Pacific Palisades was part of a five-acre parcel purchased by the magazine from the Will Rogers estate expressly for the Case Study House program. Two additional Case Study houses on the site, one by designer Rodney Walker and another by architect Richard Neutra, were completed in 1948 and 1949.

After the announcement of Case Study houses #8 and #9 in 1945, the Eameses worked out the plan and model for #8, later known as the Eames House, which consisted of two structures: a living space and a working space. The original plans submitted to *Arts & Architecture* magazine in 1945 show the residence, a rectangular box, separated from the studio, which was set into the hill and shaded by eucalyptus trees. The residence, placed at an angle to the studio, was elevated on two steel supports and cantilevered out beyond them (engineered by Edgardo Contini), providing an unobstructed view of the ocean across the meadow. The proposal was referred to as the "Bridge House," because the house bridged the meadow from the hill in the background.

However, the final plan and the constructed buildings are quite different from the original conception. After the materials for constructing the house were delivered to the site, Charles changed his mind (influenced perhaps by his visit in November 1947 to an exhibition of the work of Mies van der Rohe at The Museum of Modern Art) about the siting of the buildings and worked on a new plan that used the same amount of steel but enclosed more space. In the revised plan, published in the May 1949 issue of *Arts & Architecture*, the house and studio are aligned with a concrete retaining wall built along the base of the hill. The two structures are separated by an open court and face the ocean diagonally. Each space was conceived as a series of uniform bays (each seven and one-half by twenty feet). The house, which was built according to this plan, has eight bays, plus an overhang; the court has four, and the studio, five.

To achieve the maximum sense of space, the three-bayed living room rises seventeen feet. The strict

Color sketches by Ray for the Eames House's exterior panels

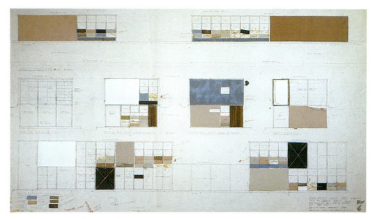

Drawings of the Eames House elevations with notations for the exterior panel treatments

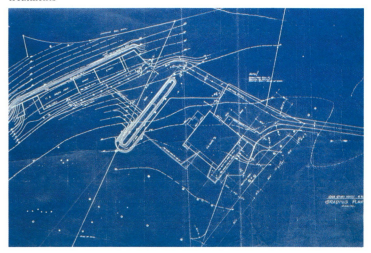

Site plan for Case Study Houses #8 and #9 (Eames and Entenza houses)

Case Study houses construction sign

A photograph by John Entenza of Charles and Ray on the steel frame of the Eames House

June–July 1948: Billy Wilder and his wife, Audrey, on their honeymoon trip to Lake Tahoe. Charles and Ray accompanied them, photographing Virginia City and Lake Tahoe

modular system of the structures resulted in cubelike spaces in the living room and studio. The lower level also includes a sitting corner and kitchen, dining, and utility areas. The second floor has two baths and a bedroom with sliding panels opening onto a view of the living room. The bedroom can be divided by sliding panels into an additional sleeping space. The studio is also a two-story space with a storage and sleeping area on the balcony above. A bathroom and darkroom are on the ground level below the balcony.

The house represented a significant departure from Charles's St. Louis architecture of the middle and late 1930s (p. 24). By the 1940s Charles had become more familiar with the work of Walter Gropius, Mies van der Rohe, Marcel Breuer, and other European modernist architects. He was certainly influenced by the two-story plan and the treatment of the exterior elevations of the I. M. Pei and E. H. Duhart house entry in the 1943 competition "Designs for Postwar Living," which was sponsored by *Arts & Architecture* and juried by Charles. Through John Entenza he had also learned much about the Southern California architecture of the international modernists Richard Neutra, Raphael Soriano, and Rudolf Schindler and of the architects working on Case Study houses (Thornton Abell, Whitney Smith, Sumner Spaulding, and John Rex, among others).

Construction was begun on the Eames House in early 1949, four years after the plan was announced. In order to preserve the natural beauty of the site's meadow and to maintain the protective advantage of its eucalyptus trees, a building lot for the house was excavated behind the trees adjacent to a hillside. A 175-foot-long, 8-foot-high steel-reinforced concrete retaining wall was built parallel to the slope of the hill. The excavated earth from the hillside was then shifted to the property line between the Eames and Entenza (Case Study House #9) houses, where an earthen berm was formed.

The buildings were constructed of machined, off-the-shelf parts. The frame consists of four-inch steel H-columns and twelve-inch steel open-web bar joists. The framing required eleven and a half tons of steel and was erected in one and a half days (a total of ninety man-hours). In some places, diagonal bracing of the frame was achieved with tension rods and turnbuckles. Truscon open-webbed joists and Ferroboard steel decking form the ceiling, which is exposed throughout the house and studio. Charles later estimated that the outside construction (non-Eames Office) costs of the house and studio were $1.00 per square foot, whereas normal residential construction with traditional wood framing would at that time have cost $11.50 per square

The Eames House under construction, seen from the hillside

View through the studio to the Eames House

Charles and his daughter, Lucia

Architect Kenneth Acker and his family

Interior wood framing

Back view of the Eames studio and house

Front view of the Eames studio and house steel framing

Charles and Ray at the site of the Eames House with staff members Verla Shulman, Charles Kratka, Don Albinson, and Frederick Usher

foot. Considerable additional cutting and welding detail on the interior of the house and fitting of the windows were performed by the Eames Office staff, especially Don Albinson.

The objective was to emphasize the structure, exposing as much of it as possible and to create a light and open interior space using readily available industrial materials. Charles wanted the walls, floor, and roof to be visually "thin"; each element resting against another without any apparent support, as if each plane had come to rest in that position.

Once the house and studio were completed, all the steel sections, the metal sash, and the flashing were painted a warm dark gray to unify the structural elements. Within the exterior walls of this neutral gray web, the contrasting stucco, cemesto, asbestos, and plywood panels were painted white, blue, red, black, or a middle-value gray. Transparent, translucent, and wired glass were used in the window sections.

The interior of the 1,500-square-foot Eames House includes large, dramatic vertical areas and intimate, small enclosed spaces. The living room is a two-story space occupying the south end of the house; the west wall is lined with vertical strips of birch. Adjacent to it— and contrasting with it—is a small seating alcove (similar in treatment to the "inglenooks" often included in Eliel Saarinen houses), under the balcony of the second floor, complete with built-in sofas and storage cabinets. The lower floor is shared by a dining area on the northwest side of the house, a kitchen, and a utility room. The kitchen can be closed off from the living area by an accordion-folding partition.

A spiral staircase leading to the second floor of the house is lighted by a square wired-glass skylight. The stairs are made from sections of steel beam formed into flanges, welded onto a pipe collar, and fitted into position on a vertical column. Plywood treads are secured to the flanges. The bedroom gallery looks out over the two-story living room and can be closed off by sliding diffusion screens made of Pylon, a translucent glass cloth laminate. Two baths are adjacent to the bedroom area.

The interior of the 1,000-square-foot studio contains a two-story space, which was used as a general work area and a sleeping area, with a bathroom and darkroom below. The studio eventually became another living area. In the early years it was used for making films and planning projects, but as the filmmaking became more complex and involved more people, more room was needed. In 1958 the Herman Miller Furniture Company moved out of 901 Washington Boulevard in Venice; from that point on, all projects were worked on at the Eames Office in the 901 building, a few miles from the house.

Top: Exterior painting around turnbuckle cross-bracing. Middle: Interior glazing detail. Above: View of the Eames House from the south, just after it was completed

Eames House and studio interior details, including the stairwell, window treatments, and living room

Kenneth Acker was employed as the architect of record and the draftsman for the Eames House. Lamport-Cofer-Salzman, Inc., was the general contractor for both the Eames and the Entenza houses. Craig Ellwood, who later designed a Case Study house too, estimated the building costs and the structural steel for both houses.

Charles and Ray moved into the house on Christmas Eve 1949. Objects, books, and toys collected for use in films and projects became part of their surroundings. Over the years they used the house for working and as a retreat, enjoying the meadow (which they left in its natural state) and its inhabitants—quail, sparrows, possums, snakes, mockingbirds—and the sound of the sea. Their feelings for the house and its site above the Pacific Ocean were expressed in a film made five years after its completion (pp. 198–199).

The Eames House was given the American Institute of Architects Twenty-Five Year Award in 1978, and The Los Angeles Conservancy nominated it to the Los Angeles Cultural Heritage Commission in 1986. Over the years a visit to the house has become an important stop for students of architecture and design and for professional architects and designers visiting Los Angeles. Interest in the house has extended beyond Southern California; it has been looked upon by architects all over the world as the model for the "off-the-shelf" approach to building, an approach that is independent of climate and place. The architectural critic and historian Reyner Banham, remembering the impact the house had at the time of its construction, wrote: "The Eames House had a profound effect on many of my generation in Britain and Europe....For most of two decades it has shared with Rodia's towers in Watts the distinction of being the best-known and most-illustrated building in Los Angeles."

The house has a unique presence in the Case Study House program; it stands out by virtue of its approach to the stated requirements of the program (pp. 48–49), its use of industrial materials for residential construction, its height, its shape, its use of interior space, its siting, and its distinctive use of pure color on its exterior walls. In the AIA award citation, the architect A. Quincy Jones wrote, "Designed by its owners, [the house] is at once an intensely personal statement and a pioneering adventure in merging technology and art. Despite its spareness and economy, it provides a subtle richness of pattern, color, and texture, and a sense of unity of nature which have successfully withstood the test of time."

Ray lived in the house continuously from 1949 until her death in 1988; she opened the house to hundreds of interested visitors, students, teachers, and professional architects throughout that time.

Top two rows: Views of the house interior, including the living room, dining room, seating alcove, kitchen. Above: Courtyard between the house and the studio

Overleaf: House and studio exterior viewed from the meadow. Foldout: Details of the Eames House and studio from 1949 to 1978, photographed by Charles

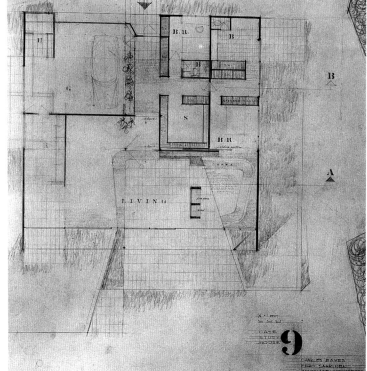

Preceding pages: Eames and Entenza houses under construction. Top: Front view of the framed-in Entenza House. Above: Model of the Entenza House

Top: Steel framing of the Entenza House. Above: Entenza House plan

Staff: 1949
901 Washington Boulevard
Kenneth Acker
Don Albinson
Frances Bishop
Jay Connor
Charles Kratka
Harlan Moore
Marion Overby
Verla Shulman
Harry Soderbloom
Frederick Usher

John Entenza and Alfred Auerbach, marketing consultant to the Herman Miller Furniture Company, standing under the steel framing of the Entenza House

1950

Arts & Architecture Case Study House #9

House #9, designed by Eero Saarinen and Charles for John Entenza, the sponsor and originator of the Case Study House program, shares a three-acre tract of land with the Eames House in Pacific Palisades (pp. 106–121). Although the structural system in the Entenza House was the same as in the Eames House—four-inch steel H-columns and twelve-inch open-web bar joists—the structure of the Entenza House is concealed. All that is visible of the twelve steel columns that support the entire structure are four four-inch columns positioned in the center of the house to allow cross bracing. The roof is a flat slab supported by the open steel trusses; the interior ceiling is birch wood strips. The differences in the treatment of the structure between the Entenza and Eames houses were used to demonstrate that industrial materials and methods could be adapted to widely divergent personal requirements and environmental needs. John Entenza was a single man who often worked at home. He wanted both an office and a place where he could entertain the growing numbers of people he met as a writer and speaker and as editor and publisher of *Arts & Architecture*.

The plan of the 1,600-square-foot Entenza House emphasizes the horizontal flow of space as opposed to the vertical definition of the Eames structure. In the Entenza House a simple frame encloses a maximum amount of space. The one-story house has seven rooms: a large living and dining area, a study, two bedrooms, a kitchen, two bathrooms, and a garage. The living area dominates the plan and design of the house, providing a space that can be used both for entertaining and for working. The thirty-six-foot-long room was designed to be flexible and adaptable, accommodating large and small gatherings, with the freestanding fireplace as its focal point. Situated on the south side of the house, the room can be opened to the meadow and has a full ocean view. There are outdoor living areas running the length of the side of the house that faces the sea, adjacent to the kitchen and master bedroom. The square-foot cost of the Entenza House was substantially higher than that of the Eames House, due in part to the amount of interior detailing and finishing involved in enclosing the structural members.

Unlike the Eames House, the Entenza House has been added to and modified in the years since its completion. John Entenza lived in the house until it was sold in 1955 to Eddie Lipps.

Exterior views of the Entenza House

Staff: 1949
901 Washington Boulevard
Kenneth Acker
Don Albinson
Frances Bishop
Jay Connor
Charles Kratka
Harlan Moore
Marion Overby
Verla Shulman
Harry Soderbloom
Frederick Usher

Fred Usher, Ray, Don Albinson, Kenneth Acker, and Charles light up the "galaxy" ceiling fixture in the office

Left and right: Front and back covers of the catalog from the *Modern Living* exhibition with drawings by Saul Steinberg

1949

An Exhibition for Modern Living

An Exhibition for Modern Living, designed, organized, and directed by architect and designer Alexander Girard for the Detroit Institute of Arts and supported financially by the J. L. Hudson Company, presented an array of contemporary housewares and objects—handmade and machine-made furniture, glass, kitchen equipment, flatware, utensils, toys, tools, and jewelry. According to Edgar Kaufmann, Jr., writing in the catalog to the exhibition, it was "the most comprehensive statement yet made in favor of modern design rooted in the necessities and character of the American community today."

Girard's overall plan for the exhibition consisted of seven rooms, each designed and furnished by a different designer: the Eameses, Alvar Aalto, Florence Knoll, George Nelson, Bruno Mathsson, Jens Risom, and Eero Saarinen. The rooms were arranged around a central garden terrace furnished by Van Keppel Green, furniture designers and manufacturers. Other areas in the exhibition included a Hall of Objects, a section on the background of modern design with a written commentary by the historian John Kouwenhoven, and a mural by Saul Steinberg with graphic commentary on the eccentricities of people, furniture, and architecture.

George Nelson described the Eames room as "not so much a literal presentation of a room as an expression of an attitude, conveyed through the use of a special personal vocabulary." An important feature of the room was "La Chaise," the full-scale mock-up of the molded plastic chaise submitted to The Museum of Modern Art "Low-Cost Furniture" Competition in 1948 (pp. 96–101). Molded plywood dining chairs were arranged around a folding table with rod legs; a folding table was hung on the back wall. The Eames Storage Units (pp. 126–129) made their public debut here. The light fixture (the "galaxy"), designed by Don Albinson and made of rods projecting from a central sphere with a light affixed to each end, was much copied after the show but never produced commercially by the Eames Office. Objects and graphics were hung on a display wall studded with a grid of pegs and a pipe system of conduit provided additional lighting; both systems were used again in the Dunne office interior in 1952 (p. 166). Plants, a kite, a Mexican mask, paper flowers, Japanese teacups, and a mural of a photograph by Charles of High Sierra bark, were included in the room. The exhibition opened on September 9, 1949, and closed November 20, 1949.

Opposite above: Ray's color plan of the Eames Office room display
Opposite: View of the completed exhibition room

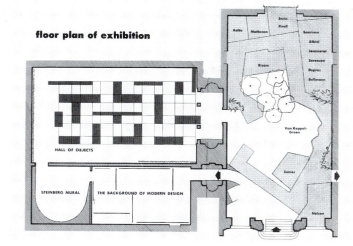

Exhibition floor plan

Ray's color sketch of an Eames Storage Unit

Eames Storage Units desk shown in the exhibition

January: Charles and Ray visit designer Alexander Girard in Grosse Point, Michigan. Charles speaks at the Detroit Museum of Art and shows slides of Eames work in progress.

Staff, 1950
901 Washington Boulevard
Kenneth Acker
Don Albinson
Frances Bishop
Jay Connor
Charles Kratka
Harlan Moore
Marion Overby
Verla Shulman
Harry Soderbloom
Frederick Usher

Left: Cover of the summer 1950 issue of *Portfolio* magazine with a cut-paper collage of a kite by Charles and Ray. The issue contained an article on the work of the Eames Office

1950

Eames Storage Units

The Eames Storage Units (ESU), a system of lightweight, modular storage cabinets constructed of plastic-coated plywood, lacquered Masonite, and chrome-plated steel framing, were another example of the office's effort to design and produce economical household furniture using industrial production techniques. Like the earlier Case Goods, which were made entirely out of wood (pp. 66–67), the standardized parts of the ESU were entirely interchangeable and could be easily adapted to a variety of office uses or residential storage needs in living rooms, dining rooms, and bedrooms. They could also be stacked and serve as room dividers. ESU quite obviously showed its industrial antecedents; no attempt was made to disguise or soften the off-the-shelf look of the components.

The units were available in single or double bays in the 100 Series (one unit high), the 200 Series (two units high), and the 400 Series (four units high) and in a desk system. The basic single-bay unit was 20 ⅝ inches high, 24 inches wide, and 16 inches deep. The double-bay unit was 47 inches wide. Desks came in widths of 44 and 60 inches and were 29 inches high. The framing consisted of chrome-plated, cold-rolled steel angles with resistance-welded diagonal rod bracing. Although the metal framework was standardized, a customer could choose from many options in designing the configuration of the storage units. Shelf tops, made of ¾-inch plywood, were available with an upper veneer of birch, walnut, or solid black plastic laminate. Drawers were made of plywood, and the sliding doors were produced in black laminate, white glass cloth, or a thin birch plywood with a vacuum-pressed circular "dimple" design. Generally, ⅛-inch Masonite with a baked enamel finish, produced in eight colors (including brilliant blue, red, and yellow), was used for filler panels. Perforated metal backs were also available.

The Herman Miller Furniture Company began marketing the Eames Storage Units in 1950. The cabinets were originally sold as a knockdown product, requiring the customer to screw and bolt the parts together. Because assembly tended to be laborious, Herman Miller later offered the storage units fully assembled. A new and sturdier leg with a triangular support designed to withstand the rigors of shipping replaced the steel-angle leg of the knockdown version. Production of the ESU continued until 1955.

Opposite: ESU variations, photographed in 1951, showing the different combinations of unit types and heights, open or with drawers

An installation of ESU configurations in the Herman Miller Furniture Company showroom in Los Angeles

An early prototype ESU desk, which eventually was equipped with drawers and a filing system

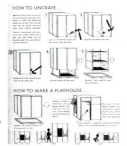

Right: A pamphlet describing a shipping carton designed by the Eames Office for the Eames Storage Units. The carton could be used as a child's playhouse

Children playing in a carton village of Herman Miller boxes

Completed units, ready for shipping

ESU with sliding "dimpled" front panels and early steel-angle legs

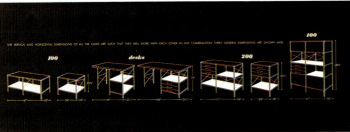

ESU brochure designed by the Eames Office

Above: Two ESU configurations demonstrating the units' storage options

ESU drawer and sliding-panel wood unit with the revised legs, 1952

Brochure showing some possible ESU variations

The opening installation of the *Good Design* exhibition at the Chicago Mart

Good Design installation at The Museum of Modern Art

Entrance to the "Hall of Light" at the Chicago Mart

Staff: 1950
901 Washington Boulevard
Kenneth Acker
Don Albinson
Frances Bishop
Jay Connor
Charles Kratka
Harlan Moore
Marion Overby
Verla Shulman
Harry Soderbloom
Frederick Usher

Susan Girard, Alexander Girard, Edgar Kaufmann, Jr., Jeremy Lepard, Charles, Taka, and Ray posing during installation of the *Good Design* exhibition

Alexander Girard, Ray, and Charles during installation of the *Good Design* exhibition

Charles, Susan Girard, Alexander Girard, Ray, and Edgar Kaufmann, Jr., at the Girard home in Grosse Point, Michigan

1950

The *Good Design* Exhibition Program

The *Good Design* exhibition program began as a partnership between The Museum of Modern Art in New York City and the Merchandise Mart in Chicago, the first time an art museum and a wholesale merchandising center had joined forces to present "the best new examples in modern design in home furnishings." The program called for three shows a year: one during the Chicago winter furniture market in January, an update coinciding with the June summer market, and a November show based on the previous two exhibitions. The January and June shows were held in the mart in Chicago; the final show opened simultaneously in Chicago and at the museum in New York City. The program began in 1950 and continued for five years.

Edgar Kaufmann, Jr., director of the Department of Architecture and Design at The Museum of Modern Art, directed the program and headed the three-person selection committees. Meyric Rogers of the Art Institute of Chicago and Alexander Girard joined him in choosing the objects for the 1950 shows. Their mandate was to consider "design intended for present-day life, in regard to usefulness, to production methods and materials, and to the progressive taste of the day." Each year a designer of note was selected to design the installation. The inaugural installation in Chicago, which opened on January 17, 1950, was designed by the Eames Office. Finn Juhl, Paul Rudolph, and Alexander Girard each designed succeeding shows. The fifth show was a composite of items selected from the previous four shows.

The 5,300-square-foot space in Chicago was divided by the Eameses into a series of "pavilions," each designated by a color scheme and separated by lighting and by transparent partitions of rope, chain, and string. Black metal folding gates were placed at the entrance, and the uncovered ductwork and pipes of the building were treated as decorative elements. Visitors then entered the "Hall of Light," a display of beautifully designed utilitarian objects from the past and paintings and sculpture on loan from the Art Institute of Chicago, which Charles felt conveyed a sense of timeless appropriateness. "Good Design" objects—contemporary furniture, appliances, utensils, flatware, tools, implements, textiles, and rugs—were arranged on walls and tables, and on the carpeted floor. In November the Eameses installed the exhibition in New York City. It opened on November 21, 1950, and closed on January 28, 1951.

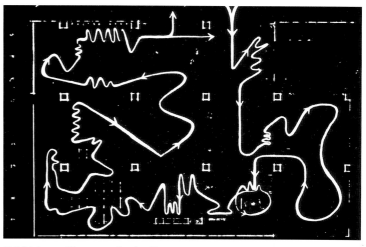

Exhibition traffic pattern for the Chicago installation

Ray and Edgar Kaufmann, Jr., arranging exhibition objects in the Chicago *Good Design* exhibition

Good Design objects on display at The Museum of Modern Art

Staff: 1950
901 Washington Boulevard
Kenneth Acker
Don Albinson
Frances Bishop
Jay Connor
Charles Kratka
Harlan Moore
Marion Overby
Verla Shulman
Harry Soderbloom
Frederick Usher

Charles posing in the mock-up for the Carson Pirie Scott windows

Ray's sketch for the Carson Pirie Scott window treatment

An Eames Office model of the Carson Pirie Scott window

View of the installed Carson Pirie Scott window

View of the *Good Design* window designed by Herbert Matter

1950

Carson Pirie Scott Windows

In 1950 the Carson Pirie Scott department store in Chicago invited four designers—Charles, George Nelson, Edward Wormley, and Eero Saarinen—each to design a street-level window devoted to their recently produced furniture. The only stated limitations were the size of the window and the requirement that the design could be executed by the store's staff.

In George Nelson's words, the Saarinen (which was designed by Herbert Matter) and Eames windows were treated as "semiabstract three-dimensional compositions...each relied on the furniture forms themselves for the shapes used as decoration." The Eames window displayed Eames furniture manufactured by the Herman Miller Furniture Company in a way that emphasized the shape of individual pieces. Blown-up paper shadows of the molded plywood chair were created and displayed along with table legs casting silver shadows. A group of plywood folding screens, a sculpture, and other objects were included. Herman Miller logos and a photograph of Charles were placed on the rear wall. The Eames Office designed the window and provided a ⅛-inch scale model to the Carson Pirie Scott staff to use as an installation guide.

A second window was designed later in the year to complement and publicize the opening of the first *Good Design* exhibition (pp. 130–131). Some of the furnishings and objects from the show were displayed in a setting designed by the Eames Office that reflected the flavor and spirit of the exhibition.

The appearance in a major department store of the so-called "modern" furniture testified to the growing popularity of the work of postwar designers and to the marketability of the furniture to general consumers. The furniture was also beginning to be copied by other manufacturers (in mostly bad imitations), indicating that its appeal had extended beyond specialized designers and architects.

Staff: 1950
901 Washington Boulevard
Kenneth Acker
Don Albinson
Frances Bishop
Jay Connor
Charles Kratka
Harlan Moore
Marion Overby
Verla Shulman
Harry Soderbloom
Frederick Usher

Designers Alvin and Elaine Lustig, friends and colleagues of the Eameses', photographed by Charles

Mercedes and Herbert Matter; Herbert was a photographer and designer and a former member of the Molded Plywood Division

1950

Herman Miller Furniture Company Graphics

In 1950 the Eames Office produced several print advertisements for the Herman Miller Furniture Company to announce the new Eames Storage Units (pp. 126–129). The ads emphasized the key feature of the system: the interchangeability of parts, which made the units usable in numerous configurations. The advertisement reproduced here appeared in *Architectural Forum* in October 1950; small drawings superimposed on the photographs point out the versatility of the furniture. The office also designed a brochure on the ESU, combining photographs and drawings to detail the available options in the modular storage system. Packing boxes with graphics were produced as well.

Charles Kratka, a member of the Eames Office, provided the inspiration and carried out the ideas for the advertisements designed by the office in this period. The graphics were planned to keep the reproduction costs within a small budget, and the magazines were chosen on the basis of their influence and standing in architecture and interior design circles.

Advertisement designed by Charles Kratka emphasizing the multiple options available with the Eames Storage Units

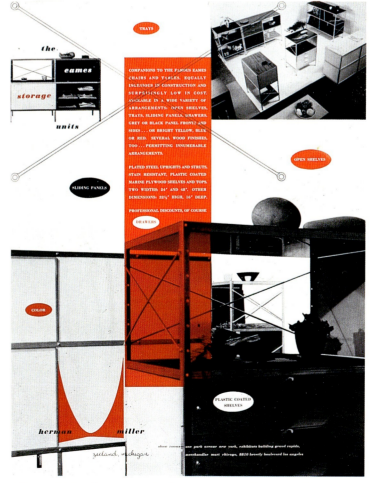

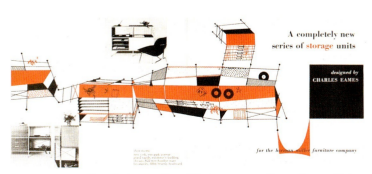

Brochure designed by Charles Kratka and Ray to announce Eames Storage Units

A Herman Miller advertisement for the Eames Storage Units using Eames Office photographs

133

Staff: 1950
901 Washington Boulevard
Kenneth Acker
Don Albinson
Frances Bishop
Jay Connor
Charles Kratka
Harlan Moore
Marion Overby
Verla Shulman
Harry Soderbloom
Frederick Usher

Eero and Lily Saarinen, photographed by Charles

1950

Film: *Traveling Boy*

Traveling Boy was the Eameses' first film. Although it was completed in 1950, it has never been shown publicly, only to audiences of friends and staff. The film tells a simple story using toys as central characters: a Japanese windup boy carrying a suitcase has a series of encounters with other windup toys and objects. The cast consisted of toys the Eameses had on hand, including Japanese and German windup animals and games and toys found in junk shops. Large numbers used on circus posters and images from Saul Steinberg drawings share the limelight with Polish-made puppets bought in Chicago and toys from F.A.O. Schwarz in New York City and from Chinatowns across the country.

Traveling Boy was made because Charles and Ray wanted to use the 16mm movie projector lent to them by a friend, the screenwriter Philip Dunne, while he was on location in Argentina. The film was shot with a rented 16mm movie camera that did not have close-up lenses. Charles made cardboard extension rings to shoot close-ups, and he recalculated the exposures. A makeshift system of plywood and wooden dowel rewinds was devised to hold film reels so the film could be cut and edited. The *Traveling Boy* footage has no main title and no narration or musical accompaniment. Three endings were filmed, but no choice was made among them.

The Eameses produced their first films by taking time out at night and on the weekends from the demands and deadlines of other work, and consequently some of the early films took years to complete. Help was voluntary in this period; the cost of paying staff was too great. Using windup toys proved to be a maddening process; during rehearsals everything worked according to plan, but when the camera was running and expensive film was being exposed, the toys often balked and stopped moving. The technique of using toys in films continued through the years. Several such films were planned: in the early 1950s some footage was shot on a film entitled *Come to the Fair*; preliminary work was done on a film about the alphabet; and Charles collected toy boats for a film that was in the planning stages for years. *Tops* (pp. 346–347), the last Eames toy film, was started in 1957 and finally finished in 1969. (Running time, *Traveling Boy*: 11 minutes, 45 seconds; color.)

Above: A sequence of frames (reading top to bottom left, top to bottom right) from scenes in *Traveling Boy*. Opposite: Two frames from the beginning of *Traveling Boy*. The frames were photographed from 16mm-film footage

Staff: 1950
901 Washington Boulevard
Kenneth Acker
Don Albinson
Frances Bishop
Jay Connor
Charles Kratka
Harlan Moore
Marion Overby
Verla Shulman
Harry Soderbloom
Frederick Usher

Ray with the model for the Wilder House

Billy and Audrey Wilder with the model for their house

1950

The Billy Wilder House

In late 1949, when the Eames Case Study House was almost completed, Charles and Ray were asked by film director Billy Wilder to design a house for him on a hilltop property in Beverly Hills, California. The plans extend the ideas and principles used to define the Eames House (pp. 106–121) and show a large rectangular structure (approximately 4,600 square feet), modular in plan and built of prefabricated, off-the-shelf steel parts. Spaces with high ceilings and glass walls allowed the interior to be filled with natural light. The plans included a two-story living area, dining areas, a study, three bedrooms, three bathrooms, dressing rooms, and utility rooms. The house was to be surrounded by concrete paved sections and planting areas. The entrance was via a large, paved parking platform. Four-inch steel H-columns and twelve-inch open-web bar joists were to be used for the framing. However, the structural elements of the Wilder House were to be more concealed than in the Eames House. The house was designed to require low maintenance; the plan included a walk-through service area, where all utilities could be monitored and serviced. A model was constructed and preliminary plans drawn up, but the house was never built. Kenneth Acker was the licensed architect employed by the office as a planner and draftsman.

The objective in this house, as in the Eames House, was to use industrial technology to provide what Charles called an "unselfconscious" enclosure that would satisfy the essentials for comfortable living. Such a structure could then be made into a personal statement by the occupant, who could fill it with the accessories of his or her own life. Designed for a different life-style and on a grander scale than the Eames House, the Wilder House was one of the last architectural commissions that Charles would undertake (pp. 155, 189). When asked why he turned away from the practice of architecture, Charles said: "That's partially the result of my chickening out. Architecture is a frustrating business. You work on an idea, but standing between you and the event are many traps. The finance committee, the contractor, the subcontractor, the engineer, even politicians—all of them can really cause the concept to degenerate." Although Charles continued "to think of [myself] functionally as an architect," his attention turned from architecture per se to other projects where he "had a more direct relationship with the end product"—film, furniture, and exhibition design.

Opposite top: Charles's site drawing for the Wilder House. Opposite: Wilder House model

Above: Exterior and interior details of the house model showing the living room and seating area

Staff: 1950
901 Washington Boulevard
Kenneth Acker
Don Albinson
Frances Bishop
Jay Connor
Charles Kratka
Harlan Moore
Marion Overby
Verla Shulman
Harry Soderbloom
Frederick Usher

Jim Eppinger, Sales representative for Herman Miller Furniture Company

Irv Green, Sol Fingerhut, and Ralph Huhn of Zenith Plastics, who introduced their fiberglass technology to the Eames Office

1950–1953

Plastic Armchair

The Eameses had first used fiberglass cloth and plastic resin material (which they had found in war-surplus stores) as screens in Case Study House #8. The office had also experimented with plastic resins before submitting chair designs and prototype chairs of stamped metal to The Museum of Modern Art's "International Competition for Low-Cost Furniture Design" in 1948 (pp. 96–101). During the war, Zenith Plastics (later to become Century Plastics), of Gardena, California, had used fiberglass to reinforce plastic on radar domes for airplanes. The Eames Office, attempting to lower the production costs of the chairs designed in stamped metal for the "Low-Cost Furniture" competition, contacted Zenith to learn more about fiberglass technology. In a cooperative effort, after the competition was juried and the winners announced, Zenith and the Eames Office began adapting the stamped metal armchair design submitted to the competition to the requirements of fiberglass technology. The armchair was chosen for

Above: Original plaster-of-paris mockup of the proposed stamped metal chair from the "Low-Cost Furniture" competition. Opposite: Plastic chairs and shipping cartons

Top: Early translucent production model of the plastic armchair with reinforced embedded cord edge. Above: Production model of the plastic armchair with thick opaque plastic and new "boot" glides at the ends of the legs

A figure drawn by artist Saul Steinberg on "La Chaise" plaster mold during a visit to the Eames Office

A figure drawn by Steinberg that extends from a chair shell to the office floor

Top: Plastic armchair with "Eiffel Tower" base. Above: Plastic armchair with low rod base

Top: Plastic armchair with wood and wire base. Above: Plastic armchair with low rod base and upholstered cover

Right: The cover of the winter 1950–1951 issue of *Everyday Art Quarterly*, which featured Eames plastic armchairs in an article entitled "Useful Objects"

Staff member Verla Shulman at the beach, making ad hoc use of a legless armchair

development over the side chair because converting it to mass production presented the greatest tooling challenge. Jim Eppinger, representing the Herman Miller Furniture Company, negotiated a contract with Zenith for making the production die for manufacturing the first 2,000 plastic armchair shells. The first fiberglass chairs, which were shown in Herman Miller's Chicago showroom, were laid up by hand by Zenith technicians. One of the first chairs was exhibited in the 1950 *Low-Cost Furniture Competition* exhibition and pictured in the exhibition catalog.

Mass-producing the molded fiberglass chairs involved a tremendous amount of design and tooling effort, a long period of product development, and considerable investment on the part of both Zenith and Herman Miller. Work continued over a three-year period. The Eames staff worked with Zenith management (Sol Fingerhut, Milt Brucker, and Irv Green) on adapting the design of the chair and on innovations in the chair's engineering. The basic technology involved forming the fiberglass material with male/female metal molds using a hydraulic press. As usual, one of Charles's requirements was that the material (in this case fiberglass) be expressed honestly and unselfconsciously; the armchair was the first one-piece plastic chair whose surface was left uncovered and not upholstered.

In 1950 Zenith began mass-producing the fiberglass-shell armchairs for Herman Miller, who offered them for sale that year. The chairs were first available in three colors—greige, elephant-hide gray, and parchment. Later, a variety of colors was offered, with a choice of several possible bases—rod-legged, cast aluminum pedestal, swivel, wire-strut, wood-legged, and wood-rocker on wire strut—attached with rubber shock mounts. The armchair could be ordered with a low wire base or with tall wood legs and a foot ring, to be used at a bar or drafting table. Although the rocker version of the armchair was not offered for sale after 1968, until 1984 it was given as a gift by Herman Miller to every employee who became a parent. The plastic shell became available in an upholstered (fabric or vinyl) version a year after the introduction of the chair. Over the years, the plastic chair has undergone some modifications: the curve of the back has become sharper and upholstery is now glued to the plastic shell. In 1961 the chair shells were modified and used in the La Fonda group (pp. 252–253), and in 1963 the armchair and side chair shells were used in a tandem seating system (p. 280). The investment of time, effort, and money in its development has been justified; it has been a popular, much-used (and imitated), inexpensively priced piece of furniture. The chairs are still produced by Herman Miller, Inc.

Drafting-height swiveling plastic armchair and rocker-base armchair with and without pad

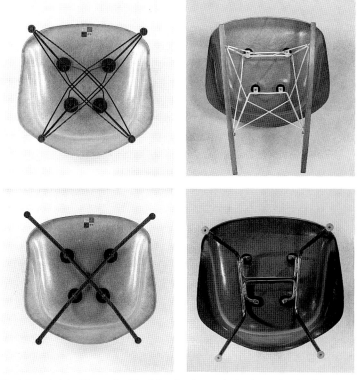

Top left and right: The underside of the plastic armchair wire and rocker bases. Above left and right: The underside of the early "X" base and the production model "H" base

Staff: 1950
901 Washington Boulevard
Kenneth Acker
Don Albinson
Frances Bishop
Jay Connor
Charles Kratka
Harlan Moore
Marion Overby
Verla Shulman
Harry Soderbloom
Frederick Usher

1950–1953

Plastic Side Chair

After the successful adaptation of the stamped metal armchair to plastic (pp. 138–141) the metal side chair submitted to the "Low-Cost Furniture" competition was developed by the Eames staff for production by Zenith Plastics. The problems of transferring the design from metal to plastic had been mastered in the development of the armchair; other details relevant to the side chair were more easily resolved. The side chair shells, made of Zenaloy (a plastic resin reinforced with fiberglass), were introduced in the natural fiberglass finish and later produced in a range of colors. Soon after production of the chairs began, an upholstered fabric cover worked out in the office with Alexander Girard was made available. The cover, a sturdy, relatively inexpensive hopsacking material, was used in its natural tan color or dyed black, red, blue, green, or yellow. The "harlequin" pad cover with its V-shaped insets at the side of the seat was made of this fabric in various colors.

As with the armchairs, the side chairs were offered with several interchangeable supports—wood legs, rod legs, wire struts, a cast aluminum pedestal with casters, and birch rockers on wire struts—all attached with rubber shock mounts. The concept behind these shell chairs was the same as that underlying other Eames furniture produced to date—that mass-produced, standardized parts could be combined in different ways to meet the unique needs of each customer. The plastic side chair is still available from Herman Miller, Inc.

Plastic side chair with upholstered pad

Plastic side chair with "harlequin" pad

Production model of the plastic side chair

Plastic side chair variations

Plastic side chair with "Eiffel Tower" base

Plastic side chair in its rocker version with an upholstered pad

Plastic side chair with an upholstered pad and a wire base

Underside of chair with the "Eiffel Tower" base

Plastic sidechair with a hopsack pad. A wire was sewn around the inside edge of the pad to hold it in tension on the chair

Artists Hedda Sterne and Saul Steinberg during a visit to the office

Two photographs by Charles of a Saul Steinberg drawing (far right) projected onto the head and shoulders of Steinberg's wife, Hedda Sterne, and Ray, and then rephotographed as part of an experiment with projected masks

Top: Eames Office staff wearing cardboard mock-ups of the toy masks. Above: Prototype of the frog mask

Prototype of the rooster mask

Right: A Saul Steinberg "diploma" made for Charles. Charles, who had left college without graduating, had a speaking engagement at a university and was asked to supply his diplomas. Steinberg furnished him with one

Left: Ray with Konrad Wachsman (an architect and designer of prefabricated industrialized building elements and a longtime friend of the Eameses') wearing Chinese masks

Staff: 1950
901 Washington Boulevard
Kenneth Acker
Don Albinson
Frances Bishop
Jay Connor
Charles Kratka
Harlan Moore
Marion Overby
Verla Shulman
Harry Soderbloom
Frederick Usher

1950

Toy Masks

Charles always maintained that the reason he and Ray began to design and make toys was a simple one: they wanted them for their grandchildren and the children of staff members and friends. In a 1972 interview Charles said of the toys: "The motivation behind most of the things we've done was either that we wanted them ourselves or we wanted to give them to family and friends. And the way to make that practical is to have the gifts manufactured."

The first toys designed in the office for mass production were a number of large head and body masks for children and adults. In the late 1940s and early 1950s, the Eameses were using masks as props in exhibitions and photographs and in theatrical skits with friends. They also experimented with projecting 35mm transparencies onto peoples' heads to create a masklike blend of the two-dimensional image with a three-dimensional form.

Don Albinson, along with other staff members, began developing large, brightly colored animal forms, which were mocked up in cardboard and paper. Some of the bird, fish, and animal heads and bodies extended down the torso and could be worn as costumes. Additional paper elements were attached to the basic cardboard form, and decorative details were added in bright primary colors. The masks were to be manufactured and sold (by Tigrett Enterprises, a Tennessee toy manufacturer) as kits of die-cut shapes that could be colored and assembled by the buyer. However, the masks did not proceed past the developmental stage.

Color sketches for toy masks

Top left: Don Albinson's son Jon wearing a bird mask. Top right: Don Albinson's son Eric in a turtle costume. Middle: Eagle and rooster masks. Above left: Frog mask. Above right: Clown face

A Herman Miller showroom setting of George Nelson furniture

Eames plastic armchairs and rockers in a setting with a Giacometti sculpture, tumbleweeds, and a photomural

An article about the Eames House entitled "A Designers Home of His Own" is published in the September 11, 1950 issue of *Life* magazine.

Staff: 1950
901 Washington Boulevard
Kenneth Acker
Don Albinson
Frances Bishop
Jay Connor
Charles Kratka
Harlan Moore
Marion Overby
Verla Shulman
Harry Soderbloom
Frederick Usher

1950

Herman Miller Furniture Company Showroom

Working in collaboration with George Nelson, Herman Miller's design director, the Eames Office designed and installed the interiors and furniture groupings for Herman Miller's showroom in Los Angeles throughout the 1950s and the early 1960s. The interior spaces of the showroom were reorganized for each opening, which usually coincided with the introduction of a new item or line of furniture. New settings were arranged to feature the pieces recently added to Herman Miller's catalog and to incorporate other furniture and fabrics from the Nelson and Girard design offices. Much of the new furniture introduced during this period was designed by the Eames Office. The Eames plastic armchairs and side chairs and a variation on the Eames folding table (pp. 81–83), available in square and rectangular versions and in dining and occasional table heights, with legs of round, tapered wood, were introduced in the 1950 opening.

The showroom floor was divided into several areas by partitions on which photomurals were mounted. The environments for the furniture groupings included household items and toys, plants and flowers, and folk art collected by the Eameses and their staff, as well as paintings and sculpture on loan from galleries. The Eameses always used an eclectic mix of objects in their showroom installations and delighted in finding things of beauty and interest in dime stores, ethnic groceries, hardware and specialty shops, and war-surplus outlets. They rotated many of the same objects through their showrooms, their films, and exhibitions.

Eames plastic chairs with a dowel-legged table introduced in 1950

A variety of Eames Storage Unit configurations

Wall with tumbleweeds gathered by the Eameses in the California desert

Plywood chairs and tables in a setting with Nelson cabinets

Staff: 1950
901 Washington Boulevard
Kenneth Acker
Don Albinson
Frances Bishop
Jay Connor
Charles Kratka
Harlan Moore
Marion Overby
Verla Shulman
Harry Soderbloom
Frederick Usher

Charles and Ray photograph their reflection in the window of their house

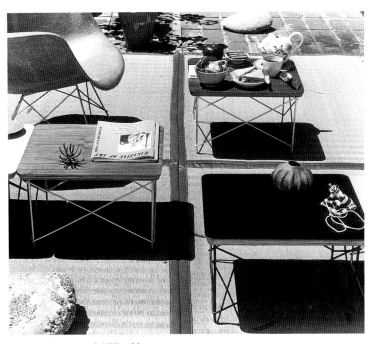

Outdoor setting with LTR tables

Low Table Wire Base (LTR)

1950

Low Table Wire (or Rod) Base (LTR)

By 1950 the Eames Office had used metal rod bases for several pieces of furniture, including the plywood lounge and dining chairs (DCM and LCM) and the round and folding tables. They had experimented with rod bases for the large lounge chair (pp. 64–65) and had tried many wire and rod configurations for the chairs in the "Low-Cost Furniture" competition (pp. 96–101).

In 1950 new, small rectangular occasional tables (Low Table Wire or Rod Base—LTR) were designed for manufacture using the processes and materials already developed for other furniture under production. The tabletops, made of ¾-inch plywood covered with a black or white plastic laminate or a natural wood veneer, are supported by two U-shaped metal rods attached to the tabletop with four screws. Resistance-welded metal cross-bracing provides stability. The edges of the table are beveled at a twenty-degree angle to expose the stripes of the plywood layers. The bases were used also for an elliptical table (p. 149) and for some Girard tables. Other tabletop surfaces, including gold and silver leaf, and patterned papers impregnated with a protective coating, were tried but discarded as impractical for mass production. The Herman Miller Furniture Company began producing the LTR in 1950 but eventually discontinued all of the variations except for the table with a white laminate top, which is still being made.

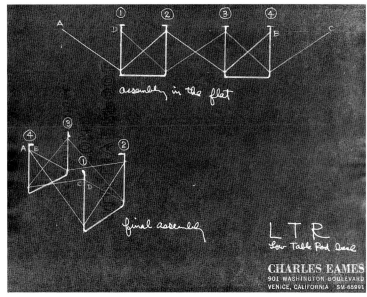

Charles's drawing of the base specifications

February and March: Eames furniture is included in *Design for Use, USA*, an exhibition at the Salon des Arts Ménagers in the Grand Palais, Paris, France.

Staff: 1951
901 Washington Boulevard
Don Albinson
Dale Bauer
Jay Connor
Charles Kratka
Clayton Lewis
Phil Lewis
Jill Mitchell
Tom Okamoto
Mariea Poole
Verla Shulman
Harry Soderbloom
Kipp Stewart
Frederick Usher
Leola Walker

Right: The Eames Office was asked by the Anheuser-Busch Company to redesign its Budweiser logo and packaging. Charles recommended keeping the existing logo, and the Eames Office provided a new package

1951

Elliptical Table Rod Base (ETR)

The Elliptical Table Rod Base (ETR) was designed both as an extension of and in contrast to the Low Table Wire Base (LTR) and was manufactured from the same materials. A long, low coffee table large enough to hold a variety of items, it fit comfortably in front of a long sofa or chairs. The table, which can be used with the LTR, had a dramatic presence and required a large amount of visual and physical space for it to be seen and used to best effect.

Don Albinson has recalled that the objective was to make a long, low table by bridging two LTR bases with a flat plane and that various shapes were tried. The ultimate choice, a dramatic 89-inch-long ellipse, was made of a plywood core with a twenty-degree-angle beveled edge. The plastic laminate top was made in black only.

The Herman Miller Furniture Company manufactured the elliptical table from 1951 to 1964.

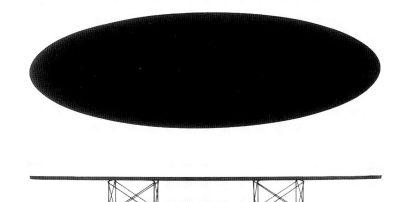

Above: Top and side views of the elliptical table

The elliptical table

149

Unpadded wire mesh side chair with an "Eiffel Tower" base

Staff: 1951
901 Washington Boulevard
Don Albinson
Dale Bauer
Jay Connor
Charles Kratka
Clayton Lewis
Phil Lewis
Jill Mitchell
Tom Okamoto
Mariea Poole
Verla Shulman
Harry Soderbloom
Kipp Stewart
Frederick Usher
Leola Walker

An early American wood blackbird sculpture, a piece of folk art used by the Eameses on many occasions, among a group of wire mesh chairs

1951–1953

Wire Mesh Chair

The possibility of making a formed wire mesh chair was first considered at the time the office was refining the fiberglass-reinforced chairs (pp. 138–141). The wire mesh seat—formed in the same shape as the plastic side chair—was another example of the adaptation of industrial technology to the production of furniture. The method of joining the wire members together was based on the resistance-welding technique used in making wire drawers, which had already been adapted to the LTR base (p. 148).

Although metal mesh chairs had been made by other designers and manufacturers, the Eames version is lighter in weight as a result of the spacing of the structural units. The rim is formed of a heavier wire than the seat and is doubled for extra strength and stability, an innovation that received the first American mechanical patent for design. Like the molded plastic chairs, the wire mesh seats are supported by a variety of bases made in wood or metal or a combination of both. The chair was available upholstered with padding fully covering the molded wire shell or with a two-piece shaped pad that partially covered the back and seat, providing a visual contrast to the lines of wire. The interchangeable pieces were available in tweed hopsack, black or tan glove leather, vinyl or textured cotton, or a "harlequin" pattern. Banner Metals of Compton, California, manufactured the wire shells and bases for the Herman Miller Furniture Company. Don Albinson, Fred Usher, and Dale Bauer were the Eames staff members who worked on the development of the chairs. Herman Miller marketed the wire mesh chairs from 1951 to 1967.

Experimental mock-up of the wire chair

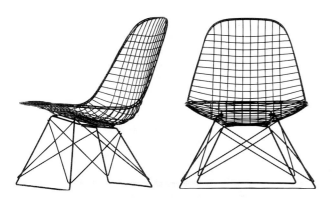

Wire chairs with low wire base

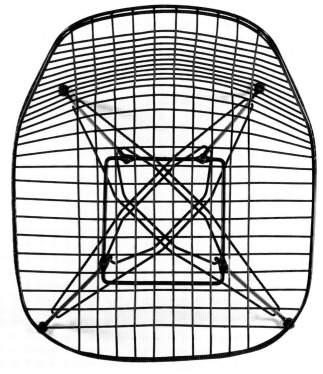

Top view of wire chair with an "Eiffel Tower" base

June: Charles gives a lecture entitled "Design, Designer, and Industry" at the first International Design Conference at Aspen, Colorado. Edgar Kaufmann, Jr., and George Nelson also give talks. Charles's lecture is published in the December issue of *Magazine of Art*. The Aspen Design Conference convenes every summer to present talks and symposia on design and related matters. Charles's last lecture to the conference was in June 1978, just before his death in August.

Charles seated at the folding table on a wire mesh chair during an office celebration of his birthday

Staff members Fred Usher and Jill Mitchell working out pattern details for the pad for the wire mesh chair

Left and right: An assortment of wire chairs with a variety of bases and two-piece pads

June 21: The plastic chair (pp. 138–143) is given the First National Industrial Designers Institute Award.

Drafting-height wire chair with swivel wood base and footrest

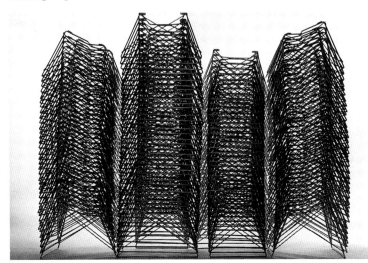

Nested low wire bases

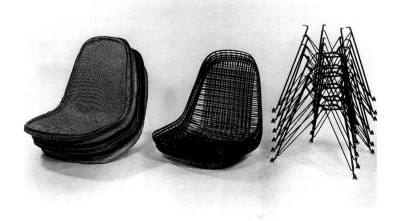

Top: Drafting-height and rocker wire chairs. Middle: Wire chair with "Eiffel Tower" base. Above: Nested pads, seats, and bases

Staff: 1951
901 Washington Boulevard
Don Albinson
Dale Bauer
Jay Connor
Charles Kratka
Clayton Lewis
Phil Lewis
Jill Mitchell
Tom Okamoto
Mariea Poole
Verla Shulman
Harry Soderbloom
Kipp Stewart
Frederick Usher
Leola Walker

Staff member Don Albinson and the wire sofa

Left: Tea ceremony at the Eames House with guests, including (from the left) Isamu Noguchi, Ray, Shirley Yamaguchi, Charlie Chaplin (fifth from the left), Iris Tree (seventh from the left), and Ford Rainey (far right)

1951

Wire Sofa

Using the same materials and technology developed for the wire chair (pp. 150–153), Eames Office staff member Don Albinson produced a prototype for a folding sofa made of wire mesh. It was designed for assembly by the buyer: a series of four collapsible wire struts on runners supported the sofa framework, three cloth-hinged cushions with button-tufted upholstery were attached to the metal framework at the back of the top and the front and back of the seat. The high back of the sofa was removable for shipping.

The wire sofa had a lightweight, airy quality and a whimsical appearance, especially when seen without its cushions. Although all of its specifications met the time-honored Eames requirements for furniture design and the office and the Herman Miller Furniture Company were enthusiastic about its sales potential, the sofa was never manufactured. Although it was conceived as an economical, knockdown item made of industrial materials, the actual factory construction of the sofa's wire framework required too much labor to be practical for mass production. Only the prototypes of the two sizes of sofa illustrated here were produced. The concept and basic form, however, were used later in the design of the Eames Sofa Compact (pp. 190–191).

Top: Back view of the wire sofa. Middle: Front view of the wire sofa Above: Wire sofa in the folded position

Two-seater version of the wire sofa, without pad

Staff: 1951
901 Washington Boulevard
Don Albinson
Dale Bauer
Jay Connor
Charles Kratka
Clayton Lewis
Phil Lewis
Jill Mitchell
Tom Okamoto
Mariea Poole
Verla Shulman
Harry Soderbloom
Kipp Stewart
Frederick Usher
Leola Walker

Charles looking through a viewing access in the Kwikset model

1951

Kwikset House

Through an Eames acquaintance, Bernard Cerlin, the Kwikset Lock Company of Anaheim, California, commissioned the Eames Office to design a low-cost, prefabricated house to be constructed with off-the-shelf parts and hardware, manufactured in quantity, and sold as a kit. The office proposed a house that was modular in plan. The front facade was designed as a modular metal framework into which the door and panels of translucent and wired glass were fitted. The one-story structure had a curved roof made of sections of plywood supported by curved and laminated plywood beams. The beams and other structural members were to be left exposed. The open plan of the interior was divided by freestanding storage walls into a living and dining area, a kitchen, enclosed bathrooms, and two bedrooms. The kitchen and bathrooms were at the sides of the structure, and the utilities were grouped together. The large living room opened out to a garden.

A one-inch scale model of the house was constructed and furnished with miniature Eames furniture. Soon after the model was completed, the Kwikset company changed hands, however, and though the plan and the projected costs of construction met the conditions of the original proposal, a prototype house was not built.

In the design of the Kwikset House, the Eames Office extended the industrial principles used in designing the two 1949 Case Study houses and the 1950 Billy Wilder House to satisfy the requirement that the house be entirely factory prefabricated. Unlike the Eames, Entenza, and Wilder houses, a minimum of interior finishing was called for and in theory, at least, could be done easily by the house owner. The house was designed for the mild Southern California climate; the openness of the interior, the wall and floor materials, and the detailing were similar in treatment to many of the Case Study houses of the time designed by other architects. The office also drew upon Don Albinson's experiences in living in a prefabricated house in the San Fernando Valley, which was designed by Konrad Wachsmann and Walter Gropius and built by the General Panel Corporation of California. Kwikset locks and hardware, used in Case Study houses and advertised in *Arts & Architecture* magazine, were part of the package.

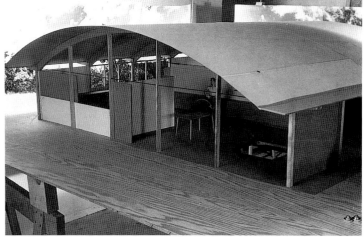

One-inch model of the Kwikset House

View into the living and dining area of the house showing scale models of Eames Storage Units and plywood tables

Living room of the Kwikset model with Eames Storage Units and a wire sofa

Staff: 1951
901 Washington Boulevard
Don Albinson
Dale Bauer
Jay Connor
Charles Kratka
Clayton Lewis
Phil Lewis
Jill Mitchell
Tom Okamoto
Mariea Poole
Verla Shulman
Harry Soderbloom
Kipp Stewart
Frederick Usher
Leola Walker

Staff member Jill Mitchell and her daughter Dinah with an early prototype of The Toy

Charles with an early prototype of The Toy

Tissue paper box kite made by Charles and Ray for their friends, the Bouverie family

1951

The Toy

"The Toy" was a package of colored geometric panels that were, according to the label, "Large-Colorful-Easy to Assemble-For Creating A Light, Bright Expandable World Large Enough To Play In and Around." Designed for adults, teenagers, and children to use as sets for amateur theatrics and parties, as room decoration, or as tents and houses for other toys and objects, the kit included square and triangular panels, thin wooden dowels with pierced ends, and pipe cleaners for connectors. Made of a recently developed plastic-coated, moisture-resistant paper, the panels had folded sleeves on the sides and came in bold colors—green, yellow, blue, red, magenta, and black. They could be arranged in a variety of ways to create open or enclosed architectural environments. Components of The Toy could be easily assembled by sliding the perforated dowels through the sleeves along the panels' edges. Pipe cleaners were passed through the perforations and twisted together to join the panels.

The original package was a large, flat box, thirty by fifty inches; the panels were flat, rigid shapes. On the suggestion of a sales representative from Sears, Roebuck and Company, the package was reduced in size and changed to a hexagonal cardboard tube, thirty inches long and three and one-half inches in diameter, and the panels were made of flexible paper that could be rolled for packaging. The Toy was manufactured by Tigrett Enterprises in Jackson, Tennessee, and was included in the Sears, Roebuck catalog for several seasons. It was featured in a July 16, 1951, article in *Life* magazine.

The Toy was the second time the Eames Office ventured into designing and manufacturing toys for the general market, but it was the first that was actually manufactured and sold in retail outlets. For the Eameses, designing toys was serious business. Play and pleasure were to be taken seriously; as much or more could be learned from such activity as from work. Charles felt that a good toy contained in it clues to the era in which it was produced, and good toys were always part of the Eames Office surroundings—a resource to be drawn upon in the solution of many problems. As much consideration was given to the design of toys as to the furniture and other projects; they were always designed to convey messages about process, materials, or the world of "good things." The toys were designed in tandem with the work on furniture, films, and other projects, and they were usually an offshoot of an experiment with the properties of some material or the extension of a current interest.

Opposite: Ray with an early prototype version of The Toy that was made of cardboard triangles; square sections were added later to allow larger volumes to be constructed with fewer pieces

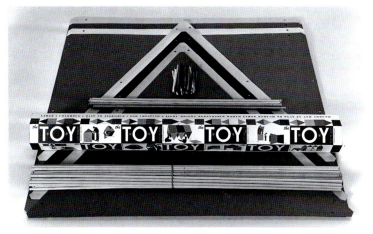
Above: The Toy package and contents; the packaging shows various suggestions for assembling The Toy

Top two rows: Assembling The Toy. Above: The Toy constructed as a children's theater

herman miller, zeeland michigan

Staff: 1951
901 Washington Boulevard
Don Albinson
Dale Bauer
Jay Connor
Charles Kratka
Clayton Lewis
Phil Lewis
Jill Mitchell
Tom Okamoto
Mariea Poole
Verla Shulman
Harry Soderbloom
Kipp Stewart
Frederick Usher
Leola Walker

Verla Shulman, Ray, Amanda Dunne, Charles, and Charles Kratka with the plastic chairs

Charles, Hugh De Pree, Alfred Auerbach, Jim Eppinger, D. J. De Pree, Max De Pree, and George Nelson at a Herman Miller Furniture Company meeting

1951

Herman Miller Furniture Company Graphics

By 1951 three lines of Eames seating were being manufactured by the Herman Miller Furniture Company: molded plywood chairs, molded plastic chairs, and wire chairs. Each line was being advertised as comfortable and durable seating for the home or office.

After the introduction of the wire chair (pp. 150–153) in 1951, the Eames Office produced a series of advertisements detailing its formal and functional characteristics. Using photographs and diagrams, the ads showed that the wire chair could be ordered with one of six different bases— wood or metal, high or low, swivel or rocker—and with a variety of fabric covers. The photographs for the ads were shot by Charles; the graphic production was carried out by Charles Kratka and Ray. The ads appeared in *Interiors*, *Architectural Forum*, and *Arts & Architecture* magazines as well as in other trade periodicals. Descriptive folders about the furniture designed at the Eames Office were also available through Herman Miller.

Above: An advertisement showing the three lines of Eames chairs. Opposite: Full-page advertisement for the plywood chair

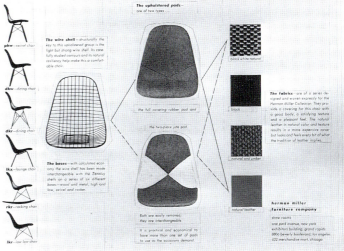

Top: An advertisement explaining the features of the wire chair. Above: Pad options for the wire chair

Staff: 1951
901 Washington Boulevard
Don Albinson
Dale Bauer
Jay Connor
Charles Kratka
Clayton Lewis
Phil Lewis
Jill Mitchell
Tom Okamoto
Mariea Poole
Verla Shulman
Harry Soderbloom
Kipp Stewart
Frederick Usher
Leola Walker

Charles and staff members Charles Kratka, Don Albinson, Ray, and Fred Usher with the Macy 4-Room props

1951

Macy 4-Room Display

The Macy 4-Room Display was a point-of-sale campaign designed to advertise Eames and Nelson furniture in Macy's department store in Chicago and in the Herman Miller Furniture Company showroom in Grand Rapids, Michigan. The 4-Room Display, developed by Eames staff members Charles Kratka and Fred Usher for Herman Miller, showed Eames and Nelson furniture for four different room arrangements—living room, dining room, bedroom, and child's room—exemplifying how the furniture could be used in a home. At the center of the display, four freestanding, double-sided panels provided graphics and information about the furniture. Four large circus poster numbers fixed to rigid panels were placed on the ceiling above the stand to identify each room. Additional circus poster imagery and Charles's photographs were included in the graphics.

The Eames Office constructed the elements for the 4-Room Display, assembled the components, and installed them in the Chicago branch of Macy's.

Top: Chicago installation of the Macy 4-Room Display. Above: Graphic panel explaining the 4-Room furniture layout

4-Room installation plan with central dividing panels and ceiling numbers

Staff: 1952
901 Washington Boulevard
Don Albinson
Dale Bauer
Charles Kratka
Clayton Lewis
Phil Lewis
Jill Mitchell
Mariea Poole
Verla Shulman
Frederick Usher
Leola Walker

1952

The Little Toy

"The Little Toy" was a small variation of The Toy (pp. 156–157). In contrast to The Toy, which was designed as a building toy for children and adults to play "in," The Little Toy was designed for adults and children to play "with"—to make small sets, tents, and houses to use with other toys and objects. Instead of the flexible paper panels used in The Toy, The Little Toy package consisted of modular square and triangular panels made of heavy cardboard with pierced corners, square and triangular wire frames, and small pieces of colored, coated bell wire. The open wire frames and solid 8- or 10-ply cardboard shapes could be joined together with the coated wire to make a variety of structures. Little Toy panels came in a range of bright, solid colors as well as in silk-screened and perforated geometric patterns.

The Little Toy reflects the Eameses' interests in modular space and in adapting readily available, off-the-shelf materials to new and unexpected uses, as well as their love of circus graphics and forms.

The Little Toy was manufactured by Tigrett Enterprises until 1961.

Little Toy constructions with animals and toy autos

Top: Components of The Little Toy. Middle and above: Assembling The Little Toy

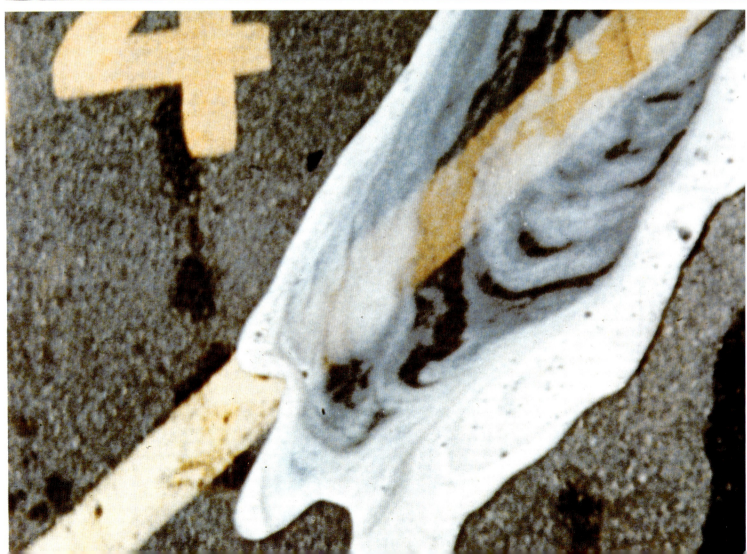

June: Charles speaks to the Michigan Society of Architects in Detroit, Michigan.

Staff: 1952
901 Washington Boulevard
Don Albinson
Dale Bauer
Charles Kratka
Clayton Lewis
Phil Lewis
Jill Mitchell
Mariea Poole
Verla Shulman
Frederick Usher
Leola Walker

Blacktop film-cutting with Charles's homemade editing equipment

1952

Film: *Blacktop*

Blacktop, the Eameses' second film, is a cinematic exploration of abstracted imagery—the movement of water over an asphalt schoolyard, a blacktop. After watching a janitor wash down a schoolyard across the street from the Venice office, Charles was intrigued with the variety and apparent randomness of the movement of the water as it crept across the asphalt—one variation laid over another— and he decided to film the process in live action. With Don Albinson handling the hose and the movement of the water in the schoolyard, Charles shot the film with a hand-held 16mm Cine-Special camera, filling the frame with close-up imagery. As the image could not be viewed directly through the shooting lens in the Cine-Special camera, Charles had to adjust continuously for parallax viewing—a challenge for an amateur cinematographer.

In *Blacktop*, Charles wanted, for the first time in his films, to use dissolves as transitions between scenes. As Charles was still an amateur at film editing, he called Ted Fogelman at Consolidated Film Industries for advice. Over the phone, Fogelman explained about A and B rolls and other intricacies of film production. Then Charles, using a primitive system of handcrafted rewinds, edited the cut film and synchronized it to Bach's Goldberg Variations, played by Wanda Landowska, by reading the optical track for visual clues to see where the music changed tempo. As Ray said later, "Miraculously, many of the [visual] points coincided as if [the music] had been written for the film."

In 1957 *Blacktop*, without its music track, was shown on "Stars of Jazz," a Los Angeles television program featuring local and nationally known jazz musicians in live performance (p. 211). *Blacktop* has no narration. It won an Edinburgh International Film Festival Award in 1954.

Blacktop stands alone in the catalog of Eames films. It uses no toys, actors, or objects; it was not made to present a concept to a client or to make a point about a particular idea. The film is a live-action extension of the still-life studies of the seashore Charles made in his first years in California using a 4x5 camera to record close-ups of tide pools and the natural textures of the water and the sand. Many of the 35mm images used in Lecture I (pp. 50–51) were close-up studies of with a similar abstract quality. (Running time, *Blacktop*: 11 minutes; color.)

Above: A sequence of frames (reading top to bottom left, top to bottom right) from scenes in *Blacktop*. Opposite: Two frames from *Blacktop*. The frames were photographed from 16mm-film footage

163

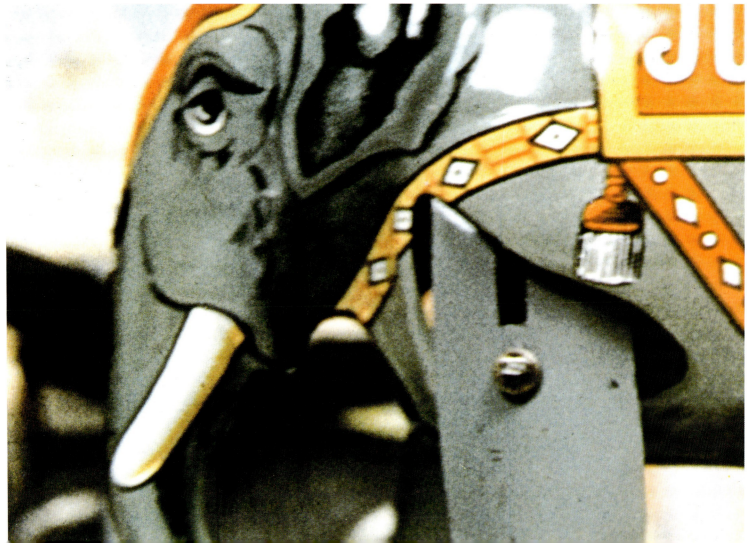

Staff: 1952
901 Washington Boulevard
Don Albinson
Dale Bauer
Charles Kratka
Clayton Lewis
Phil Lewis
Jill Mitchell
Mariea Poole
Verla Shulman
Frederick Usher
Leola Walker

1952

Film: *Parade, or Here They Come Down Our Street*

Parade is a live-action pageant of mechanical toys, animals, puppets, cars, lead soldiers, and dolls—all set in motion. Toy buildings and photographic and painted images of city streets serve as backdrops. The film titles and scenery were drawn by five-year-old Sansi Girard, daughter of architect and designer Alexander Girard.

Parade's genesis lies in the 1950 film *Traveling Boy* (pp. 134–135). *Parade* was the first film for public showing made by the Eameses to use objects and toys as the primary characters. Festive elements from circuses, carnivals, and holiday parades are combined into an exuberant procession set to the music of John Philip Sousa's "Radetsky March," "Stars and Stripes Forever," and the "March of the Gladiators." As the parade ends and the last puppet looks up at the sky, a red balloon drifts upward and the music fades out.

Parade was shot with volunteer help at night and on weekends in the studio at the Eames House. In his book *Business As Unusual*, Hugh De Pree of the Herman Miller Furniture Company recalls spending a night at the studio—after a day working at the Eames Office on Herman Miller business—helping Charles, Ray, and Billy Wilder wind up toys for the film until three in the morning. All the elements were set up and photographed on a tabletop. Toys and objects of various sizes were photographed from different angles and distances (at the toy spectator's eye level) to create the effect of a "real" parade.

Parade was the first Eames film to be shot using bar charts to detail picture action and music tempo. After *Traveling Boy* and *Blacktop*, which were shot first and then cut to the music, Charles wanted to photograph his next film within the confines of a given score and to utilize more disciplined shooting techniques. The toys, paper ornaments, and objects were drawn from the Eames and Girard collections and from those of staff members. The film has no narration. It is in general circulation.

Parade won an Edinburgh International Film Festival Award in 1954. (Running time, *Parade*: 6 minutes; color.)

Above: A sequence of frames (reading top to bottom left, top to bottom right) from scenes in *Parade*. Opposite: Two frames from *Parade*. The frames were photographed from 16mm-film footage

Staff: 1952
901 Washington Boulevard
Don Albinson
Dale Bauer
Charles Kratka
Clayton Lewis
Phil Lewis
Jill Mitchell
Mariea Poole
Verla Shulman
Frederick Usher
Leola Walker

The "Old Writers Building" on the Twentieth Century Fox studio lot

1952

Philip Dunne Office

In 1952 Philip Dunne, head screenplay writer at Twentieth Century Fox, asked the Eameses to redesign the interior of his office in the "Old Writers Building," a European-inspired cottage on the movie studio's lot, which doubled for the studio as a set for shooting exteriors. The L-shaped space was to accommodate a conference area and a small seating arrangement. In the Eames plan the two areas were defined by the placement of furniture, most of which was designed and produced in the Eames Office. A built-in sofa similar to the one in the Eameses' own house (pp. 106–121) occupied a corner near the entry in the seating area. A Saarinen womb chair, a marble-topped occasional table, and a telephone stand built from standardized parts (similar in principle to the ESU; pp. 126–129) completed the lounge space. The conference area was defined by a large plywood-topped table with wood dowel legs and wire struts. A drafting table made from ESU parts was placed behind it. Plywood dining chairs and a drafting-height plastic armchair completed the furnishings.

Behind the sofa, a grid of studs (the system was first used in *An Exhibition for Modern Living*; pp. 124–125) was set into the wall to accommodate a changing picture gallery of photographs of Dunne's wife, Amanda. An Argentinian bola collected by Dunne while on location in South America was hung on an adjacent wall. Light fixtures were suspended from an exposed conduit of ceiling pipe, a similar design to the lighting system used in *An Exhibition for Modern Living*. A special feature of the room was the tackboard for mementos and family photos that Dunne liked to have close at hand. A paper kite, plants, baskets, and flowers were added as final details.

Top and middle: Seating areas in the Dunne office. Above: Desk area

Staff: 1952
901 Washington Boulevard
Don Albinson
Dale Bauer
Charles Kratka
Clayton Lewis
Phil Lewis
Jill Mitchell
Marlea Poole
Verla Shulman
Frederick Usher
Leola Walker

"Tiger" Saito, editor of *Japan Today* magazine, visits the Eames House. Saito introduced the Eameses' work to the Japanese public through his articles

Right: Pacific Northwest Indian sculpture of a whale resting on Eames metal chair bases before the folk-art piece, a favorite of the Eameses', was installed in the Herman Miller showroom

1952

Herman Miller Furniture Company Showroom

On the occasion of the introduction of the wire chair (pp. 150–153), the interior display areas of the Herman Miller showroom in Los Angeles were redesigned to include the new Eames collection, new furniture from the George Nelson, and fabrics by designer Alexander Girard. The black-and-white Eames Storage Units and the calf-hide plywood chairs were included. As in past installations (pp. 102–105, 146–147), the furniture was surrounded by a variety of objects—a Mexican piñata, a wooden sculpture of a whale from the Pacific Northwest (suspended from the ceiling), a wall of seed packets purchased at a local nursery, shells, Indian kites and reels, desert flora, flowers, plants, and table accessories. On one wall, the entire Herman Miller catalog was mounted page by page. As in other installations and exhibitions, the objective was not to show actual room settings but to create an "attitude" of home or office by the use of objects and images. The catholic tastes and discerning eye of Alexander Girard had a great influence on the Eameses in this period, and the eclectic mix of what Charles called "good stuff" always included commonplace things that took on new meaning and significance by virtue of their placement with other, more exotic objects. After a Herman Miller opening, many of the props—a radar antenna, tumbleweeds, seed packets—appeared in the offices, studios and classrooms of many a designer, shop proprietor, or design student.

View of the showroom with the suspended whale sculpture

Top: Groupings of Eames and Nelson furniture. Middle and above: The catalog wall and the wall of seed packets

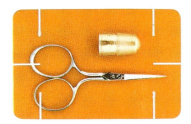   

  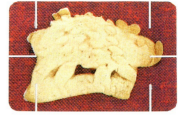 

Title card, picture deck	Straight pins	Spools of thread	English Victorian pillboxes
Nosegay of flowers	Early American toy locomotive	Japanese penny toy cars	School pens, pencils, brush
Gold thimble and embroidery scissors	Chinese pincushion	Buttons	Japanese toy fish game
German porcelain marbles	Eighteenth-century ribbon bow	Old cigar box	Inlaid candies from Strasbourg
Tassels of French bell pulls	Embroidered Portuguese trinket box	Garden vegetables	Watch hands
Medicine	French and English measures and rules	Boar-shaped cookie	Moths and butterflies
Old Japanese paper dolls	Ends of chalk	Old American toy railroad station	Czechoslovakian blown glass beads

Metronome	Chinese dominoes	German toy boat	Old lace
Lockets	Peeling paint	Mexican string	Chinese abacus
Red-tipped kitchen matches	Walnut	United States coins	Crab
Chinese "baby" firecrackers	Apple on Meissen dish	Chinese patchwork quilt	American Indian kachina doll
Snail shell on sand	Austrian wax angel	Christmas tree ornament	Nineteenth-century building blocks
Wax crayons	East Indian doll	Wooden comb from Zaire (Bakuba tribe)	Balancing toy; Buster Brown and tiger
Herbs and spices	Giant glass marble	German wood doll	Asterisk motif, reverse side of all cards

November 2: Charles delivers a lecture at Long Beach City College in Long Beach, California, and shows an early, unfinished version of the film *A Communications Primer* (pp.182–183).

A structure using the House of Cards picture deck

Suji Masumoto, Edward Masumoto, and Sokosen, later to be known as Soshitsu Sen (a Japanese tea master), visit with Ray

A structure using the House of Cards pattern deck. Overleaf: Assembly of House of Cards pattern and picture decks

Title card, pattern deck	Pink tissue paper	Japanese gold foil	Dark green flint paper
English marbled paper	Yellow paper	Rose paper	Chinese printed paper
Japanese rice paper	Firecracker paper	Printed fabric	Japanese printed paper
Chartreuse flint paper	Turkey feather	Packing paper	Colored paper
Chinese firecracker paper	Early American printed paper	Printed quilt pattern	Lavender tissue paper
Black glazed paper	American marbled paper	Pink Slatex paper	Florentine printed paper
Asterisk motif, reverse side of all cards	Chinese paper	Punched paper	Chinese paper

French marbled paper
Printed paper
Chinese printed paper
Victorian lithograph decoupage
Printed paper
English Cockerell paper
Italian printed paper

Green flint paper
Japanese printed paper
Chinese foil butterfly
Paper assemblage
Chinese printed paper
Flint paper (green square)
Printed paper

Japanese printed paper
Paper assemblage
Chinese wax-printed paper
Orange tissue paper
Japanese printed paper
Yellow green tissue paper
Victorian lithographed decoupage

French marbled paper
Magenta flint paper
Japanese printed paper
Chinese tea-chest paper
Chinese wax-printed paper
Japanese printed paper
Paper assemblage

Eames furniture is included in the *Good Design* exhibition at the Crocker Art Gallery, Sacramento, California.

Staff: 1952
901 Washington Boulevard
Don Albinson
Dale Bauer
Charles Kratka
Clayton Lewis
Phil Lewis
Jill Mitchell
Mariea Poole
Verla Shulman
Frederick Usher
Leola Walker

1952

House of Cards

The House of Cards consists of two decks of fifty-four playing-size cards. Each card has six slots, two on either side and one at both ends, so they may be locked together with other cards to create three-dimensional structures of various shapes and sizes. The cards in the first deck, the "pattern deck," are printed on one side with a pattern or a texture photographed from textured or colored surfaces (such as printed papers, fabrics, Victorian decoupage, Chinese paper and paper cuts, and marbled paper). The reverse side of each card is printed with a black asterisk.

The second deck, or "picture deck," which was produced later, consists of images of "good things" gathered from many sources: "familiar and nostalgic objects from the animal, mineral, and vegetable kingdoms," including toys, common household items (scissors, thimbles, twine, and buttons), coins, marbles, jewelry, and lace. On the reverse of the picture cards are gray green asterisks on a white ground. The objects and patterns were chosen from dozens of possibilities; much care and anguish went into the final choices. Each selection had to pass inspection by Ray, the office staff, and Alexander Girard, who made the final choices.

House of Cards was printed by American Playing Card and distributed by Tigrett Enterprises. Eventually, both decks were sold together in a package designed by the Eames Office. The original cards were produced until 1961. The German company Otto Maier later produced a composite "medium-size" House of Cards—a thirty-two-card set selected from the pattern and picture decks. Printed on 8-ply card stock, the cards measured 4 ½ by 6 ⅞ inches and were slotted for assembly into structures. The picture deck was issued in Europe in 1960 and again in 1986 by Otto Maier.

Charles and Ray's view of toys was never frivolous. There was always a point to be made and something to be learned by both adults and children. While the toys were appealing on a purely sensory level, a closer look revealed messages about the things human beings make and use and the everyday objects we take for granted but no longer see as useful *and* beautiful. Charles returned again and again, in toys, films, slide shows, and exhibitions, to the message that we have only to look at our immediate surroundings and the things we use and love for a deep and lasting appreciation of *art* in its truest form.

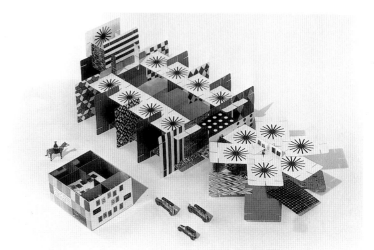

Opposite top: Picture deck structure. Opposite: Pattern deck card box and card structure

Above: Pattern deck cards in a variety of structures

Staff: 1953
901 Washington Boulevard
Don Albinson
Dale Bauer
Charles Kratka
Parke Meek
Jill Mitchell
Mariea Poole
Phillip Ransom
Bill Sahara
Verla Shulman
Deborah Sussman
Frederick Usher
Leola Walker

Charles's office

1953

A Rough Sketch for a Sample Lesson for a Hypothetical Course

In 1952 designer George Nelson was invited by Lamar Dodd, chairman of the Department of Fine Arts at the University of Georgia in Athens, to help develop a new educational policy. After an initial summer meeting with Dodd and the faculty committee, Nelson suggested that Charles be called in. After visiting classes and assessing the undergraduate curriculum, Nelson and Charles agreed that a reexamination of the department's priorities was in order. They stressed that the primary challenge of an arts teacher is to "foster understanding and creative capacity so that these qualities could be employed in any situation."

Nelson and Charles's objective was to establish principles for effectively communicating course material to the student in the shortest possible time. Confusion, misunderstanding, and hostility resulted from the initial presentation of the ideas to the faculty, convincing Nelson and Charles to propose a "sample" imaginary course as a demonstration of what they were advocating—an awareness of relationships between seemingly unrelated phenomena that would "decompartmentalize" the curriculum and make effective use of the resources of the entire university. Using "high-speed techniques such as film, slides, sound, music, narration," they designed a course (entitled "Art X" by Nelson) whose stated goals included "the breaking down of barriers between fields of learning...making people a little more intuitive ...increasing communication between people and things." The Rockefeller Foundation agreed to fund the lesson and Edgar Kaufmann, Jr., was enlisted as a consultant. Alexander Girard joined the group to help prepare the presentation.

The lesson was divided into three "packages" to be produced by the three designers over the next five months, at the end of which they would convene at the university for the first presentation. The result of this combined effort was an experimental multimedia "lecture" entitled *Communication*, in which graphics, film segments, slides, music, and synthetic smells were accompanied by the commentary of Charles and Nelson. The technically complex lesson involved a lot of equipment and required eight people to make the presentation. Although Nelson referred to the lesson as "Art X," the Eames Office always called it "A Rough Sketch for a Hypothetical Course." The lesson was a significant milestone in Charles's approach to presenting information in audiovisual form.

Opposite top: Charles's lecture at the second presentation of the Sample Lesson, which was given at UCLA in May 1953. Opposite: George Nelson delivering his commentary at UCLA

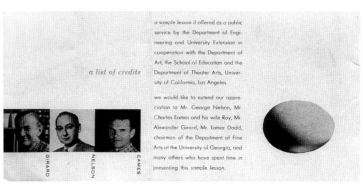

Front and back of the Sample Lesson brochure designed by Jerome Gould, a Los Angeles graphic designer, for the UCLA Extension program

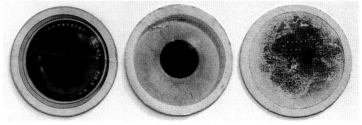

Tickets to the UCLA Sample Lesson designed by Jerome Gould

View of lecture hall with graphic panels

Staff: 1953
901 Washington Boulevard
Don Albinson
Dale Bauer
Charles Kratka
Parke Meek
Jill Mitchell
Mariea Poole
Phillip Ransom
Bill Sahara
Verla Shulman
Deborah Sussman
Frederick Usher
Leola Walker

Writer Larry Bachman and Charles, colleagues and friends since the days at MGM

1953

Film: *Bread*

Two parts of an early version of the later Eames film *A Communication Primer* (pp.182–183) were used to set the stage for the central message of the Sample Lesson. *Bread*, in the form of an Eames slide show, was first shown at the University of Georgia as a preview of another possible lesson, and it was made into a short film for the UCLA presentations. The film looked at the subject of bread from a variety of standpoints—in Charles's words, "the way bread is used in nutrition, bread as an art, bread as a political tool, bread as a symbol." Live-action shots of the different shapes, forms, and ethnic varieties of bread were accompanied by the Sonata 'a Cinque by Malipiero and the Trio for Violin, Cello, and Harp by Jacques Ibert. As the film was being shown at UCLA, the aroma of baking bread was introduced into the lecture room via the air-conditioning ducts, a feat orchestrated by Alexander Girard and Ray. *Bread* is not narrated and was not released commercially.

Six performances of the Sample Lesson (pp. 176–177) were given at the University of Georgia in January 1953, and three more presentations were given five months later at the University of California, Los Angeles, sponsored by the Department of Engineering and the University Extension program. According to George Nelson, "Sample Lesson produced both confusion and enlightenment, generated enthusiasm and hostility." Nevertheless, the approach to teaching was used by a few instructors; in 1957 Nelson wrote that the faculty at the University of Georgia had used the Sample Lesson as a model to develop more than thirty lessons over the next few years.

Charles felt that there was an urgent need to break down barriers and to explore connections and continuities among disciplines in our increasingly specialized society. He returned to the Sample Lesson theme many times in lectures given to schools and university groups; it was one of the underlying messages in his 1970–1971 Norton Lectures (pp. 355–362). The Sample Lesson was the first time Charles used multimedia techniques and was his first use of slides projected in multiples (two- and three-screen passes). It marked the beginning of his use of the word "sketch" in the working titles for many projects and the use of the concept as a model for investigating other design problems that Charles felt were basically open-ended in nature. (Running time, *Bread*: 6 minutes, 30 seconds; color.)

A sequence of frames (reading top to bottom left, top to bottom right) from scenes in *Bread*. The frames were photographed from 16mm-film footage

Staff: 1953
901 Washington Boulevard
Don Albinson
Dale Bauer
Charles Kratka
Parke Meek
Jill Mitchell
Mariea Poole
Phillip Ransom
Bill Sahara
Verla Shulman
Deborah Sussman
Frederick Usher
Leola Walker

1953

Herman Miller Furniture Company Graphics

Whenever the need arose, the Eames Office prepared graphics—advertisements, brochures, instruction booklets, and packaging—for the Herman Miller Furniture Company. On occasion, point-of-sale campaigns were prepared for shops and furniture stores carrying Eames furniture to demonstrate graphically the variety of configurations and the range of possibilities available in the three lines of Eames chairs.

One point-of-sale promotional piece was a freestanding system of graphic panels that showed the leg and seat combinations, the types of available pads, and the range of colors and finishes for plywood, plastic, and wire chairs. Designed to be installed in the middle of a display of chairs, the knockdown panel system was provided to each retail outlet.

A pegboard with cards illustrating different chairs was another device designed to solve the problem of showing all the possible combinations and options available in Eames chairs. Each card featured one of the chair variations.

Top: Circular arrangement of various Eames chairs. Above: Eames chairs with point-of-sale display panels

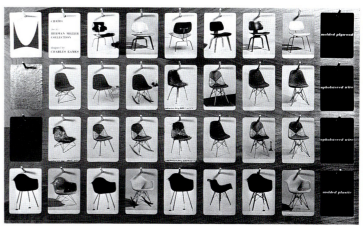

Pegboard showing Eames chair options

179

Staff: 1953
901 Washington Boulevard
Don Albinson
Dale Bauer
Charles Kratka
Parke Meek
Jill Mitchell
Mariea Poole
Philip Ransom
Bill Sahara
Verla Shulman
Deborah Sussman
Frederick Usher
Leola Walker

A set of blocks designed by the Eames Office for Tigrett Enterprises (but not manufactured)

Ray working with blocks and card toys

1953

Giant House of Cards

The Giant House of Cards, a large-scale version of the House of Cards (pp. 168–175), was a deck of twenty cards, each seven by eleven inches, made of 8-ply cardboard. The cards, larger and more rigid than their predecessors, allowed larger volumes to be enclosed. Each card in the set was printed on one side with graphic images—drawings, photographs or historical engravings—that were, according to the box label, "Colorful Panels to Build With * Each With a Graphic Design Taken from the Arts * The Sciences * The World Around Us." The images—including an architectural column, an engraving of snowflakes, a scroll of calligraphy, a classic letter construction, a blow-up of an eggshell in halftone dots, a mathematical model— were chosen from dozens of candidates as examples of the richness of our historical visual traditions and of the world around us. Squares of brilliant colors on white fields (chosen with the help of Alexander Girard) were printed on the reverse side of each card. As in the original House of Cards, each card had six slots for locking; other toys and objects could be used in the card structures. Charles Kratka executed the graphics with assistance from Deborah Sussman.

The Giant House of Cards was manufactured by Tigrett Enterprises in Chicago. Production was discontinued in 1961 when the company went out of business.

Opposite: Front faces of the Giant House of Cards. Top to bottom left: Method of constructing the Roman letter "A"; The three process colors used in printing; Type used as a decorative border from a printer's specimen book; Enlarged halftone print of an eggshell; Patterns of straight lines joining points on the perimeter of a circle; Drawing by Piranesi of Corinthian pilaster capital and column; Path of a free-swinging column. Top to bottom middle: Printer's screens graded from black to white; Old astronomical engraving surrounded by telescopic photograph; Various cuts of gemstones; Enlargements of snowflakes; Diagram of the principal ester that gives the apple its flavor and aroma; Geometric development of a spiral and photo of a chambered nautilus shell; Steel engraving from Diderot's encyclopedia of old watch works. Top to bottom right: Exercise in drawing perspective; Perspective drawing of a chalice by Paolo Uccello (fifteenth century); Methods of constructing an ellipse from the *Dictionary of Architecture*,1811; Graphic representation of an icosahedron (a twenty-sided geometric solid); Numbers enlarged from a German type-specimen book; Diagram of prevailing water currents in the South Pacific; Card Boxtop

Top: A child, wearing a horse's head costume, playing with the Giant House of Cards. Middle: A Giant House of Cards setup. Above: Children building a structure with the Giant House of Cards

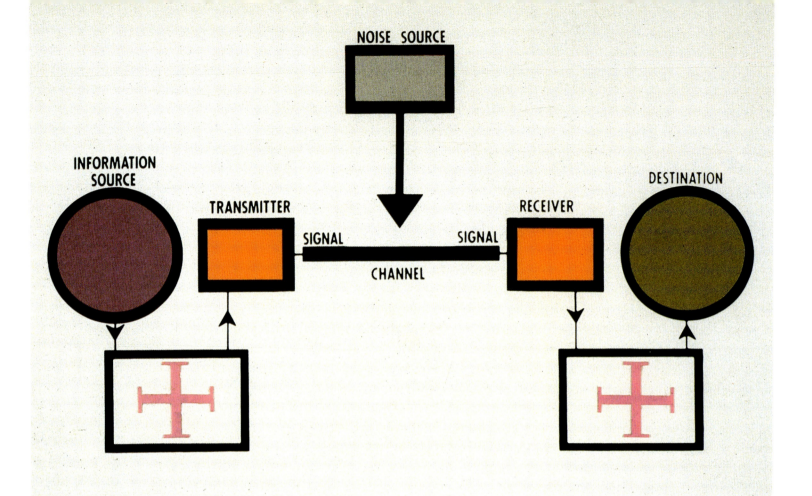

May 31: Charles delivers a talk and shows slides of current Eames Office work at the All-City Los Angeles Art Festival.

Staff: 1953
901 Washington Boulevard
Don Albinson
Dale Bauer
Charles Kratka
Parke Meek
Jill Mitchell
Mariea Poole
Phillip Ransom
Bill Sahara
Verla Shulman
Deborah Sussman
Frederick Usher
Leola Walker

A picnic at the Eames House with present and former staff members Don Albinson, Milton Driggs, Ray, Harry Soderbloom, Georgia Cunningham, and Ada Franchesca

1953

Film: *A Communications Primer*

A Communications Primer was the first film production by the Eames Office to include outside consultants and resources in significant ways. The film was based on the communications theory outlined in the 1949 book *The Mathematical Theory of Communication* by Claude Shannon. The film uses Shannon's Input/Output diagram and the theory of signal processing as its basis. Elements of the film were included in the Sample Lesson presentations at the University of Georgia and UCLA (pp. 176–178). It was subsequently refined and completed.

Charles wanted this film to inspire greater appreciation of the broad meaning of "communication" and to advocate the breakdown of barriers between various disciplines. The film was an Eames attempt to interpret and present current ideas on communications theory to architects and planners in an understandable way and to encourage their use as tools in planning and design. He sent a print of the film to Ian McCallum, editor of the British journal *Architectural Review*, and in an accompanying letter proposed the application of communications theory to architecture. He went on to explain how such theories have unlimited potential for calculating and managing the multiplicity of factors and relationships involved in architecture and planning.

The film was warmly received by British and European architects and architectural critics. Although the film is more than thirty years old, it is still used to teach the concepts of communications theory. Claude Shannon used it in his classes, and the IBM Corporation began using it in the 1950s to acquaint its personnel with Shannon's work. *A Communications Primer* was the first Eames film to combine live action, still photography, and animation and the first to credit the office staff. It was written and narrated by Charles. Elmer Bernstein composed and conducted the music, the first of many scores he wrote for Eames films. It is also the first Eames film in which actors are used. From the beginning, actors in Eames films were drawn mainly from the office staff, their families, and friends, or from the Herman Miller staff. Only occasionally were professional actors employed. *A Communications Primer* is in general circulation. (Running time, *A Communications Primer*: 22 minutes, 30 seconds; color.)

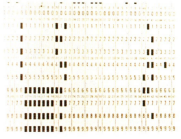

Above: A sequence of frames (reading top to bottom left, top to bottom right) from scenes in *A Communications Primer*. Opposite: Two images from *A Communications Primer*. The frames were photographed from 16mm-film footage

Staff: 1953
901 Washington Boulevard
Don Albinson
Dale Bauer
Charles Kratka
Parke Meek
Jill Mitchell
Mariea Poole
Phillip Ransom
Bill Sahara
Verla Shulman
Deborah Sussman
Frederick Usher
Leola Walker

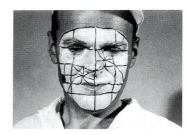

Charles wearing face makeup for Halloween

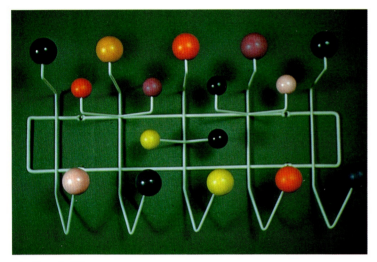

The Hang-It-All

1953

Hang-It-All

The "Hang-It-All," a device for hanging things, was designed for Tigrett Enterprises's Playhouse Division. A mass-production system for the simultaneous welding of wires, the same manufacturing technique that inspired the low table bases (p. 148) and wire chair (pp. 150–153), was used for the Hang-It-All. Short rods, on a metal framework, each capped with a wooden ball, served as hooks on which an assortment of children's belongings—mittens, scarves, jackets, dolls, slingshots, skates, and knapsacks—could be hung. The framework and rods were white, and the two sizes of wooden balls were painted bright colors—red, yellow, pink, blue, magenta, ocher, green, or violet.

The Hang-It-All was distributed by Tigrett by direct mail and advertised in periodicals, including *The New Yorker*. The graphics for the box, tag, and advertisement were designed in the Eames Office by Ray, Deborah Sussman, and Jill Mitchell. Several thousand Hang-It-Alls were made and sold, but production stopped when Tigrett went out of business in 1961.

A child's room with the Hang-It-All, the House of Cards, and the Little Toy

Top: Hang-It-All envelope, which contained the framework's assembly screws
Above: A Hang-It-All in use

Staff: 1953–1954
901 Washington Boulevard
Don Albinson
Dale Bauer
Charles Kratka
Parke Meek
Jill Mitchell
Mariea Poole
Philip Ransom
Bill Sahara
Verla Shulman
Deborah Sussman
Frederick Usher
Leola Walker

1953–1954

Berkeley Course

In late 1953 Charles was invited by William Wurster, architect and dean of the School of Architecture at the University of California, Berkeley, to restructure the first-year design course for the school's beginning architecture students. Wurster originally asked him to tackle a graduate course, but Charles felt it was most important to make an impact on thinking and practice during the first months a student was in the program. For the required course in design, given to 125 students, a series of lab problems was designed challenging the students to think in new terms about design and structure and to connect experiences and events, history and practice. Charles had three basic guidelines: "the objective of each problem should be limited; the process of solution had to be within the scope of the student; and there had to be a practical basis for evaluating the results." Lectures were delivered monthly, beginning in December 1953 and ending in April 1954. In between the lectures, students were to solve the lab problems on their own or with the help of teaching assistants.

The Eameses spent three days a month on the Berkeley campus; all of the preparation for class problems, lectures, and critiques was accomplished in the office in Venice to allow other work to continue. In a preliminary trial of the lab problems, the office staff was given the class problems to solve. The two- and three-screen slide shows, *Railroad, Townscape, Seascape,* and *Road Race* (pp. 186–187), were shot and assembled for the classes. The images on this page are slides of the students' work.

Although Charles had chosen not to teach a graduate course because he felt that the attitudes of graduate students would be too solidified by that point, he discovered that the graduate students auditing the course were the most enthusiastic about it, often working on the problems on an extracurricular basis. He felt that the freshmen and sophomores for whom the class was designed were, in some cases, mystified by the problems and the Eames approach. Charles continued to lecture in universities on a limited basis, but with the exception of a ten-week course he gave at UCLA in early 1977 as a University of California Regent's Professor, the Berkeley course was his only long-term teaching commitment; the work in the office required too much of his concentration and time.

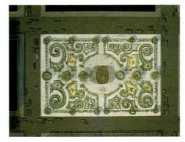

Above: A selection of images of student work from five separate class projects in structure and planning

Photographs taken by Charles at the third Aspen Design Conference, Aspen, Colorado. Right: Museum of Modern Art Director of Design and Architecture Edgar Kaufmann, Jr., and architect Alexander Girard

Staff: 1953–1954
901 Washington Boulevard
Don Albinson
Dale Bauer
Charles Kratka
Parke Meek
Jill Mitchell
Mariea Poole
Phillip Ransom
Bill Sahara
Verla Shulman
Deborah Sussman
Frederick Usher
Leola Walker

Top left to right: Designers George Nelson and Alvin Lustig, Container Corporation chairman Walter Paepcke and Mrs. Paepcke, technologist Buckminster Fuller. Above left to right: Designer and painter Herbert Bayer, architect James Fitch, designer Max Bill and Bina Bill, painter and teacher Gyorgy Kepes

1953–1954

Slide Shows: *Railroad, Townscape, Seascape, Road Race*

Four two- and three-screen slide shows were assembled for a course Charles gave to beginning architecture students at the University of California, Berkeley, in 1953 and 1954 (p. 185). Of the four, *Townscape* and *Railroad* remain essentially in their original form; *Seascape* is still partially assembled, but *Road Race* no longer exists (although some of the images have been incorporated into other projects). A race sequence drawn from the early *Road Race* slide show was also incorporated into the *Think* film presentation at the IBM pavilion for the New York World's Fair in 1964–1965 (pp. 284–291).

Railroad is a two-screen presentation of images of the railroad featuring close-ups of trains and cars, tracks, railroad ties, conductors and other railroad workers, train equipment, and graphics. Train and yard noises were recorded and used as accompaniment.

Townscape, a three-screen slide show, is composed of close-up details of urban architecture—storefronts, road signs, street markings, graphics, manhole covers, and overhead wires. A sound track of city noises—snatches of random conversations overheard on the street, sounds from bars and shops, and traffic noises—accompanies the slides. The last part of the track incorporates a recording of Gertrude Stein reading "The Living and the Dead," a passage from her essay "The Making of Americans."

Seascape is a two-screen show of images of the sea and shore shot along the California coast, accompanied by recorded sounds of the wind and the sea. *Road Race* was a sequence of images of the last automobile race to be held in Golden Gate Park in San Francisco. It was accompanied by the live sounds of the event.

All of the slides for the shows were taken by Charles. Some were drawn from the Eameses' growing library of photographic images and some were shot specifically for the Berkeley class. The slide shows, taken together, addressed favorite Eames themes: "continuities" and "connections," or how parts come together to express the whole. The shows were used, along with films, poetry, and text readings, to provide an environment within which the problems for the class were set up and discussed. Charles also used the shows outside the class context in lectures and talks to other groups.

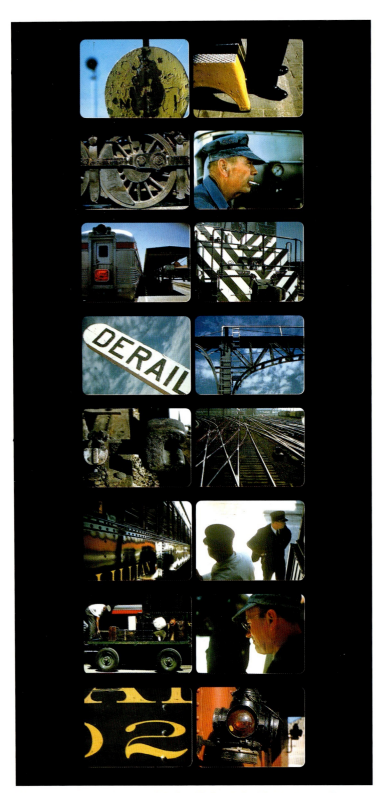

A sequence of images from the slide show *Railroad*. Each left-right pair of images was shown simultaneously in the two-screen presentation

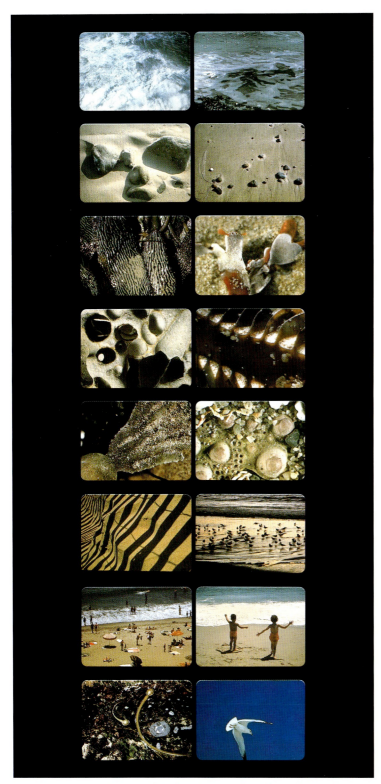

A sequence of images from the slide show *Seascape*. Each left-right pair of images was shown simultaneously in the two-screen presentation

A sequence of images from the slide show *Townscape*. Each trio of images was shown simultaneously in the three-screen presentation

Staff: 1954
901 Washington Boulevard
Don Albinson
Dale Bauer
Parke Meek
Mariea Poole
Phillip Ransom
Lita Rocha
Bill Sahara
Verla Shulman
Deborah Sussman
Leola Walker

Ray preparing the set for a photographic session featuring the Sears Compact Storage unit

Actress Audrey Wilder and the "starlight" mirror

1954

Sears Compact Storage

A prototype compact storage unit was designed for Sears, Roebuck and Company to provide inexpensive, small-scale portable closet space. Made of composition board, the storage system had two bays into which railings and shelves could be mounted. A folding accordion door, mounted into the unit with a piano hinge, closed across the front. The unit, designed to exploit the potential of mass-production techniques and to use low-cost materials, was to be manufactured by the Herman Miller Furniture Company. As with the Eames Storage Units (pp. 126–129), it was to be sold as a knockdown item and assembled by the buyer. Units could be combined to create additional storage space. The "starlight," a mirror with small theatrical makeup lights placed around its edges, was an optional feature in the system.

The knockdown closets were never manufactured. However, the work on storage systems led eventually to the 1961 Eames Contract Storage units (pp. 264–265).

Top: Assembled storage unit. Above: Storage unit in use

Left: Staff members Don Albinson and Dale Bauer assembling a unit
Right: Audrey Wilder demonstrating the storage unit's flexible curtain door

July 3: Charles and Ray attend the Annual Art Conference and Festival of Films at Long Beach State College in Long Beach, California. The theme of the conference is the "Role of Art in Public Schools."

Staff: 1954
901 Washington Boulevard
Don Albinson
Dale Bauer
Parke Meek
Mariea Poole
Phillip Ransom
Lita Rocha
Bill Sahara
Verla Shulman
Deborah Sussman
Leola Walker

1954

Max De Pree House

In 1954 the Eames Office designed a house for Max De Pree, the son of D. J. De Pree who later became the chairman of Herman Miller, Inc. The Zeeland, Michigan, house is an all-timber, rectangular structure with two stories and a detached garage. The front facade is a modular grid with repeated vertical elements. An open balcony and railing, covered by the flat overhanging roof, extend across the back of the second story, looking onto a garden and a wooded area. The major part of the design work on this structure was accomplished by Don Albinson; the interiors of the house were also designed by the Eames Office.

The house was designed in the same spirit of economical construction as the Kwikset House (p. 155), but among the design constraints was the restriction that the house be built entirely by local craftsmen, many of whom had emigrated from Holland— "old-world" artisans who could give special and skillful attention to the details of wood construction. Built in 1954, the house shared many stylistic characteristics (though adapted to a colder winter climate) with the *Arts & Architecture* magazine Case Study houses built in California in the same period (including a modular, open floor plan). The original design included plans for several future extensions to the house, all of which were added in later years. The De Pree family lived in the house until it was sold in 1975 to the Rynbrandt family, who continue to live there.

Front view of the completed house

Top: Four photographs of the house model. Middle: Completed house and site showing the open balcony. Above: Four views of the interior and exterior of the completed house

The Eameses' friend and colleague Dorothy Jeakins sitting in the Sofa Compact

Charles and Ray are awarded the "Decimo Diploma di Medaglia d'Oro" for their work in design at the *Triennale di Milano* held in Milan, Italy.

Staff: 1954
901 Washington Boulevard
Don Albinson
Dale Bauer
Parke Meek
Mariea Poole
Phillip Ransom
Lita Rocha
Bill Sahara
Verla Shulman
Deborah Sussman
Leola Walker

A photograph taken for a Herman Miller advertisement of the Sofa Compact in a dentist's office setting

1954

Sofa Compact

The Eames Sofa Compact is a high-backed sofa based on the design of a sectional seating unit built into an alcove of the living room in the Eames House (pp. 106–121). The compact, portable version is supported by square-sectioned, chrome-plated steel legs and a frame of black-enameled steel. It was designed for use in domestic and commercial settings.

The Sofa Compact is also an adaptation and extension of the ideas developed in the 1951 prototype wire sofa (p. 154). The new version had fewer parts, eliminated much of the hand labor needed to manufacture the wire sofa, and was less expensive to produce. It was called "Sofa Compact" because it was designed to ship in a small box instead of requiring a large, half-empty crate; the entire upright back section can be folded down for shipping or storage.

The unique high back of the Sofa Compact is divided into two horizontal urethane foam pads with a cord welting detail. These and the seat pad, which rests on a steel and wire-spring armature, can be upholstered in leather, vinyl, or a choice of fabrics. The sofa has an interesting profile and none of the bulk of an upholstered couch. It adapts to a variety of environments, and though not designed for lounging per se, it has proven its serviceability in the home or in office waiting rooms. Introduced in 1954, the sofa is still manufactured by Herman Miller, Inc. Eames staff members Don Albinson and Dale Bauer developed the Sofa Compact and designed the tooling for its manufacture.

The Sofa Compact was the last piece of "low-cost" furniture attempted by the office. The plywood, plastic, and wire chairs were designed with low retail cost as one of the major constraints; in successive furniture designed by the Eames Office this objective became less important as a determining factor in the design process, but the goal of cost-effective mass-manufacturing remained an important consideration in Eames furniture development. Although Charles was never satisfied that the lowest possible retail cost had been achieved in his plywood, plastic, and wire furniture, he moved on to other interests, primarily expressed in film production and exhibition design. The design of furniture continued to be an important part of the office operation, but it was never again its sole preoccupation.

Top: Sofa framework. Middle: Folded sofa. Above: Open sofa

May 25: Charles speaks and shows slides of current office work at a museum benefit, the "Uncommon Market" at the Pasadena Museum of Art, Pasadena, California.

Staff: 1954
901 Washington Boulevard
Don Albinson
Dale Bauer
Parke Meek
Mariea Poole
Phillip Ransom
Lita Rocha
Bill Sahara
Verla Shulman
Deborah Sussman
Leola Walker

A sequence of frames (reading top to bottom left, top to bottom right) from scenes in *S-73* (Sofa Compact). The frames were photographed from 16mm footage

1954

Film: *S-73* (Sofa Compact)

The film *S-73* was made to explain the design and function of the Eames Sofa Compact (pp. 190–191) to the Herman Miller Furniture Company's sales force and to dealers and merchants. "S-73" was the designation given to the sofa in the Herman Miller catalog (it is now "473"). Regular-time and stop-motion footage shows a sofa being assembled (it was packaged and shipped as a knockdown) and demonstrates its portability and flexibility in a number of situations.

The film was written and narrated by Charles. The music is by Elmer Bernstein. Friends and Eames Office and Herman Miller staff members were the "cast" for the film. The film is not in general circulation, but Herman Miller still uses it on occasion.

Charles always maintained that he used film primarily as a tool for communicating information. When discussing his approach to the medium, he often said: "They're not experimental films, they're not really films. They're just attempts to get across an idea." *S-73* was the first of many films made by the Eames Office to demonstrate or introduce a project to a client and the first designed to be used by the client itself to inform its staff. Film was Charles's favorite method for getting lots of information across in a very short time to an audience whose concentration he could control and focus; captive in a darkened room, most people hesitate to interrupt. For Charles, putting information in film form provided a strict discipline for structuring ideas and presenting them in short capsules. (Running time, *S-73*: 10 minutes, 40 seconds; color.)

The Eames films *Blacktop* and *Parade* win awards at the Edinburgh International Film Festival.

Staff: 1954
901 Washington Boulevard
Don Albinson
Dale Bauer
Parke Meek
Mariea Poole
Phillip Ransom
Lita Rocha
Bill Sahara
Verla Shulman
Deborah Sussman
Leola Walker

1954

Stadium Seating

In its first attempt to design a multiple-seating system for public spaces, the Eames Office used the fiberglass-reinforced plastic side chair and armchair shells it had developed between 1950 and 1953. The plastic shells were mounted on cast aluminum spiders with rubber shock mounts, and the spiders were secured to a steel beam. Prototypes of rows of side chair shells were produced, as were rows of seats that alternated side and armchair shells.

The work on the stadium seating system was the first attempt by the office to develop seating expressly for nonresidential markets, in this case, schools, stadiums, and airports. Earlier ventures into the office market involved only variations on existing systems (the ESU desk and the drafting and office chair versions of the plastic chair). It was apparent from the prototype that mass-production techniques developed for earlier fiberglass chairs could be adapted to multiple-seating systems and that such seating would have great advantages over the wooden chairs and bleachers commonly used in outdoor settings or in other situations where they would receive heavy wear, such as the large waiting rooms and terminals being developed to accommodate the increasing numbers of air travelers.

This early solution to public seating on a mass scale was developed only through the prototype stage. However, the office returned to the idea in the early 1960s and completed a system for use in Chicago's O'Hare and Washington's Dulles airports (pp. 274–275).

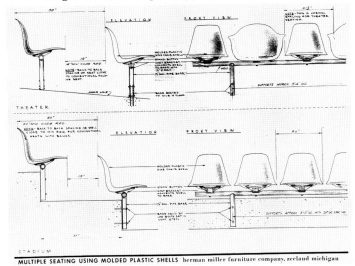

Stadium seating specifications

Top: Prototype of side chair shells in a multiple-seating system. Middle: Armchair and side chair combination seating. Above: Detail of seat support

Staff: 1954
901 Washington Boulevard
Don Albinson
Dale Bauer
Parke Meek
Mariea Poole
Phillip Ransom
Lita Rocha
Bill Sahara
Verla Shulman
Deborah Sussman
Leola Walker

1954

Herman Miller Furniture Company Graphics

By 1954 molded plywood, wire, and plastic Eames chairs in all their variations were selling in furniture stores and specialty shops across the United States. The Eames Office continued to produce Herman Miller's print advertisements for trade journals and professional magazines and to design point-of-sale graphics for showrooms and stores. Deborah Sussman and Ray produced the ad layouts and illustrations.

The "Polyhedron" was designed to accompany groupings of Eames chairs and was a further refinement of an earlier point-of-sale chair display (pp. 158–159). Approximately three feet in diameter, it consisted of six square cardboard panels and eight brightly colored triangular insets joined with fasteners at twelve points to make a cuboctahedron. The square faces were illustrated with black-and-white photographs of Eames furniture—chairs, tables, the Sofa Compact, storage units—in six different room settings. The Polyhedron's instructions suggested that the assembled geometric form be suspended above a twelve-foot-wide circle of fourteen different Eames chairs. The Polyhedron was distributed to Herman Miller showrooms and other dealers as a knockdown package to be assembled on site.

Showroom advertisement with the Polyhedron

 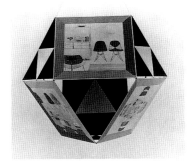  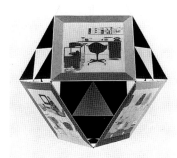

Above: Views of the Polyhedron's faces with photographs of Eames furniture used in different contexts. Opposite: Full-page advertisement for Eames chairs with sketch details of connections and fabrication information

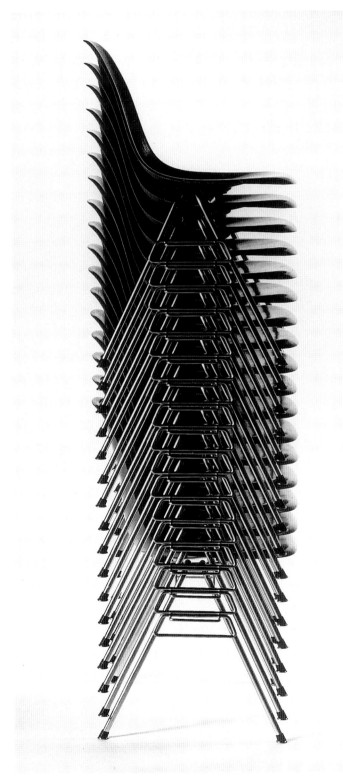
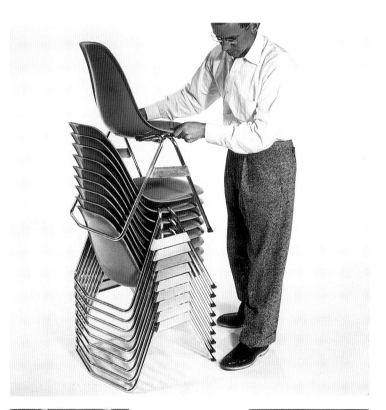
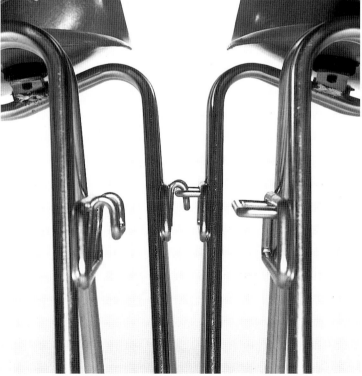

Profile view of Eames stacking chairs

Top: Dale Bauer with an early prototype version of the stacking chair. Above: Two chair legs linked together by hooks (rear) and two unattached chairs showing hooking system (foreground)

Staff: 1955
901 Washington Boulevard
Don Albinson
Dale Bauer
Neil Carlson
Parke Meek
Mariea Poole
Bill Sahara
Verla Shulman
Deborah Sussman
Leola Walker

1955

Stacking Chair

The molded plastic side chair shell, first produced in 1950 (pp. 142–143), was used as the seat for a new stacking chair the Eames Office developed in 1954. The early prototype version shown here had a U-shaped rear leg and a metal clip at the sides (joined to the front and rear legs) for stacking and fastening. In a revised design, a fiberglass-reinforced polyester shell was attached with rubber shock mounts to rod legs of bent steel tubing. A U-shaped hook welded to the legs allows such chairs to be stacked vertically or joined to one another in horizontal rows—a compact, sturdy, and flexible solution to the problem of storing and using large numbers of chairs in a limited amount of space. For easy moving and convenient storage, several chairs can be stacked on a wheeled dolly designed by the office to accompany the chairs. Staff members Don Albinson and Dale Bauer were responsible for the development of the chair and the mass-production tooling.

Herman Miller has continuously produced and marketed the chairs since 1955. Stacking chairs are available in a number of colors (crimson, ocher, parchment, ultramarine, and raw umber). The chair legs have nylon self-leveling glides and are coated black or have a zinc finish. The practicality and simplicity of the chair has made it extremely popular for use in meeting rooms, classrooms, and auditoriums as permanent or temporary seating.

Linking together a row of stacking chairs

Top: Production model of the Eames stacking chair. Above: Assembly of stacking chairs

HOUSE

Staff: 1955
901 Washington Boulevard
Don Albinson
Dale Bauer
Neil Carlson
Parke Meek
Mariea Poole
Bill Sahara
Verla Shulman
Deborah Sussman
Leola Walker

Charles and Ray at the entry to the Eames House

1955

Film: *House—After Five Years of Living*

House is a cinematic exploration of the Eames House and Studio (pp. 106–121) made five years after Charles and Ray began living there. Created entirely from still images shot as 35mm transparencies by Charles from 1949 to 1955 (and transferred to film by Parke Meek), the film takes the viewer from dawn to dusk; from the site—a hillside and meadow overlooking the Pacific Ocean—to the house exterior and through the interior (the living room, balcony, studio, courtyard, and kitchen), lingering on objects, flowers, plants, and details in each area. The tempo of the image sequences builds as the film moves from living areas to studio work spaces.

House was made as an exercise in looking at architecture through the medium of film. Charles felt that details could be shown more effectively by using sequences of still images than by panning a movie camera through a room. He chose his own house for the experiment because he had already photographed a large number of slides of it and could easily fill in additional images.

The music was composed by Elmer Bernstein, who carefully timed the score to sequences of still images; when the slides were transferred to film, their progression was timed to the recorded track. The slides were recorded sequentially on 35mm motion-picture film by an animation stop-motion camera, a technique that allowed Charles to edit in the fade-ins, fade-outs, lap dissolves, and color correction processes ordinarily handled by a film laboratory.

Rather than a step-by-step record of each room, the film is a visual tone poem that leaves the viewer with a feeling for the qualities and atmosphere of the house. The close-up shot, a technique that rapidly became an Eames trademark, is used here to "experience" the house by concentrating on its parts and details—objects, folded textiles, shells, a flower against a window pane, rain on the windows, leaves on the path, architectural details—the way a person might see the house, changing focus from close to far with each glimpse. *House* is a romantic document; though begun as an experiment in photographing architecture, its most revealing message is the unspoken expression of the Eameses' feeling for their home. *House* has no narration. The film is in general circulation. (Running time, *House*: 10 minutes, 40 seconds; color).

Above: A sequence of frames (reading top to bottom left, top to bottom right) from scenes in *House*. Opposite: Two frames from *House*. The frames were photographed from 16mm-film footage

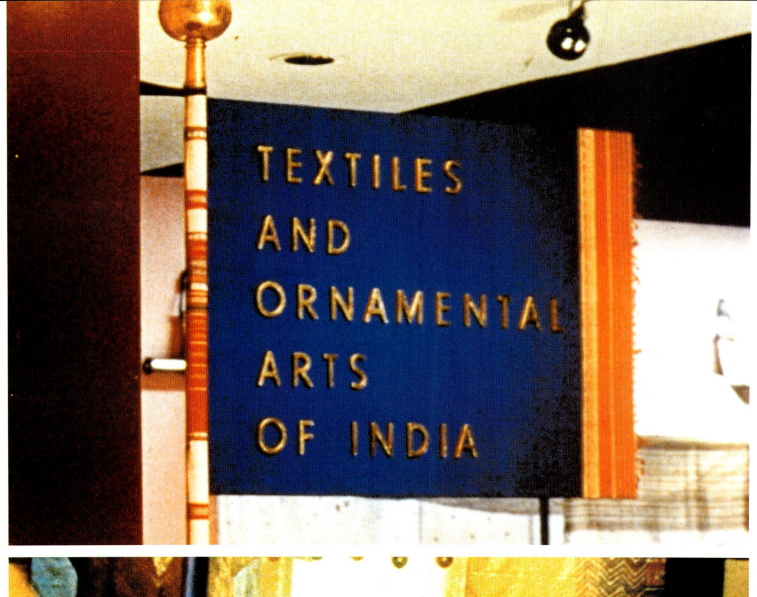

May 26: Charles receives an honorary doctorate of fine arts from the Kansas City Art Institute, Kansas City, Missouri.

Staff: 1955
901 Washington Boulevard
Don Albinson
Dale Bauer
Neil Carlson
Parke Meek
Mariea Poole
Bill Sahara
Verla Shulman
Deborah Sussman
Leola Walker

Alexander Girard during the installation of the exhibition *Textiles and Ornamental Arts of India*

Mrs. Pupul Jayakar, representative of the Indian Ministry of Commerce and Industry

Musician Ali Akbar Khan

1955

Film: *Textiles and Ornamental Arts of India*

Textiles and Ornamental Arts of India is a cinematic record of an exhibition designed and installed by Alexander Girard at The Museum of Modern Art in New York City in 1955. Girard and Edgar Kaufmann, Jr., then director of Architecture and Design at the museum, gathered the material for the exhibition from private and museum collections in India and Europe.

The film was made by the same slide-to-film technique employed in the production of *House* (pp. 198–199). Using a sequence of 35mm still-image transparencies transferred to film by staff member Parke Meek, the film takes the viewer through the rooms of the exhibition, combining long views with close-up details of the displayed objects and textiles to reveal the colors, textures, and visual richness of Indian traditional arts.

The narration for the film was written by Charles with Mrs. Pupul Jayakar, a representative of the Indian Ministry of Commerce and Industry. It was read by Mrs. Jayakar and Edgar Kaufmann, Jr. The music is "A Morning Raga" from an Angel recording, with Ali Akbar Khan playing the sitar and Chatur Lal the tabla. The film is in general circulation.

The production of the film marked the beginning of the Eameses' lifelong interest in India and Indian culture. Intrigued by the variety of Indian ornamental arts and by Girard's dramatic exhibition plan, Charles arranged with Kaufmann to shoot slides of the rooms and objects during the installation. (Shooting live-action film would have been too great an interruption in the installation process.) After the opening, Charles photographed visitors to the show. Charles's objectives were to extend the audience for the exhibition, as it could be seen by relatively few people in its museum run, and to provide a full-screen, close-up look at exotic objects and textiles rarely seen outside a museum context. The film is a good example of the cross-fertilization process that was characteristic of the Eames-Girard relationship from its inception in 1946 to Charles's death in 1978 and of the important role that Edgar Kaufmann, Jr., had assumed as an enthusiastic supporter of Charles's work, beginning in 1949 (pp. 124–125). Charles and Ray's friendship with Mrs. Jayakar led to other work in India (pp. 232–233, 294–299) and long-term relationships with several prominent Indians. (Running time, *Textiles and Ornamental Arts of India*: 11 minutes; color.)

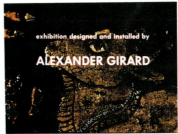

Above: A sequence of frames (reading top to bottom left, top to bottom right) from scenes in *Textiles and Ornamental Arts of India*. Opposite: Two frames from *Textiles and Ornamental Arts of India*. The frames were photographed from 16mm-film footage

Staff: 1955
901 Washington Boulevard
Don Albinson
Dale Bauer
Neil Carlson
Parke Meek
Mariea Poole
Lita Rocha
Bill Sahara
Verla Shulman
Deborah Sussman
Leola Walker

Right: A photograph by Charles of Dionne and Richard Neutra in Germany. In November 1954 Charles, sculptor Richard Lippold, painter Robert Motherwell, designer George Nelson, and architect Richard Neutra were invited to visit Germany by the German Cultural Exchange Program

1955

Film: *Two Baroque Churches in Germany*

Two Baroque Churches is a cinematic exploration of two mid-eighteenth-century examples of German baroque architecture—the churches Vierzehnheiligen (north of Nuremberg) and Ottobeuren (west of Munich). The film was produced by the same technique of transferring 35mm slides to film footage employed in *House* (pp. 198–199) and *Textiles and Ornamental Arts of India* (pp. 200–201).

The slides were photographed by Charles during a cultural exchange trip the Eameses took to Germany with George Nelson, Richard Lippold, Robert Motherwell, and Richard Neutra. After returning home, Charles began to develop a script for the film and to work out the image continuity. The slides chosen for the film (296 in all) were transferred to film by staff member Parke Meek. In the introductory narration Charles describes the unique features of each church while close-up images of the architectural details are seen in rapid succession.

As in *House*, images of details are played against an occasional long shot, conveying a sense of the fabric of the structure and the fusion of architecture, sculpture, music, and philosophy that signified the baroque period in Germany. Baroque organ music accompanies the film. It was performed and recorded at Vierzehnheiligen and Maria Limbach, another German baroque church. Toccata in C Minor by Georg Muffat was played on an eighteenth-century organ by Walter Korner at Vierzehnheiligen; the Prelude and Fugue in D Minor by Anton Murchauser and the *Aria Pastoral* by Valentin Rathgeber were played by Rudolph Zartner at Maria Limbach. The film is in general release. (Running time, *Two Baroque Churches*: 10 minutes, 30 seconds; color.)

Above: A sequence of frames (reading top to bottom left, top to bottom right) from scenes in *Two Baroque Churches*. The frames were photographed from 16mm-film footage

Staff: 1955
901 Washington Boulevard
Don Albinson
Dale Bauer
Neil Carlson
Parke Meek
Mariea Poole
Lita Rocha
Bill Sahara
Verla Shulman
Deborah Sussman
Leola Walker

August: Charles on location in Newfoundland, Nova Scotia, shooting scenes for the film *The Spirit of St. Louis* (p. 210)

1955

Slide Show: *Konditorei*

At the suggestion of Billy Wilder and another friend, Frank Perls, the Eameses visited the Conditorei Kreutzmann (a pastry and coffee shop) in Munich during a cultural exchange trip they made to Germany. They were so impressed with the perfection of the cafe's operation and the elegance of its pastries that they persuaded the proprietor to let them photograph the shop's behind-the-scenes workings one night. Shooting began at 9:00 P.M. and continued through the night in the basement bakery. In addition to recording the preparation, decoration, and serving of pastries, Charles photographed the storefront and some architectural details, the waitresses' uniforms, and the serving utensils and china—in short, the art and character of the German coffee shop.

On returning home, Charles used the photographs to make a three-screen, thirty-two-pass (ninety-six images were seen in sets of threes) slide show accompanied by baroque music. For the Eameses, the ritual forms and organizational harmony of the pastry shop revealed distinctive aspects of the German sensibility; the *Two Baroque Churches* film (p. 202) and the *Konditorei* slide show are good examples of Charles's interest and delight in finding connections and continuities in the experiences of everyday life.

Above: A sequence of three-image passes (reading top to bottom) from the slide show *Konditorei*

Sansi Girard using The Coloring Toy

Staff: 1955
901 Washington Boulevard
Don Albinson
Dale Bauer
Neil Carlson
Parke Meek
Mariea Poole
Lita Rocha
Bill Sahara
Verla Shulman
Deborah Sussman
Leola Walker

A photograph by Charles of Eero Saarinen photographing his wife, Aline, and their newborn son, Eames

Charles with his grandson Byron Atwood

1955

The Coloring Toy

"The Coloring Toy" was designed for and manufactured by Tigrett Enterprises. The box contained card-stock sheets, coloring crayons, and butterfly clips: "All the ingredients for a kind of fun that children have enjoyed for a long time." Each sheet was printed with a variety of outlined die-cut shapes for children to color, punch out, and attach together to make abstract or realistic figures, objects, or architectural structures. To quote from the instruction sheet "Note to Parents," (itself a good example of Charles's feelings about the true function of toys):

> The purpose of The Coloring Toy is to provide a sort of jet assist into a world of color, drawing, shapes, and play. This is a world discovered and rediscovered by all children and is their own creation. The Coloring Toy does not presume to make artists out of children or to teach them how to play (children are far ahead of us on both counts). But we do hope that the contents of this box and the clues it offers will stimulate the use of these and other materials in an ever-expanding variety of ways.

The Coloring Toy was an outgrowth of the toy masks project started by the Eames Office in 1950 (pp. 144–145). Staff member Deborah Sussman designed many of the elements while the Eameses were on a trip in Germany. The box cover reproduced examples of coloring by Sansi Girard (Alexander Girard's daughter) and staff members Lita Rocha and Deborah Sussman.

Top left and right: Children coloring die-cut shapes from The Coloring Toy kit and a selection of colored-in shapes. Above left and right: Eight sheets of die-cut shapes from the kit (sold by Tigrett Enterprises in toy and gift stores until 1961)

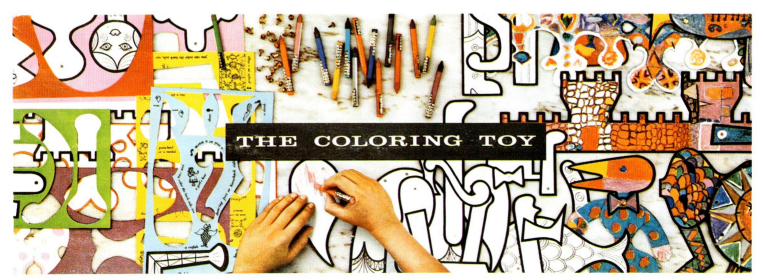

The box-top label for The Coloring Toy

205

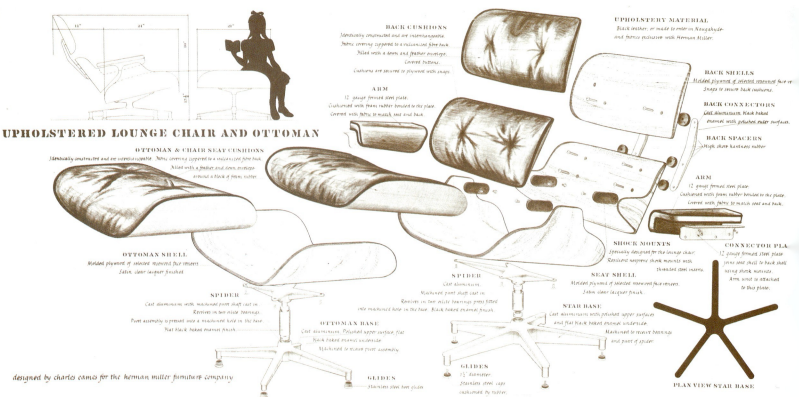

Top: The lounge chair at the Eames House. Above: Exploded drawing of lounge chair components by Charles Kratka (with hand lettering by Sister Corita Kent of Immaculate Heart College)

May 12: Charles lectures on the "converging forces in design" at the University of California, Los Angeles.

Staff: 1956
901 Washington Boulevard
Don Albinson
Sue Atkinson
Dale Bauer
Parke Meek
Mariea Poole
Bill Sahara
Verla Shulman
Deborah Sussman
Leola Walker
John Whitney

Philippa and Miranda Dunne, daughters of screenwriter Philip Dunne, in the Eames lounge chair, 1956

Stockbroker John Meyer, a friend of Charles's, posing in the Eames lounge chair for a Herman Miller advertisement

1956

Lounge Chair and Ottoman

The Eames lounge chair is often referred to as a twentieth-century interpretation of the nineteenth-century English club chair, a chair that Charles hoped would have the "warm receptive look of a well-used first baseman's mitt." It is the culmination of the Eames effort to design a handsome and comfortable lounging chair. The chair's evolution dates from prototypes Eero Saarinen and Charles submitted to The Museum of Modern Art's "Organic Design in Home Furnishings" competition in 1940, and its ancestors include the 1946 experimental all-plywood lounge chair (pp. 64–65).

The lounge chair departs from earlier Eames efforts to create economical mass-produced furniture. Though Charles and Albinson hoped that the retail cost of the chair would be within reach of a wide audience, the chair's design required combining factory technologies with expensive hand labor and craftsmanship. (The level of skill in working with plywood that made it possible to produce the lounge chair had developed to a high degree at Herman Miller in the years since the first plywood chairs were manufactured.) In addition, although certain components of the lounge chair and ottoman are interchangeable, the chair has more individual pieces than other examples of Eames furniture and—unlike the plywood dining and lounging chairs—pads are used on the seat, back, and ottoman for added comfort.

The developmental work on the prototype and the production tooling was done by Don Albinson. The original production chair was made of rosewood; the current version is produced in walnut. The chair is composed of three molded plywood shells; the ottoman of one. Both chair and ottoman were originally padded with leather cushions filled with down, duck feathers, and foam; they now are filled with dacron and foam. The armrests also are padded with foam and covered in leather. The chair and ottoman rest on cast aluminum swivel bases with polished and matte black surfaces; the aluminum back braces are finished the same way. The connections between the two back shells and between the arm and seat are made with rubber shock mounts, giving the chair the resiliency of other Eames seating.

The lounge chair and ottoman were designed for the Herman Miller Furniture Company, which began marketing them in 1956. They are still in the Herman Miller catalog.

Top: Front view of the lounge chair. Middle: Back view of the lounge chair
Above: (left and right): profile and end views of the ottoman

Charles delivers lectures on design at Los Angeles public high schools and junior colleges.

Staff: 1956
901 Washington Boulevard
Don Albinson
Sue Atkinson
Dale Bauer
Parke Meek
Mariea Poole
Lita Rocha
Bill Sahara
Verla Shulman
Deborah Sussman
Leola Walker
John Whitney

Above: A sequence of frames (reading top to bottom left, top to bottom right) showing Dick Hoffman assembling the lounge chair and trying it out in *Eames Lounge Chair*. The frames were photographed from 16mm-film footage

1956

Film: *Eames Lounge Chair*

Eames Lounge Chair is a short, stop-motion film account of how the Eames lounge chair (pp. 206–207) is assembled and then dismantled and packed for shipment. (Charles had first used stop-motion footage, a technique that makes use of time-lapse photography, in the kachina doll sequence in the 1952 film *Parade*.) The film records the piece-by-piece assembly of the chair, shows a few people trying it out, and concludes with it being disassembled and packed for shipment.

Just before the Herman Miller Furniture Company formally introduced the chair at a showroom press conference in New York City, Charles and Ray were invited to appear on the "Today Show," which was hosted by the television personality Arlene Francis. The Eameses decided to make a short film to show on the television program that demonstrated the chair's design and assembly. The film was produced over a weekend in the Venice office: Elmer Bernstein was called upon to improvise a music track on the piano, and the actor in the film, Dick Hoffman, was the Herman Miller employee responsible for assembling the chairs. Model Nan Martin and staff member Deborah Sussman make cameo appearances. There is no narration.

The film and the chair were shown, along with examples of other Eames chairs, on the morning television program, and Charles was interviewed by Francis. The film was subsequently used by Herman Miller to demonstrate the chair to its sales force. Charles considered the film to be a good example of "spontaneous production," a favorite Eames term to define a project that was conceived as an answer to an immediate and pressing need and produced and delivered without the luxury of long deliberation time. *Eames Lounge Chair* is in general circulation. (Running time, *Eames Lounge Chair*: 2 minutes, 15 seconds; black and white.)

The Eames Office is awarded the "Merit for Excellence in Furniture Design" by the American Institute of Decorators.

Staff: 1956
901 Washington Boulevard
Don Albinson
Sue Atkinson
Dale Bauer
Parke Meek
Mariea Poole
Lita Rocha
Bill Sahara
Verla Shulman
Deborah Sussman
Leola Walker
John Whitney

1956

Stephens Speaker

In 1956 Bernard Cirlin and William Berlant of Stephens Trusonic, Inc., manufacturers of high-fidelity audio components, asked Charles to redesign the enclosures for their equipment. (Cirlin had previously brought the Kwikset House project to the office in 1951.) Working closely with Stephens engineers, Don Albinson devised an arrangement of baffles inside the speakers that amplified and improved the sound and produced four design solutions for enclosures that incorporated the plywood-molding techniques developed for the early chairs and the Case Goods system (pp. 66–67).

One design, christened the "Quadraflex Speaker," was chosen to be the production model. The speaker is raised on a cast aluminum pedestal base, identical in form to the base used on the ottoman for the lounge chair (pp.206–207). The speaker itself is set into the center of a square wooden case. According to Albinson, the objective was to design a speaker system that worked "logically and properly with the way sound itself works."

The exterior casing is made of molded walnut plywood; the screen covering the speaker is a detachable woven cloth. Unlike other speakers on the market, the Stephens model, introduced in the period when high-fidelity sound systems were becoming popular, was designed as a piece of furniture handsome enough to sit alongside other furniture in living rooms or studios. Stephens manufactured and marketed this speaker for several years. Herman Miller supplied the pedestal bases.

Front view of the production-model speaker

Speaker prototype

Two speaker prototypes

209

Charles lectures at the California Institute of Technology, Pasadena.

Staff: 1957
901 Washington Boulevard
Don Albinson
Sue Atkinson
Dale Bauer
Dolores Cannata
Parke Meek
John Neuhart
Mariea Poole
Lita Rocha
Bill Sahara
Robert Staples
Deborah Sussman
Leola Walker
John Whitney

A selection of images photographed by Charles on *The Spirit of St. Louis* locations in the United States and Europe

1957

Film Montage: *The Spirit of St. Louis*

The Spirit of St. Louis, a Warner Brothers feature film released in 1957, tells the story of Charles Lindbergh's historic flight across the Atlantic Ocean to France in 1927. Charles (Eames) was asked by the film's director, Billy Wilder, and the producer, Leland Hayward, to produce a film montage to be used as a link between scenes and to handle the second film unit, which customarily shoots scenes not involving principal actors. Working on location and in the studio, the second unit provided location shots and backup material for the primary action. Charles designed and directed the photography of the plane-building montage in which the plane is constructed. The montage includes a sequence of close-up views of the Ryan Aircraft Company staff drawing plans, detailing the engineering, and constructing and fabricating the plane—attending to the details of putting the movie's *Spirit of St. Louis* together.

While on location for the film in Nova Scotia, Ireland, Spain, Egypt, Algiers, and France, Charles took aerial shots from an opening in the belly of a plane flown by the stunt pilot Paul Mantz. He also photographed the behind-the-scenes action of movie production. Some of these images appear on this page; many were later incorporated into his slide show *Movie Sets* (p. 362) assembled for the Norton Lectures at Harvard University.

Staff: 1957
901 Washington Boulevard
Don Albinson
Sue Atkinson
Dale Bauer
Dolores Cannata
Parke Meek
John Neuhart
Mariea Poole
Lita Rocha
Bill Sahara
Robert Staples
Deborah Sussman
Leola Walker
John Whitney

Right: Oskar Morgenstern, a Princeton economics professor who with John von Neumann wrote the book *The Theory of Games in Economic Behavior*, and his family on a visit to the Eames House. Charles consulted the book in making the film *A Communications Primer*. He met Morgenstern later and invited him to visit

1957

Film: *Stars of Jazz*

"Stars of Jazz," a weekly Los Angeles television show hosted by Bobby Troup that featured local and national jazz musicians performing live, explored ways of expanding the visual dimensions of music by using film and other visual media as backdrops for their musical performances. In 1957 the film *Blacktop* (pp. 162–163) was borrowed from the Eameses to use on one of the program's live sessions. Instead of playing the film's original sound track, jazz pianist Oscar Peterson improvised with his own music. As the film was shown, Peterson's hands were seen playing on a keyboard superimposed on one side of the television image, providing a counterpoint to the movement of water.

At the end of the performance the producers announced that the Eameses were working on a new piece of film for the following week's program, an announcement that came as a complete surprise to Charles and Ray, who were watching the program as it was broadcast. They decided to try to meet the deadline and hurriedly began work on a film about spinning tops that they had been thinking about for some time. Working with staff member Parke Meek in the studio at their house, the Eameses produced enough footage for the short segment. Though shot in black and white, this footage is the precursor of *Tops* (pp. 346–347), their 1968 color film, and shows close-ups of a variety of spinning tops. The television film, referred to in the Eames Office as the *Stars of Jazz*, was not narrated and had no recorded music track. No records have been found identifying the musicians whose improvisations accompanied it on the program. It was broadcast in 1957 on ABC. (Running time, *Stars of Jazz*: 3 minutes, 1 second; black and white.)

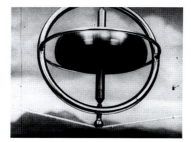 

 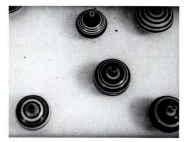
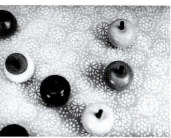 

Above: A sequence of frames (reading top to bottom left, top to bottom right) from scenes in *Stars of Jazz*. The frames were photographed from 16mm-film footage

Staff: 1957
901 Washington Boulevard
Don Albinson
Sue Atkinson
Dale Bauer
Dolores Cannata
Parke Meek
John Neuhart
Mariea Poole
Lita Rocha
Bill Sahara
Robert Staples
Deborah Sussman
Leola Walker
John Whitney

Right: Charles and staff member Parke Meek prepare to photograph the storage system designed by Alexander Girard for the Alcoa Forecast Program while Girard and his wife, Susan, assemble it. Charles and Meeke shot both live-action footage and stills of the system; the still photographs were used in magazine advertisements for Alcoa

1957

Film: *Day of the Dead*

Day of the Dead explores the special objects and rituals of the annual Mexican celebration of All Souls' Day, which is observed on the first day of November. The film examines the Mexican philosophy of death and the ways in which the people have come to terms with mortality. A rich variety of folk objects, created each year for the celebration, are shown in detail.

The impetus and inspiration for the film came from Alexander Girard, who wanted to find and photograph (and collect) the fantastic "stuff" (a favorite Eames and Girard term for describing "good things") still being made for the All Souls' Day celebration. He persuaded the Museum of International Folk Art in Santa Fe to back the production. Charles had seen the celebration during his stay in Mexico in the 1930s and remembered the intense involvement of villagers in the local festival. After some preliminary work, the scope of the film was expanded to examine the Mexican attitude toward death as well as of the ritual and popular objects used in the celebration.

The film was created from 35mm slides transferred to film (using the technique developed for *House* and other films); live-action footage was also used for a short segment showing a procession of folk-art toys and objects. Some of the slides were shot in Mexico by the Eameses and staff member Deborah Sussman, who also acquired Mexican folk art and researched the story. Additional images were photographed by Charles, and the live-action sequences were shot at the Girard's house in Santa Fe. The title panel for the film was designed by Deborah Sussman with type and typographic ornaments found in Mexico. The original narration was read by Alma Usher; the final version by Edgar Kaufmann, Jr. Charles wrote the text with Kaufmann and Girard, and the accompanying guitar music, derived from Mexican folk music, was composed and performed by Laurindo Almeida.

Day of the Dead won an award at the San Francisco International Film Festival in 1958. It is in general circulation. (Running time, *Day of the Dead*: 15 minutes; color.)

Above: A sequence of frames (reading top to bottom left, top to bottom right) from scenes in *Day of the Dead*. Opposite: The title panel for *Day of the Dead* and an opening image from the film. The frames were photographed from 16mm-film footage

January: The Eames Office is awarded the 100th Anniversary Gold Medal for "craftsmanship and excellence in furniture design and execution," by the American Institute of Architects.

June: An article by Charles entitled "The Making of a Craftsman" is published in the magazine *Asilomar*.

Staff: 1957
901 Washington Boulevard
Don Albinson
Sue Atkinson
Dale Bauer
Delores Cannata
Parke Meek
John Neuhart
Mariea Poole
Lita Rocha
Bill Sahara
Robert Staples
Deborah Sussman
Leola Walker
John Whitney

Charles and Ray with a panel detailing the office history that was made for the A. I. A.

1957

Film: *Toccata for Toy Trains*

In this film, in which toys and objects are the featured players, toy trains of various vintages, styles, sizes, and materials are used to tell a simple story of a journey: the cars travel from railyard and roundhouse through countryside and villages to a station.

The opening segment of the film was written and narrated by Charles, who used the opportunity to make a point about toys: "In a good old toy there is apt to be nothing self-conscious about the use of materials. What is wood is wood; what is tin is tin; and what is cast is beautifully cast. ...It is possible that somewhere in all this is a clue to what sets the creative climate of any time, including our own."

The railroad was an important part of Charles's boyhood in St. Louis (p. 17), and as an adult he was intrigued by nineteenth- and early twentieth-century toy trains, which were made in all kinds of materials and sizes. The gift from Billy Wilder of an Ives locomotive, the "Grand Duke," stimulated Charles to begin acquiring train elements for a film that would make a point about the unselfconscious use of material, a favorite theme in all Eames work. The idea of a film combining trains with other props and toys germinated for several years; in 1956 the Eameses began shooting the first segments with the assistance of the office staff (Parke Meek, Deborah Sussman, and John Whitney) and occasional help from other volunteers. A number of sets were drawn and built by the office staff, and the entire film was shot on an eight-foot tabletop in the studio at the Eames House. The trains, toy people, backgrounds, buildings, and other props, drawn from many collections, including those of the Eameses and the Girards, were pushed and pulled by hand to simulate locomotion; the film segments were then edited to make the motion appear to be continuous. In this film, Charles made full use of his love of shooting close-ups of details. He used the camera to manipulate the relative size of the trains, which in reality are of many different sizes, so that they appear to be close in scale.

The music for the film was composed and conducted by Elmer Bernstein, who also suggested the film's title. The film has won a number of awards—at the Edinburgh International Film Festival in 1957; at the Melbourne Film Festival in 1958; and at the American Film Festival in 1959. *Toccata for Toy Trains* is in general circulation. (Running time, *Toccata for Toy Trains*: 14 minutes; color.)

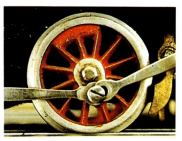

Opposite: Two frames from the beginning of *Toy Trains*. Above: A sequence of frames (reading top to bottom left, top to bottom right) from scenes in *Toccata for Toy Trains*. The frames were photographed from 16mm-film footage

Charles and Ray in the studio at the Eames House surrounded by toys and props used in *Toccata for Toy Trains*

A greeting for Charles's fiftieth birthday pinned on a window at the Eames House

Two-page layout by Deborah Sussman for a mock-up of a proposed Eames Office book on toy trains

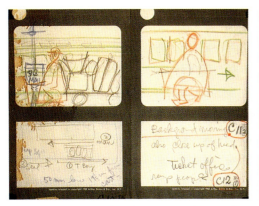 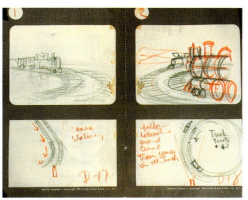 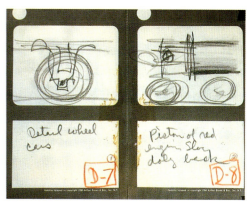

Above left and center: Charles's storyboard for the film specifying station scenes and locomotives passing on a bend in the track. Right: Storyboard of close-ups of a locomotive

Top: Charles, Parke Meek, and John Whitney lining up the camera. Above: Ray checking a scene by looking through the camera lens

Top: Charles adjusting the "Hero" train. Above: Charles making a camera setting

GPRR

GRIFFITH PARK RAILROAD

NOW!

REAL RAILROADING IN MINIATURE

OPEN

The Greatest in the Country

RIDE

CHILDREN 15c   AT LOS FELIZ & RIVERSIDE DR.   20c ADULT

The Eames Office is awarded the "Diploma di Gran Premio" for the Lounge Chair (pp. 206–207) at the *Eleventh Triennale di Milano*, Milan, Italy.

Staff: 1957
901 Washington Boulevard
Don Albinson
Sue Atkinson
Dale Bauer
Dolores Cannata
Parke Meek
John Neuhart
Mariea Poole
Lita Rocha
Bill Sahara
Robert Staples
Deborah Sussman
Leola Walker
John Whitney

Griffith Park Railroad owner Sam Bornstein in the GPRR yard

Topping off the Griffith Park diesel shed with a Christmas tree, 1956

Pat Southern, GPRR station manager, with Eames Office staff members Sue Atkinson, Deborah Sussman, and Don Albinson at the grand opening of the redesigned railroad

1957

Griffith Park Railroad

Sam Bornstein, operator of a miniature railroad concession at Griffith Park in Los Angeles, asked Charles to design the station and railyard through which the train (one-fifth life-size) passed on its journey. In addition, the office designed the concession's graphics—tickets, a poster, and signage. The station house, painted olive drab, red, and black, was inspired by Victorian railway architecture and the graphics by Victorian typography. Other architectural elements and props along the route—a water tower, utility and storage sheds, side stations, trestles, signal posts, and oil drums—were built in the office to the same scale as the train. Don Albinson and Dale Bauer were responsible for the design and construction of the yard buildings; Deborah Sussman developed the typography and color for the signs, tickets, and the station facade; John Neuhart designed the poster.

Bornstein continued to operate the Griffith Park Railroad until 1961, when his lease was terminated. A second Bornstein train ride in Kansas City's Swope Park, including a "Children's World" (with interactive games), was to have been designed by the office but did not go beyond the preliminary development stage. The Eameses' work at the Griffith Park site was drastically altered by Bornstein's successor and then removed entirely.

Top: The GPRR train station. Above two rows: Graphics designed by Deborah Sussman for the entrance to the GPRR

Above: The GPRR train passing through the utility yard. Opposite: Griffith Park Railroad poster designed at the time of the opening by John Neuhart

GPRR utility yard

Staff: 1957
901 Washington Boulevard
Don Albinson
Sue Atkinson
Dale Bauer
Dolores Cannata
Parke Meek
John Neuhart
Mariea Poole
Lita Rocha
Bill Sahara
Robert Staples
Deborah Sussman
Leola Walker
John Whitney

Staff member Deborah Sussman's early visualization of the solar machine

John Neuhart, Charles, and Ray with the solar machine

Staff members Don Albinson, Robert Staples, and John Neuhart photographing the finished solar machine in the meadow next to the Eames House

1957

Alcoa Solar Do-Nothing Machine

In 1957 Charles was asked by the advertising agency Ketchum, MacCleod and Grove to participate in the "Forecast Program," an advertising campaign for Alcoa (Aluminum Company of America). Charles and other designers were invited to help promote aluminum by creating new aluminum products to be photographed for magazine advertisements. The Eames Office was asked specifically to design an aluminum toy. Its approach to the problem was to investigate the use of solar energy in combination with the lightweight, reflective properties of aluminum. In their first scheme they used an aluminum parabolic reflector, which boiled water, making steam to run an engine that moved the parts of the toy. Eddie Lipps (owner of the Entenza House), who was an engineer by profession, introduced his neighbors, the Eameses, to photovoltaic cells made by the International Rectifier Corporation, which simplified the problems of energy source. After many months of experimentation with the cells, the office came up with the "Solar Do-Nothing Machine," a device that converted sunlight into electrical energy to run motion displays.

The solar machine consisted of a twenty-four-inch elliptical aluminum platform supporting ten motion displays topped with pinwheels and star shapes of colored anodized aluminum. A freestanding reflector screen of polished aluminum strips captured sunlight and reflected it onto two panels of twelve photovoltaic cells, converting the light into electrical energy. The energy was conducted by wires to six small, one-and-a-half-volt motors (placed on aluminum pedestals) that drove a series of pulleys and belts that caused the aluminum shapes mounted on the pedestals to revolve.

Many staff members, including Don Albinson and Parke Meek, worked on the solar machine. In the summer of 1957 John Neuhart continued its development and with Don Albinson constructed the final machine delivered to the client. Although the solar machine "did nothing" and was not a product to be marketed and sold, it provided an early working demonstration of the potential union between aluminum and solar energy. The solar machine was featured in Alcoa's 1957-1958 advertising campaign in a variety of monthly and weekly periodicals (the first advertisement was in *Time* magazine) and in a feature article in *Life* magazine (March 24, 1958).

Opposite top: The solar machine photographed in the meadow at the Eames House. Opposite: Charles with the solar machine seen from behind

A mock-up of an early prototype of the solar machine

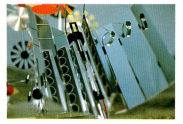

Middle two rows: Close-up details of the solar machine's motion-tree forms, the solar reflector, and the aluminum tree-form turning. Above: The solar machine in motion

December: Charles and Ray visit Ahmedabad, India, to begin their research for the India Report (pp. 232–233).

Staff: 1957
901 Washington Boulevard
Don Albinson
Sue Atkinson
Dale Bauer
Dolores Cannata
Parke Meek
John Neuhart
Mariea Poole
Lita Rocha
Bill Sahara
Robert Staples
Deborah Sussman
Leola Walker
John Whitney

The making of the film *The Information Machine* marked the beginning of the Eameses' long association with the IBM Corporation. Eliot Noyes, who had met Charles in 1940 during The Museum of Modern Art's "Organic Design in Home Furnishings" competition and had kept in touch through the years, became design director at IBM and brought Charles into the corporation on numerous occasions, beginning with the *Feedback* film commission (p. 251), which was temporarily shelved to produce *The Information Machine*. IBM, in addition to the Herman Miller Furniture Company, became the Eameses' major client.

1957

Film: *The Information Machine: Creative Man and the Data Processor*

The Information Machine was produced for the IBM Corporation to be shown in its pavilion at the 1958 Brussels World's Fair. Intended as an introduction to the electronic computer, the film uses animation to depict the computer as the culmination of centuries of tools and systems man has developed to process information. For *The Information Machine* film Charles synthesized and extended the concepts of information theory he presented in his 1953 film *A Communications Primer* (pp. 182–183) and explored how humans have gone about the process of solving problems before and after the advent of the electronic computer.

The story of the human need to process and communicate larger and more complex amounts of information is depicted in animated sequences in which people learn to manipulate abstractions with increasing sophistication and skill. *The Information Machine* was the first completely animated film produced by the Eames Office. It was also their first film commissioned by a client (Eliot Noyes, then design director for IBM, brought the project to the office)—all of the earlier Eames films originated in the office itself or were extensions of other projects. *The Information Machine* also was the first Eames project completed for the IBM Corporation, and the first to give screen credit to office staff members.

The narration was written by Charles and was read by Vic Perrin. Dolores Cannata drew the animated sequences, and the film was shot in the office by Parke Meek and John Whitney (who in his own right is also an important experimental filmmaker) on an animation stand. Elmer Bernstein wrote the original score. The film won an award at the Edinburgh International Film Festival in 1958. *The Information Machine* is in general circulation.

The production of *The Information Machine* marked a pivotal point in the direction in which the work in the office would move in succeeding years. In Charles's words, "The office would be more and more concerned with the way information is handled." Furniture, toys, and graphics would continue to be important, but the ordering of information in film, exhibitions, and books became the Eameses' major preoccupation. (Running time, *The Information Machine*: 10 minutes; color.)

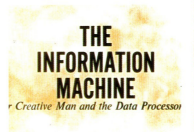

Above: A sequence of frames (reading top to bottom left, top to bottom right) from scenes in *The Information Machine*. Opposite: A drawing by Dolores Cannata from *The Information Machine*. The frames were photographed from 16mm-film footage

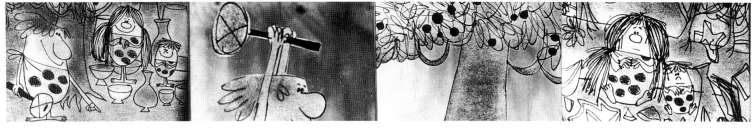

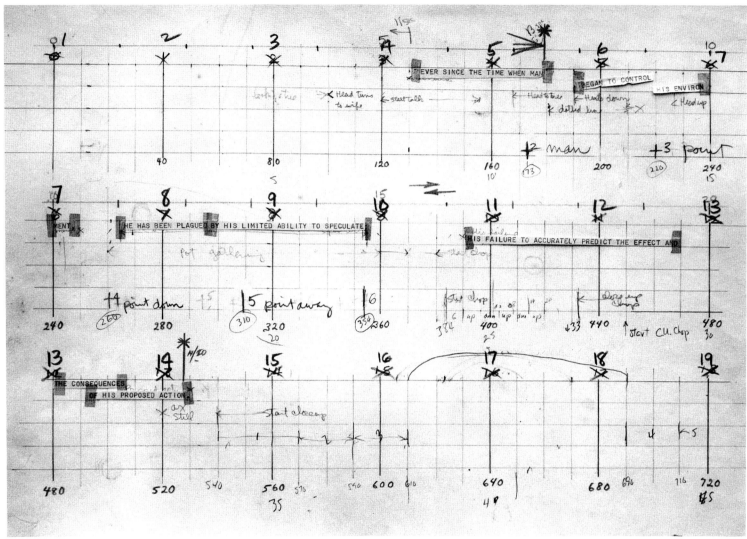

Top: Frames from the beginning of the film depicting early man's difficulties with predicting events. Above: Bar chart used to chart the relationship of the film's dialogue to the action in the illustration above

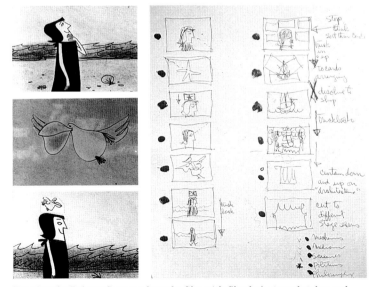

Drawings by Dolores Cannata from the film with Charles's story sketches and notations

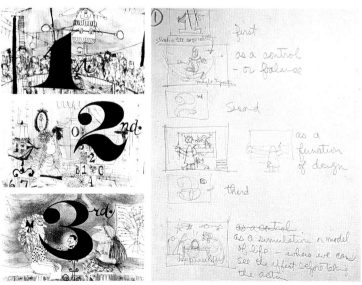

Drawings by Dolores Cannata from the film with Charles's sketches. The sequence depicts significant moments in people's ability to manipulate and use information

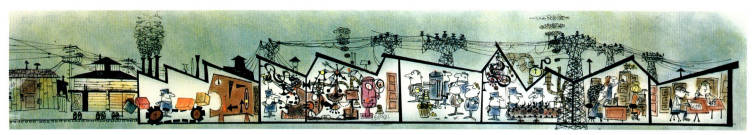
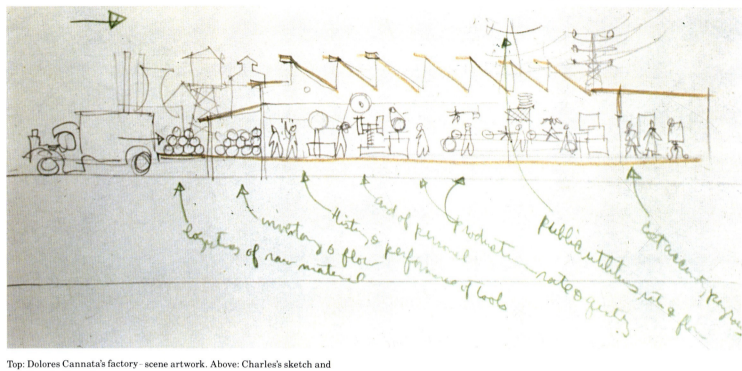

Top: Dolores Cannata's factory-scene artwork. Above: Charles's sketch and notations for the action

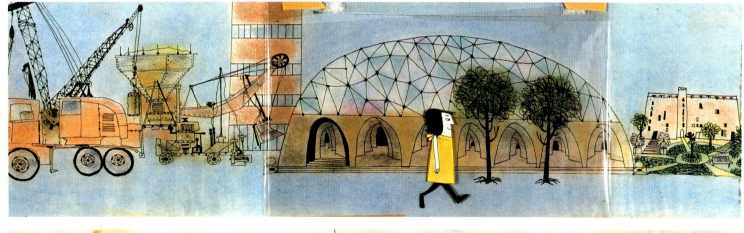
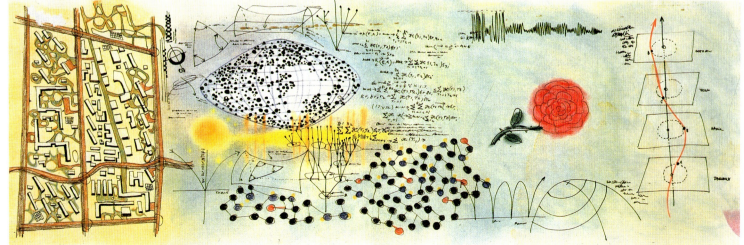

Top and above: Two scenes from the end of the film summing up the ways the computer is used in daily life

January 15-17: Charles delivers a talk to the California Council of the American Institute of Architects in Monterey, California.

Staff: 1958
901 Washington Boulevard
Don Albinson
Sue Atkinson
Dale Bauer
Ellie Bogardus
Lucia Capacchione
Selby Daley
Carlos Diniz
Glen Fleck
Charles Fraser
Dan Greenberg
Ella Hogan
Nancy Kane
Sylvia Kennedy
Ed Leavitt
Parke Meek
John Neuhart
Peter Pearce
Mariea Poole
Carl Ronay
Marvin Rubin
Bill Sahara
Robert Staples
Frederick Swenson
Richard Usher
Leola Walker
John Whitney

1958

Aluminum Group Furniture

At times in its development, the "Aluminum Group" of Eames furniture was called the "leisure group" or the "indoor-outdoor group." The inspiration for a collection of aluminum furniture developed out of conversations between Charles and Alexander Girard about the lack of high-quality outdoor furniture available on the market. The first aluminum chairs were produced as a special project for Girard and Eero Saarinen's Irwin Miller House in Columbus, Indiana (Girard was designing the interiors). By 1958, the Herman Miller Furniture Company was manufacturing the Eames line of aluminum furniture and marketing it for use in outdoor or indoor domestic and institutional contexts. Don Albinson, Dale Bauer, and Bob Staples were the Eames staff members most closely involved in the project. Some later adaptations in the furniture bases were designed by Peter Pearce.

The first aluminum lounge chairs were available in striped blue, gray, green, or brown saran weaves (a plastic cloth) designed by the Eames Office and Alexander Girard. The fabric was laid into the chair side members with triple-layer folds at the seat, back, and head areas. This tripling-up provided additional support for the seat and back and reduced sagging. A heat-sealed Koroseal (a naugahyde) was later substituted for saran. After additional experimentation, an upholstery "sandwich"—a front and back layer of naugahyde or fabric, an inner layer of stiff vinyl-coated nylon (Fiberthin), and a ¼-inch layer of vinyl foam—ultrasonically welded together in parallel transverse ribs at 1 ⅞-inch intervals (the melting vinyl of the foam and Fiberthin binds the laminated assembly together) was adopted as the production standard for the chair.

The current Aluminum Group consists of a high-back, tilt-swivel lounge chair (with or without arms), a low- and high-back, tilt-swivel desk chair with an adjustable seat (with or without arms), a low-back side chair (with or without arms), an ottoman, a coffee table, and a dining table. Each of the chair's side ribs is a curved, one-piece, die-cast aluminum member; two "flaring spreaders," or "antlers," are screwed into the frames at the back and under the seat, connecting the two ribs. A technical achievement of the Aluminum Group is the way the continuous plane of the seat-back upholstery is held tautly within grooves along the aluminum frames and rolled tightly at the ends. This was accomplished by sewing a stiff strip of plastic (Royalite) along the edges of the upholstery and then working it into the grooves with the

Opposite: Back view of the Aluminum Group Chair production model. A new Eames laminate-topped coffee table is in the background

A room setting of early Eames indoor-outdoor seating

Early indoor-outdoor chair prototype with polyester saran covering showing the lapped fabric area

March: Charles receives the "Alumni Award" from his alma mater, Washington University, St. Louis, Missouri.

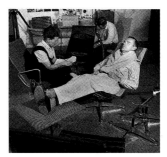

Ray, Don Albinson, and Charles with examples of the Aluminum Group furniture

Charles and Ray examining the sling locations to be covered by fabric lapping

Charles and the "antler" seat section and base pedestal

frames turned inward. The frames were then flipped over, pulling the fabric in place under tension. The aluminum spreaders are screwed into position to keep the chair sides a fixed distance apart. The back stretcher is also a carrying handle and the seat stretcher a support for the pedestal base.

The high and low tables, supported by cast aluminum pedestal bases, originally trapezoidal in section and later elliptical in form, were available in Botticino marble, slate, or white glass. Today they are produced with several hardwood veneers or plastic laminated tops. Herman Miller still manufactures the chairs and ottoman in eight different fabrics, including vinyl. In addition to the bright, polished aluminum finish originally designed for the chair frames, they are available with cool tone, warm tone, or eggplant gloss frames.

The Eames Office had used aluminum in earlier chair and table bases and had attempted for the "Low-Cost Furniture Design" competition (pp. 96–101) to stamp chair shells out of aluminum sheets. However, the Aluminum Group chairs were the office's first use of the material for structural side members and represented a major departure from the concept of the chair as a solid shell. The chair sling of heat-sealed naugahyde was also a new application for that material, which up to then had been used primarily as an upholstery covering.

A series of round tables was introduced at the same time as the Aluminum Group. Made in two heights (dining and coffee table). the tables were produced in diameters ranging from 30 inches to 54 inches and in thicknesses of $7/8$-inch and $1/16$-inches. The surface of the tabletop was covered with white laminate and finished with a black extruded-vinyl edge; other surfaces were available by special order from Herman Miller. The polished aluminum bases for the tables were the same as those used for the Aluminum Group chairs, and the supporting column was black steel. Other variations in tabletop surfaces and column treatment were added in succeeding years. Herman Miller still makes the tables.

May: *Interiors* magazine publishes an article by Charles, "Designing the Indoor/Outdoor Leisure Group."

Charles and Don Albinson checking a detail on an aluminum chair side member

Robert Staples shaping a cast side member for an aluminum chair

Examples of prototypes in the development of the aluminum side member. Top to bottom: final pattern, early casting pattern, early prototype

Dale Bauer and Don Albinson connecting spreaders to side members

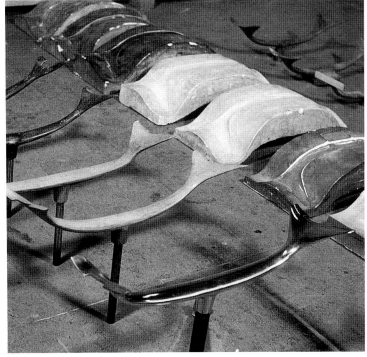
Various stages of "antler" spreader development

Don Albinson inserting a Royalite strip into the upholstery

March: *Family Circle* magazine publishes an article by Charles, "Have Great Love or Profound Discipline."

Right: Immaculate Heart College sisters Thecia, Seconda, Mary Corita Kent, and Magdalen Mary during the Eames Office filming of *Herman Miller at the Brussels World's Fair*. The Eameses maintained a close relationship with these art instructors at the Los Angeles college

Sister Mary Corita Kent photographing Charles photographing a scene for the film *Herman Miller at the Brussels World's Fair*

Staff: 1958
901 Washington Boulevard
Don Albinson
Sue Atkinson
Dale Bauer
Ellie Bogardus
Lucia Capacchione
Selby Daley
Carlos Diniz
Glen Fleck
Charles Fraser
Dan Greenberg
Ella Hogan
Sylvia Kennedy
Nancy Kane
Ed Leavitt
Parke Meek
John Neuhart
Peter Pearce
Mariea Poole
Carl Ronay
Marvin Rubin
Bill Sahara
Robert Staples
Richard Swenson
Frederick Usher
Leola Walker
John Whitney

1958

Film: *Herman Miller at the Brussels World's Fair*

In 1958, on returning from a trip to India, Charles and Ray visited the opening of the Brussels World's Fair (where their film *The Information Machine* was playing in the IBM pavilion and their furniture was being used in rest areas in the U.S. pavilion; pp. 222–225). They shot a series of 35mm slides documenting the pavilion, including its Saul Steinberg murals and visitors relaxing in chairs provided by Herman Miller. As a surprise for Herman Miller, the Eameses decided on their return to California to make a film from these slides showing the fair, in particular the visitors relaxing in the Eames-Herman Miller furniture.

The still images were arranged in a sequence and filmed using the slide-to-film technique developed for previous films. Pickup shots of specific furniture details were made at the Eames Office. Herman Miller knew nothing about the film until it was shown in a special preview at the Eames Office. It was subsequently used by Herman Miller for its customers and staff members. The accompanying score is a Riverside Company recording of music performed by the Herbie Mann Sextet, Chet Baker, and The Wind. There is no narration. The film is in general circulation. (Running time, *Herman Miller at the Brussels World's Fair*: 4 minutes, 30 seconds; color.)

A sequence of frames (reading top to bottom left, top to bottom right) from scenes in *Herman Miller at the Brussels World's Fair*. The frames were photographed from 16mm-film footage

October: Charles lectures to the American Institute of Architects.

November: Charles delivers a talk to the Kansas City Art Institute, Kansas City, Missouri.

Staff: 1958
901 Washington Boulevard
Don Albinson
Sue Atkinson
Dale Bauer
Ellie Bogardus
Lucia Capacchione
Selby Daley
Carlos Diniz
Glen Fleck
Charles Fraser
Dan Greenberg
Ella Hogan
Nancy Kane
Sylvia Kennedy
Ed Leavitt
Parke Meek
John Neuhart
Peter Pearce
Mariea Poole
Carl Ronay
Marvin Rubin
Bill Sahara
Robert Staples
Richard Swenson
Frederick Usher
Leola Walker
John Whitney

1958

Film: *The Expanding Airport*

The Expanding Airport was produced for the architectural and engineering team of Eero Saarinen, Ellery Husted, Amman & Whitney, and Burns & McDonnell as part of their presentation for the design of the new Washington International Airport, later named Dulles Airport. The plan proposed by Saarinen and his associates for the terminal eliminated the long connecting hallways common to many airports and instead recommended buslike vehicles, called "mobile lounges," that would move passengers from central departure gates to planes on the airfield. The film demonstrates the advantages for both the public and the airlines of parking the planes on the field conveniently near service centers: airport efficiency would increase and passengers would be saved long walks with heavy luggage.

The film, designed to aid Saarinen in a detailed presentation, was begun before the mechanics of the lounges were completed. It was produced in stages, the first of which was shown to a client meeting of airline presidents at which Saarinen presented his new concept. Subsequent segments were shown to the client as progress on the lounges and the film was made (with markers in the footage indicating forthcoming scenes). Although the project was approved and started before the film was actually completed, the Eames Office produced a final version with all scenes intact.

The film is composed primarily of animation by Glen Fleck with some sequences of black and white still photography transferred to film. The film was written with Glen Fleck and narrated by Charles. The accompanying music was composed of phrases chosen from a variety of popular tunes and combined for the sound track. The film is not in general circulation. (Running time, *The Expanding Airport*: 9 minutes, 30 seconds; color.)

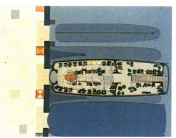
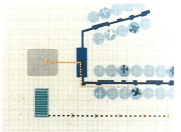

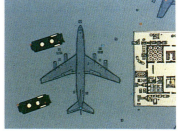

A sequence of frames (reading top to bottom left, top to bottom right) from scenes in *The Expanding Airport*. The frames were photographed from 16mm-film footage

Right: Buckminster Fuller in India, photographed by Charles after the two met by chance. They toured the countryside in search of indigenous architecture, which Charles photographed

Staff: 1958
901 Washington Boulevard
Don Albinson
Sue Atkinson
Dale Bauer
Ellie Bogardus
Lucia Capacchione
Selby Daley
Carlos Diniz
Glen Fleck
Charles Fraser
Dan Greenberg
Ella Hogan
Nancy Kane
Sylvia Kennedy
Ed Leavitt
Parke Meek
John Neuhart
Peter Pearce
Mariea Poole
Carl Ronay
Marvin Rubin
Bill Sahara
Robert Staples
Richard Svenson
Frederick Usher
Leola Walker
John Whitney

People, places, and artifacts photographed in India by Charles. Though the India photographs were not included in the India Report itself, they were used in the *Nehru* exhibition (pp. 294–299) and in the Norton Lectures at Harvard (pp. 360–361) in 1971, and in many other slide-show presentations

1958

India Report

Charles and Ray's involvement with India began with their work on the film *Textiles and Ornamental Arts of India*, a cinematic record of the 1955 exhibition at The Museum of Modern Art (pp. 200–201). While making the film, they became friends with Mrs. Pupul Jayakar, India's representative at the exhibition. In 1957 the government of India and its leader, Jawaharlal Nehru, expressed concern about the impact of Western design and technology on Indian culture. Charles, on Mrs. Jayakar's recommendation, was invited to visit the country, evaluate the problem, and recommend a course of action. Charles accepted the assignment and he and Ray journeyed throughout India, meeting individuals from all disciplines and taking hundreds of photographs (a representative selection is seen here). The result of his initial study, the "India Report," was submitted to the Indian government in 1958. Among the report's recommendations was the establishment of an "Institute of Design Research and Service" that would aid small industries in the production of "quality" consumer goods.

The report begins with excerpts from the Bhagavad Gita, the Sanskrit poem, about the importance of work for its own sake rather than for a selfish interest in results:

> You have the right to work, but for the work's sake only. You have no right to the fruits of work. Desire for the fruits of work must never be your motive in working. Never give way to laziness, either.
>
> Perform every action with your heart fixed on the Supreme Lord. Renounce attachment to the fruits. Be even-tempered in success and failures, for it is this evenness of temper that is meant by Yoga.
>
> Work done with anxiety about results is far inferior to work done without such anxiety, in the calm of self-surrender.
>
> Seek refuge in the knowledge of Brahman.
>
> They who work selfishly for results are miserable.

Charles used the passages from the Bhagavad Gita as the inspiration for his approach to the solution to India's contemporary problems. He felt that in the search for solutions to the problems that challenge traditional life in India there must be a search for "quality," arrived at through the "design process." A design institute, he

Right: Kamaladevi Chattopadhyay (recipient of the Charles Eames Award), Ray, and Vinay Jha, director of the National Institute of Design at the award ceremony in Ahmedabad, India, December 19, 1987

proposed, an arm of the government, carefully organized and dedicated to an awareness of the qualities and problems inherent in everyday life, could assist in dealing with the changes occurring in India, which, he felt, were "changes in *kind*, not in degree." These revolutionary changes, caused primarily by advances in communication in the modern world, were, Charles stated, "something that affects a world, not a country." He recommended that "despite such changes, the same attention to quality evident in traditional Indian society and philosophy should be applied to contemporary design problems. [Of all the objects] we have seen or admired during our visit to India, the lota, that simple vessel of everyday use (a traditional water jug), stands out as perhaps the greatest, the most beautiful." New designs for modern India should provide the same "tremendous service, dignity, and love" as the lota.

The report also recommended that a board of governors for the institute be drawn from representatives of many disciplines—sociology, engineering, philosophy, architecture, economics, communications, physics, and history, among others. Later sections of the report detailed the kinds of faculty, trainees, projects, service aspects, and physical plant the design center required. It was suggested that the institute would also have the capacity to produce exhibitions, books, posters, and television programs for the government.

On the basis of the Eames India Report, the National Institute of Design was founded in 1961 in Ahmedabad. It was considered to be the first institution for industrial design, education, training, and service to be established in the developing world. Over the years, the Eameses maintained a close relationship with the institute and its members. Guests from the institute visited the office regularly, and on the occasion of its twenty-fifth anniversary, the institute announced an award to be made to an individual "who has substantially contributed to design thinking and practice, and to the ideals of 'service, dignity, and love' called for in the India Report." Called the Charles Eames Award, it commemorates the designer who wrote the original plan and had a profound impact not only on the institute in India but on the profession as a whole. The award, first made in December 1987 to Kamaladevi Chattopadhyay, is to be given every two years.

Madame Chattopadhyay was the unanimous choice of the jury as a representative of "the values Charles Eames brought to the profession of design," through "the contribution she has made to a national awareness of and priority for the importance of inherited values and aesthetics in a new environment."

The Eameses' trip to India and their three-months of travel and study were funded by the Ford Foundation.

People, places, and artifacts photographed in India by Charles

November 14: Charles delivers a talk to the Los Angeles Art Directors Club, Los Angeles, California.

The Eames film *Day of the Dead* receives an award at the San Francisco International Film Festival, San Francisco, California.

Staff: 1958
901 Washington Boulevard
Don Albinson
Sue Atkinson
Dale Bauer
Ellie Bogardus
Lucia Capacchione
Selby Daley
Carlos Diniz
Glen Fleck
Charles Fraser
Dan Greenberg
Ella Hogan
Nancy Kane
Sylvia Kennedy
Ed Leavitt
Parke Meek
John Neuhart
Peter Pearce
Mariea Poole
Carl Ronay
Marvin Rubin
Bill Sahara
Robert Staples
Richard Swenson
Frederick Usher
Leola Walker
John Whitney

A sequence of frames (reading top to bottom left, top to bottom right) from scenes in *De Gaulle Sketch*. The frames were photographed from 16mm-film footage

1958

Film: *De Gaulle Sketch*

De Gaulle Sketch consists of filmed sequences of still photographs that appeared in the French and American popular press during the height of the Algerian insurrection, from May 15 to June 1, 1958. The photographs, gathered from *Le Monde* and the *Paris Journal* and *Life* magazines, are a record of the polarization of French politicians into left and right factions and of Charles de Gaulle's rise to power. The film was produced and edited in a week. John Neuhart collected the images as Charles developed the story line. They then laid out each scene, and planned the scene-by-scene camera animation; Parke Meek and John Whitney shot the film on the office animation stand. The close-ups revealed the halftone dots of the newspaper images. Because of the speed with which the film was produced, Charles considered it to be an excellent demonstration of economical construction—doing the best possible job within the constraints of time and the availability of material. As he said on numerous occasions, "The best you can do between now and Tuesday is still a kind of best you can do."

The film was made for Leland Hayward as an example of a series of proposed film bridges intended for use on CBS News' year-end wrap-up. The bridges were designed to provide a visual introduction to the news events of the preceding year. Although the proposal was not executed, the *De Gaulle Sketch* was used by Eric Sevareid in his 1960 news recap of the 1950s. It was also included in a slightly modified version in the television program "The Fabulous Fifties," shown in 1960 on CBS.

The photographic images are accompanied by the popular French song "The Poor People of Paris." There is no narration. The film is in general circulation. (Running time, *De Gaulle Sketch*: 2 minutes; black and white.)

January 1–4: Charles and Ray attend a conference sponsored by UCLA on "Communication in Science and Industry" in Lake Arrowhead, California.

January 27: Charles lectures to the Costume Council of the Los Angeles County Museum of Art, Los Angeles, California.

Staff: 1959
901 Washington Boulevard
Don Albinson
Gordon Ashby
Barbara Baldwin
Dale Bauer
Ruby Beasley
Richard Bungay
Dolores Cannata
Colin Cantwell
Lucia Capacchione
Nick Chaparos
Selby Daley
Steve Escalante
Ella Hogan
Nancy Kane
Sylvia Kennedy
James Knapp
Jeremy Lepard
Parke Meek
John Neuhart
Peter Pearce
Mariea Poole
Leonard Reiter
Carl Ronay
Bill Sahara
Miyoko Sasaki
Robert Staples
Frederick Swenson
Richard Usher
Leola Walker
John Whitney
Ann Wright

Jeremy Lepard, Charles, and Gordon Ashby shooting the Revell Toy House model

Detail of the Revell Toy House's model furniture

1959

Revell Toy House

A model house kit, in ¾-inch scale and completely furnished with miniature Eames furniture and accessories, was designed by the Eames Office for the Revell Company, a toy manufacturer. The company wanted to include in its line of toy products a "modern house." The kit was to include a system of modular units of structural grids and panels to be manufactured by Revell out of injection-molded plastic. Rooms and spaces of varying sizes could be built into one- and two-level structures.

For the prototype version shown here, a kit was produced containing molded plastic side chairs and armchairs on pedestal bases, circular tables with pedestal bases, Aluminum Group chairs and ottomans, sofa compacts, and various Case Goods units, along with miniature rugs, grass, trees, plants, and decorative objects. Although the preliminary work was completed in ¾-inch scale, it was decided that the kit should be made in 1-inch scale instead. Production of the toy house was not carried further with Revell, however, because Charles felt that there were too many potentially difficult and unresolved production problems in manufacturing the kits. The Herman Miller Furniture Company, which intended to use the house kit as a furniture layout planning tool and as a demonstration item for its sales force, eventually produced its own planning kit, complete with ½-inch scale models of furniture represented in its production line.

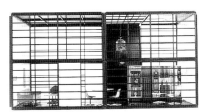

Final prototype modular units, which could be used horizontally or vertically (to create multiple-story houses)

Top to bottom: Two elevations and plan view of the Revell Toy House model

March 23: Eames Office receives an award for the stacking chair (pp. 196–197) from the National Industrial Design Council of Canada.

April: Charles delivers the Lethaby Lectures (named after the Arts and Crafts designer William R. Lethaby) at the Royal College of Art, London, England.

Staff: 1959
901 Washington Boulevard
Don Albinson
Gordon Ashby
Barbara Baldwin
Dale Bauer
Ruby Beasley
Richard Bungay
Colin Cantwell
Dolores Cannata
Lucia Capacchione
Nick Chaparos
Selby Daley
Steve Escalante
Ella Hogan
Nancy Kane
Sylvia Kennedy
James Knapp
Jeremy Lepard
Parke Meek
John Neuhart
Peter Pearce
Mariea Poole
Leonard Reiter
Carl Ronay
Bill Sahara
Miyoko Sasaki
Robert Staples
Frederick Swenson
Richard Usher
Leola Walker
John Whitney
Ann Wright

1959

Film: *Kaleidoscope Shop*

Kaleidoscope Shop was produced for a lecture given by Charles at the Royal College of Art in London. Asked by the college to include pictures of the Eames Office in his presentation, he brought with him a filmed kaleidoscopic tour of 901 Washington Boulevard photographed by a movie camera fitted with a special system of mirrors designed to shoot kaleidoscopic images. The camera was developed in the office by Charles, Parke Meek, and Jeremy Lepard and was used again to make the film *Kaleidoscope Jazz Chair* in 1960 (p. 250).

Kaleidoscope Shop opens with a single view of a desk in the office reception area. Then the camera pans horizontally across the reception office and the scene dissolves into a kaleidoscopic image, beginning a tour through the rest of the building—graphic layout rooms, film production spaces, offices, and the furniture development and tool shop.

Charles was uncomfortable about being asked to show pictures of the office. The fractured images that the special kaleidoscopic camera produced (giving very little actual information) were a kind of Eames "joke"; he had complied with the request from the Royal College but had not violated his own sense of privacy.

Calliope music from a merry-go-round on the pier in Santa Monica accompanies the images. There is no narration. The film is not in general circulation. (Running time, *Kaleidoscope Shop*: 4 minutes; color.)

901

Venice

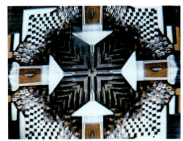

A sequence of frames (reading top to bottom left, top to bottom right) from scenes in *Kaleidoscope Shop*. The frames were photographed from 16mm-film footage

April 14: Charles delivers the "Annual Discourse" at the Royal Institute of British Architects, London, England.

Right: Photographs by Charles of Bill Ballantine of the Ringling Brothers' Barnum & Bailey Circus, and his wife, Roberta

Staff: 1959
901 Washington Boulevard
Don Albinson
Gordon Ashby
Barbara Baldwin
Dale Bauer
Ruby Beasley
Richard Bungay
Dolores Cannata
Colin Cantwell
Lucia Capacchione
Nick Chaparos
Selby Daley
Steve Escalante
Ella Hogan
Nancy Kane
Sylvia Kennedy
James Knapp
Jeremy Lepard
Parke Meek
John Neuhart
Peter Pearce
Mariea Poole
Leonard Reiter
Carl Ronay
Bill Sahara
Miyoko Sasaki
Robert Staples
Richard Swenson
Frederick Usher
Leola Walker
John Whitney
Ann Wright

1959

Film: *Time & Life Building International Lobby*

Henry Luce, chairman of Time Inc., invited Charles to design a lobby for Time's New York City offices to be used by international correspondents returning from assignments around the world. Charles presented the proposal in film form. The film, the third "study" film developed by the Eames Office presenting the basic concept and design of a project (before or after the project's completion) to clients, was not completed beyond the first study stage. It was shown in conjunction with presentation of a model of the lobby made by the Eames Office and brought to New York City by Charles; live-action footage helped him explain the lobby's basic functions and key features. Though the international lobby did not go beyond the proposal stage, in 1960 the Eames Office completed other lobbies for Time Inc. in its New York offices.

The film has no narration or music track and is not in general circulation. (Running time, *Time & Life Building International Lobby*: 2 minutes, 43 seconds; color.)

A sequence of frames (reading top to bottom left, top to bottom right) from scenes in *Time & Life Building International Lobby*. The frames were photographed from 16mm-film footage

Top: View of the Moscow Fair auditorium showing the seven screens displaying *Glimpses of the U.S.A.*. Above: Interior view of the Buckminster Fuller geodesic dome

Charles receives the Alcoa Industrial Design Award for his use of aluminum in the Aluminum Group furniture

Staff: 1959
901 Washington Boulevard
Don Albinson
Gordon Ashby
Barbara Baldwin
Dale Bauer
Ruby Beasley
Richard Bungay
Dolores Cannata
Colin Cantwell
Lucia Capacchione
Nick Chaparos
Selby Daley
Steve Escalante
Ella Hogan
Nancy Kane
Sylvia Kennedy
James Knapp
Jeremy Lepard
Parke Meek
John Neuhart
Peter Pearce
Mariea Poole
Leonard Reiter
Carl Ronay
Bill Sahara
Miyoko Sasaki
Robert Staples
Richard Swenson
Frederick Usher
Leola Walker
John Whitney
Ann Wright

Charles, designer George Nelson, and Jack Masey (of the United States Information Agency) studying an early screen configuration for the Moscow presentation

1959

Film: *Glimpses of the U.S.A.*

In 1958 designer George Nelson was approached by the United States Information Agency to design the American National Exhibition in Moscow for the 1959 U.S.S.R.-U.S.A. exchange in Sokolniki Park, the first cultural exchange between the two countries since the Russian Revolution. His task was to provide a setting for the display of American manufactured products. As a complement to the product exhibition, Nelson and Jack Masey of the United States Information Agency asked the Eameses to produce a film on "a day in the life of the United States," which would serve as an introduction to the exhibition. The Eames Office proposed a multiscreen presentation called *Glimpses of the U.S.A.*

The Eames production was presented simultaneously on seven large screens and composed of more than 2,200 still and moving images designed to provide a visual expression of the complexity and diversity of American life. Various configurations of screens were tried before the final decision was made to use seven. The number of images to be seen had to be too many to comprehend individually, but not so many that the information would be confusing or hard to follow.

To produce the multiscreen display, thousands of photographs were amassed. Charles, staff members, and friends and associates photographed many of the still photographs and live-action film sequences. Others were made available by various photo archives—Time Inc., Curtis Publishing, Cowles Magazines, Inc., Photo Researchers, Inc., Magnum Photos—and by individual

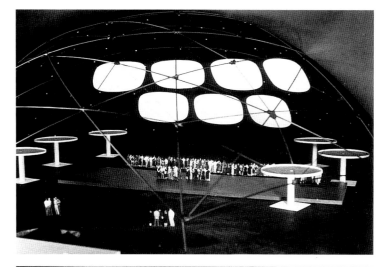

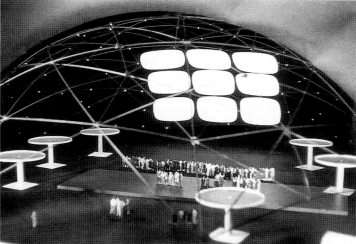

Projection simulation in the ½-inch scale model of the auditorium

Top to bottom: Three views of the ½-inch scale study models of early screen configurations used for planning *Glimpses of the U.S.A.*

Right: A picture of the Eames Office staff taken for an article on Charles in the August 15, 1959 issue of *Vogue* magazine. Left to right: Don Albinson, Nancy Kane, Charles Fraser, Parke Meek, Richard Swenson, Robert Staples, Charles, Ray, Peter Pearce, Sylvia Kennedy, Dale Bauer, and John Neuhart

John Whitney, Charles, Ray, Parke Meek, and John Neuhart standing in the one-fifth-life-size scale projection model of the Moscow auditorium

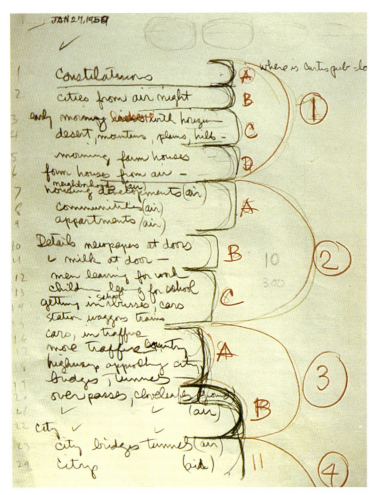

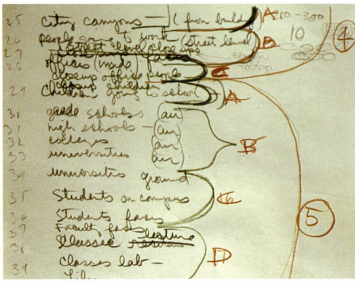

Above: Two pages of Charles's script development and image breakdown for *Glimpses of the U.S.A.*

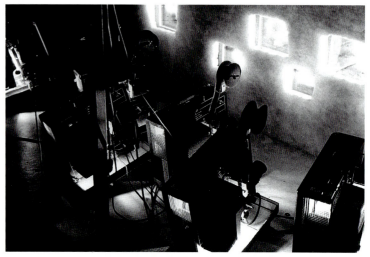

Top and middle: Lucia Capacchione and John Neuhart organizing images for *Glimpses of the U.S.A.* Above: Seven 35mm strip projectors installed in the Eames Office to simulate the seven-screen showing

September 7–9: Charles attends a conference sponsored by UCLA on "The Systems Approach in Planning for Future Living" in Lake Arrowhead, California.

October: Charles delivers lectures at the American Institute of Architects and the University of Washington, Seattle

Charles and Ray leaving for Moscow with the film reels of *Glimpses of the U.S.A.* in hand

Left: Group portrait of the *Glimpses of the U.S.A.* design and production crew the morning after final production shooting. Front row, left to right: John Neuhart, Parke Meek, John Whitney, Robert Staples. Middle row: Charles and Ray. Back row: Miyoko Sasaki, Don Albinson, Dale Bauer, Nancy Kane, Richard Swenson, Lucia Capacchione, Nick Chaparos, and Peter Pearce

photographers—including Ernest Braun, Ferenc Berko, Ezra Stoller, Todd Walker, Eliot Noyes, and Charles Guggenheim. The images were selected to illustrate such aspects of daily life as where Americans live, work, and play, how they get around, what they eat, and how they dress. The presentation also included live-action segments of industrial processes—milling and refining—and a scene from the Billy Wilder film *Some Like It Hot*. The concluding images in the show were images of partings—goodnights, symbols of love and friendship—and the last image was of a bunch of forget-me-nots. It was discovered during the show's run that the Soviets also regard the flower as a symbol of friendship and loyalty. As the audience recognized the flower, they could be heard saying "*nezabutki*"—"forget-me-not."

The images were combined into seven separate 35mm film reels projected simultaneously onto the 20-by-30-foot screens installed in a 250-foot-diameter geodesic dome designed by Buckminster Fuller. Spectators stood to view the thirteen-minute presentation. *Glimpses of the U.S.A.* was shown sixteen times a day, from 10:00 A.M. to 10:00 P.M., for the duration of the fair. The film was never shown outside the U.S.S.R. John Neuhart, Parke Meek, Jeremy Lepard, Lucia Capacchione, Robert Staples, and John Whitney were the Eames staff members involved in the planning and direction of the production. Elmer Bernstein composed the music.

Exhibits of American architecture, painting, sculpture, and photography (including the Edward Steichen *Family of Man* photography exhibition) were seen for the first time by the people of Russia. The product display area in the American pavilion was the site of the Nixon-Khrushchev "kitchen debate." (Running time, *Glimpses of the U.S.A.*: 10 minutes)

The seven interlocked 35mm projectors used in the Moscow showing of *Glimpses of the U.S.A.*

Above: Assembled composites of seven-screen configurations showing landscapes, suburban housing, automobile traffic, dinner scenes, and goodnight scenes from everyday life in America

October 29, 1959–March 17, 1960: Charles participates in the lecture series "Impact of Scientific Change" at the University of California, Los Angeles.

November 10: Charles and George Nelson deliver a talk and slide show on the U.S. exhibition in Moscow to the American Institute of Architects, Southern California Chapter, Los Angeles, California.

Left: The office makes a proposal for a "Birthday House" for Hallmark Cards to be constructed in a park in Kansas City. The house was to be used for birthday celebrations. The project did not go forward

Staff: 1959
901 Washington Boulevard
Don Albinson
Gordon Ashby
Barbara Baldwin
Dale Bauer
Ruby Beasley
Richard Bungay
Dolores Cannata
Colin Cantwell
Lucia Capacchione
Nick Chaparos
Selby Daley
Steve Escalante
Ella Hogan
Nancy Kane
Sylvia Kennedy
James Knapp
Jeremy Lepard
Parke Meek
John Neuhart
Peter Pearce
Mariea Poole
Leonard Reiter
Carl Ronay
Bill Sahara
Miyoko Sasaki
Robert Staples
Richard Swenson
Frederick Usher
Leola Walker
John Whitney
Ann Wright

1959

Herman Miller Furniture Company Showroom

In 1959 Aluminum Group chairs and ottomans with the early saran fabric slings were formally introduced in new settings in the Herman Miller showroom in Los Angeles. Other Eames and Nelson furniture, including a miniature drawer cabinet, was shown in groupings with new objects and fabrics by Alexander Girard.

The showroom was designed to provide an "indoor-outdoor" setting for the multiple-use Aluminum Group. A large papier-mâché tree, made by Eames staff member Lucia Capacchione and several of her fellow students at Immaculate Heart College (the Eameses had a close and long-lasting friendship and mutual assistance relationship with the college's art instructors, Sister Magdalen Mary and Sister Mary Corita Kent), stood in the center of the showroom. A torn-paper collage mural of trees, also made by the Capacchione group, provided a backdrop for a furniture grouping. A row of small trees in Architectural Pottery planters designed by Los Angeles designer John Follis were placed along the side of one furniture area. Other objects used in this installation included new Eames "finds"—a crystal chandelier (hung in the front window), mirrors, obelisks, and toy towers brought from Moscow.

The periodic redesigning of the Los Angeles showroom usually brought the Girards from Santa Fe to help arrange the new furniture settings and to add new folk art and objects to the mix of props; Girard could always be counted on to make fast decisions in the last-minute push. The relationship between the Girards and the Eameses was always marked by a spirit of cooperation and mutual assistance. The skills and temperaments of the designers complemented each other, and Charles made regular use of Girard's keen eye for form and color, his sensitive handling of textiles, and his skill in arranging objects; in turn, Charles assisted in the development of Girard furniture and photographed his exhibitions and installations extensively (Girard seldom recorded his own work), providing a remarkable record of his colleague's work.

Opposite top: Aluminum Group lounge tables and the Eames plywood lounge chair in the redesigned showroom. Opposite: Aluminum Group dining chairs with the early saran sling arranged around an Eames laminate-topped dining table with an Aluminum Group base

Top and middle: Views of showroom interiors: mural and tree made by Lucia Capacchione. Above: Lounge chair with fabric-covered upholstery

January 15: Charles delivers a talk to the Southern California Chapter of the Association of Interior Designers at the Pasadena Art Museum, Pasadena, California.

Staff: 1960
901 Washington Boulevard
Gordon Ashby
Dale Bauer
Ruby Beasley
Richard Bungay
Bruce Burdick
Lucia Capacchione
Nick Chaparos
Selby Daley
Richard Donges
Glen Fleck
John Follis
Ella Hogan
Robert Hostick
Nancy Kane
James Knapp
Jeremy Lepard
Paul Levine
Ron Maidenberg
Nicholas Maremont
Parke Meek
John Neuhart
Keith Olson
Noel Dave O'Malley
Peter Pearce
Mariea Poole
Kenneth Rang
Michael Raugh
Leonard Reiter
Bill Reithard
Carl Ronay
Don Ronay
Bill Sahara
Miyoko Sasaki
Robert Staples
Richard Swenson
Leola Walker
Jerry White
John Whitney

View of the exhibition *20 Years of Eames Chairs*, installed by Elaine Sewell and Don Albinson, which opened in January at the Pasadena Art Museum, Pasadena, California

1960

Films: "The Fabulous Fifties"

"The Fabulous Fifties" was a television program broadcast on January 22, 1960, on the CBS network. The program, produced by Leland Hayward for CBS, recapped the significant events of the 1950s and included six film segments made by the Eames Office. The short film segments, designed as visual interludes to be shown between appearances by celebrity guests (including Julie Andrews, Rex Harrison, Jackie Gleason, Shelley Berman, Elaine May, and Mike Nichols), and made use of animation, live-action, and still photography. Charles and Ray each won an Emmy Award in "Graphics" for their work on "The Fabulous Fifties."

Film segments:

Gift from the Sea is a sequence of still images of the seashore. Quotations from Anne Morrow Lindbergh's popular 1952 book of the same name are narrated by Leora Dana. (Running time: 3 minutes, 30 seconds; black and white.)

Music of the Fifties is a series of still and live-action imagery drawn from newspapers, publicity photographs, record covers, and photos. The film is accompanied by a medley of the most popular songs of the 1950s (chosen on the basis of sales of sheet music and records) collected and arranged by Jay Blackton. The segment introduced a quick-cutting technique to television. *Music of the Fifties* is in general circulation. (Running time: 9 minutes, 25 seconds; black and white.)

De Gaulle Sketch, originally produced in 1958 for CBS News (p. 234), was modified slightly for inclusion in "The Fabulous Fifties" telecast. The principal personalities, two years after the 1958 version was made, were still very much a part of current events. *De Gaulle Sketch* is in general circulation. (Running time: 2 minutes; black and white.)

Dead of the Fifties is a visual record of well-known personalities in the arts, the sciences, government, and sports who died in the 1950s. The piece is accompanied by an Elmer Bernstein dirge. The prologue, written by Charles, is narrated by Henry Fonda. *Dead of the Fifties* is in general circulation. (Running time: 4 minutes, 40 seconds; black and white.)

Comics of the Fifties is a brief overview of popular comic strips from the daily and Sunday newspapers of the 1950s. Stills selected from the comics themselves are accompanied by appropriate sound effects recorded by Elmer Bernstein. (Running time: 3 minutes, 30 seconds; black and white.)

"Where Did You Go?" "Out" "What Did You Do?" "Nothing" is based on the book by Robert Paul Smith about a small boy and his daily adventures. When asked, "Where did you go?" he replies, "Out." To the question, "What did you do?" he says, "Nothing." Drawings and animation are by Dolores Cannata. Music is by Elmer Bernstein. (Running time: 4 minutes; black and white.)

A sequence of frames (top to bottom left) from *Gift from the Sea* and (top to bottom right) from *Music of the Fifties*, photographed from 16mm-film footage

February 15: Charles speaks to the UCLA Industrial Design Association, Los Angeles, California.

March 11: Charles presents a three-screen slide show on the *Moscow Fair Exhibition* to the Janus Society of the J. Paul Getty Museum, Malibu, California.

April 18: Charles delivers a talk to the UCLA Art Association, Los Angeles, California.

Staff member Dolores Cannata working on the animation for *"Where Did You Go?" "Out" "What Did You Do?" "Nothing"*

Choir robes designed by Ray for Hope College in Holland, Michigan

A sequence of frames (top to bottom left) from *De Gaulle Sketch* and (top to bottom right) from *Dead of the Fifties*, photographed from 16mm-film footage

A sequence of frames (top to bottom left) from *"Where Did You Go?" "Out" "What Did You Do?" "Nothing"* and (top to bottom right) from *Comics of the Fifties*, photographed from 16mm-film footage

245

Time & Life Building lobby reception area

June 6: Charles receives an award for excellence in design from the Philadelphia Museum College of Art, Philadelphia, Pennsylvania.

Ray receives an honorary master's degree in art from her alma mater, the May Friend Bennett School in Millbrook, New York.

Right: A view of the exhibition *Chairs from Machines* at the Isetan Department Store in Tokyo, Japan. The exhibition featured Eames, Nelson, and Girard furniture mass-produced by the Herman Miller Furniture Company

Staff: 1960
901 Washington Boulevard
Gordon Ashby
Dale Bauer
Ruby Beasley
Richard Bungay
Bruce Burdick
Lucia Capacchione
Nick Chaparos
Selby Daley
Richard Donges
Glen Fleck
John Follis
Ella Hogan
Robert Hostick
Nancy Kane
James Knapp
Jeremy Lepard
Paul Levine
Ron Maidenberg
Nicholas Maremont
Parke Meek
John Neuhart
Keith Olson
Noel Dave O'Malley
Peter Pearce
Mariea Poole
Kenneth Rang
Michael Raugh
Leonard Reiter
Bill Reithard
Carl Ronay
Don Ronay
Bill Sahara
Miyoko Sasaki
Robert Staples
Richard Swenson
Leola Walker
Jerry White
John Whitney

1960

Time & Life Building Lobbies

Henry Luce, chairman of Time Inc., commissioned the Eames Office to design three lobbies for offices in the newly constructed Time & Life Building at Rockefeller Center in New York City. The project developed out of Luce's earlier plan for a lobby and debriefing center for overseas correspondents, for which the Eames Office had produced a model and film proposal (p. 237). The Eames Office designed the main reception lobby on the twenty-seventh floor and two smaller lobbies on the twenty-eighth and twenty-ninth floors. On each floor an elevator opened onto a hallway that led to the lobby. The office designed the floor, ceiling, wall, and lighting treatments, as well as the furniture, which was produced especially for the lobbies by the Herman Miller Furniture Company.

The lobbies served two main purposes: as waiting areas during business hours and as after-hours relaxation areas for staff members working late. The main lobby was a rectangular space divided by a reception desk in the center. On one side of the desk was a lounge area with cast aluminum and black leather chairs (pp. 248–249) and turned walnut stool/tables. A magazine display case, made of walnut, occupied one wall, and vertical walnut panels served to separate the lobby from the hallway. A conference area on the far side of the desk contained a Thonet bentwood table and chairs. A light wall for viewing transparencies was included. The same furniture was used in each lobby.

The lobby walls were covered with photo murals and mosaics made of small, multicolored glass tesserae. The murals were blowups of halftone reproductions in color and black and white—recognizable at close range only as halftone dots; from the distance of the elevators they could be seen as complete photos from *Time* and *Life* magazines. The Ravenna mosaic tile walls were essentially variations of white, gray, and yellow (one color for each floor). A Berber rug completed the setting.

Gordon Ashby was the principal designer of the lobbies; he was assisted by Charles Wychoff in New York City.

Above: Charles, John Neuhart, Ray, Robert Staples, Parke Meek, and Gordon Ashby posing with lobby mock-ups

View into lobby from hallway showing the reception desk, the magazine rack, a photo blowup, and a seating area

June 13: Charles is made a Benjamin Franklin Fellow by the Royal Society for the Encouragement of Arts, Manufactures, and Commerce, London, England.

July 8: Charles receives a Royal College of Art honorary diploma and is made a Fellow of the Royal College of Art, London, England.

September: Charles speaks to the Art Directors' Club of San Francisco, San Francisco, California.

September 21: Charles participates in the Photo-Journalism Conference, Asilomar, California.

Right: An advertisement for the Herman Miller Furniture Company showing the Aluminum Group furniture in different room settings

John Neuhart, Ray, Charles, and Jeremy Lepard photographing an advertisement (left) for the Herman Miller Furniture Company

Time-Life Chair production models and walnut stool

October: Charles and Ray receive the first annual Kaufmann International Design Award, New York City. The award is designed by Danish designer Finn Juhl.

Right: An Eames Office group photo on Charles's fifty-third birthday. Left to right: Robert Staples, Nancy Kane, Charles, Glen Fleck, Ray, Gordon Ashby, Bill Reithard, Mariea Poole, Richard Donges, Robert Hostick, Peter Pearce, Lucia Capacchione, Dale Bauer, Michael Raugh, John Neuhart, and Richard Bungay

Staff: 1960 901 Washington Boulevard Gordon Ashby Dale Bauer Ruby Beasley Richard Bungay Bruce Burdick Lucia Capacchione Nick Chaparos Selby Daley Richard Donges Glen Fleck John Follis Ella Hogan Robert Hostick Nancy Kane James Knapp Jeremy Lepard Paul Levine Ron Maidenberg Nicholas Maremont Parke Meek John Neuhart Keith Olson Noel Dave O'Malley Peter Pearce Mariea Poole Kenneth Rang Michael Raugh Leonard Reiter Bill Reithard Carl Ronay Don Ronay Bill Sahara Miyoko Sasaki Robert Staples Richard Staples Leola Walker Richard Swenson Jerry White John Whitney

1960

Time-Life Chair and Stool

A padded leather swivel chair, later manufactured by the Herman Miller Furniture Company as executive seating, was designed for the Time & Life Building lobbies (pp. 246–247) to satisfy the need for a comfortable chair that was smaller than the lounge chair (pp. 206–207) and that could also be used as a conference chair. The chair is made of molded plywood, polished aluminum, leather upholstery, and foam padding. Unlike the lounge chair, however, the plywood core is hidden within the leather upholstery seat and back, which are bolted to the cast aluminum side frames. The pedestal base has an elliptical cross-section and is finished with nylon glides.

Herman Miller offers the chair as part of a line called "Eames Executive Seating." Two related chairs with adjustable seat heights closely resemble the Time-Life Chair in proportions: a swivel lounge and a tilt-swivel lounge. Eames Executive Seating comes upholstered in several types of fabric or leather. Peter Pearce, Dale Bauer, Robert Staples, and Bill Reithard produced the prototypes. The chairs are still in the Herman Miller catalog.

In 1961 Herman Miller introduced the Eames Executive Desk Chair, a modified version of the Time-Life Chair. By narrowing the width of the seat and back, reducing the length of the seat pad, making the seat height adjustable, and adding a tilt-swivel base, the lobby chair was transformed into a desk chair. The legs are provided with casters or glides.

In 1972 the American chess grand master Bobby Fischer specifically requested the Time-Life Chair to sit in during his match with the Russian Boris Spassky in Reykjavik. (Fischer considered it to be a chair in which he could really concentrate.) Spassky then demanded one as well, and a second Time-Life Chair was hurriedly acquired by the tournament's sponsors.

Ray designed four solid walnut stools for the Time & Life Building lobby to serve as low tables or seats. The upper and lower sections of the stools are identical, but the center sections are each turned differently, creating four different profiles. Herman Miller began producing the stools in 1960 and continues to manufacture three variations. They are now made in several pieces of wood, laminated, and pinned together.

Top: Production models of the walnut stool. Above: Time-Life Chair and stool setting

Time-Life Executive Desk Chair

Staff: 1960
901 Washington Boulevard
Gordon Ashby
Dale Bauer
Ruby Beasley
Richard Bungay
Bruce Jurdick
Lucia Capacchione
Nick Chaparos
Selby Daley
Richard Donges
Glen Fleck
John Follis
Ella Hogan
Robert Hostick
Nancy Kane
James Knapp
Jeremy Lepard
Paul Levine
Ron Maidenberg
Nicholas Maremont
Parke Meek
John Neuhart
Keith Olson
Noel Dave O'Malley
Peter Pearce
Mariea Poole
Kenneth Rang
Michael Raugh
Leonard Reiter
Bill Reithard
Carl Ronay
Don Ronay
Bill Sahara
Miyoko Sasaki
Robert Staples
Richard Swenson
Leola Walker
Jerry White
John Whitney

Staff member Parke Meek editing *Kaleidoscope Jazz Chair*

Charles and Ray in the living room of their house

1960

Film: *Kaleidoscope Jazz Chair*

Kaleidoscope Jazz Chair employs the technique first designed in 1959 to produce the film *Kaleidoscope Shop* (p. 236): photographing through a mirror system to achieve radial kaleidoscopic images. Charles made the film to experiment further with the kaleidoscopic effect; he liked the richness of the fractured image and decided to try a second film on another subject.

Jazz Chair has two parts: the first shows fast-moving kaleidoscopic images of chairs, objects, and materials photographed in the Eames Office using the mirror technique; in the second part the kaleidoscopic images of the office dissolve into a sequence of stop-motion shots of Charles and Ray seated in multicolored plastic chairs.

The film is accompanied by a jazz track composed and arranged by Dick Marx. The film was used occasionally for publicity purposes by Herman Miller. It is not in general circulation. (Running time, *Kaleidoscope Jazz Chair*: 6 minutes, 30 seconds; color.)

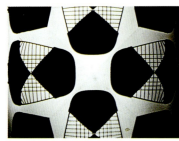

A sequence of frames (reading top to bottom left, top to bottom right) from scenes in *Kaleidoscope Jazz Chair*. The frames were photographed from 16mm-film footage

Toccata for Toy Trains (pp. 214–217) receives the Eleventh Annual Scholastic Teacher's Award.

Right: Staff members Parke Meek, Jeremy Lepard, and Charles photograph architect Bill Reid, who plays a sea captain in the film *Introduction to Feedback*

A clown posing in an Eames Lounge Chair (pp. 206–207) in the film *Introduction to Feedback*

Staff: 1960
901 Washington Boulevard
Gordon Ashby
Dale Bauer
Ruby Beasley
Richard Bungay
Bruce Burdick
Lucia Capacchione
Nick Chaparos
Selby Daley
Richard Donges
Glen Fleck
John Follis
Ella Hogan
Robert Hostick
Nancy Kane
James Knapp
Jeremy Lepard
Paul Levine
Ron Maidenberg
Nicholas Maremont
Parke Meek
John Neuhart
Keith Olson
Noel Dave O'Malley
Peter Pearce
Mariea Poole
Kenneth Rang
Michael Raugh
Leonard Reiter
Bill Reithard
Carl Ronay
Don Ronay
Bill Sahara
Miyoko Sasaki
Robert Staples
Richard Swenson
Leola Walker
Jerry White
John Whitney

1960

Film: *Introduction to Feedback*

Introduction to Feedback, made for the IBM Corporation, is one of a series of films proposed by the Eames Office to explain computers and the principles underlying their operation. Such films were intended for school and institutional uses. Begun in the mid-1950s as a sequel to *A Communications Primer* (pp. 182–183), *Introduction to Feedback* would have been the first Eames project completed for IBM. It was shelved temporarily, however, so that the film *The Information Machine* (pp. 222–225) could be made in time to be shown by IBM at the Brussels World's Fair in 1958.

The subject of *Introduction to Feedback* is the principle of feedback—the cycle by which performance is measured, evaluated against desired results, and corrected for future performance. The film draws analogies between the function of the feedback principle in everyday situations and the way it works in the modern electronic computer. Situations as simple as a girl adapting her moves in a game of jacks and as complex as the mechanical operation of a ball governor regulating a steam engine were filmed to demonstrate the process.

The film uses live-action, animation, and still photography. The script was written by Charles and narrated by Vic Perrin. The score was composed by Elmer Bernstein. The film is in general circulation and is part of the IBM film collection. No additional films in the projected series were made.

The film won awards in 1961 at the Festival International du Film du Montreal and the International Filmwoche in Mannheim, West Germany, and at the Melbourne Film Festival in 1963. (Running time, *Introduction to Feedback*: 10 minutes, 40 seconds; color.)

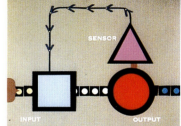

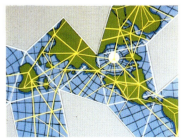

A sequence of frames (reading top to bottom left, top to bottom right) from scenes in *Introduction to Feedback*. The frames were photographed from 16mm-film footage

January 20: Charles lectures to the San Diego Art Guild at the Art Center, La Jolla, California.

Staff: 1961
901 Washington Boulevard
Gordon Ashby
Dale Bauer
Michael Birman
Thomas Bouck
Richard Bungay
Lucia Capacchione
Gladys Chernik
Ozelia Clement
Stan Croner
Dorothy Danziger
Annette Del Zoppo
Richard Donges
Rod Dyer
Patrick Fitzgerald
Glen Fleck
Archer Goodwin
Ella Hogan
Robert Hostick
Robert Inman
Nancy Kane
Jeremy Lepard
Myrna Lyons
Harry McQuiston
Parke Meek
Robert Nakamura
John Neuhart
Eliot Noyes, Jr.
Noel Dave O'Malley
David Parry
James Parsons
Peter Pearce
Mariea Poole
Kenneth Rang
Bill Reithard
Gordon Rollins
Carl Ronay
Don Ronay
Bill Sahara
Richard Sherwin
George Spacek
Robert Staples
Dorothy Stotland
Deborah Sussman
Leonard Taylor
Lewis Vanderbeken
Leola Walker
Christopher Whorf
Don Wright
Marcia Zintner

1961

La Fonda Chair

Two new chairs, known as "La Fonda" chairs, resulted from a collaboration between Alexander Girard and the Eames Office. The chairs were made for the La Fonda del Sol restaurant, which was designed by Girard and opened in 1961 in New York City's Time & Life Building.

The chairs, manufactured by the Herman Miller Furniture Company for the restaurant and later added to its product line, were made of reinforced fiberglass and were molded in shapes similar to those of the 1951 plastic armchairs and side chairs (pp. 138–141, 142–143). Girard specified that the back of the dining chair not be visible above the tabletops, so the shell was lowered to comply with his request. The texture of the seats and the configuration of the pedestal base differ from the earlier chairs: a gel coat was introduced into the shell mold before the fiberglass was added to achieve a matte finish (in which the fibers are not visible).

The armchair shells were upholstered in one of several solid-colored Herman Miller wool fabrics and vinyls, and the edges were framed in charcoal vinyl. Side chairs used in the restaurant's cocktail area were upholstered in glove leather. The upholstery system with the vinyl edge, which was first used in the La Fonda chairs, later became the standard method of upholstery for all fiberglass shell chairs in the Eames line, replacing the original wire restraining system. For the restaurant chairs, the four-columned pedestal base, elliptical in cross-section and attached to the seat with rubber shock mounts, was cast in two pieces bolted together at the bottom. The vinyl edges were produced in several colors, including red, blue, orange, and green. The cast aluminum base was ball-burnished and anodized a dark gray-black. In the production model chair, the base was assembled from four castings and welded together at the top and bottom. The shells have also been used in tandem seating systems in airports. The La Fonda base armchair can still be special-ordered from Herman Miller, Inc. Eames staff members responsible for developing the La Fonda group included Don Albinson, Peter Pearce, and Bill Reithard.

Opposite: Production model of the La Fonda side chair

La Fonda group of side chairs and armchairs

A production model of the La Fonda chair and an Eames plastic side chair showing the difference in the height of the backs

La Fonda armchairs and side chairs with the prototype of a La Fonda table that did not go into production

Staff: 1961
901 Washington Boulevard
Gordon Ashby, Dale Bauer, Michael Birman, Thomas Bouck, Dick Bungay, Lucia Capacchione, Gladys Chernik, Ozelia Clement, Stan Croner, Dorothy Danziger, Annette Del Zoppo, Richard Donges, Rod Dyer, Patrick Fitzgerald, Glen Fleck, John Follis, Archer Goodwin, Ella Hogan, Robert Hostick, Robert Inman, Nancy Kane, Jeremy Lepard, Myrna Lyons, Harry McQuiston, Parke Meek, Robert Nakamura, John Neuhart, Eliot Noyes, Jr., Noel Dave O'Malley, David Parry, James Parsons, Peter Pearce, Mariea Poole, Kenneth Rang, Bill Reithard, Gordon Rollins, Carl Ronay, Don Ronay, Bill Sahara, Richard Sherwin, George Spacek, Robert Staples, Dorothy Stotland, Deborah Sussman, Leonard Taylor, Lewis Vanderbeken, Leola Walker, Christopher Whorf, Don Wright, Marcia Zintner

Ray and Charles with the final ½-inch scale model of the exhibition

1961

Exhibition: *Mathematica: A World of Numbers...and Beyond*

Mathematica was the first major exhibition produced by the Eames Office. It was designed for the March 1961 opening of a new science wing at the California Museum of Science and Industry in Los Angeles and was the first exhibition in the new space. The IBM Corporation, approached by the museum to contribute to the new wing, asked Charles to propose a suitable exhibition. Charles responded with a plan for an exhibition that would explain fundamental mathematical concepts with interactive devices and graphics. He outlined its purpose:

> [The exhibition] should be of interest to a bright student and not embarass the most knowledgeable...One of the best kept secrets in science is how unpompous scientists are at their science, and the amount of honest fun that for them is part of it. In doing an exhibition, as in *Mathematica*, one deliberately tries to let the fun out of the bag. The catch is that it can't be any old fun but it must be a very special brand. The excitement, or joke, must be a working part of the idea. The fun must follow all of the rules of the concept involved.

The 3,000-square foot exhibition is organized around several kinds of experiences. At the entrance to the exhibition, the Model Showcase houses demonstrations of a range of mathematical phenomena. The central area of the exhibition space is dominated by nine interactive displays dealing with topology, probability, the laws of minimal surfaces, projective geometry, celestial mechanics, and multiplication. In each of the interactive displays a visitor presses a button to activate the demonstration. When the button is pressed in the Probability Machine, 30,000 plastic balls fall through a maze of 200 steel pegs, randomly forming the classic bell curve. In the Multiplication Cube, a cube composed of 512 electric light bulbs illuminates the answers to multiplication problems entered sequentially on a keyboard by the visitor. On the Moebius Band display a red arrow travels around the double-sided surface. The principles these exhibits demonstrate mechanically are also explained by graphic panels with text and illustrations.

The participatory displays are enclosed by two 50-foot walls, a "History Wall" and an "Image Wall." The

Opposite top: Entrance to *Mathematica*. Opposite: View into the exhibition's model showcase

Top: The History Wall. Above: The Image Wall

Ray and Charles photographing an early ¼-inch scale model of the exhibition

Raymond Redheffer of the UCLA mathematics department and staff member Glen Fleck discussing the exhibition with Charles

Top to bottom: Three views of an early ¼-inch scale study model of the exhibition

Top: Plan view of ½-inch scale model showing details of the exhibition layout. Middle: View of the model showcase. Above: View of the Projective Geometry display and the Moebius Band

Right: Dean McKay of IBM wearing an Eames Office medal made in honor of his birthday and standing in front of the mock-up of the History Wall timeline

John Follis working on the mock-up of the fifty-foot History Wall

History Wall is a timeline that documents the evolution of mathematics (primarily Western) from A.D. 1100 to 1950—a chronology in words and images of biographies of mathematicians and the major milestones and developments in mathematical concepts. The timeline also includes key historical events. On the Image Wall, photographs and diagrams provide visual demonstrations of mathematical principles. Suspended from the ceiling over the entire central area are panels displaying quotations by mathematicians. The exhibition originally included five "peep shows" (pp. 260–261), two-minute films about mathematical concepts projected in individual viewing devices.

The office spent a year researching the exhibition, drawing especially on the collections of Butler Library at Columbia University in New York City for visual materials. Raymond Redheffer of the Department of Mathematics at the University of California, Los Angeles, was the project consultant. Glen Fleck, Redheffer, and Charles developed the content and storyline of the exhibition, and John Neuhart worked with Ray and Charles on graphic production. Gordon Ashby, working with Charles, designed the devices and the layout of the exhibition space.

IBM continues to sponsor and maintain the exhibition. *Mathematica* celebrated its twenty-fifth anniversary in 1986 with a party at the museum. No major changes have been made in its twenty-eight-year history (with the exception of the addition of two "Scholar's Walk" stands and fun-house mirrors from the IBM pavilion at the New York World's Fair and four interactive computer programs designed by Neuhart Donges Neuhart that expand on concepts treated in the show). The original materials remain, except for the "peep shows," which were removed in 1962 because of mechanical difficulties with the viewing devices.

A duplicate *Mathematica* exhibition, with minor modifications in the floor plan, was installed in late 1961 at the Museum of Science and Industry in Chicago. It remained there until November 1980 and was then moved to the Boston Museum of Science, where it opened in November 1981. Elements of the show were also on view at the New York World's Fair in 1964 and 1965, at the Time & Life Building in New York City, and subsequently, with the addition of a large outdoor Probability Machine, at the Pacific Science Center in Seattle. *Mathematica* has been visited by thousands of people and for many of them it has been their first introduction to mathematics. It has often been used as the model for exhibitions on science; its longevity and continuing popularity are proof of its value and of the solidity of the scholarship that went into its development.

Top: Mock-up of the Probability Machine. Above: Charles and Deborah Sussman working on the layout of the History Wall

Staff member Dale Bauer finishing the installation of the Image Wall

Staff member Nick Chaparos working on a model showcase display

A soap-solution dipping device for demonstrating minimal surfaces

A section of the Model Showcase containing mathematical forms representing theoretical areas of mathematics

Interactive Multiplication Cube for demonstrating the multiplication functions of squaring and cubing

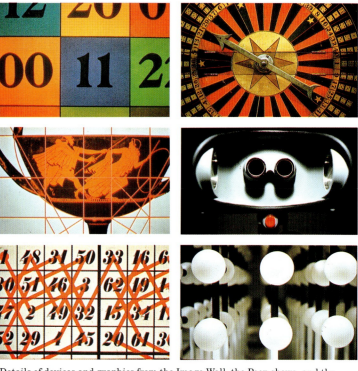
Details of devices and graphics from the Image Wall, the Peep shows, and the Multiplication Cube

Staff member Gordon Ashby and an early prototype of the exhibition's celestial mechanics device

Staff member Robert Staples and Charles working on the interactive display that explains the Moebius band

Probability Machine and the graphic panel explaining the laws of probability

Visitors watching the traveling spheres in the Celestial Mechanics device. A button is pushed to project the spheres one-by-one into elliptical orbits

Visitors looking into the Projective Geometry device. Several viewing apertures in the device provide views of different projections

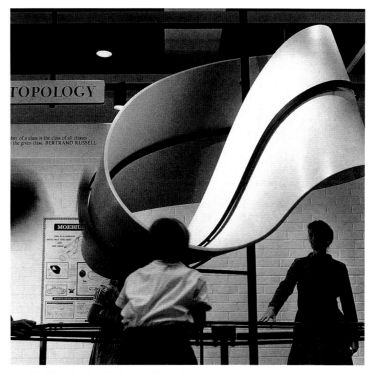

The Moebius Band with its traveling red arrow. The arrow is started on its path by pushing a button

Staff members Glen Fleck and Deborah Sussman examining the graphics for the film *Symmetry*

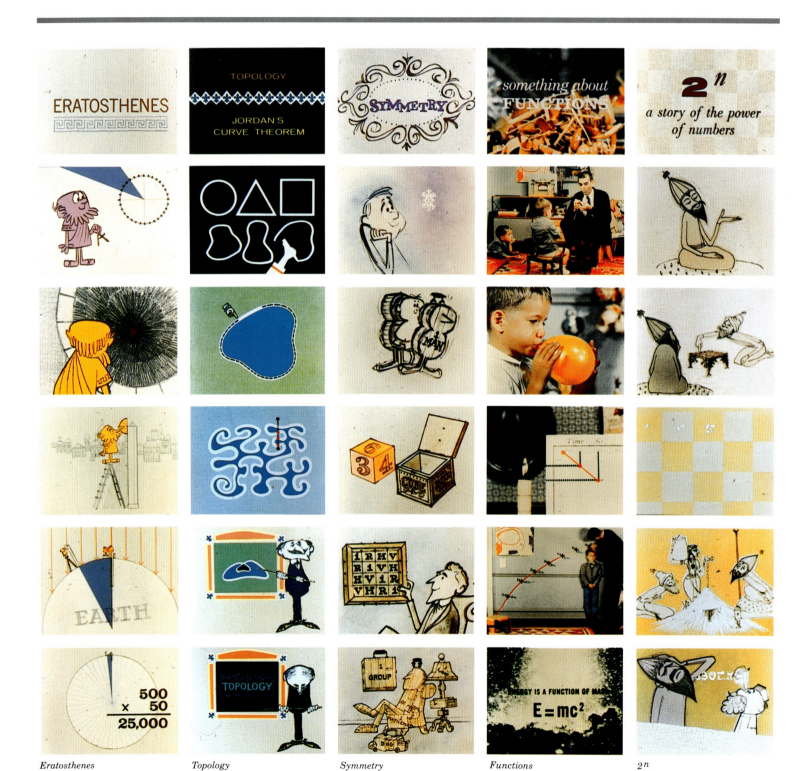

Eratosthenes   *Topology*   *Symmetry*   *Functions*   *2^n*

A sequence of frames selected from scenes in the *Mathematica* peep shows. The frames were photographed from 16mm-film footage

Staff: 1961
901 Washington Boulevard
Gordon Ashby
Dale Bauer
Michael Birman
Thomas Bouck
Richard Bungay
Lucia Capacchione
Gladys Chernik
Ozelia Clement
Stan Croner
Dorothy Danziger
Annette Del Zoppo
Richard Donges
Rod Dyer
Patrick Fitzgerald
Glen Fleck
Archer Goodwin
Ella Hogan
Robert Hostick
Robert Inman
Nancy Kane
Jeremy Lepard
Myrna Lyons
Harry McQuiston
Parke Meek
Robert Nakamura
John Neuhart
Eliot Noyes, Jr.
Noel Dave O'Malley
David Parry
James Parsons
Peter Pearce
Mariea Poole
Kenneth Rang
Bill Reithard
Gordon Rollins
Carl Ronay
Don Ronay
Bill Sahara
Richard Sherwin
George Spacek
Robert Staples
Dorothy Stotland
Deborah Sussman
Leonard Taylor
Lewis Vanderbeken
Leola Walker
Christopher Whorf
Don Wright
Marcia Zintner

1961

Films: *Mathematica* Peep Shows

Five films were made to accompany the *Mathematica* exhibitions at the California Museum of Science and Industry and the Museum of Science and Industry in Chicago. With the exception of *Functions* (photographed in live action and in animation) the films are composed entirely of animation, drawn in large part by Glen Fleck. The films were called "peep shows" because they were first shown in devices designed to accommodate one viewer. They were intended for a short attention span; each two-minute film explored one mathematical concept and could be seen as many times as the viewer needed to understand the idea. The individual viewing devices were replaced by small theater areas, and eventually the peep shows were taken out of the exhibition because the technology for showing continuous 8mm loop films was not up to the wear and tear of exhibition use. People waiting to see the films also slowed traffic moving through the exhibition. The films were part of the IBM film collection, through which they were made available to schools.

Music for the films was composed and performed by Elmer Bernstein. *Eratosthenes* is narrated by Vic Perrin. The other four films are narrated by Charles. All of the scripts were written by Charles and Glen Fleck. Raymond Redheffer was the mathematics consultant. (Running time, each film: 2 minutes; color.)

The Peep Shows:

Eratosthenes is about the system devised by the Greek mathematician for measuring the circumference of the earth.

Topology explores the Jordan Curve Theorem devised by the mathematician Camille Jordan to describe simple closed curves.

Symmetry is about the mathematical ordering of form and the symmetrical properties of objects.

Something About Functions explains concepts behind mathematical functional relationships.

2^n is a story about the exponential growth of numbers raised to powers.

Young viewer watching a peep show

Lucia Eames Demetrios and her children, Lucia, Carla, and Byron, at the individual viewing devices

April 27: Charles delivers a lecture entitled "Architecture and Science" at the Third Annual Congress of the Institute of Contemporary Art, London, England.

Right: Objects in Charles's office. Charles worked at an adjustable, wooden drafting table, and his office contained an eclectic mix of folk art, books, prints, engravings, and photographs culled from projects or gathered on his travels

Seating area in the Herman Miller showroom featuring Eames plastic chairs, an Eames laminate-topped coffee table, a Time-Life chair, George Nelson cabinets, Alexander Girard fabrics, and an Eames low table

Staff: 1961
901 Washington Boulevard
Gordon Ashby
Dale Bauer
Michael Birman
Thomas Bouck
Richard Bungay
Lucia Capacchione
Gladys Chernik
Ozelia Clement
Stan Croner
Dorothy Danziger
Annette Del Zoppo
Richard Donges
Rod Dyer
Patrick Fitzgerald
Glen Fleck
Archer Goodwin
Ella Hogan
Robert Hostick
Robert Inman
Nancy Kane
Jeremy Lepard
Myrna Lyons
Harry McQuiston
Parke Meek
Robert Nakamura
John Neuhart
Noel Dave O'Malley
Eliot Noyes, Jr.
David Parry
James Parsons
Peter Pearce
Mariea Poole
Kenneth Rang
Bill Reithard
Gordon Rollins
Carl Ronay
Don Ronay
Bill Sahara
Richard Sherwin
George Spacek
Robert Staples
Dorothy Stotland
Deborah Sussman
Leonard Taylor
Lewis Vanderbeken
Leola Walker
Christopher Whorf
Don Wright
Marcia Zintner

Architect Alexander Girard and Susan Girard in their Santa Fe, New Mexico home

1961

Herman Miller Furniture Company Showroom

In 1961 the Time-Life and La Fonda chairs (pp. 248–249, 252–253) were introduced into the market at the Herman Miller Furniture Company showroom in Los Angeles. The Eames Office redesigned the interiors and provided settings for their new furniture, a new upholstered chair designed by George Nelson, and recently designed fabrics by Alexander Girard. The walnut stools from the Time & Life Building lobbies were also introduced at this opening. Other previously introduced Eames and Nelson furniture was included.

A stationary carousel figure of a centaur dressed as a British soldier (complete with helmet and medals) was the centerpiece of the room. Other props for the new showings included a large black-and-white poster incorporating the initials of Herman Miller designers and the De Prees and a large photomural of an engraving used in the *Mathematica* exhibition—two world globes surrounded by a landscape of geometric solids (from *Heck's Iconographic Encyclopedia*, which was published in the nineteenth century).

The Eameses added props to each new showroom installation to soften and personalize the space and to keep it from looking like a standard furniture display room. There was usually no particular message inherent in the choice of props; they were usually new objects that the Eameses or the Girards had found on their travels. Occasionally, something from an office project, such as the *Mathematica* poster, would be added. It was this seemingly casual mix of assorted objects and new furniture that made the Herman Miller showrooms interesting, unique, and memorable.

Eames Lounge Chair in a setting with Girard fabrics and Nelson cabinets

Carousel figure holding a bouquet in the entrance to the showroom

May 11: Charles lectures to the School of Architecture, Arizona State University, Tempe, Arizona.

La Fonda armchairs and side chairs are included in the *California Design 8* exhibition at the Pasadena Art Museum, in Pasadena, California.

Staff: 1961
901 Washington Boulevard
Gordon Ashby
Dale Bauer
Michael Birman
Thomas Bouck
Richard Bungay
Lucia Capacchione
Gladys Chernik
Ozelia Clement
Stan Croner
Dorothy Danziger
Annette Del Zoppo
Richard Donges
Rod Dyer
Patrick Fitzgerald
Glen Fleck
Archer Goodwin
Ella Hogan
Robert Hostick
Robert Inman
Nancy Kane
Jeremy Lepard
Myrna Lyons
Harry McQuiston
Parke Meek
Robert Nakamura
John Neuhart
Eliot Noyes, Jr.
Noel Dave O'Malley
David Parry
James Parsons
Peter Pearce
Mariea Poole
Kenneth Rang
Bill Reithard
Gordon Rollins
Carl Ronay
Don Ronay
Bill Sahara
Richard Sherwin
George Spacek
Robert Staples
Dorothy Stotland
Deborah Sussman
Leonard Taylor
Lewis Vanderbeken
Leola Walker
Christopher Whorf
Don Wright
Marcia Zintner

Staff members Peter Pearce and Don Albinson testing the ECS foldup chair prototype

1961

Eames Contract Storage

Eames Contract Storage units were designed to replace most of the furniture needed in a dormitory or in other institutional residences. ECS, as it was called, included space for sleeping, working or studying, and storage. The self-contained system was designed to be a comfortable, organized, and durable living arrangement for students. ECS had five parts—three closets, a desk unit, and a folding bed—any combination of which could be purchased from the Herman Miller Furniture Company. The units were delivered as a knock down item, ready to be bolted onto two standard Unistrut sections mounted horizontally on a wall at the top and bottom of the unit. The Contract Storage unit was elevated off the floor by nine inches, leaving the top and bottom open for ventilation.

The storage closets came fully outfitted with wire shelves and drawers, coat hooks, towel bars, and lights. The sleeping mattress rested on a pivoting counterbalanced birch slab, which when closed matched the solid-core birch doors of the closets. The only area left open was the desk, which was provided with a built-in light, tackboard, and filing cabinet. The detailing of the system was extensive; door handles were made of polished cast aluminum, extruded aluminum strips formed continuous hinges at the sides of each unit, and the fir plywood partitions had a black phenolic plastic coating embossed with a gridlike design to resist scratches and dents. Don Albinson, Dale Bauer, Bob Staples, and Peter Pearce were responsible for the developmental work on ECS.

Herman Miller began marketing the system in 1961, and it was installed in dormitories on college campuses— including Purdue University, Southern Illinois University at Carbondale, and the University of Michigan at Ann Arbor. It was also installed at the Charlotte (North Carolina) YWCA and the Zeller Clinic in Peoria, Illinois. Though the system had great potential as a dormitory solution, federal support for such facilities at educational institutions was halted, and as more students began living off-campus in the 1960s, the need for new dorms declined drastically. As a result, sales declined and ECS was discontinued in 1969.

Opposite top: ECS production model with cabinet doors closed. Opposite: Open cabinet doors showing the configuration of the storage system

ECS storage system showing various components

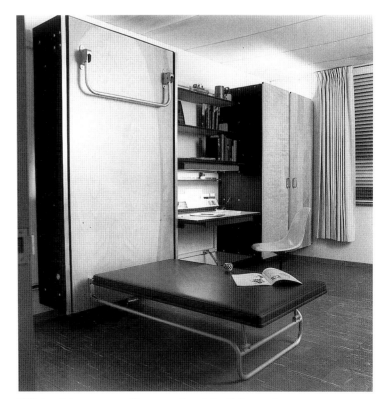

ECS closed storage area with an experimental pull-down sofa

September: Charles lectures to the British Architectural Students Association Conference on Architectural Education, Durham, England.

October: The films *Introduction to Feedback* and *Kaleidoscope Shop* win awards at the Internationale Filmwoche in Mannheim, West Germany.

Left: Exhibition fabricator Robert Shultz supervising the installation of the second *Mathematica* exhibition in the Museum of Science and Industry, Chicago, Illinois. Right: A view of the Chicago installation of *Mathematica*

Staff: 1961
901 Washington Boulevard
Gordon Ashby
Dale Bauer
Michael Birman
Thomas Bouck
Richard Bungay
Lucia Capachione
Gladys Chernik
Ozelia Clement
Stan Croner
Dorothy Danziger
Annette Del Zoppo
Richard Donges
Rod Dyer
Patrick Fitzgerald
Glen Fleck
Archer Goodwin
Ella Hogan
Robert Hostick
Robert Inman
Nancy Kane
Jeremy Lepard
Myrna Lyons
Harry McQuiston
Parke Meek
Robert Nakamura
John Neuhart
Eliot Noyes, Jr.
Noel Dave O'Malley
David Parry
James Parsons
Peter Pearce
Mariea Poole
Kenneth Rang
Bill Reithard
Gordon Rollins
Carl Ronay
Don Ronay
Bill Sahara
Richard Sherwin
George Spacek
Robert Staples
Dorothy Slotland
Deborah Sussman
Leonard Taylor
Lewis Vanderbeken
Leola Walker
Christopher Whorf
Don Wright
Marcia Zintner

1961

Film: *ECS*

Produced for the Herman Miller Furniture Company, *ECS* was made as a sales tool to introduce the functions and design properties of the Eames Contract Storage Units and to demonstrate the system for prospective customers. A portion of the film is devoted to the hardware and the detailing of the cabinetry. The narration, written and read by Charles, includes an often-quoted statement Charles made about the design process, one that he later used in other contexts:

> The details are not details, they make the product just as details make the architecture—the gauge of the wire, the selection of the wood, the finish of the castings— connections, the connections, the connections. It will in the end be these details that provide service to the customer and give the product its life.

In a later interview Charles expanded on the "connections" theme: "Eventually everything connects—people, ideas, objects, etc., ... the quality of the connections is the key to quality per se."

ECS uses both live-action footage and animation. Jeremy Lepard organized the production and Glen Fleck designed the animated sequences. Buddy Collette composed the original score, which was performed by the Chico Hamilton quintet. The film is not in general circulation. (Running time, *ECS*: 10 minutes, 30 seconds; color.)

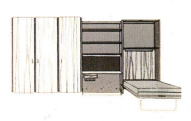 
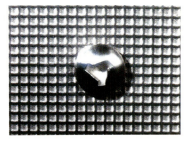 

A sequence of frames (reading top to bottom left, top to bottom right) from scenes in *ECS*. The frames were photographed from 16mm-film footage

November 16: Charles speaks to the Professional Photographers of Northern California.

Eames films *Mathematica* Peep Shows, *House*, and *Introduction to Feedback* win awards at the Montreal International Film Festival, Montreal, Canada.

Staff: 1961
901 Washington Boulevard
Gordon Ashby
Dale Bauer
Michael Birman
Thomas Bouck
Richard Bungay
Lucia Capacchione
Gladys Chernik
Ozelia Clement
Stan Croner
Dorothy Danziger
Annette Del Zoppo
Richard Donges
Rod Dyer
Patrick Fitzgerald
Glen Fleck
Archer Goodwin
Ella Hogan
Robert Hostick
Robert Inman
Nancy Kane
Jeremy Lepard
Myrna Lyons
Harry McQuiston
Parke Meek
Robert Nakamura
John Neuhart
Eliot Noyes, Jr.
Noel Dave O'Malley
David Parry
James Parsons
Peter Pearce
Mariea Poole
Kenneth Rang
Bill Reithard
Gordon Rollins
Carl Ronay
Don Ronay
Bill Sahara
Richard Sherwin
George Spacek
Robert Staples
Dorothy Stotland
Deborah Sussman
Leonard Taylor
Lewis Vanderbeken
Leola Walker
Christopher Whorf
Don Wright
Marcia Zintner

Charles and Parke Meek photographing Bill Reithard modeling a section of the La Fonda chair

1961

Slide Show: *Tivoli*

Tivoli, a ninety-two-image, single-screen slide show, was composed of photographs shot during a visit by Charles and Ray to Tivoli Gardens in Copenhagen, Denmark, on the first day of the garden's annual spring opening in 1959. The slide show includes general views of the park and its attractions—flowers, ponds, lights, restaurants, and a fireworks display. It was assembled as an example of a pleasant experience spent, according to Ray, "in a magical, enchanting atmosphere of play and relaxation for all ages." An urban playground, encircled by the city of Copenhagen but quite separate from it, the park offers to its visitors, a commedia dell'arte theater, musical performances, and other entertainments without relying on gadgets, rides, and special effects to attract visitors.

The energy, grace, and charm of Tivoli Gardens made a lasting impression on the Eameses, and Charles used them as models for the planning and design of the public spaces in the IBM pavilion at the New York World's Fair in 1964.

Tivoli was assembled into a slide show after the Eameses returned to their Venice office. The show was seen only by friends, staff, and clients.

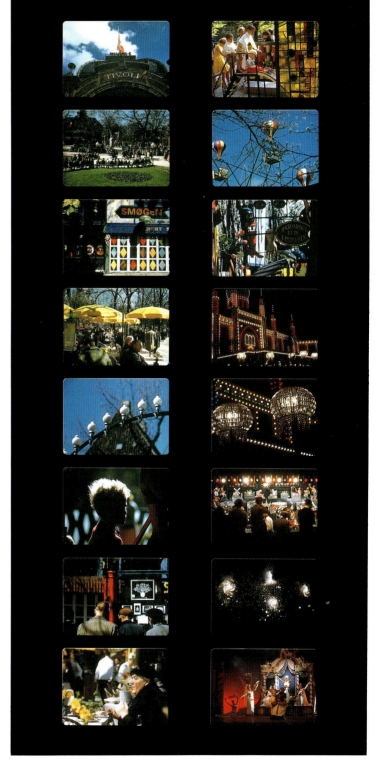

A selection of images (reading top to bottom left, and top to bottom right) from the single-screen slide show *Tivoli*

267

February: Charles lectures to the Friends of Art in Grand Rapids, Michigan.

Staff: 1962
901 Washington Boulevard
James Abbott
Gordon Ashby
Arthur Case
Stan Croner
Dorothy Danzinger
Annette Del Zoppo
Richard Donges
Gwen Dotzler
Glen Fleck
Archer Goodwin
John Heaney
Kazuo Higa
Ella Hogan
Nancy Kane
Joy Kinser
Joan Longdon
Harry Loucks
Amelia Marks
Harry McQuiston
Kenneth Meade
Parke Meek
Robert Mitchell
Ruth Munns
Robert Nakamura
Mariea Poole
Phillip Rich
Don Ronay
Bill Sahara
Michael Sand
James Sommers
George Spacek
Robert Staples
Deborah Sussman
Henrik Wahlfors
Leola Walker
Samuel Weiss
Christopher Whorf
Albert Woods
Don Wright
Yu Yoshioka

Bill Lightfield, Dorothy Jeakins, staff member Glen Fleck, and Charles planning the shooting script for *The Good Years* segments

A sequence of frames (reading top to bottom left, top to bottom right) from *Meet Me in St. Louis* (photographed from 16mm-film footage)

1962

Film: *The Good Years*

The Good Years is the collective title given to three short film sequences made for a CBS television special produced by Leland Hayward. Shown in 1962, the special presentation dealt with three historical events that occurred just after the beginning of the twentieth century. The idea and title for the show were taken from the book *The Good Years – From 1900 to the First World War*, by Walter Lord. Of the three segments, only *Meet Me in St. Louis* is in general circulation.

Film segments:

Panic on Wall Street, produced for the Eames Office by Chris Jenkins, is about the 1907 Wall Street financial crisis in which President Theodore Roosevelt and financier J.P. Morgan played major roles. The film uses historical photographs and animation. (Running time: 5 minutes; black and white.)

San Francisco Fire uses historic photographs and live-action photography to depict events surrounding the 1906 San Francisco earthquake and fire. The film looks at the city before the earthquake and shows how it marshaled its forces to fight and then recover from the three-day fire. Costume designer Dorothy Jeakins worked on the production design. Music is by Elmer Bernstein and the narration by Henry Fonda. (Running time: 4 minutes, 45 seconds; black and white.)

The subject of the *Meet Me In St. Louis* sequence is the Louisiana Purchase Centennial Exposition of 1904. Historic photographs are used to provide a glimpse of the fair and the events associated with it. The music is *Meet Me in St. Louis*, conducted by Elmer Bernstein. (Running time: 2 minutes; black and white.)

The Good Years was the Eameses' second television production in conjunction with Leland Hayward, a longtime friend of theirs and a collaborator on other projects.

In films such as *House* (pp. 198–199) and *Two Baroque Churches* (p. 202), the office had developed techniques for making short films whose message was essentially visual in nature. In The Fabulous Fifties (pp. 244–245), made for Hayward in 1960, they had first successfully adapted the technique to the requirements of television's small-screen format.

Staff member Robert Nakamura adjusting set lighting

Charles directing Dorothy Jeakins in a scene from *San Francisco Fire*

Archer Goodwin, Charles, and Ray on the set for *The Good Years*

A sequence of frames (reading top to bottom left, top to bottom right) from *San Francisco Fire* (photographed from 16mm-film footage)

A sequence of frames (reading top to bottom left, top to bottom right) from *Panic on Wall Street* (photographed from 16mm-film footage)

Seated audience in *The House of Science* theater

June: Charles delivers the commencement address and is awarded an honorary doctorate of fine arts by the College of Arts and Crafts, Oakland, California.

June: Charles lectures at the International Film Producers Association National Conference at UCLA in Los Angeles, California.

Staff: 1962
901 Washington Boulevard
James Abbott
Gordon Ashby
Arthur Case
Stan Croner
Dorothy Danziger
Annette Del Zoppo
Richard Donges
Gwen Dotzler
Glen Fleck
Archer Goodwin
John Heaney
Kazuo Higa
Ella Hogan
Nancy Kane
Joy Kinser
Joan Longdon
Harry Loucks
Amelia Marks
Harry McQuiston
Kenneth Meade
Parke Meek
Robert Mitchell
Ruth Munns
Robert Nakamura
Mariea Poole
Phillip Rich
Don Ronay
Bill Sahara
Michael Sand
James Sommers
George Spacek
Robert Staples
Deborah Sussman
Henrik Wahlfors
Leola Walker
Samuel Weiss
Christopher Whorf
Albert Woods
Don Wright
Yu Yoshioka

Composer Elmer Bernstein and Charles discussing the music for *The House of Science*

1962

Film: *The House of Science*

In 1960 the Eames Office was asked by the United States Department of State to create a film to be shown in the United States Science Exhibit at the 1962 Century 21 World's Fair in Seattle, Washington.

The House of Science multiscreen film presentation was produced as an introduction to the government's five pavilions, each of which dealt with a different aspect of science. Multiple images were projected onto six screens arranged along the concave wall of one pavilion's auditorium. A projection the size of the combined six screens made a seventh image. The presentation was designed to convey to the visitor "the excitement, the diversity, and the richness of the scientific discipline."

The film show began on a single screen with a four-minute animated sequence that portrayed the historical evolution of the sciences with an architectural allegory, the "House of Science." The earliest sciences—mathematics, biology, natural philosophy, astronomy, and medicine—were represented as architectural structures. As the sciences developed and became more specialized, the structures grew and divided, with the architecture

The House of Science audience seated below the projection wall

Top: A six-screen configuration of working notations by several scientists. Above: A six-screen configuration of telescopes from *The House of Science*

271

Staff member Glen Fleck and Ray working on the layouts for *The House of Science* animation sequence

Staff member Robert Mitchell working on the animated sequences

Staff members Gordon Ashby and Glen Fleck working on the graphic development of *The House of Science*

Staff members Robert Staples, Glen Fleck, and Deborah Sussman reviewing animation production

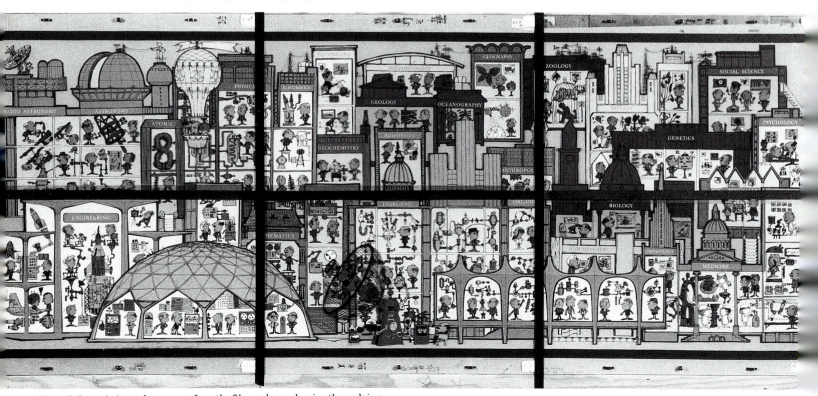

Top and above: Animated sequences from the film prologue showing the evolving "houses of science" and the fully developed structure representing the state of science

Lisa Ponti of *Domus* magazine and Charles at the Eames House. The Eameses' work was published regularly in *Domus* magazine

Consultant F. Hamilton Wright preparing a blackboard notation

Staff member Annette Del Zoppo keeping track of the production shooting

changing in style to reflect historical progression. As the structures expanded, the single-frame image was gradually accompanied by images on all six screens, and the House of Science grew into a city of buildings whose complexity paralleled that of the modern scientific world. The remainder of the multiscreen presentation, which played for nine minutes, was a still-image and live-action exploration of the contemporary scientific landscape, including photographs of scientists, their laboratories and offices, and their tools and equipment. The narration examined the nature of the scientific attitude and the exponential growth of science in this century.

The importance of viewing science as art was a long-standing preoccupation of Charles's. To quote from the film's narration:

> Science is essentially an artistic or philosophical enterprise carried on for its own sake. In this it is more akin to play than to work. But it is quite a sophisticated play in which the scientist views nature as a system of interlocking puzzles....High on the list of prerequisites for being a scientist is a quality that defines the rich human being as much as it does the man of science, that is, his ability and his desire to reach out with his mind and his imagination to something outside himself.

The theater for *The House of Science* occupied the first of six pavilions designed by Minoru Yamasaki. The interior was elliptical in shape. The lower section of the walls was lined with a light-colored, hardwood paneling; one side of the plaster upper section of the thirty-four-foot-high wall served as a giant screen. The images were shown from seven 35mm projectors set in painted faceted openings in the opposite wall. Visitors either sat on the carpeted floor or stood during the showing.

The history of science section was written and animated by Glen Fleck, who worked with Thomas S. Kuhn, a historian of science at the University of California and the primary consultant to the Eames Office on this project. Assistance was also provided by a number of expert consultants, including Abraham Kaplan, Helen Wright, Albert Hibbs, and Malcolm Gordon. Gordon Ashby executed the architectural allegory; Robert Mitchell assisted with the animation. Laurence Harvey read the narration, and Elmer Bernstein wrote the original score.

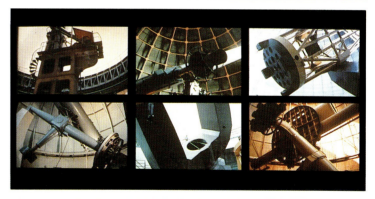
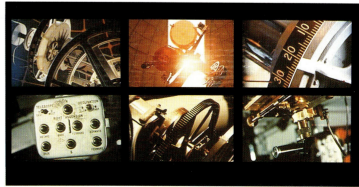
A selection of six-screen configurations from *The House of Science*

Charles receives the Gold Key Award from the National Home Fashions League.

Staff: 1962
901 Washington Boulevard
James Abbott
Gordon Ashby
Arthur Case
Stan Croner
Dorothy Danzinger
Annette Del Zoppo
Richard Donges
Gwen Dotzler
Glen Fleck
Archer Goodwin
John Heaney
Kazuo Higa
Ella Hogan
Nancy Kane
Joy Kinser
Joan Longdon
Harry Loucks
Amelia Marks
Harry McQuiston
Kenneth Meade
Parke Meek
Robert Mitchell
Ruth Munns
Robert Nakamura
Mariea Poole
Phillip Rich
Don Ronay
Bill Sahara
Michael Sand
James Sommers
George Spacek
Robert Staples
Deborah Sussman
Henrik Wahlfors
Leola Walker
Samuel Weiss
Christopher Whorf
Albert Woods
Don Wright
Yu Yoshioka

Jim Sommers and Robert Staples working on the seat assembly for the Tandem Sling Seating

Jim Sommers resting after loading Tandem Sling Seating units on a truck

1962

Eames Tandem Sling Seating

The Eames Office began to experiment with mass-seating systems for schools and institutions in 1954. The first attempts followed the designs of the prototype for stadium seating (p. 193), using a single steel support to join a series of seat shells. In 1958 the architect Eero Saarinen asked the Eames Office to address the need for comfortable, sturdy, and attractive public seating for Dulles Airport in Washington, D.C. At the same time, C.F. Murphy Associates, the architects of two new terminal buildings at Chicago's O'Hare Airport, were searching for good-looking seating that was strong, durable, resistant to wear, and easy to maintain and repair. They contacted Robert Blaich at the Herman Miller Furniture Company, who in turn brought the O'Hare problem to the Eames Office. The solution for both O'Hare and Dulles airports—The Eames Tandem Sling Seating—was developed in collaboration with C.F. Murphy and the Special Products Division of Herman Miller.

The sling system consists of single or double (back-to-back) rows of two to ten seats made of black or colored heat-sealed Naugahyde held between polished aluminum castings (a further development of the Aluminum Group sling system) and secured to a continuous steel T-beam. The interchangeable seat and back pads are constructed with the same heat-sealing process developed for the Aluminum Group (pp. 226–229). Here, however, the heat-sealed lines define triangular and trapezoidal areas and weld together the individual upholstery sandwiches of vinyl foam, Naugahyde, and Fiberthin nylon. The polished aluminum chair frames, legs, and arm supports are assembled with mechanical joints. The armrests are a hard black urethane.

A prototype of the tandem seating, built in the Eames Office by Dale Bauer, Peter Pearce, Richard Donges, and Robert Staples, was subjected to rigorous testing at the Herman Miller Technical Center. The seat pad underwent a series of stress tests, which included having a one-hundred-pound padded weight dropped onto its surface fifteen thousand times from a height of five inches. The system went into production in 1962. Eames Tandem Seating was installed first in O'Hare and Dulles airport terminals and later in airports around the world. Herman Miller still produces the seating units in single rows of two to six or in double rows of ten and twelve. They also manufacture a table attachment that can be substituted for a seat.

Opposite top: Tandem Sling Seating production model. Opposite: Installation of Tandem Sling Seating at Chicago's O'Hare Airport

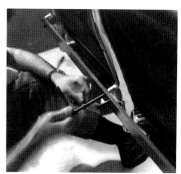
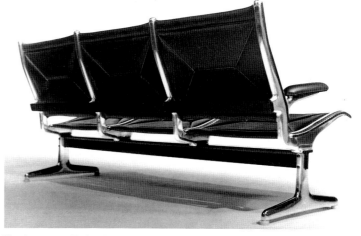

Top three rows: Richard Donges and Peter Pearce assembling a prototype sling seat. Above: Back view of the Tandem Sling Seating unit

September: Charles lectures at Wayne State University, Detroit, Michigan.

September: Charles lectures at the Industrial Design Institute, Detroit, Michigan.

A Herman Miller, Inc., stock certificate designed by Deborah Sussman and used until 1970 when Herman Miller became a public company

Staff: 1962
901 Washington Boulevard
James Abbott
Gordon Ashby
Arthur Case
Stan Croner
Dorothy Danziger
Annette Del Zoppo
Richard Donges
Gwen Dotzler
Glen Fleck
Archer Goodwin
John Heaney
Kazuo Higa
Ella Hogan
Nancy Kane
Joy Kinser
Joan Longdon
Harry Loucks
Amelia Marks
Harry McQuiston
Kenneth Meade
Parke Meek
Robert Mitchell
Ruth Munns
Robert Nakamura
Mariea Poole
Phillip Rich
Don Ronay
Bill Sahara
Michael Sand
James Sommers
George Spacek
Robert Staples
Deborah Sussman
Henrik Wahlfors
Leola Walker
Samuel Weiss
Christopher Whorf
Albert Woods
Don Wright
Yu Yoshioka

1962

Film: *Before the Fair*

Before the Fair was made for Herman Miller, Inc., after the close of the 1962 Seattle World's Fair. The film shows the last-minute preparations being executed for the fair's opening. Herman Miller furniture is seen as it was used on the fairgrounds in rest areas around the pavilion. *Before the Fair* was not planned in advance; it was shot and assembled in the same spontaneous mode as *Herman Miller at the Brussels World's Fair*.

Beginning with *S-73* (Sofa Compact; p. 192), the Eames Office provided Herman Miller with in-house films about the purpose and design qualities of Eames furniture that the company used to instruct its sales staff and to show to clients. However, *Before the Fair* (like its counterpart *Brussels* film; p. 230), was used by Herman Miller less for instructional reasons than for publicity and advertising. The film also provided a glimpse of the Seattle fair to Herman Miller employees and Eames Office staff who could not go to the actual event.

Before the Fair is composed of a series of 35mm slides transferred to film. The photographs were shot at the site by Charles and by staff members Deborah Sussman and Glen Fleck, who were in the midst of installing *The House of Science* in the United States Science Exhibit Pavilion at the fair. Photographs of construction crews, the nearly completed exhibit buildings, and the myriad shapes, colors, and textures of the festival site are paced to the constantly accelerating music of Gavin Gordon's "The Rake's Progress." There is no narration. The film is not in general circulation. (Running time, *Before the Fair*: 6 minutes, 45 seconds; color.)

A sequence of frames (reading top to bottom left, top to bottom right) from scenes in *Before the Fair*. The frames were photographed from 16mm-film footage

September: Charles serves on the jury of the London *Daily Mirror*'s "First International Furniture Design" competition, London, England.

Eames Office designs a preliminary plan and model for the Vatican's pavilion at the New York World's Fair.

Staff: 1962
901 Washington Boulevard
James Abbott
Gordon Ashby
Arthur Case
Stan Croner
Dorothy Danziger
Annette Del Zoppo
Richard Donges
Gwen Dotzler
Glen Fleck
Archer Goodwin
John Heaney
Kazuo Higa
Ella Hogan
Nancy Kane
Joy Kinser
Joan Longdon
Harry Loucks
Amelia Marks
Harry McQuiston
Kenneth Meade
Parke Meek
Robert Mitchell
Ruth Munns
Robert Nakamura
Mariea Poole
Phillip Rich
Don Ronay
Bill Sahara
Michael Sand
James Sommers
George Spacek
Robert Staples
Deborah Sussman
Henrik Wahlfors
Leola Walker
Samuel Weiss
Christopher Whorf
Albert Woods
Don Wright
Yu Yoshioka

Film producer Julian Blaustein and Charles discussing plans for the IBM pavilion

Archer Goodwin, Charles, and George Spacek lining up a shot for the IBM presentation films

1962–1963

Films: *IBM Fair Presentation #1* and *#2*

There are two *IBM Fair Presentation* films. The first presents the Eames Office's preliminary design proposals for the IBM pavilion at the 1964 New York World's Fair. This film uses photography and animation to present the concept, architecture, and overall look of the pavilion and to convey an impression of the exposition's spirit and content. This version of the film was made expressly to introduce the project to IBM's senior executives.

The film begins with a view of the actual fair site at Flushing Meadows, New York, and then examines the Eames Office model of the IBM pavilion. Shots of the model display areas are followed by an animated simulation of the film presentation planned for the pavilion's theater. The animated sequences were done by Glen Fleck. The film is not in general circulation. (Running time, *IBM Fair Presentation Film #1*: 5 minutes; color.)

IBM Fair Presentation Film #2 is a revised version of the first film and details the modifications and additions that were agreed upon after the original proposal was viewed. Made after another year of work on the project, it shows many of the pavilion's features in greater detail and is a further refinement of the original design guidelines. The Kor-ten "trees" that formed a canopy over the outdoor exhibition area of the pavilion are defined in more detail, as are the People Wall and the Ovoid Theater (pp. 284–291).

The narration was written and performed by Charles. The music is "A Fine Day," played by the Chico Hamilton quintet and Buddy Collette. The film is not in general circulation. (Running time, *IBM Fair Presentation Film #2*: 4 minutes, 45 seconds; color.)

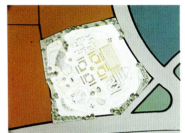

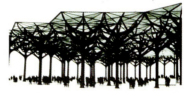

A sequence of frames (reading top to bottom left) from scenes in *IBM Fair Presentation Film #1* and (reading top to bottom right) *IBM Fair Presentation Film #2*. The frames were photographed from 16mm-film footage

May: Charles delivers a lecture and shows an early version of the slide show *Movie Sets* (p. 362) and the film *Day of the Dead* (pp. 212–213) at the Pasadena Art Museum, Pasadena, California.

Domus magazine gives its first "Obelisk" award to the Eames Office for excellence in design.

Right: The cover of the May 1963 issue of *Domus* magazine, which featured an article on the work of the Eames Office

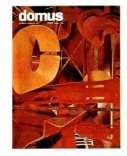

Susan Girard and Herman Miller executive Hugh De Pree at the showroom opening

Staff: 1963
901 Washington Boulevard
Hamilton Acimoto
Robert Anderson
Ray Aragon
Mary Beresford
John Blaustein
Alan Capps
Lester Churchill
Dorothy Danziger
Annette Del Zoppo
Cyril Didjurgis
Richard Donges
Glen Fleck
Archer Goodwin
Geoffrey Greib
Richard Hart
Pamela Hedley
Ella Hogan
Nancy Kane
Harry Loucks
Marvin Lyons
Parke Meek
Robert Mitchell
Robert Nakamura
Mariea Poole
Bill Sahara
Dorothy Shirely
Bill Smith
James Sommers
George Spacek
Robert Staples
Michio Suguwara
Deborah Sussman
Charles Swenson
Leola Walker
Yu Yoshioka
Gary Young
Peter Zellner

1963

Herman Miller, Inc., Showroom

In 1963 Herman Miller showrooms in New York City, Chicago, and Los Angeles were redesigned by the office for the introduction of the Eames Tandem Sling Seating. As a visual "joke," the seating system, designed for airport use, was shown against a mural enlarged from a photograph taken by Charles in a German train station. The "set," designed to give a feeling of public space, was used in all three showrooms, and included objects found in stations—cast-iron light standards, hanging signs, luggage, newspapers, and a flower store—surrounded by La Fonda tables and chairs treated in a café-style setting. Each table represented a different country, complete with printed menus, local dishes, and other table accessories reinforcing the idea of travel. Deborah Sussman collected the objects, designed the menus, and set up the New York and Chicago showrooms. Ray and Deborah developed the sets for the Los Angeles showroom. Other furniture from the Herman Miller catalog was arranged throughout the room in settings for the office and home.

In the front of the Los Angeles showroom a small branch of Alexander Girard's New York Textiles & Objects shop was installed and filled with folk art, toys, dolls, Girard fabrics, weavings, and embroideries. The small shop was enclosed by white batiste curtains. T&O, as it was called, was designed by Girard for Herman Miller as a retail home accessory shop, with merchandise selected and arranged by Girard. The opening of the first shop on East 53rd Street in New York City was followed by the establishment of branches in several Herman Miller showrooms.

Café table setting in the Chicago showroom

Opposite top: Los Angeles showroom on opening night. Opposite: Railway station photomural in the Tandem Sling Seating installation in the Chicago showroom

Middle two rows: Café table settings and the T&O Shop enclosure in the Los Angeles showroom. Above: Café table setting with the La Fonda chairs in the Los Angeles Showroom

IBM *Mathematica* Peep Shows receive the "Outstanding Film of the Year" award at the London Film Festival, London, England.

October 7: Charles speaks at a meeting of the American Institute of Architects, Memphis Regional Chapter, Memphis, Tennessee.

Staff, 1963
901 Washington Boulevard
Hamilton Acimoto
Robert Anderson
Ray Aragon
Mary Beresford
John Blaustein
Alan Capps
Lester Churchill
Dorothy Danziger
Annette Del Zoppo
Cyril Didjurgis
Richard Donges
Glen Fleck
Archer Goodwin
Geoffrey Greib
Richard Hart
Pamela Hedley
Ella Hogan
Nancy Kane
Harry Loucks
Marvin Lyons
Parke Meek
Robert Mitchell
Robert Nakamura
Mariea Poole
Bill Sahara
Dorothy Shirely
Bill Smith
James Sommers
George Spacek
Robert Staples
Michio Sugawara
Deborah Sussman
Charles Swenson
Leola Walker
Yu Yoshioka
Gary Young
Peter Zellner

Ray, Deborah Sussman, Eliot Noyes, Eli Noyes, Charles, and Glen Fleck posing with cameras in the Eames Office yard

Edgardo Contini, engineer of the "Bridge House," the first version of Case Study House #8 (pp.106–121), on a visit to the Eames Office

1963

Tandem Shell Seating

A variation on the Eames solution for public seating, Tandem Shell Seating, combines the shells developed for the plastic armchairs and side chairs (pp. 138–143) with the base developed for the Eames Tandem Sling Seating (pp. 274–275). The shells are attached to cast aluminum spiders by rubber shock mounts and then are mounted onto a black, epoxy-painted steel T-beam. The seating is available in multiple units of three, four, or five shells. Seat and table combinations are also produced; the tabletops are made of a white laminate with a dark vinyl edge.

Herman Miller began producing Tandem Shell Seating in 1963. The fiberglass-reinforced side and armchair shells are still manufactured in a variety of colors, including crimson, parchment, raw umber, red orange, ultramarine, and yellow. They are also available upholstered in vinyl or in one of several fabrics (the outer shell is made in a dark toned, neutral light, or parchment-colored polyester). The seats are edged in either a dark or light vinyl.

Top: A row of Tandem Shell Seating armchairs facing a row of Tandem Shell side chairs. Above: A view from below of side chairs in the Tandem Shell system

A mock-up of a shoe-store setting with Tandem Shell Seating built in the Eames Office for a photography session

Staff: 1964
901 Washington Boulevard
Victor Arzate
Charles Brittin
Alan Capps
Robert Carlson
Dorothy Danziger
Annette Del Zoppo
Richard Donges
Edward Duffy
Stacey Dukes
Glen Fleck
John Griffiths
Verity Grinnell
Atsuo Haida
Keith Hall
Pamela Hedley
Ella Hogan
James Homsy
Ann Hutton
Ronald Knapp
Harry Loucks
Herman Mayer
Parke Meek
Robert Mitchell
Fred Miwa
John Neuhart
Mariea Poole
Alistair Riach
James Sommers
George Spacek
Robert Staples
Michio Suguwara
Deborah Sussman
Charles Swenson
Leola Walker
Tomoko Yoshioka
Yu Yoshioka

Left: Hugh De Pree (of Herman Miller, Inc.), Willy Fehlbaum (president of the company licensed to produce Herman Miller furniture in Europe), Charles, and Ray with a School Seating unit

1964

School Seating

In addition to individual seating and the Tandem Shell Seating, the Eames Office also used fiberglass-reinforced plastic side chairs to create multiple seating units for schools. Like the Tandem Shell Seating, a system that lends itself to numerous public applications, the side shells in the School Seating system are mounted in rows on two black, epoxy-coated steel straps bent into a slight radius and clamped together (to follow the various curved risers often found in school lecture halls) by a steel spider and leg cap. In the School Seating, the aluminum leg support base forms a triangle and, like the steel beam, is coated with black epoxy. Each chair is provided with a right-hand fold-up tablet arm laminated in a neutral light formica. School seating is still produced by Herman Miller, Inc.

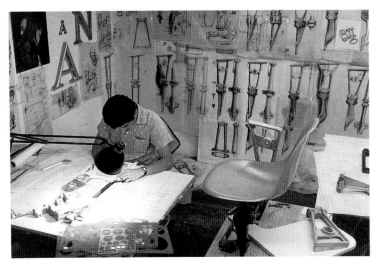

Staff member Yu Yoshioka working on design solutions for the support-member casting

Top and middle: Classroom installation showing the fixed tablet arm and fold-up tablet arm variations of the Eames School Seating. Above: Details of the seat-support casting

Right: Charles and the Japanese potter Hamada discussing plans for the IBM pavilion at the New York World's Fair. Master potter Hamada visited the Eames Office whenever he came to the United States, and Charles kept him abreast of office projects

Staff: 1964
901 Washington Boulevard
Victor Arzate
Charles Brittin
Alan Capps
Robert Carlson
Dorothy Danziger
Annette Del Zoppo
Richard Donges
Edward Duffy
Stacey Dukes
Glen Fleck
John Griffiths
Verity Grinnell
Atsuo Haida
Keith Hall
Pamela Hedley
Ella Hogan
James Homsy
Ann Hutton
Ronald Knapp
Harry Loucks
Herman Mayer
Parke Meek
Robert Mitchell
Fred Miwa
John Neuhart
Mariea Poole
Alistair Riach
James Sommers
George Spacek
Robert Staples
Michio Suguwara
Deborah Sussman
Charles Swenson
Leola Walker
Tomoko Yoshioka
Yu Yoshioka

1964

3473 Sofa

The 3473 Sofa, named after its Herman Miller catalog number, was introduced in 1964 and produced until 1973. The sofa, similar in shape to the 1954 Sofa Compact (pp. 190–191), had a high back and an angled seat, supported by symmetrical cast aluminum legs attached to an angle-iron bracing system running across the seat and from the front to the back. The cross-section of the leg casting graduated from round to elliptical and was the precursor to the support system eventually used for the Chaise (pp. 338–339). A ½-inch high, 1 ¼-inch diameter nylon glide was driven into each leg.

The seat and back of the sofa were each constructed out of a single piece of plywood with an angle molded into the back section eight inches from the top. No-sag springs in the seat were hooked together by wire clips. The pads for both seat and back were made of 3-inch urethane foam covered by a 1-inch layer of dacron. The first production sofas were upholstered in Naugahyde and later in fabrics from the Herman Miller line (or in leather by special order.) Cord welting ran around the seat and back sections and horizontally across each in two places. The indentation in the pad was formed by a piece of fabric attached to the welting on the inside, pulled and secured underneath and in the back of the sofa beneath a covering of Royalite. The 3473 Sofa combined elements from earlier Eames furniture; the height of the back and the general shape of the sofa were derived from the Sofa Compact (pp. 190–191), and the interior plywood support system and the configuration of the padded sections began with the Time-Life chairs (pp. 248–249). The amount of detailing on the sofa ultimately made it too expensive to produce. Staff members Dale Bauer, Peter Pearce, and Richard Donges were responsible for the developmental work.

Profile of the 3473 Sofa

3473 Sofa upholstered in Naugahyde

Opposite: 3473 Sofa with fabric upholstery (foreground) in Herman Miller's Los Angeles showroom

Right: Four display windows designed by the Eames Office and installed in IBM's Madison Avenue Exhibit Center to introduce the public to the IBM pavilion at the forthcoming World's Fair

Ray, Glen Fleck, and Charles developing the script for the *Think* presentation

Staff: 1964
901 Washington Boulevard
Victor Arzate
Charles Brittin
Alan Capps
Robert Carlson
Dorothy Danziger
Annette Del Zoppo
Richard Donges
Edward Duffy
Stacey Dukes
Glen Fleck
John Griffiths
Verity Grinnell
Atsuo Haida
Keith Hall
Pamela Hedley
Ella Hogan
James Homsy
Ann Hutton
Ronald Knapp
Harry Loucks
Herman Mayer
Parke Meek
Robert Mitchell
Fred Miwa
John Neuhart
Mariea Poole
Alistair Riach
James Sommers
George Spacek
Robert Staples
Michio Suguwara
Deborah Sussman
Charles Swenson
Leola Walker
Tomoko Yoshioka
Yu Yoshioka

1964–1965

IBM Corporation Pavilion for the New York World's Fair

In early 1961 Eero Saarinen and Charles began discussing concepts for a pavilion to represent the IBM Corporation at the 1964 New York World's Fair. The Eames Office began work on the project in 1962 in collaboration with Eero Saarinen's architectural firm, which, after Saarinen's death in September 1961, was directed by Kevin Roche and John Dinkeloo. Roche/Dinkeloo and Associates designed the site and the architectural planning for the one-and-a-quarter acre site, which was situated on the northwest edge of the "Pool of Industry" in Flushing Meadows, New York. The Eames Office was responsible for exhibition material, film presentations, graphics, and pavilion signage.

Charles and Saarinen had agreed that the pavilion should be "unarchitectural" and should not compete with other pavilions in design and form. Both Saarinen and Eames wanted the visitor to remember the experience and not the architecture. In the first project presentation film (pp. 277), Charles stated his general aims: "From any approach the visitor looks through trees and shrubs into an open and spacious structure. The supporting elements are so developed that they are not unlike the natural forms themselves."

Both Eero and Charles had also agreed that the fair visitor should take information and ideas away from the presentation, in addition to being entertained and amused. The pavilion site was divided into several exhibit areas, each dedicated to demonstrating the role

Opposite top: Exterior of the Ovoid Theater. Opposite: Kor-ten tree supports with the program host on an elevated platform in the foreground. Above: View of the entire IBM pavilion

Top: Exhibition areas with Eames puppet shows. Middle: Graphic panels in the Scholar's Walk. Above: The People Wall ascending into the Ovoid Theater

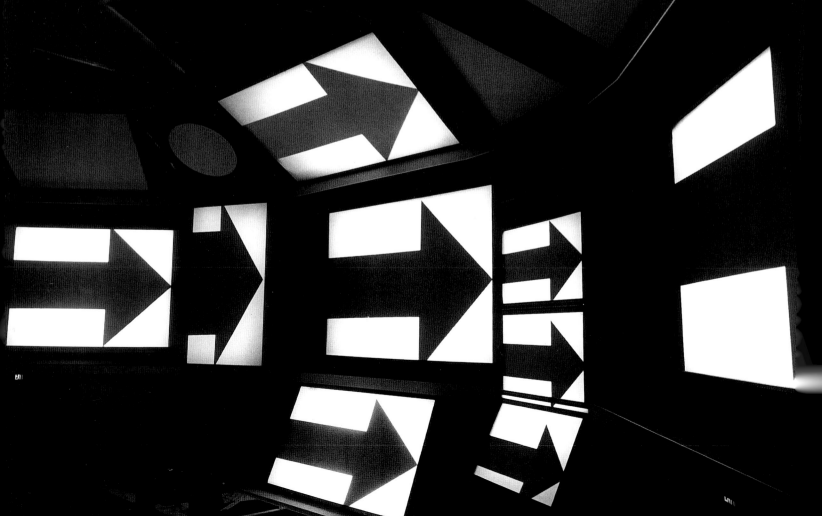

April 30: Charles lectures at the conference "Design in America," sponsored by the Ford Foundation, Princeton, New Jersey.

Ray arranging the table setting for the "Dinner Party" sequence

Charles, staff members Glen Fleck and Pamela Hedley, Ray, and writer Ralph Caplan reviewing the film storyboard for the *Think* film

of the computer in everyday life. The goal was not to teach the visitor how computers operated but to demonstrate the relationship between information processing by computers and everyday problem solving.

A large translucent plastic canopy, supported by forty-five Kor-ten steel "trees," each thirty-two feet high with spans of up to thirty-five feet, covered the smaller exhibition areas, where exhibits demonstrated how computers function in everyday life. Two of these areas included elements from the *Mathematica* exhibition—the "Scholars' Walk" (a walkway lined with graphic panels of anecdotes, poetry, cartoons, and other information about computers) and the fourteen-foot Probability Machine displayed in the "Probability Court." Three Eames Office computer-driven puppet shows, *Computer Day at Midvale*, *Sherlock Holmes in the Singular Case of the Plural Green Mustache*, and *Cast of Characters*, played under the "Pentagon Platform" canopy.

In another area, "The Typewriter Bar," visitors could try out the newest IBM typewriters. The "Computer Court" included an IBM 1460 data-processing system, one of the first to use optical character recognition for retrieval and language translation. The housings for the "Computer Court" exhibits were designed by Herb Rosenthal.

The main attraction of the IBM pavilion was a multiscreen film presentation, *Think*, shown in a large, egg-shaped structure, the "Ovoid Theater," which was raised ninety feet above the canopy and the central structure of the pavilion. While waiting in line to enter the theater and see the film, visitors were entertained by strolling musicians and then invited to sit in bleachers directly below the theater—the "People Wall." A host slowly descended from the theater above on a moving platform, greeted the audience, and prepared them for the presentation they were about to see. The bleachers (seating over four hundred people) were then elevated into the Ovoid Theater (or the "Information Machine"), where prefilm images and lights were already playing. Once the bleachers were in place, the multiscreen presentation *Think* was shown.

The host, who also ascended into the theater, acted as master of ceremonies and narrator, appearing at intervals to explain a complicated sequence and prepare the audience for the next one. *Think* dealt with the concept of modeling and the use of abstractions. Its central message had to do with problem solving and was designed to take the mystery out of computer processing: to demonstrate that the methods we use for solving complex problems—stating the problem, abstracting the essentials, trying out relationships, and

Opposite top and bottom: Two screens from the *Think* film presentation

Top to bottom: A selection of screens from *Think*

June 5: Charles receives an honorary doctorate of arts from Pratt Institute, Brooklyn, New York

The IBM pavilion outdoor seating, which was designed by the Eames Office

making decisions—are the same as those we use for solving simple ones. The difference is only in the number of decisions that must be made and acted upon. Animated, still, and live-action images demonstrating the many parts of any given problem were projected simultaneously onto fourteen large and eight small screens of different shapes and sizes. Sequences in the film dealt with problems of varying complexity, ranging from common, everyday ones—how to plan the seating for a dinner party—to complex business and scientific problems—city planning and weather prediction. Other segments on check writing, coaching football, a road race, and "twoness" were included.

The script for *Think* was developed by Glen Fleck, Ralph Caplan, and I.A.L. Diamond in cooperation with Charles. Glen Fleck worked out the storyboard. The thirty-minute presentation was shown at the fair for two seasons, the summers of 1964 and 1965. The buildings and the exhibits were dismantled at the conclusion of the fair in the fall of 1965. The Scholars' Walk panels were added to the *Mathematica* exhibition in Chicago; a duplicate set was added to the exhibition in Los Angeles. Elements from *Mathematica* were installed at the Time & Life Building in New York City, and were later transferred to the Pacific Science Center in Seattle.

Four films were made by the Eames Office as records of the fair and to extend the life of some of the ideas expressed in the fair presentations: two of the puppet shows were filmed and combined on one reel for distribution (pp. 302–303), the *Think* multiscreen film was condensed into a single-screen film (pp. 306–307), and a "souvenir" film, *IBM at the Fair* (pp. 304–305), collapsed the entire IBM World's Fair display-and-film experience into a fast-moving review.

Above: view into the IBM pavilion's garden, which surrounded the *Mathematica* exhibition area. Opposite: Details and close-ups of the IBM pavilion's exhibition area photographed by Charles

Top: Scholars' Walk panels. Middle: Visitors in the *Mathematica* area clustered around the Celestial Mechanics Machine. Above: History Wall and Scholars' Walk panels

June 13: Charles delivers a dinner address to the School of Architecture at his alma mater, Washington University, St. Louis, Missouri.

July 15: Charles lectures at Michigan State University in East Lansing.

Charles is appointed to the Conference on Good Design by the governor of California, Edmund G. Brown. The conference was convened to establish statewide guidelines to be used in matters having to do with architecture and design.

Ray and Tomoko Yoshioka working on the graphics for the IBM pavilion

Charles's secretary Pamela Hedley

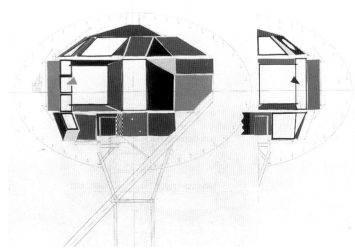

Top and middle: Charles's first concept drawings for the Ovoid Theater. Above: A drawing of a section of the Ovoid Theater

Top: Parke Meek and George Spacek working on an early model of the Ovoid Theater. Middle: Constructing a scale model of the projection screen layout in the Ovoid Theater. Above: A scale model of the multiple-projection screen configuration in the Ovoid Theater

Right: Office staff posing for a "model" photo session. To "people" their scale models, the office photographed staff members and friends and then printed the images in the scale of the exhibition model. The "model people" appear in the photo below

Top: A photograph from the model of the under-the-canopy presentation. Middle: Graphic treatments for the pavilion signage and swags and borders. Above: Robert Staples and Harry Loucks finishing a detail of the pavilion's finials

Top: Puppet show mock-up. Middle: Work on the finished puppet show mechanism. Above: Pneumatic mechanism for the Dr. Watson puppet from the Sherlock Holmes puppet show.

July 20: Charles is a member of a panel discussing "The Role of Films and Other Artistic Creations in the Teaching of Science" at the National Science Foundation Conference, University of Colorado, Boulder, Colorado.

August 6: Charles speaks at the American Association of Museums' Shows and Exhibits Workshop in New York City.

Right: Physicist Philip Morrison, whom Charles met when they served on a panel at the National Science Foundation Conference. The meeting was the beginning of a long association and friendship. Morrison often acted as a consultant on Eames Office science projects and wrote a book in 1982 expanding on the concepts in the Eames film *Powers of Ten* (pp. 336–337, 440–441)

Staff: 1964
901 Washington Boulevard
Victor Arzate
Charles Brittin
Alan Capps
Robert Carlson
Dorothy Danziger
Annette Del Zoppo
Richard Donges
Edward Duffy
Stacey Dukes
Glen Fleck
John Griffiths
Verity Grinnell
Atsuo Haida
Keith Hall
Pamela Hedley
Ella Hogan
James Homsy
Ann Hutton
Ronald Knapp
Harry Loucks
Herman Mayer
Parke Meek
Robert Mitchell
Fred Miwa
John Neuhart
Marita Poole
Alistair Riach
James Sommers
George Spacek
Robert Staples
Michio Sugawara
Deborah Sussman
Charles Swenson
Leola Walker
Tomoka Yoshioka
Yu Yoshioka

1964

Film: *The House of Science*

The House of Science is a single-screen composite of the multiscreen presentation produced to introduce the six United States science pavilions at the Seattle Century 21 World's Fair in 1962 (pp. 270–273). The film was produced with sponsorship from IBM.

Like the original 35mm production, which was shown on seven projectors to the fair audience, the composite film begins with an animated sequence depicting the historical evolution of science as an architectural allegory. The remainder of the film surveys the broad spectrum of modern science.

The narration from the Seattle presentation, written by Charles with Glen Fleck and read by Laurence Harvey, was also used for this single-screen film. The music was composed and conducted by Elmer Bernstein. Thomas S. Kuhn served as consultant. The film is in general circulation. (Running time, *The House of Science*: 14 minutes; color.)

A sequence of frames (reading top to bottom left, top to bottom right) from scenes in *The House of Science*. The frames were photographed from 16mm-film footage

Charles is invited by the Indian government to serve as a consultant on an Indian national memorial to Jawaharlal Nehru.

November: The American Institute of Architects presents an award to Eero Saarinen and Associates and the Eames Office for the design of the IBM pavilion at the New York World's Fair.

Staff: 1964
901 Washington Boulevard
Victor Arzate
Charles Brittin
Alan Capps
Robert Carlson
Dorothy Danziger
Annette Del Zoppo
Richard Donges
Edward Duffy
Stacey Dukes
Glen Fleck
John Griffiths
Verity Grinnell
Atsuo Haida
Keith Hall
Pamela Hedley
Ella Hogan
James Homsy
Ann Hutton
Ronald Knapp
Harry Loucks
Herman Mayer
Parke Meek
Robert Mitchell
Fred Miwa
John Neuhart
Mariea Poole
Alistair Riach
James Sommers
George Spacek
Robert Staples
Michio Sugawara
Deborah Sussman
Charles Swenson
Leola Walker
Tomoko Yoshioka
Yu Yoshioka

Mathematica exhibition (pp. 254–259) elements from the New York World's Fair are installed in the New York Time & Life Building

1964

Segmented Base Tables

In 1964 the Eames Office designed a table with a single segmented base, constructed of modular units, that could support tops of different lengths and widths. The base, similar in form to the pedestal support on the La Fonda chair and table (pp. 252–253), consists of one or more tubular steel columns joined at the bottom by steel spreaders and cast aluminum legs. The configuration of the base and the number of elements required varies with the size and shape of the tabletop. Each pedestal column slides into a cast aluminum spider, which is then screwed into the wood tabletop. At the bottom, the column is joined to the legs, and a single bolt running the length of the pedestal secures the base to the table.

Herman Miller, Inc., has been selling segmented base tables since 1964. The strength and versatility of the base design has made it possible to produce tables ranging from five to twenty-two feet in length. These individual work surfaces or conference tables are available with round, rectangular, or oval ("super-ellipse") tops in hardwood veneers, plastic laminates, or Italian white marble. All the tops, which are 11/16-inch thick, are edged in a light, dark, or warm-toned vinyl. Robert Staples and Richard Donges developed the segmented table system.

An early prototype of the segmented base table with the column-leg units cast in one piece standing behind an occasional table with the La Fonda base

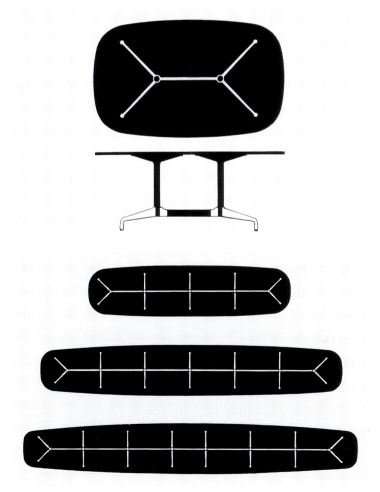

Top: Plan and elevation of the segmented base table production model
Above: A diagram of the segmented base table expansion scheme

April 1: Charles is the keynote speaker at California Governor Edmund G. Brown's Advisory Committee on Design.

April 14: Charles is awarded the President's Medal by the New York Art Director's Club in New York City for excellence in design.

April 19: Charles is made a member of the Industrial Designers of America.

Staff: 1965
901 Washington Boulevard
Bob Anderson
Victor Arzate
Joseph Bernstein
Charles Brittin
Roger Conrad
Annette Del Zoppo
Richard Donges
Glen Fleck
Russell Frears
Kenneth Grobecker
Karl Haeuser
Atsuo Haida
Keith Hall
Lars Hanson
Margaret Harris
Pamela Hedley
Ella Hogan
Ann Hutton
Don Jim
Brent Jordan
Harry Loucks
Parke Meek
Virgil Mirano
Larry Needleman
Sheldon Nemoy
John Neuhart
Mariea Poole
Harry Robbins
James Sommers
Robert Staples
Michio Suguwara
Deborah Sussman
Yu Yoshioka

Charles and Ray taking photographs in India

Ray and Indira Gandhi, then India's minister of culture, reviewing exhibition materials at the National Institute of Design in Ahmedabad, India

1965

Exhibition: *Nehru: His Life and His India*

When Charles and Ray first went to India in 1958 in preparation for their proposal to establish an Indian institute of design (pp. 232–233), they were impressed by the extent of Prime Minister Jawaharlal Nehru's interests and the scope of his vision for the future of his country. When Indira Gandhi, shortly after her father's death in 1964, expressed an interest in organizing a traveling exhibition on his life, the Eames Office was commissioned to plan a memorial that would reflect Nehru's commitment to India and the Indian people and that could be seen by people outside the boundaries of the country as well as by the Indians themselves. Entitled *Nehru: His Life and His India*, the exhibition traveled in India, England, and the United States.

Although the exhibition could have been assembled more easily in California, Charles felt that the project was a good opportunity for the members of the National Institute of Design at Ahmedabad and the Eames Office to work together on something of mutual interest. The Eames Office collected materials and equipment and put together a traveling darkroom and other facilities to be shipped to the National Institute of Design. Ray, Deborah Sussman, Robert Staples, and Bob Anderson worked for three months in Ahmedabad with the institute, which was under the direction of Gautam and Gira Sarabhai. They were joined for short periods by Glen Fleck and Charles. Alexander Girard supervised the exhibition display of textiles and objects. Production was then completed in New York City, and the exhibition was first installed in the

Opposite: Exhibition opening night in Los Angeles. Above left: Exhibition poster. Above right: The "Nehru rose"

Top and middle: Two views of the exhibition from above. Above: A section of the exhibition on Nehru's marriage

S. Dillon Ripley, chairman of the Smithsonian Institution, at the opening of the *Nehru* exhibition in Washington, D.C.

Top left and right, middle left and right, above left and right: Views of the exhibition installed in Los Angeles, New York, and London showing graphic panels, entry area, and the Nehru timeline

Architect and designer Alexander Girard and Eames staff member Robert Staples working on fabric panels and panel assemblies for the *Nehru* exhibition

Charles and longtime friend and colleague architect and engineer Konrad Wachsman at the Eames Office

Union Carbide Building on Park Avenue.

The exhibition tells the story of Nehru's life, including his early life and marriage, his work on behalf of Indian independence, and his political relationships with British and Indian leaders before independence and after he became the state's first prime minister. The exhibition was housed in large, open spaces, divided into sections by partitions. Pavilions draped with fabric, display islands, and large display panels defined the sections, each of which dealt with a period or specific event in Nehru's life. More than 1,200 small and large photographs and 30,000 words of text, drawn mostly from Nehru's own writings and speeches, illustrated Nehru's career and goals. Artifacts collected in India were part of the exhibition, including Nehru's journals and personal memorabilia. A "History Wall" of words and images provided a decade-by-decade account of Nehru's life and chronicled political and cultural events in India and the world during his lifetime. Indira Gandhi and other members of the family assisted in the selection of documents and quotations. The exhibition ended its tour in Delhi, where it remains on permanent display.

The construction of the exhibits used materials indigenous to India. Teak pole structures with cast brass fasteners served as supports for large photo or graphic panels, and the backs of the panels, which were visible, were lined with Indian fabrics. Sandbag weights, covered in a variety of Indian cottons, stabilized the vertical poles and were disguised as cushions. The large, laminate-surfaced, freestanding wall panels were framed at both ends by fabric-covered uprights supported by weighted bolsters; brass medallions surrounded brass nail heads.

Exhibition venues: Union Carbide Building, New York City, February 1965; Royal Festival Hall, London, June 1965; Smithsonian Institution, Washington, D.C., October 1965; California Museum of Science and Industry, Los Angeles, March 1966; Delhi, India, 1966.

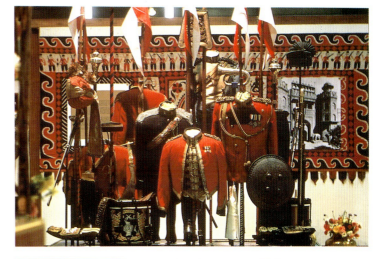

Top: A view of the costume area showing British army uniforms. Middle: Nehru's personal artifacts. Above: Close-ups of Indian objects and a display structure

A selection of images photographed in India by Charles. Many of the images were used in the India slide show assembled for the Norton Lectures in 1971 (p. 361)

April 23: Charles lectures at the First Unitarian Church, St. Louis, Missouri, on the importance of eliminating "discontinuities" from personal and institutional life.

April 27: Charles lectures at the Cranbrook Academy of Art, Cranbrook, Michigan, on current projects in the Eames Office.

Staff: 1965
901 Washington Boulevard
Bob Anderson
Victor Arzate
Joseph Bernstein
Charles Brittin
Roger Conrad
Annette Del Zoppo
Richard Donges
Glen Fleck
Russell Frears
Kenneth Grobecker
Karl Haeuser
Atsuo Haida
Keith Hall
Lars Hanson
Margaret Harris
Pamela Hedley
Ella Hogan
Ann Hutton
Don Jim
Brent Jordan
Harry Loucks
Parke Meek
Virgil Mirano
Larry Needleman
Sheldon Nemoy
John Neuhart
Mariea Poole
Harry Robbins
James Sommers
Robert Staples
Michio Sugawara
Deborah Sussman
Yu Yoshioka

Parke Meek, Charles, and Virgil Mirano during a shooting session for the film *Westinghouse in Alphabetical Order*

1965

Film: *Westinghouse in Alphabetical Order*

In the early 1960s Charles became a consultant to Westinghouse Electric Corporation on matters of corporate design. He and designer Paul Rand were brought into the company by Eliot Noyes, who served as a design consultant to both Westinghouse and the IBM Corporation. Discussions about producing a film for Westinghouse began several years before the project was finally completed. Westinghouse originally wanted the Eames Office to produce a film about its design program; instead, Charles convinced them to sponsor a film showing their extensive product line—a far more diversified output than the refrigerators, light bulbs, and fans for which the company was popularly known.

Using live-action and still images selected in large part from the company's archives, annual reports, magazine advertisements, and other sources, the film documents the full range of Westinghouse's mid-1960s line, showing the products (ranging from small household appliances made for the retail market to enormous generators and turbines made for industrial use) in alphabetical order by corporate inventory name. The multitude of products is presented in quick succession, accompanied by a choral group singing the name of each item as it is shown.

The film is a good example of Charles's fondness for packing as much information as possible into a presentation. The quick-cut technique was used here to cover the entire Westinghouse inventory, which was represented by photographs of varying style and format (the Eames Office photographed only a few items). The music acts as a bridge between items and as a unifying element for the visual material. The "libretto" was assembled by Victor Arzate, and the music was composed and conducted by Elmer Bernstein. The film has no narration and is not in general circulation. (Running time, *Westinghouse in Alphabetical Order*: 12 minutes; Color.)

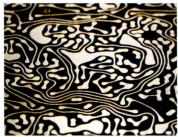

A sequence of frames (reading top to bottom left, top to bottom right) of Westinghouse products chosen from scenes in *Westinghouse in Alphabetical Order*. The products are seen one at a time in the film. The frames were photographed from 16mm-film footage

May 3: Charles lectures to architectural students at the University of Oregon in Eugene.

May 4: Charles speaks at an architectural students' seminar, Portland, Oregon.

Staff: 1965
901 Washington Boulevard
Bob Anderson
Victor Arzate
Joseph Bernstein
Charles Brittin
Roger Conrad
Annette Del Zoppo
Richard Donges
Glen Fleck
Russell Frears
Kenneth Grobecker
Karl Haeuser
Atsuo Haida
Keith Hall
Lars Hanson
Margaret Harris
Pamela Hedley
Ella Hogan
Ann Hutton
Don Jim
Brent Jordan
Harry Loucks
Parke Meek
Virgil Mirano
Larry Needleman
Sheldon Nemoy
John Neuhart
Mariea Poole
Harry Robbins
James Sommers
Robert Staples
Michio Suguwara
Deborah Sussman
Yu Yoshioka

Charles and the office staff celebrate the Fourth of July with glasses designed by Deborah Sussman

1965

Film: *The Smithsonian Institution*

This film was made for the Smithsonian Institution, with sponsorship from the IBM Corporation, for a special celebration of the two-hundredth anniversary of the birth of James M. Smithson, a French-born English citizen and chemist who bequeathed money to found the institution. (Smithson, who never visited America, left half a million dollars "to the United States of America, to found at Washington, under the name of the Smithsonian Institution, an establishment for the increase and diffusion of knowledge among men.") The film chronicles Smithson's life, the events that led to the establishment of the institution by an act of Congress in 1846, and the efforts of other individuals who helped define the Smithsonian's character and goals. Historical moments are reenacted, and the film concludes with a glimpse of the vast collections in the "nation's attic."

The film, which was the first time the full story of the Smithsonian had been compiled as a movie, required a shooting session at the Royal Academy in London (of Smithson artifacts and records) and considerable researching of the Smithsonian collections; these tasks were organized by Glen Fleck, with assistance from Karen Loveland of the Smithsonian.

The Smithsonian Institution is composed primarily of live-action footage with the addition of some still images. Several Smithsonian curators acted in the historical sequences, re-creating events from the institution's past. Glen Fleck wrote the script with Charles. The film was narrated by Walter Cronkite and Alistair Cooke, with a closing statement by S. Dillon Ripley, Secretary of the Smithsonian. The music was composed by Elmer Bernstein. The film has not had a wide audience and is not in general circulation. (Running time, *The Smithsonian Institution*: 20 minutes, 30 seconds; color.)

A sequence of frames (reading top to bottom left, top to bottom right) from scenes in *The Smithsonian Institution*. The frames were photographed from 16mm-film footage

May 6: Charles lectures at the School of Architecture, University of California, Berkeley.

Staff: 1965
901 Washington Boulevard
Bob Anderson
Victor Arzate
Joseph Bernstein
Charles Brittin
Roger Conrad
Annette Del Zoppo
Richard Donges
Glen Fleck
Russell Frears
Kenneth Grobecker
Karl Haeuser
Atsuo Haida
Keith Hall
Lars Hanson
Margaret Harris
Pamela Hedley
Ella Hogan
Ann Hutton
Don Jim
Brent Jordan
Harry Loucks
Parke Meek
Virgil Mirano
Larry Needleman
Sheldon Nemoy
John Neuhart
Mariea Poole
Harry Robbins
James Sommers
Robert Staples
Michio Sugawara
Deborah Sussman
Yu Yoshioka

1965

Film: *Computer Day at Midvale*

Computer Day at Midvale is a film record of one of two electronically controlled puppet shows made by the Eames Office for the IBM pavilion (pp. 284–291) at the 1964–1965 New York World's Fair. The puppet shows, which were seen in small theaters on the grounds of the pavilion, were used at the fair to convey basic information about new technology in a traditional and entertaining way. They were filmed by the Eames Office during the fair to document the performances.

In the imaginary town of Midvale, the mayor and a computer expert, Dr. Miles White, appear before the townspeople to commemorate the installation of the town's first computer. The mayor arrives at some erroneous conclusions about the way computers work, conclusions that reflect some common misconceptions. These misunderstandings are then corrected by the computer expert. The puppets in this film were really automatons, controlled and programmed by a complex mechanism built into the puppet set.

The puppets' dialogue was written by Glen Fleck and I.A.L. Diamond and spoken by Herbert Vigran and John Erwin. The theater and sets were designed by Deborah Sussman and Gordon Ashby. The music was written (slightly off-key) by Elmer Bernstein for Midvale's Charles W. Babbage Junior High School Marching Band. The film is in general circulation. On the same reel is a film of the second puppet show, *The Singular Case of the Plural Green Mustache*. (Running time, *Computer Day at Midvale* plus *The Singular Case of the Plural Green Mustache*: 9 minutes; color.)

A sequence of frames (reading top to bottom left, top to bottom right) from scenes in *Computer Day at Midvale*. The frames were photographed from 16mm-film footage

September 30: Charles is the keynote speaker at the National Meeting of the Industrial Design Society of America, New York City.

Staff: 1965
901 Washington Boulevard
Bob Anderson
Victor Arzate
Joseph Bernstein
Charles Brittin
Roger Conrad
Annette Del Zoppo
Richard Donges
Glen Fleck
Russell Frears
Kenneth Grobecker
Karl Haeuser
Atsuo Haida
Keith Hall
Lars Hanson
Margaret Harris
Pamela Hedley
Ella Hogan
Ann Hutton
Don Jim
Brent Jordan
Harry Loucks
Parke Meek
Virgil Mirano
Larry Needleman
Sheldon Nemoy
John Neuhart
Mariea Poole
Harry Robbins
James Sommers
Robert Staples
Deborah Sussman
Michio Sugawara
Yu Yoshioka

1965

Film: *Sherlock Holmes in the Singular Case of the Plural Green Mustache: Based on the Characters by Sir Arthur Conan Doyle in Which Sherlock Holmes Uses His Mastery of 2-Valued Logic to Solve a Baffling Problem*

This is the film record of the second of two computer-run puppet shows in the IBM pavilion at the New York World's Fair in 1964–1965 (see opposite page). The film uses the characters of Sherlock Holmes and Dr. Watson to demonstrate by example an important concept in computer programming. Holmes solves a crime by his usual method of deduction, which is a method structurally identical to the Boolean logic (a symbolic way of stating a problem in terms of true or false decisions) used in programming the electronic digital computer.

The dialogue was written by Glen Fleck and spoken by Hillary Wontner and Patrick O'Moore. Deborah Sussman and Gordon Ashby designed the set and the puppets. The music included sound effects and was composed by Elmer Bernstein. (Running time, *Computer Day at Midvale* plus *The Singular Case of the Plural Green Mustache*: 9 minutes; color.)

A sequence of frames (reading top to bottom left, top to bottom right) from scenes in *The Singular Case of the Plural Green Mustache*. The frames were photographed from 16mm-film footage

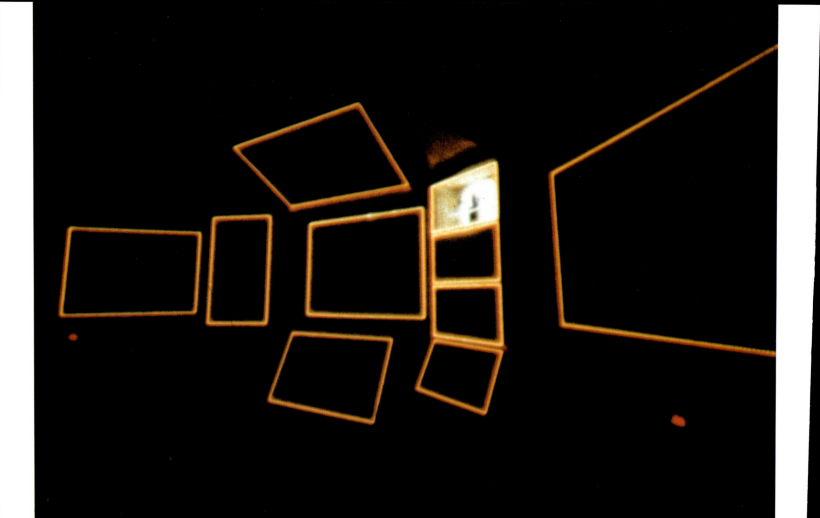

October 15: Charles serves as a member of the Design Forum, "Good Design, Good Business," London, England.

Staff: 1965
901 Washington Boulevard
Bob Anderson
Victor Arzate
Joseph Bernstein
Charles Brittin
Roger Conrad
Annette Del Zoppo
Richard Donges
Glen Fleck
Russell Frears
Kenneth Grobecker
Karl Haeuser
Atsuo Haida
Keith Hall
Lars Hanson
Margaret Harris
Pamela Hedley
Ella Hogan
Ann Hutton
Don Jim
Brent Jordan
Harry Loucks
Parke Meek
Virgil Mirano
Larry Needleman
Sheldon Nemoy
John Neuhart
Mariea Poole
Harry Robbins
James Sommers
Robert Staples
Michio Sugawara
Deborah Sussman
Yu Yoshioka

IBM design consultant Eliot Noyes during a visit to the Eames Office

1965

Film: *IBM at the Fair*

IBM at the Fair was made as a film souvenir of the IBM pavilion at the 1964–1965 New York World's Fair (pp. 284–291). The film is composed of live-action film footage and still photographs shot by cameraman Mike Murphy, Charles, and members of the Eames Office staff during the run of the fair. Fast-cutting and time-lapse photography create a high-speed montage of visitors moving through the various attractions in the pavilion, revealing patterns of movement not apparent in real-time footage. There is a brief glimpse of the People Wall being lifted into the Ovoid Theater, where the multiscreen film *Think* was shown. Other exhibition elements—graphics from the *Mathematica* exhibition and two electronic puppet shows—are seen briefly in this quick tour.

IBM at the Fair is another of the films Charles made to capture the mood and atmosphere of a passing event; the pace is lively, and although the viewer is not given much hard documentary information, a sense of celebration is conveyed.

IBM at the Fair includes some glimpses of Charles and Ray, Eames Office staff members, and IBM personnel. Richard Sargeant is the pavilion host. There is no narration; the musical score was composed by Elmer Bernstein. The film is in general circulation. (Running time, *IBM at the Fair*: 7 minutes, 30 seconds; color.)

Above: A sequence of frames (reading top to bottom left, top to bottom right) from scenes in *IBM at the Fair*. The frames were photographed from 16mm-film footage. Opposite: Two frames from the beginning of *IBM at the Fair*

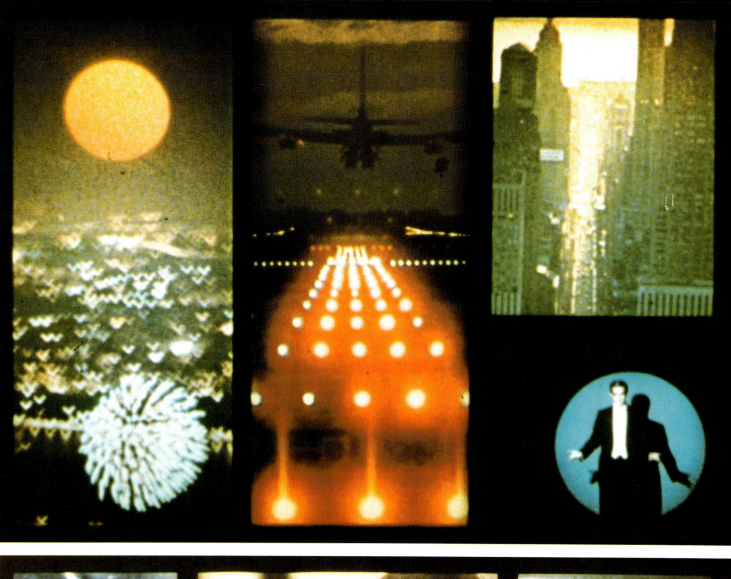

February 15: Charles speaks at Harvard University, Cambridge, Massachusetts, on general issues in contemporary design.

February: Charles lectures at the University of California, Davis, and shows slides of the current work in the office.

Staff: 1966
901 Washington Boulevard
Duane Alt
Charles Brittin
John Carter
Annette Del Zoppo
Richard Donges
Robert Falck
Glen Fleck
Russell Frears
Frank Gardony
Arnold Ginsburg
Sansi Girard
Keith Hall
Lars Hanson
Pamela Hedley
Ella Hogan
Ann Hutton
N. A. Ingrid
Ingrid Levy-Huneberg
Parke Meek
Virgil Mirano
Eugene Morris
Kenneth Nelson
Sheldon Nemoy
John Neuhart
Benjamin Nye
David Olney
Theodore Orlan
Mariea Poole
Tom Schiller
Linda Shibuya
Robert Staples
Michio Suguwara
Deborah Sussman
Peter Valdez

1966

Film: *View from the People Wall*

View from the People Wall is a 16mm single-screen composite of the multiscreen film presentation *Think*, which was shown in the Ovoid Theater of the IBM pavilion at the 1964–1965 New York World's Fair (pp. 284–291). Charles felt that the message of *Think* was valuable enough to warrant reworking the material into a film that would have a larger circulation and a longer life than the fair presentation. The single-screen film also serves as a record of the screening in the theater, which was dismantled at the end of the fair in 1965. The film was sponsored by the IBM Corporation.

The subject of *View from the People Wall* is the process of problem solving. The film begins with an explanation of the "Information Machine"—Charles's device for presenting information in fragments so that viewers are compelled to see new relationships among events, objects, and people. The narrative accompanying the images points out the parallels between solving simple and complicated problems and then demonstrates that complex problems are solved by the computer with the same logical procedures that people use to solve simple ones.

The original narration and music from *Think* were repeated for this composite film, which was adapted by Glen Fleck. The host from the fair presentation, Richard Sargeant, is the film's primary narrator. The film is in general circulation. (Running time, *View from the People Wall*: 13 minutes; color.)

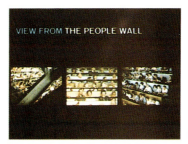 

Above: A sequence of frames (reading top to bottom left, top to bottom right) from scenes in *View from the People Wall*. The frames were photographed from 16mm-film footage. Opposite: Two frames from the beginning of *View from the People Wall*

April 15: Charles delivers a talk at Ohio University, Athens.

Staff: 1966
901 Washington Boulevard
Duane Alt
Charles Brittin
John Carter
Annette DelZoppo
Richard Donges
Robert Falck
Glen Fleck
Russell Frears
Frank Gardony
Arnold Ginsburg
Sansi Girard
Keith Hall
Lars Hanson
Pamela Hedley
Ella Hogan
Ann Hutton
N.A. Ingrid
Ingrid Levy-Huneberg
Parke Meek
Virgil Mirano
Eugene Morris
Kenneth Nelson
Sheldon Nemoy
John Neuhart
Benjamin Nye
David Olney
Theodore Orlan
Mariea Poole
Tom Schiller
Linda Shibuya
Robert Staples
Michio Suguwara
Deborah Sussman
Peter Valdez

The Eames Office produces a main title for the United States Information Agency film *Horizontes*

1966

Smithsonian Carousel

The History and Technology Division of the Smithsonian Institution asked the Eames Office to design the housing for a nineteenth-century carved wooden carousel in its collection. The structure, which was to be located on the Mall in Washington, D.C., near the Smithsonian buildings, needed to be open and accessible during the day and visible but protected at night.

The Eames Office solution, based on wooden structures Charles had seen in New England, was a faceted glass pavilion with glass doors that opened like fins during the day but could be closed and locked at night. The carousel, lighted for nighttime viewing, could be seen through the glass partitions. Architect Philo Jacobsen developed the glass structure.

A model was built and photographed, and the plans were drawn up, but the project was set aside after it was decided that maintenance of the carousel and the pavilion building would be too difficult and costly.

Top: Smithsonian carousel. Middle: Model of the proposed Eames Office glass enclosure. Above: Carousel animals

April 30: Charles receives an honorary diploma from the Eurodomus-Genoa Fair at the *First International Exhibition of the Modern House*, Genoa, Italy.

Staff:1966
901 Washington Boulevard
Duane Alt
Charles Brittin
John Carter
Annette Del Zoppo
Richard Donges
Robert Falck
Glen Fleck
Russell Frears
Frank Gardony
Arnold Ginsburg
Sansi Girard
Keith Hall
Lars Hanson
Pamela Hedley
Ella Hogan
Ann Hutton
N.A. Ingrid
Ingrid Levy-Huneberg
Parke Meek
Virgil Mirano
Eugene Morris
Sheldon Nelson
Kenneth Nemoy
John Neuhart
Benjamin Nye
David Olney
Theodore Orlan
Mariea Poole
Tom Schiller
Linda Shibuya
Robert Staples
Michio Sugawara
Deborah Sussman
Peter Valdez

Left: The cover of the September 1966 issue of *Architectural Design*, which featured the work of Charles Eames. The article included contributions by Peter and Alison Smithson, Geoffrey Holroyd, and Michael Brawne

1966

Film: *The Leading Edge*

The Leading Edge was made for the Boeing Aircraft Company's campaign to obtain the contract to build the Supersonic Transport plane (SST) for the U.S. government. One of a number of films commissioned by Boeing to explain various aspects of the aircraft, the Eames Office film demonstrated the degree to which computers are used to support design development and production in an aerospace manufacturing facility. Boeing's use of the computer for modeling products and systems coincided with Charles's long-standing interest in computer manipulation of information and in computer modeling as a method for working out problems in design.

The Leading Edge was shown along with the SST films made by other filmmakers in congressional hearings to provide information and inspire confidence in Boeing's ability to build the planes. Boeing was granted the contract, but public concern with the problem of excessive noise and supersonic blasts forced indefinite postponement of the project.

The film is composed entirely of live-action footage of aircraft-manufacturing equipment and technology photographed on location at the Boeing plant in Seattle, Washington. The narration, written by Glen Fleck with Charles and read by Sandy Kenyon, describes the approach taken by the Boeing Corporation in setting up design and manufacturing procedures for new products. The score is by David Raksin. The film is not in general circulation. (Running time, *The Leading Edge*: 11 minutes, 15 seconds; color.)

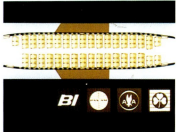

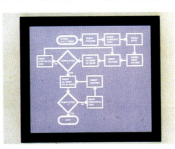

A sequence of frames (reading top to bottom left, top to bottom right) from scenes in *The Leading Edge*. The frames were photographed from 16mm-film footage

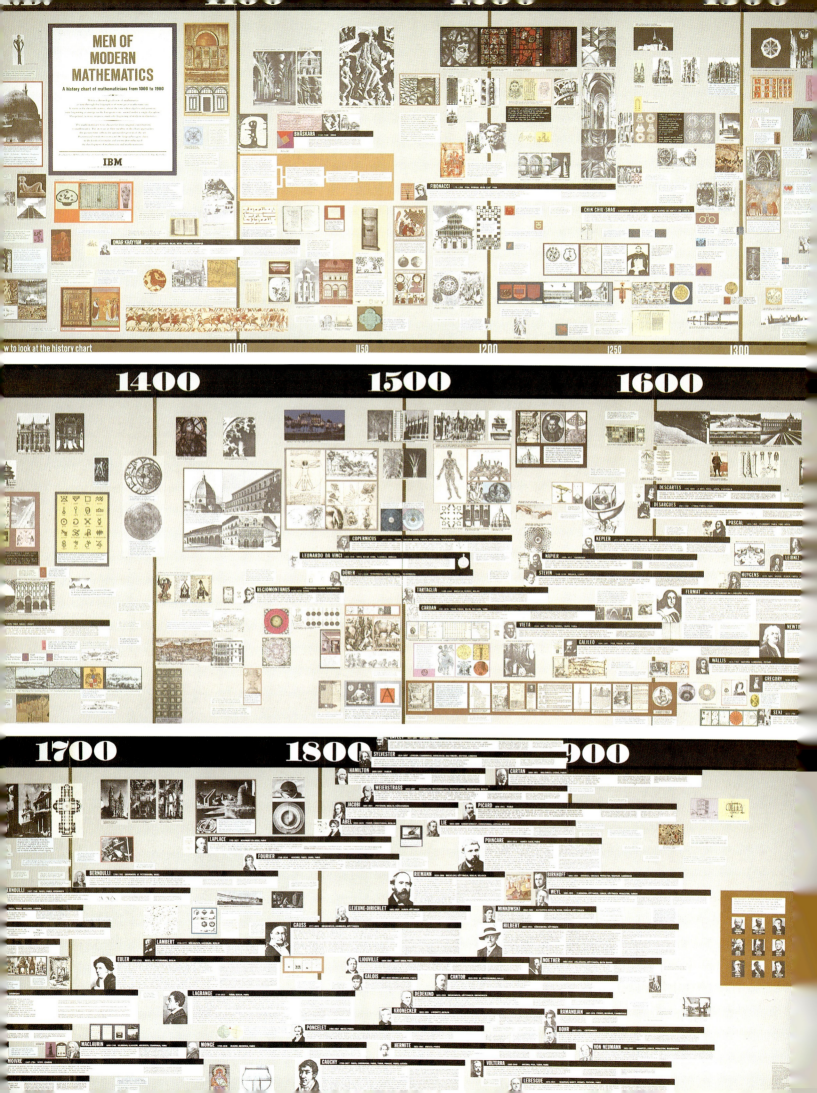

Left: *Mathematica* exhibition elements from the IBM pavilion at the 1964–1965 New York World's Fair and from the Time & Life Building lobby installed in the Pacific Science Center, Seattle, Washington (where they remained on display until 1980)

Staff: 1966
901 Washington Boulevard
Duane Alt
Charles Brittin
John Carter
Annette Del Zoppo
Richard Donges
Robert Falck
Glen Fleck
Russell Frears
Frank Gardony
Arnold Ginsburg
Sansi Girard
Keith Hall
Lars Hanson
Pamela Hedley
Ella Hogan
Ann Hutton
N.A. Ingrid
Ingrid Levy-Huneberg
Parke Meek
Virgil Mirano
Eugene Morris
Kenneth Nelson
Sheldon Nemoy
John Neuhart
Benjamin Nye
David Olney
Theodore Orlan
Mariea Poole
Tom Schiller
Linda Shibuya
Robert Staples
Michio Suguwara
Deborah Sussman
Peter Valdez

1966

Timeline: "Men of Modern Mathematics"

Produced for the IBM Corporation, the "Mathematica" timeline is a slightly modified, printed version of the History Wall from the *Mathematica* exhibition (pp. 254–259). It was printed on one wide 48-by-73 ½-inch perforated sheet, which was meant to be separated horizontally into two, attached together, and made into a wall chart 2 feet wide by 12 feet 2 ⅞ inches long. Twenty color runs were required to print the chart.

The title graphic on the chart describes the printed timeline (in keeping with the original History Wall) as a "chronological view of mathematics as seen through the biographies of some great mathematicians." Its subject is the development of mathematics in the Western world from 1100 to 1950. The biographies, separated into life and work sections and including portraits and text, were adapted from the original History Wall. Illustrations and text blocks describing significant historical and cultural events surround the biographical panels, and illustrations with captions outlining major historical milestones are positioned on the lower section of the chart as a general reference.

As in the exhibition's History Wall, the biographies and mathematical notes were researched and written by Raymond Redheffer of the Department of Mathematics at UCLA. IBM has distributed the chart to schools since 1966.

MEN OF MODERN MATHEMATICS

A history chart of mathematicians from 1000 to 1900

This is a chronological view of mathematics as seen through the biographies of some great mathematicians. It starts in the eleventh century, about the time when algebra and geometry were beginning to emerge on the European scene, united under a single discipline. This period, in many respects, marks the beginning of modern mathematics.

The mathematicians were chosen for their original contributions to mathematics. The increase in their number as the chart approaches the present time reflects the spectacular growth of the art. Pictures and words that surround the biographies give clues to the kinds of attitudes and events that influenced the development of mathematics and mathematicians.

Produced for IBM by the office of Charles Eames. Biographies and mathematical notes by Ray Redheffer.

IBM

© Copyright 1966 International Business Machines Corporation, Armonk, N.Y.

The timeline title panel

| Portrait | Name | Date of birth & death | Place of birth | Where he worked |

 **PASCAL** 1623-1662 CLERMONT; PARIS, PORT ROYAL

ATTENDING NO SCHOOL, BLAISE PASCAL LEARNED CLASSICS FROM HIS FATHER, GEOMETRY BEING WITHHELD UNTIL THE BOY, AGE 12, DISCOVERED A THEOREM ON HIS OWN. HIS "PROVINCIAL LETTERS," COMPOSED AFTER HE LEFT SCIENCE FOR THEOLOGY, ARE A GLORY OF FRENCH PROSE.

Pascal's concise essay on conics, written at 16, contains contributions to projective geometry rivaling those of his teacher, Desargues. This was followed three years later by his adding machine, and still later by probability developed jointly with Fermat.

Personal biography — **Mathematical achievements**

Above: Panel from the printed timeline displaying biographical information on the French mathematician Blaise Pascal. Opposite: The printed timeline (divided into three sections for inclusion in this volume)

Views of the showroom: Top: La Fonda and Aluminum Group furniture with the Anchor block mural. Above: A section of the Nelson layout of Herman Miller's museum collection with photographs of the designers

June 25: Charles speaks at the "Design Around Us" conference at Stanford University, Palo Alto, California.

Staff: 1966
901 Washington Boulevard
Duane Alt
Charles Brittin
John Carter
Annette Del Zoppo
Richard Donges
Robert Falck
Glen Fleck
Russell Frears
Frank Gardony
Arnold Ginsburg
Sansi Girard
Keith Hall
Lars Hanson
Pamela Hedley
Ella Hogan
Ann Hutton
N. A. Ingrid
Ingrid Levy-Huneberg
Parke Meek
Virgil Mirano
Eugene Morris
Kenneth Nelson
Sheldon Nemoy
John Neuhart
Benjamin Nye
David Olney
Theodore Orlan
Mariea Poole
Tom Schiller
Linda Shibuya
Robert Staples
Michio Suguwara
Deborah Sussman
Peter Valdez

Staff member Russell Frears working on a model of the Herman Miller showroom

Deborah Sussman and Ray installing objects in the furniture showroom

1966

Herman Miller, Inc., Showroom

To celebrate their New York City branch's move to new office and showroom facilities at 600 Madison Avenue in New York City, Herman Miller asked George Nelson, Alexander Girard, and the Eameses to collaborate on the interior planning of the new space and the installation of new furniture settings, props, and graphics. Each designer planned part of the showroom: Nelson was responsible for the architecture of the overall space, a museumlike display of examples of Herman Miller's classic furniture, as well as for groupings of his Action Office system (a flexible system of panels, desks, and storage areas for offices). Girard arranged the displays of his new fabrics and his "Textiles & Objects" collection (folk art and accessories on sale in the Herman Miller Textiles & Objects shops.) The Eames Office (Deborah Sussman and Russell Frears) designed the display for the furniture areas. The installation was later re-created in Herman Miller's Chicago and Los Angeles showrooms.

Eames furniture featured in the showroom included versions of the Tandem Seating systems—with fiberglass-shell chairs, armchair shells and La Fonda armchair and side chair shells, La Fonda chairs and tables, and the Sofa Compact. Plywood chairs and other furniture from the Herman Miller catalog designed by each of the three designers were distributed throughout the installation. In the New York City showroom each structural column was given a unique graphic treatment. One was covered by a cracked mirror; another appeared to be a stack of seats; others were covered with photographic murals of trees, trompe l'oeil patterns, shadows of people on a sidewalk, Palmer Cox toys, and a photo of gyrating teenagers. An architectural drawing, enlarged to the size of a mural, was hung behind a row of Eames School Seating; a photographic mural of an Anchor block structure (a nineteenth-century building toy) and another of a group of trees provided backdrops for other furniture. A mock-up of a photographer's studio, complete with lights and camera, no-seam paper backdrop, ladder, stools, tripods, and a photographer's black head covering stood ready for use in a corner.

The Los Angeles showroom featured Eames Tandem Seating systems, Eames Contract Storage units and segmented tables, Aluminum Group furniture, Girard's La Fonda and L'Etoile furniture, and Nelson furniture.

Although the 1966 installation was the last major showroom designed by the Eames Office, the Eameses continued to design settings on occasion until 1976, when Herman Miller moved from the Beverly Boulevard location to the Pacific Design Center.

Top: Eames furniture placed among the graphic columns. Middle: The Anchor block mural. Above: Graphic columns of a stack of seats and Palmer Cox toys with Nelson, Girard, and Eames furniture

Staff: 1966
901 Washington Boulevard
Duane Alt
Charles Brittin
John Carter
Annette Del Zoppo
Richard Donges
Robert Falck
Glen Fleck
Russell Frears
Frank Gardony
Arnold Ginsburg
Sansi Girard
Keith Hall
Lars Hanson
Pamela Hedley
Ella Hogan
Ann Hutton
N.A. Ingrid
Ingrid Levy-Huneberg
Parke Meek
Virgil Mirano
Eugene Morris
Kenneth Nelson
Sheldon Nemoy
John Neuhart
Benjamin Nye
David Olney
Theodore Orlan
Mariea Poole
Tom Schiller
Linda Shibuya
Robert Staples
Michio Suguwara
Deborah Sussman
Peter Valdez

The Italian architect Gio Ponti, Charles, and unidentified guests

The Eames Office develops a proposal for the Time & Life Building's plaza, New York City

1966–1969

National Aquarium Proposal

On October 9, 1962, an act of Congress authorized the development of a National Fisheries Center and Aquarium. The center's mandate was to be a focus of scientific research committed to the display of aquatic life for "educational, recreational, cultural, and scientific purposes." The aquarium was to be situated one mile south of the Mall, on the island that forms East Potomac Park in Washington, D.C. Kevin Roche, John Dinkeloo and Associates, the architectural firm awarded the contract for the aquarium proposal, commissioned the Eames Office to design the aquarium exhibitions, graphics, films, and other related materials. In 1966 Stewart Udall, Secretary of the Interior, presented the joint Roche Dinkeloo/Eames proposal to a congressional committee.

The Eames Office produced flat graphic panels and a scale model for the proposal, which included the exterior design of the building and plans for the 166,000 square feet of exhibition, gallery, research, and administrative space. The aquarium consisted of three major areas: a ground level, divided into a modular arrangement of concourse, live-specimen galleries, orientation areas, special exhibits, offices, and research areas; an open upper terrace conceived as a large aquatic garden with various exhibits; and a one-hundred-foot-high greenhouse containing three ecosystems.

Conservation was the underlying concept behind the proposed aquarium exhibits. The stated aim was to demonstrate that everyone can help preserve and protect the environment by, in Charles's words, "coming to have a

Above: Plan view of the model of the aquarium. Opposite: One-inch scale model of the aquarium

Top: Orientation area of the aquarium model. Middle: The stairway from the lower level to the upper concourse. Above: A view into the entrance of the National Aquarium

Myra Maxwell working on the National Aquarium Species Wall, photographed in 1969

more informed respect for it." The displays of aquatic life were to have included "birds, insects, amphibians, and growing plants, with special stress on the delicate balance among them."

Warren J. Wisby, director of the National Fisheries Center and Aquarium, was the major force behind the project. Malcolm Gordon of UCLA served as scientific consultant to the Eames Office.

Large tanks with complete habitats of marine life were maintained in the Eames Office as part of the Eameses' effort to understand scientists' views of the aquatic world and make them accessible to the exhibition visitor. Many photographs and a large quantity of live-action footage were taken of the marine life in the tanks, including all of the scenes in the film *A Small Hydromedusan* (p. 350).

Although Congress had appropriated funds for the aquarium, a moratorium was placed on all government building in Washington. Thus, the plans for the aquarium were not developed beyond the proposal stage. In 1967 the Eames Office produced a film detailing the aquarium proposals (p. 318), and in 1969 a booklet on the aquarium (pp. 340–341) was designed and produced containing a synopsis of the major points covered in the original proposal. In spite of the continuing efforts of all involved, the aquarium project was canceled by the Nixon administration after the departure of Secretary of the Interior Walter J. Hickel, a proponent of the aquarium proposal.

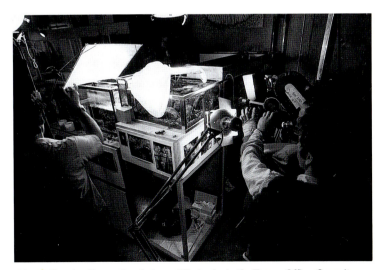

Above: Shooting live-action footage of the tanks in the Eames Office. Opposite: Photographs of marine life in tanks at the Eames Office

Top: Staff member Sam Passalacqua photographing marine life. Middle: Staff member Charles Brittin preparing to photograph the greenhouse area of the model. Above: A preliminary layout of the Species Wall

February 23: Charles lectures at the School of Architecture, University of Illinois, Carbondale.

Charles is a consultant on plans for a new campus at Immaculate Heart College, Los Angeles, California.

Staff: 1967
901 Washington Boulevard
Charles Brittin
Judith Bronowski
Paul Bruhwiler
Barbara Charles
Richard Claybour
Darryl Conybeare
Annette Del Zoppo
Richard Donges
Jan Eisenbart
Wayne Elgar
Glen Fleck
Marlene Gerloff
Gary Gregson
Keith Hall
Lars Hanson
Pamela Hedley
Robert Helfrich
Ella Hogan
Ann Hutton
David Jack
John Kuiper
Carl Magnusson
Parke Meek
Sergio Miranda
Virgil Mirano
Michael Monchette
Kenneth Nelson
Pat Naritomi
David Olney
Theodore Orlan
Antti Paatero
Sam Passalacqua
Mariea Poole
Frank Romero
Mark Rosenthal
Adrienne Russell
Charles Saunders
Robert Staples
Frank Styduhar
Michio Suguwara
Deborah Sussman
Peter Valdez
Clinton Wade
Rosa Zaldivar

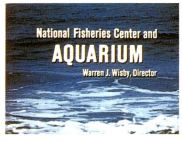

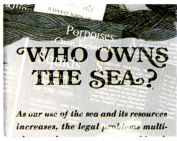

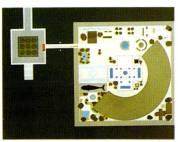

A sequence of frames (reading top to bottom left, top to bottom right) from scenes in *National Fisheries Center and Aquarium*. The frames were photographed from 16mm-film footage

1967

Film: *National Fisheries Center and Aquarium*

National Fisheries Center and Aquarium is a film report commissioned by Stewart Udall, Secretary of the Interior, and developed later for his successor, Walter J. Hickel, to assist them in their efforts to promote the proposed National Fisheries Center and Aquarium in Washington, D.C. (pp. 314–317). In 1969 a booklet by the same title (pp. 340–341) was developed from the film.

The film sets forth the objectives of the center, shows its chosen locale in East Potomac Park on the banks of the Potomac River, describes the building's architectural program, and gives a guided tour through a model of the galleries and exhibits. According to Charles's narration, "the principal goal [of the exhibition center] is much the same as science: to give the visitor some understanding of the natural world. If the National Aquarium is as good as it can be, it will do just that."

National Fisheries was made from still photos and transparencies transferred to film, live-action location photography, and footage of the model and of live marine specimens filmed in the Eames Office. Additional animated sequences were drawn by Glen Fleck. Charles wrote and read the narration. Accompanying music was composed by Buddy Collette and performed by guitarist Herb Ellis. The film is in general circulation. (Running time, *National Fisheries Center and Aquarium*: 10 minutes, 30 seconds; color.)

Staff: 1967
901 Washington Boulevard
Charles Brittin
Judith Bronowski
Paul Bruhwiler
Barbara Charles
Richard Claybour
Darryl Conybeare
Annette Del Zoppo
Richard Donges
Jan Eisenbart
Wayne Elgar
Glen Fleck
Marlene Gerloff
Gary Gregson
Keith Hall
Lars Hanson
Pamela Hedley
Robert Helfrich
Ella Hogan
Ann Hutton
David Jack
John Kuiper
Carl Magnusson
Parke Meek
Sergio Miranda
Virgil Mirano
Michael Monchette
Pat Naritomi
Kenneth Nelson
David Olney
Theodore Orlan
Antti Paatero
Sam Passalacqua
Mariea Poole
Frank Romero
Adrienne Russell
Mark Rosenthal
Charles Saunders
Robert Staples
Frank Styduhar
Michio Suguwara
Deborah Sussman
Peter Valdez
Clinton Wade
Rosa Zaldivar

1967

Slide Show: *G.E.M.*

Originally entitled *Excellence, G.E.M.*, or *Government, Education, and Management*, was a 345-image, 3-screen, (115-pass) slide show. It was first seen in Miami, Florida, in March 1967 at an IBM Corporation "Corporate Recognition Event" for the IBM's "Hundred Percent Club." The images and narration addressed favorite Eames lecture topics: the need to look anew at familiar details that are often taken for granted and "excellence"—commitment to work and an understanding of the true meaning of "quality." Charles made the following comments as the slides were shown:

> One could be sure that in the past when a man would rise to the point of producing work of great quality, it was not through any conscious attempt to excel but rather because he cared about what he was doing—he was committed to his work. This has become something rare—because being committed means becoming involved and to become involved means giving something of oneself. It is only the rare ones today who seem to care that much. Yet, that quality that makes for excellence—that commitment—is more important to us today on a daily operational basis than perhaps ever before.
>
> At least one of the reasons this is true is quite simple. The nature of the problems we face changes even as we work with them. We cannot tell from what disciplines or from what art the preparation for the next step will come. We cannot fall back on the lore of the art because that lore does not yet exist. There is, however, a tradition that is held in common by natural philosophers, explorers, pioneer woodsmen—anyone who in his daily life has been compelled to face new problems. That is a tradition of respect and concern for the properties and the quality of everything in the world around them.
>
> To excel in the structuring of a problem we must be committed to a concern for quality in everything around us. We must learn to care deeply.

Many of the slides were pulled from previous slide shows, going back to *Lecture I* (pp. 50–51). *G.E.M.* was shown again at the April 1967 Photographers Convention in Century City, Los Angeles. With the last nine passes changed and renamed *Smithsonian Gems*, it was shown again at the Smithsonian Institution in December 1967.

A sequence of 3-image passes (reading top to bottom) from the 3-screen slide show, *G.E.M.* Each set of 3 images was used as the visual exemplification of some point in Charles's presentation

Charles is awarded the Medal of Art by the Alumni Association of the Philadelphia College of Art, Philadelphia, Pennsylvania.

May 23: Charles attends the annual reception of the Faculty of Royal Designers for Industry at the Royal Society of the Arts, London, England.

Staff: 1967
901 Washington Boulevard
Charles Brittin
Judith Bronowski
Paul Bruhwiler
Barbara Charles
Richard Claybour
Darryl Conybeare
Annette Del Zoppo
Richard Donges
Jan Eisenbart
Wayne Elgar
Glen Fleck
Marlene Gerloff
Gary Gregson
Keith Hall
Lars Hanson
Pamela Hedley
Robert Helfrich
Ella Hogan
Ann Hutton
David Jack
John Kuiper
Carl Magnusson
Parke Meek
Sergio Miranda
Virgil Mirano
Michael Monchette
Pat Naritomi
Kenneth Nelson
David Olney
Theodore Orlan
Antti Paatero
Sam Passalacqua
Mariea Poole
Frank Romero
Mark Rosenthal
Adrienne Russell
Charles Saunders
Robert Staples
Frank Styduhar
Michio Suguwara
Deborah Sussman
Peter Valdez
Clinton Wade
Rosa Zaldivar

1967

Film: *The Scheutz Machine*

The Scheutz Machine is a cinematic record of the hand-powered calculating machine—a "Difference Engine"—built by Georg and Edvard Scheutz in Sweden in 1853. The machine, one of two built, was based on the plans for the Difference Engine designed by Charles Babbage in England in the mid-nineteenth century. The Scheutz machine, unlike the Babbage engine, actually performed calculations; the machine in the film was used at the Dudley Observatory in Albany, New York, to calculate astronomical tables. The engine is one of the important milestones in the history of calculating and computing; it is now in the collections of the Smithsonian Institution in Washington, D.C. (Its pair is in the Science Museum in London.) The film is composed entirely of live-action, close-up footage (photographed at the Smithsonian) of the machine in action—performing calculations and printing tables.

Produced for the IBM Corporation, *The Scheutz Machine* is a model of the type of film Charles planned to use in the proposed IBM museum on computer history (pp. 328–329). The original music was "The Work Song" by Herb Alpert and the Tijuana Brass. *The Scheutz Machine* was later combined with the Babbage film (p. 326) and accompanied by music by David Spear. There is no narration, and the film is in general circulation. (Running time, *The Scheutz Machine* original length: 4 minutes, 40 seconds; color.)

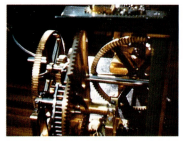

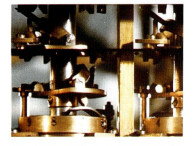

A sequence of frames (reading top to bottom left, top to bottom right) from scenes in *The Scheutz Machine*. The frames were photographed from 16mm-film footage

The Eames House is given the Grand Prix Award by the American Institute of Architects, Southern California Chapter, Los Angeles, California.

Staff: 1967
901 Washington Boulevard
Charles Brittin
Judith Bronowski
Paul Bruhwiler
Barbara Charles
Richard Claybour
Darryl Conybeare
Annette Del Zoppo
Richard Donges
Jan Eisenbart
Wayne Elgar
Glen Fleck
Marlene Gerloff
Gary Gregson
Keith Hall
Lars Hanson
Pamela Hedley
Robert Helfrich
Ella Hogan
Ann Hutton
David Jack
John Kuiper
Carl Magnusson
Parke Meek
Sergio Miranda
Virgil Mirano
Michael Monchette
Pat Naritomi
Kenneth Nelson
David Olney
Theodore Orlan
Antti Paatero
Sam Passalacqua
Mariea Poole
Frank Romero
Mark Rosenthal
Adrienne Russell
Charles Saunders
Robert Staples
Frank Styduhar
Michio Suguwara
Deborah Sussman
Peter Valdez
Clinton Wade
Rosa Zaldivar

D. J. De Pree of Herman Miller, Inc., and Ray with the Herman Miller timeline

1967

Slide Show: *Herman Miller International*

In 1967 Herman Miller, Inc., sponsored an international conference for thirteen of its licensees from Europe, South America, and Japan. The group, invited to meet each of Herman Miller's three top designers, was taken first to New York City to meet George Nelson and then to Chicago and the Herman Miller corporate headquarters in Zeeland, Michigan. From there they traveled to Santa Fe, New Mexico, to meet architect and designer Alexander and Susan Girard and then on to Los Angeles for "A Day with Charles Eames." The group, which by then had grown to seventy-five people, including D. J. De Pree, his wife, Nellie, and sons Hugh and Max, was invited to the Eames House for a picnic lunch in a tent on the meadow. Everyone was given the Eames Office's timeline of Herman Miller's history (pp. 322–323), and after lunch the group went to the Eames Office to see films, slide shows, and works in progress. The surprise highlight of the afternoon, however, was a three-screen slide show of 156 images drawn from the group's own trip across the United States. The photographers accompanying them had been secretly sending their film to the Eames Office for inclusion in the show.

Con Boeve of Herman Miller, the organizer and leader of the tour, has described the experience:

> All of a sudden this shed that's his [Eames's] studio just resounded with a stereophonic "Stars and Stripes Forever." I mean, it just blew the roof off that place. And here on the wall is a three-screen projection going on covering the U.S. trip—including Disneyland—of all these people who were sitting there watching.
>
> They had stayed up all night, those Eames people, doing those slides. I'm telling you, it was just the most amazing thing. They cried, those licensees. They literally cried.

The show was screened once publicly. John Philip Sousa's "Stars and Stripes Forever" accompanied the slides; the show had no narration or commentary.

A sequence of 3-image passes (reading top to bottom) selected from the slide show *Herman Miller International*

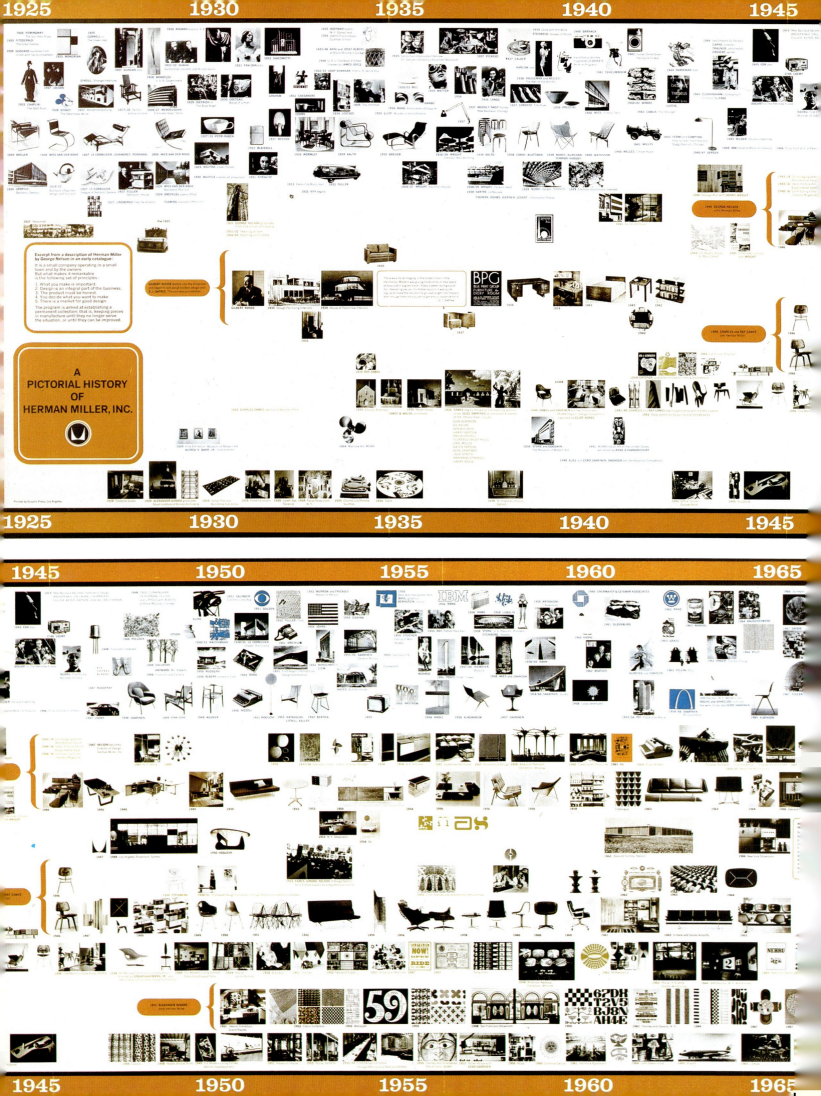

January 25: Charles attends a meeting of the board of directors of the Center for the Arts of Indian America.

February 9: Charles speaks at the Institute of Contemporary Arts, Boston, Massachusetts.

Staff: 1967
901 Washington Boulevard
Charles Brittin
Judith Bronowski
Paul Bruhwiler
Barbara Charles
Richard Claybour
Darryl Conybeare
Annette Del Zoppo
Richard Donges
Jan Eisenbart
Wayne Elgar
Glen Fleck
Marlene Gerloff
Gary Gregson
Keith Hall
Lars Hanson
Pamela Hedley
Robert Helfrich
Ella Hogan
Ann Hutton
David Jack
John Kuiper
Carl Magnusson
Parke Meek
Sergio Miranda
Virgil Mirano
Michael Monchette
Pat Naritomi
Kenneth Nelson
David Olney
Theodore Orlan
Antti Paatero
Sam Passalacqua
Mariea Poole
Frank Romero
Mark Rosenthal
Adrienne Russell
Charles Saunders
Robert Staples
Frank Styduhar
Michio Suguwara
Deborah Sussman
Peter Valdez
Clinton Wade
Rosa Zaldivar

1967

Timeline: A Pictorial History of Herman Miller, Inc.

The Eames Office produced an illustrated timeline for Herman Miller, Inc., in 1967. Beginning in 1927 and ending in 1967, the year of its publication, it shows in detail the work of designers George Nelson, Charles and Ray Eames, and Alexander Girard, from the dates of their first association with Herman Miller in 1946, late 1946, and 1951, respectively.

The timeline is divided into three horizontal strips marked vertically in ten-year increments. The top band outlines developments in the arts (painting, sculpture, architecture, design, literature, music, dance, film, theater) and the work of other designers and architects. The middle band traces events in the history of Herman Miller, Inc., starting with the work of Gilbert Rohde for Herman Miller (their first involvement with the "modern" movement in furniture) in the 1930s. The professional biographies of Nelson, the Eameses, and Girard, including their work for Herman Miller and other major projects, occupy the bottom band.

The 14 ½-by-42-inch wall chart was printed in three colors by Graphic Press in Los Angeles. Deborah Sussman and Barbara Charles worked on the design and research. It was given first to the Herman Miller International group at a picnic at the Eames House on September 21, 1967, and later made available to Herman Miller clients and interested students. It is now out of print.

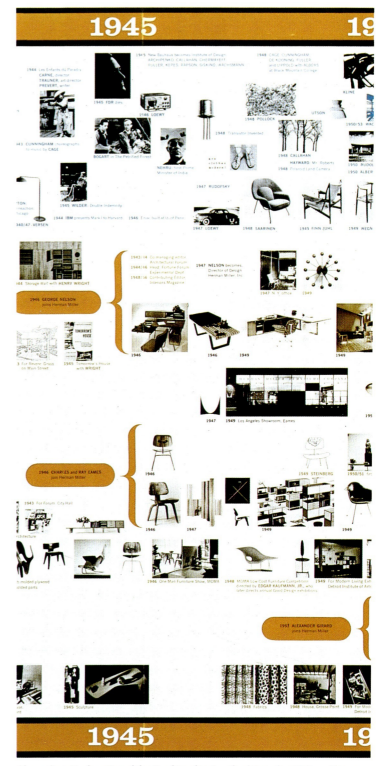

Above: A vertical section of the timeline showing the dates when Nelson, Eames, and Girard first began their association with Herman Miller. Opposite: The printed timeline (divided into two sections for this volume)

323

September 27: Charles receives the Design Medal from the Society of Industrial Artists and Designers of Great Britain, London, England.

Charles receives the Design Award from the Centro de Investigación de Diseño Industrial, Buenos Aires, Argentina, for the Aluminum Group side chair and armchair, the fiberglass chairs, the Time-Life and Executive Desk chairs, and the segmented table.

Staff: 1967
901 Washington Boulevard
Charles Brittin
Judith Bronowski
Paul Bruhwiler
Barbara Charles
Richard Claybour
Darryl Conybeare
Annette Del Zoppo
Richard Donges
Jan Eisenbart
Wayne Elgar
Glen Fleck
Marlene Gerloff
Gary Gregson
Keith Hall
Lars Hanson
Pamela Hedley
Robert Helfrich
Ella Hogan
Ann Hutton
David Jack
John Kuiper
Carl Magnusson
Parke Meek
Sergio Miranda
Virgil Mirano
Michael Monchette
Pat Naritomi
Kenneth Nelson
David Olney
Theodore Orlan
Antti Paatero
Sam Passalacqua
Mariea Poole
Frank Romero
Mark Rosenthal
Adrienne Russell
Charles Saunders
Robert Staples
Frank Styduhar
Michio Suguwara
Deborah Sussman
Peter Valdez
Clinton Wade
Rosa Zaldivar

1967

Slide Show: *Picasso*

The images for *Picasso*, a 96-slide, 3-screen (32-pass) slide show, were photographed by Charles during an impromptu, one-hour visit to an exhibition of Picasso's work at The Museum of Modern Art in New York City. The images, close-ups and details of sculpture, paintings, and drawings, provide intimate views of many of the exhibited items. The slide show, put together for friends who missed the exhibition, was also shown at a Friends of the Smithsonian meeting in 1967. At some showings, the slides were accompanied by classical music; at others, by a recorded Gertrude Stein reading from her writings on Picasso.

The *Picasso* slide show is another of Charles's attempts to capture a passing event and preserve its "essence" through photography. Beginning with the 1955 film *Textiles and Ornamental Arts of India* (pp. 200–201), these efforts were not intended to be documentary records but instead, to be visual syntheses of the "spirit" of the exhibition experience as seen through Charles's eyes.

A sequence of 3-image passes (reading top to bottom) from the slide show *Picasso*, showing details of paintings, sculpture, and drawings

Staff: 1968
901 Washington Boulevard
Carol Berryman
Charles Brittin
Judith Bronowski
Jeffrey Brosk
Paul Bruhwiler
John Bulthius
Linda Buzzell
Barbara Charles
Roger Conrad
Darryl Conybeare
Douglas Cox
Annette Del Zoppo
Raul de Brigard
Richard Donges
Raymond Duddies
Carl Duzen
Maria Ewing
Honor Field
Glen Fleck
Richard Foy
Alex Funke
Breon Gilleran
Keith Hall
Pamela Hedley
Gary Hinckley
Ella Hogan
David Jack
Joslin Jerl
Hap Johnson
Ruth Laug
Carl Magnusson
Parke Meek
William Miner
Virgil Mirano
Jill Mitchell
Pat Naritomi
David Olney
Theodore Orlan
Antti Paatero
Sam Passalacqua
Mariea Poole
Leonard Reiter
Karl Rimer
Charles Saunders
Brent Saville
Robert Staples
Michio Suguwara
Randall Walker
Henry Washington
Michael Whitney
Rosa Zaldivar
Tadas Zilius

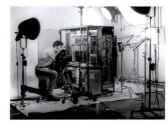

Staff member Virgil Mirano photographing a computer for the film *A Computer Glossary*

1968

Film: *A Computer Glossary Or, Coming to Terms with the Data Processing Machine*

A Computer Glossary was shown in 1968 in the IBM Corporation's pavilion at Hemisfair, the World's Fair in San Antonio, Texas. The film, another in the series of Eames Office projects promoting understanding of the electronic computer, begins with a live-action, close-up sequence depicting the path that data travels in the computer, accompanied by a sound track of professional jargon being spoken by the computer-room staff. The film goes on to introduce various terms specific to electronic data processing, thereby creating a computer glossary. Animated sequences define and illustrate the glossary (according to definitions that were valid in the mid-1960s). The graphic presentation of terms and definitions is accompanied by short, animated dramatizations of computer operations and applications.

A Computer Glossary was written by Glen Fleck and Charles with the assistance of Lynn Stoller of IBM. Glen Fleck also drew the animated sequences. Philip Abbott and Dolores Sutton read the narration, and Elmer Bernstein composed the original score. The film won a bronze medal at the Atlanta International Film Festival in 1969. It is in general circulation. (Running time, *A Computer Glossary*: 11 minutes; color.)

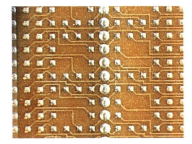

A sequence of frames (reading top to bottom left, top to bottom right) from scenes in *A Computer Glossary*. The frames were photographed from 16mm-film footage

Staff: 1968
901 Washington Boulevard
Carol Berryman
Charles Brittin
Judith Brittin
Jeffrey Brosk
Paul Bruhwiler
John Bulthius
Linda Buzzell
Barbara Charles
Roger Conrad
Darryl Cotybeare
Douglas Cox
Raul de Brigard
Annette Del Zoppo
Richard Donges
Raymond Duddles
Carl Duzen
Maria Ewing
Honor Field
Glen Fleck
Richard Foy
Alex Funke
Breon Gilleran
Keith Hall
Pamela Hedley
Gary Hinckley
Ella Hogan
David Jack
Joslin Jerl
Hap Johnson
Ruth Laug
Carl Magnusson
Parke Meek
William Miner
Virgil Mirano
Jill Mitchell
Pat Naritomi
David Olney
Theodore Orlan
Antti Paatero
Sam Passalacqua
Mariea Poole
Leonard Reiter
Karl Rimer
Charles Saunders
Brent Saville
Robert Staples
Michio Suguwara
Randall Walker
Henry Washington
Michael Whitney
Rosa Zaldivar
Tadas Zilius

A sequence of frames (reading top to bottom left, top to bottom right) from scenes in *Babbage's Calculating Machine*. The frames were photographed from 16mm-film footage

1968

Film: *Babbage's Calculating Machine or Difference Engine*

Babbage's Calculating Machine is a live-action, close-up study of the only existing Babbage Difference Engine, a machine designed in the first quarter of the nineteenth century by Charles Babbage, an English inventor and mathematician, and later built by his son, Henry. The engine, designed to calculate and print out tables of numbers for use in navigation, insurance, and astronomy, is an important artifact in computer history. Babbage is considered to be the father of the modern computer, and his Difference Engine and Analytical Machine are among the forerunners of the modern electronic computer. The film provides a rare opportunity to view the Difference Engine in action.

Babbage's Calculating Machine was produced for the "Computer Origins" section of the proposed IBM Corporation Museum (pp. 328–329). Charles, assisted by Bruce Collier of Harvard University and staff member Parke Meek, filmed the machine in the Science Museum in South Kensington, London, where it is housed. The film is the companion piece to *The Scheutz Machine* (p. 320). There is no narration; the musical accompaniment, "Alamaine" and the "Scots March," was performed by Carl Dolmetsch and the Dolmetsch Consort on an Angel recording. *Babbage's Calculating Machine* was later put on the same reel with *The Scheutz Machine*. The two films are in general release. (Running time, *Babbage's Calculating Machine*: 3 minutes, 50 seconds; black and white.)

March 17 and 24: "A Conversation with Charles Eames and Immaculate Heart College Students" is aired on NBC Television, Los Angeles, California.

Staff: 1968
901 Washington Boulevard
Carol Berryman
Charles Brittin
Judith Bronowski
Jeffrey Brosk
Paul Bruhwiler
John Bulthius
Linda Buzzell
Barbara Charles
Roger Conrad
Darryl Conybeare
Douglas Cox
Raul de Brigard
Annette Del Zoppo
Richard Donges
Raymond Duddles
Carl Duzen
Maria Ewing
Honor Field
Glen Fleck
Richard Foy
Alex Funke
Breon Gilleran
Keith Hall
Pamela Hedley
Gary Hinckley
Ella Hogan
David Jack
Joslin Jerl
Hap Johnson
Ruth Laug
Carl Magnusson
Parke Meek
William Miner
Virgil Mirano
Jill Mitchell
Pat Naritomi
David Olney
Theodore Orlan
Antti Paatero
Sam Passalacqua
Mariea Poole
Leonard Reiter
Karl Rimer
Charles Saunders
Brent Saville
Robert Staples
Michio Sugawara
Randall Walker
Henry Washington
Michael Whitney
Rosa Zaldivar
Tadas Zilius

1968

Intermediate Desk Chair

The chairs designed by the Eames Office in the last ten years of its existence were essentially refinements of previously designed pieces. The Intermediate Desk Chair, a small mobile chair, combines the structural features and materials of other Eames chairs and is based on ideas used in the Time-Life Chair and the Executive Desk Chair.

Intended primarily for the office market, the chair had back and seat pads covered with black leather or Naugahyde reinforced by stiff nylon Fiberthin slings secured to the cast aluminum side members. The cast aluminum arms were attached to the side members, joining the seat to the back. The chair had a tilt-swivel pedestal base, and its shaped legs came with casters or with glides.

Herman Miller, Inc., introduced the chair in 1968. Manufacturing the chairs proved to be too expensive, and they were discontinued in 1973.

Top: Profile of the production model of the Intermediate Desk Chair. Above: Three-quarter view of the Intermediate Desk Chair

Model view of the museum's "Presentation Area"

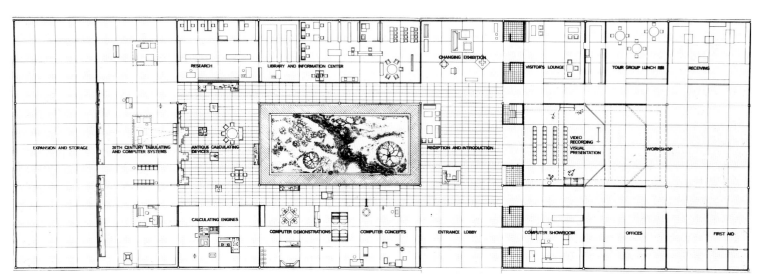

Plan view of the museum layout

March 26: Charles delivers a lecture on art and science at the U.S. Embassy in London, England.

Staff: 1968
901 Washington Boulevard
Carol Berryman
Charles Brittin
Judith Brittin
Jeffrey Bronowski
Paul Bruhwiler
John Bulthuis
Linda Buzzell
Barbara Charles
Roger Conrad
Darryl Conybeare
Douglas Cox
Raul de Brigard
Annette Del Zoppo
Richard Donges
Raymond Duddles
Carl Duzen
Maria Ewing
Honor Field
Glen Fleck
Richard Foy
Alex Funke
Breon Gilleran
Keith Hall
Pamela Hedley
Gary Hinckley
Ella Hogan
David Jack
Joslin Jerl
Hap Johnson
Ruth Laug
Carl Magnusson
Parke Meek
William Miner
Virgil Mirano
Jill Mitchell
Pat Naritomi
David Olney
Antti Paatero
Sam Passalacqua
Mariea Poole
Leonard Reiter
Karl Rimer
Charles Saunders
Brent Saville
Robert Staples
Michio Sugawara
Randall Walker
Henry Washington
Michael Whitney
Rosa Zaldivar
Tadas Zilius

Franklin McMahon, illustrator of the *IBM Museum* film

1968

Proposal and Film: *IBM Museum*

The IBM Corporation's original plan for its new corporate headquarters in Armonk, New York, included a museum to be situated on the same site. The museum was to be a repository for the collection of books and antique calculators begun by Thomas Watson, Sr., founder of IBM, and an information center about the electronic computer. It was to be open to invited guests and IBM employees. The Eames Office presented a proposal for the museum in a study film, using animated and live-action sequences, drawings, still photographs, and clips from other films to show how the museum could give "a fresh look at those historic objects and events that help place the computer in terms of our changing culture.... Ideally it would be housed in a beautifully equipped loft space with the mood of a working laboratory, where visitors could feel that they were being let in on the experience." Visitors would leave the museum "feeling a little more at home with the computer—and sufficiently at ease with the idea that they can position the computer in relation to their own daily decisions."

The proposal called for several permanent exhibition areas in which historic machines and memorabilia from IBM's collections could be shown alongside twentieth-century electronic computers. Another gallery was to provide space for temporary exhibitions on technical innovations. Included in the plan were a library and resource center, a presentation area where visitors could listen to orientation lectures and see multiscreen projections, a center where visitors could get hands-on experience with computer operations and applications, and a classroom for demonstrating the concepts and fundamentals of computing.

Although the plans and model for the proposed museum were completed by Roche Dinkeloo Architects, IBM decided not to go ahead with the project. However, elements from the research for the museum were later incorporated into other IBM projects developed by the Eames Office. *The Scheutz Machine* and *Babbage Calculating Machine* films (pp. 320, 326) were made in the course of the work on the proposal (which was carried on over many years), and much of the preparatory work on the history of the computer was incorporated into the exhibition, *A Computer Perspective*, shown in 1971 at IBM's Exhibit Center in its regional headquarters in New York City (pp. 364–369).

The film detailing the proposal, *IBM Museum*, was written by Glen Fleck with Charles. It is one of the Eames Office "study" films and is not in general circulation. (Running time, *IBM Museum*: 10 minutes; color.)

A sequence of frames (reading top to bottom left, top to bottom right) from scenes in *IBM Museum*. The frames were photographed from 16mm-film footage

329

Staff: 1968
901 Washington Boulevard
Carol Berryman
Charles Brittin
Judith Bronowski
Jeffrey Brosk
Paul Bruhwiler
John Bulthius
Linda Buzzell
Barbara Charles
Roger Conrad
Darryl Conybeare
Douglas Cox
Raul de Brigard
Annette Del Zoppo
Richard Donges
Raymond Duddles
Carl Duzen
Maria Ewing
Honor Field
Glen Fleck
Richard Foy
Alex Funke
Breon Gilleran
Keith Hall
Pamela Hedley
Gary Hinckley
Ella Hogan
David Jack
Joslin Jerl
Hap Johnson
Ruth Laug
Carl Magnusson
Parke Meek
William Miner
Virgil Mirano
Jill Mitchell
Pat Naritomi
David Olney
Theodore Orlan
Antti Paatero
Sam Passalacqua
Mariea Poole
Leonard Reiter
Karl Rimer
Charles Saunders
Brent Saville
Robert Staples
Michio Suguwara
Randall Walker
Henry Washington
Michael Whitney
Rosa Zaldivar
Tadas Zilius

Charles and Ray selecting images for *Photography & the City*

1968

Exhibition: *Photography & the City: The Evolution of an Art and a Science*

The exhibition *Photography & the City*, designed by the Eames Office, was installed in the central court, west wing, and balcony of the Arts and Industries Building of the Smithsonian Institution in Washington, D.C. The show opened on June 6, 1968, and closed January 1, 1969.

The subject of the exhibition was the influence of the photographic image on the way we view the changing composition of our cities. The large open space of the gallery was divided into subject areas by freestanding rectangular display pylons. Individual photographs and composite photomurals were mounted on the display pylons. Large overhead title panels identified various categories of urban photography on display—architecture and planning, social documentation, aerial photography, photojournalism, mapmaking, and newsreels. The work of such photographers of the urban scene as Louis-Jacques-Mandé Daguerre, Jacob Riis, Lewis Hine, Émile Zola, Dorothea Lange, Alfred Steiglitz, and Berenice Abbott was included.

The accompanying explanatory text and caption material, which included names of artists, titles, and subject headings, were kept to a minimum. Artifact cases containing vintage cameras and other historic photographic paraphernalia were included in the exhibition.

The photographs were selected from the Smithsonian and the Library of Congress and from other collections in the United States and abroad. The images were printed and mounted for the exhibition at the Eames Office. Robert Staples developed the exhibition plan, Barbara Charles and Glen Fleck did the research and writing, and Richard Donges and Staples were responsible for the installation.

Opposite: A view of the main court of the exhibition *Photography & the City*

Top: A graphic pylon explaining the impact of immigration on the composition of the city. Above: A photomural of New York City skyscrapers

A photograph by Charles of the photographer Imogen Cunningham, taken in her home

Top and above: Two views of graphic pylons in the main court area

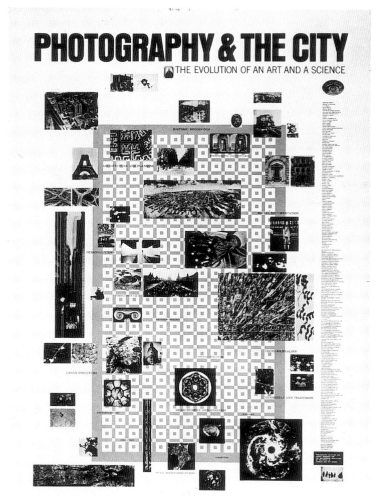

Top: Exhibition poster. Above: An artifact case housing vintage cameras and equipment

Staff members David Olney and Robert Staples installing *Photography & the City*

Staff members Darryl Conybeare, Charles, Paul Bruhwiler, and Barbara Charles reviewing the exhibition

Exhibition pylon of an urban street scene, photographed from above

Plan view of a one-inch model of the exhibition built by the Eames Office

Detail from the model showing the entry to the exhibition

333

August: Charles receives a "Special Award" from the Museum of Science and Industry in Chicago, Illinois.

Staff: 1968
901 Washington Boulevard
Carol Berryman
Charles Brittin
Judith Bronowski
Jeffrey Brosk
Paul Bruhwiler
John Bulthius
Linda Buzzell
Barbara Charles
Roger Conrad
Darryl Conybeare
Douglas Cox
Raul de Brigard
Annette Del Zoppo
Richard Donges
Raymond Duddles
Carl Duzen
Maria Ewing
Honor Field
Glen Fleck
Richard Foy
Alex Funke
Breon Gilleran
Keith Hall
Pamela Hedley
Gary Hinckley
Ella Hogan
David Jack
Joslin Jerl
Hap Johnson
Ruth Laug
Carl Magnusson
Parke Meek
William Miner
Virgil Mirano
Jill Mitchell
Pat Naritomi
David Olney
Antti Paatero
Sam Passalacqua
Mariea Poole
Leonard Reiter
Karl Rimer
Charles Saunders
Brent Saville
Robert Staples
Michio Sugawara
Randall Walker
Henry Washington
Rosa Zaldivar
Tadas Zilius

1968

Film: *The Lick Observatory, Mount Hamilton, California: A Brief Look at the Objects and People That Make Up Its Landscape*

The Lick Observatory film was made for the Commission on College Physics as a tool for acquainting students (who might never have the opportunity to visit an observatory) with an observatory environment. Using still images transferred to film, *The Lick Observatory* presents the history of astronomical research, looks at current developments in the field, and offers a glimpse of the processes and disciplines involved in astronomical research. The film begins with sequences of historical images and vintage tools and continues with scenes of modern astronomers at work in the Lick Observatory, where early astronomical instruments are used alongside modern telescopes, data-processing machines, and imaging equipment. As the images unfold in one sequence, the cogwheels, brass gauges, and instruments of a nineteenth-century telescope are seen while astronomers Philip Morrison and Albert G. Wilson discuss the importance of continuity and consistency in the investigative process.

The Lick Observatory includes other comments on the nature of the scientific quest by astronomers Albert G. Wilson, Carl A. Wirtanen, C. Donald Shane, Stanislaus Vassileskiz, and Peter S. Conti and ends with photographic portraits of some leading men and women of astronomy who—as Philip Morrison, professor of physics at the Massachusetts Institute of Technology in Cambridge, Massachusetts, remarks—continue in the tradition of working to understand "that universe that still lies beyond our understanding."

The accompanying music is a Columbia recording of Glen Gould playing J. S. Bach's *Well-Tempered Clavier*. The film is in general circulation. (Running time, *The Lick Observatory*: 8 minutes, 20 seconds; color.)

A sequence of frames (reading top to bottom left, top to bottom right) from scenes in *The Lick Observatory*. The frames were photographed from 16mm-film footage

September 10: Charles lectures at the American Institute of Interior Design, New York City.

Staff: 1968
901 Washington Boulevard
Carol Berryman
Charles Brittin
Judith Bronowski
Jeffrey Brosk
Paul Bruhwiler
John Bulthius
Linda Buzzell
Barbara Charles
Roger Conrad
Darryl Conybeare
Douglas Cox
Raul de Brigard
Annette Del Zoppo
Richard Donges
Raymond Duddles
Carl Duzen
Maria Ewing
Honor Field
Glen Fleck
Richard Foy
Alex Funke
Breon Gilleran
Keith Hall
Pamela Hedley
Gary Hinckley
Ella Hogan
David Jack
Joslin Jerl
Hap Johnson
Ruth Laug
Carl Magnusson
Parke Meek
William Miner
Virgil Mirano
Jill Mitchell
Pat Naritomi
David Olney
Theodore Orlan
Antti Paatero
Sam Passalacqua
Mariea Poole
Leonard Reiter
Karl Rimer
Charles Saunders
Brent Saville
Robert Staples
Michio Suguwara
Randall Walker
Henry Washington
Michael Whitney
Rosa Zaldivar
Tadas Zilius

1968

Washington Presentation Center

In 1967 the IBM Corporation asked the Eames Office to design a permanent installation for its "Presentation Center" in Washington, D.C. The installation was designed to show IBM's latest computer applications and the work produced by IBM-affiliated research centers and scientists. Prospective clients and other interested individuals were invited to the center to learn about IBM innovations in the various disciplines, including city planning, weather and earthquake prediction, medicine, and mathematics.

Photographs of examples of computer output, along with explanatory text, were hung on panels mounted along the hallways and on the central columns of the main presentation room. Floor-to-ceiling display panels with photographic enlargements of electronic circuitry and computer-processed pictures were also exhibited. Several workstations were set up for visitor demonstrations. These displays were to be changed to accommodate new material as it became available.

A large graphic panel depicting the history of the development of computer technology was hung in the nearby reception lounge. In the center's dining room another large panel with black and white squares, randomly patterned "according to the laws of chance" (first used by the Eames Office in the *Mathematica* exhibition), was mounted on one wall. A case for games and toys that had "at some time been analyzed mathematically" and were considered useful paradigms of problem solving was also on display in the dining center.

The center's mathematical games and toys case

Top: Seating area showing the computer history panel on the back wall. Middle: A view of the workstations and graphic panels and columns. Above: Graphic panels of computer output

335

September 22: Charles participates in the International Review of Exhibition Design at the *Third Biennial of Applied Graphic Arts*, Brno, Czechoslovakia.

Staff: 1968
901 Washington Boulevard
Carol Berryman
Charles Brittin
Judith Bronowski
Jeffrey Brosk
Paul Bruhwiler
John Bulthuis
Linda Buzzell
Barbara Charles
Roger Conrad
Darryl Conybeare
Douglas Cox
Raul de Brigard
Annette Del Zoppo
Richard Donges
Raymond Duddles
Carl Duzen
Maria Ewing
Honor Field
Glen Fleck
Richard Foy
Alex Funke
Breon Gilleran
Keith Hall
Pamela Hedley
Gary Hinckley
Ella Hogan
David Jack
Joslin Jerl
Hap Johnson
Ruth Laug
Carl Magnusson
Parke Meek
William Miner
Virgil Mirano
Jill Mitchell
Pat Naritomi
David Olney
Theodore Orlan
Antti Paatero
Sam Passalacqua
Mariea Poole
Leonard Reiter
Karl Rimer
Charles Saunders
Brent Saville
Robert Staples
Michio Sugawara
Randall Walker
Henry Washington
Michael Whitney
Rosa Zaldivar
Tadas Zilius

Ray, Charles, and Edward P. Morgan discussing plans for a television program on the Eameses' work

1968

Film: *Powers of Ten: A Rough Sketch for a Proposed Film Dealing with the Powers of Ten and the Relative Size of the Universe*

The film *Powers of Ten* is another Eames project in which the idea of exponential series is investigated. In the films *A Communications Primer* (pp. 182–183) and the *Mathematica* peep show 2^n (pp. 260–261), Charles used the system of exponential powers to visualize and make understandable very large quantities. When he came across the 1957 book by Kees Boeke, *Cosmic View: The Universe in Forty Jumps*, he decided to use it as the basis of a film investigating the relative size of things and the significance of adding zero to any number—the powers of ten.

The film translates Boeke's book into a series of continuous camera moves, starting with a scene on Earth and steadily moving away until the edge of the known universe is shown. Then the traveler moves back again to Earth, continuing down to the level of a carbon atom. The film begins with a close-up shot of a man sleeping on a golf course in Florida, "... a scene one meter wide, which we view from just one meter away." The camera pulls back at the rate of 10^{10} meters per second ("in each 10 seconds of travel the imaginary voyager covered ten times the distance he had traveled in the previous 10 seconds"). The man becomes a speck, the golf course disappears, and the planet Earth looms and diminishes. The camera moves out to a point where it shows our galaxy as one of many galaxies; it then moves back toward Earth, traveling at the same rate, revealing the microscopic skin cells on the sleeping man's wrist, thirty-six powers of ten smaller than our galaxy. We see atoms and then atomic particles. An instrument panel at the left side of the screen shows the distance traveled, the corresponding power of ten, the traveler's time, the time on Earth, and the percentage of the speed of light.

The narrator, Judith Bronowski (who also did the research for the film), describes the journey into and out of space and provides additional information. The accompanying score was composed and played by Elmer Bernstein on a Japanese synthesizer organ.

The film was produced for the Commission on College Physics as a rough exercise, or a "sketch," to be presented to an assembly of a thousand American physicists. An updated and more developed version of the film was produced in 1977 (pp. 440–441). Both films are in general circulation. (Running time, *Powers of Ten*: 8 minutes; color.)

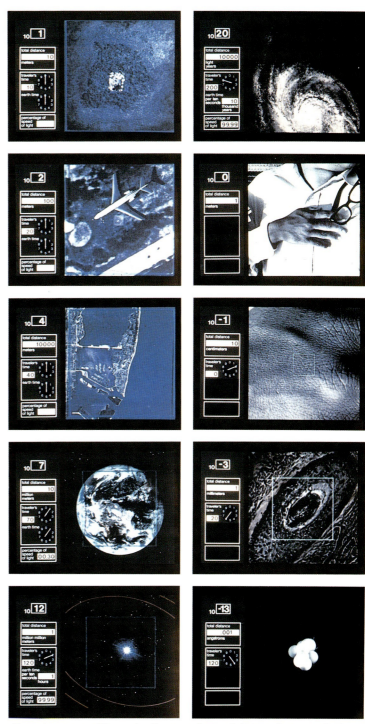

Above: A sequence of frames (reading top to bottom left, top to bottom right) from scenes in *Powers of Ten* showing the progressive moves made by the imaginary traveler into space and back. Opposite: Two frames from the beginning of *Powers of Ten*. The frames were photographed from 16mm-film footage

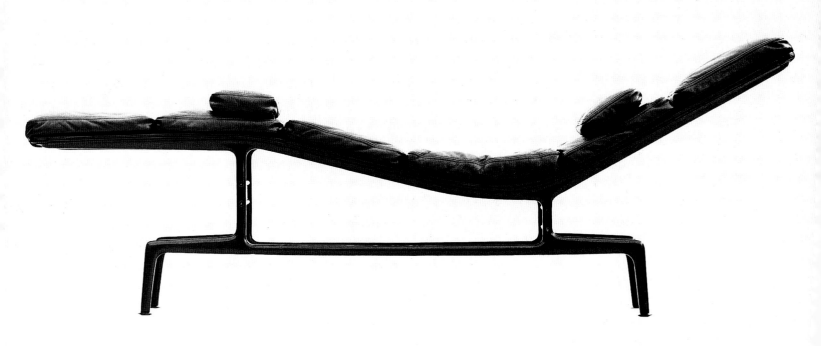

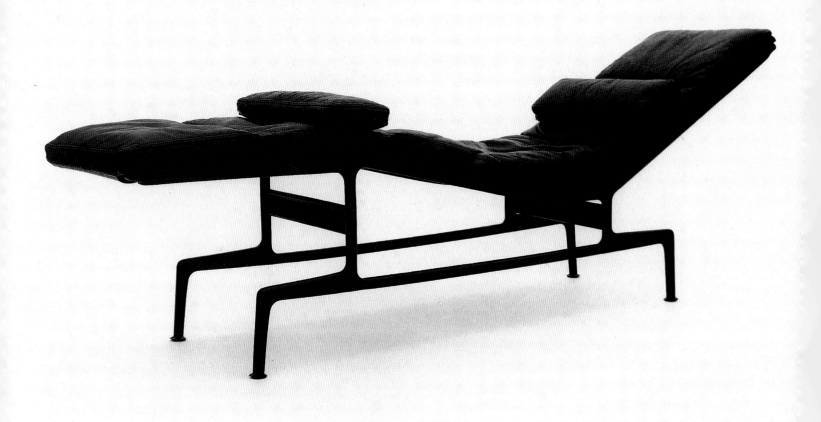

Top: Chaise profile. Above: Three-quarter view of the Chaise

November: Charles participates in a conference on design at the Musée des Arts Decoratifs, Paris, France.

Staff: 1968 / 901 Washington Boulevard / Carol Berryman / Charles Brittin / Judith Bronowski / Jeffrey Brosk / Paul Bruhwiler / John Bulthius / Linda Buzzell / Barbara Charles / Roger Conrad / Darryl Conybeare / Douglas Cox / Raul de Brigard / Annette Del Zoppo / Richard Donges / Raymond Duddles / Carl Duzen / Maria Ewing / Honor Field / Glen Fleck / Richard Foy / Alex Funke / Breon Gilleran / Keith Hall / Pamela Hedley / Gary Hinckley / Ella Hogan / David Jack / Joslin Jerl / Hap Johnson / Ruth Laug / Carl Magnusson / Parke Meek / William Miner / Virgil Mirano / Jill Mitchell / Pat Naritomi / David Olney / Theodore Orlan / Antti Paatero / Sam Passalacqua / Mariea Poole / Leonard Reiter / Karl Rimer / Charles Saunders / Brent Saville / Robert Staples / Michio Suguwara / Randall Walker / Henry Washington / Michael Whitney / Rosa Zaldivar / Tadas Zilius

Staff member Richard Donges, Charles, and Ray reviewing the side-member casting pattern

1968

Chaise

The Chaise was designed for film director and Eames friend Billy Wilder. In 1955, while on location shooting in Nova Scotia for the feature film *The Spirit of St. Louis*, Wilder took an afternoon nap in a lighthouse on an improvised bench: a 6-foot-by-12-inch plank resting on two sawhorses. Wilder remarked at the time that he needed a narrow office couch on which he could take brief afternoon naps. Charles remembered the conversation, and with Wilder's requirements in mind, the Eames Office began work several years later on the Chaise, a 17 ½-inch, armless, curved form that required Wilder to lie on his back with his arms folded over his chest while napping. After a short time, his arms would inevitably slip to the floor, waking him. The first Chaise was delivered to Wilder, who, when asked what he thought of it, replied, "If you had a girlfriend shaped like a Giacometti, it would be wonderful."

The Chaise has a sand-cast aluminum frame made of two one-piece leg and side members. A sheet of plasticized Fiberthin the length of the side members is stretched between them and held tautly in place by four spreaders—two on the uprights and two at the head and foot of the Chaise. Six cushions of urethane foam enclosed by polyester fiber batting and covered with black leather rest on the sling. Only the cushions at each end are secured to the frame; the others are attached to one another with zippers. Two loose cushions are provided for head or body support.

Herman Miller, Inc., began manufacturing the Chaise in 1968. It is still produced and is made of top-grain black leather; the aluminum frame and base are coated with an eggplant-colored nylon.

Richard Donges was responsible for the development of the Chaise.

Detail of the Chaise's seat-support area

Detail of the Chaise's rear leg

Charles, scientist Malcolm Gordon, and architect John Dinkeloo at one of the marine-life tanks in the Eames Office

Amanda and Philip Dunne with Charles by a marine-life tank in the Eames Office

Ray with painter and teacher Gyorgy Kepes

A selection of pages from the aquarium booklet

February: Charles delivers a lecture to the American Association of Physics Teachers.

Staff: 1969
901 Washington Boulevard
Donval Barnard
Henry Beer
Joan Breitman
Judith Bronowski
James Bumgardner
Jehane Burns
Linda Buzzell
Barbara Charles
Danny Clawson
Richard Coker
Darryl Conybeare
Peter Dane
Carl Daniel
Annette Del Zoppo
Richard Donges
Philippa Dunne
Maria Ewing
Honor Field
Glen Fleck
James Fletcher
Richard Foy
Alex Funke
Richard Funkhouser
Susan Gandel
Keith Hall
Ella Hogan
Barbara Janoff
Hap Johnson
Susan Kenagy
Ruth Laug
Carl Magnusson
Myra Maxwell
Parke Meek
William Miner
Virgil Mirano
Missy Morris
Pat Naritomi
David Olney
Theodore Orlan
Sam Passalacqua
Constance Pharr
Mariea Poole
Lita Redman
Karl Rimer
Norbert Rozendal
Kenneth Schuster
Mel Shockner
Robert Staples
Frederick Steady
Linda Strawn
Michio Sugiwara
Bill Tondreau
Randall Walker

Staff member Annette Del Zoppo organizing photography for the National Aquarium project

1969

Booklet: *National Fisheries Center and Aquarium*

In the preface to the booklet *National Fisheries Center and Aquarium*, Charles states that "the intention of this report is to give the reader an idea of the aims and responsibilities" of the proposed new National Aquarium in Washington, D.C. (pp. 314–317). The report describes the building and its layout and outlines the educational and research goals of the institution. Using text, illustrations, charts, and photographs, the booklet details the features of the aquarium, the theme and purpose of the proposed displays, and their significance to the visitor. The booklet also stresses the importance of conservation to the aquarium program and the stated intention to foster the public's personal involvement and interest and "to attract talented people within the discipline to take part in the aquarium program." The booklet was an offshoot of the Eames Office *National Fisheries Center and Aquarium* film and was produced as an alternative source of information about the National Aquarium. As Charles remarked, the book "was something a senator could pull out of his pocket and show to another senator."

The sixty-page limited-edition paperback report was printed in a 5 ½-inch-square format primarily for use by the Department of the Interior, then headed by Walter J. Hickel. The aquarium project was organized under the leadership of Warren J. Wisby, director of the National Fisheries Center and Aquarium. Malcolm Gordon of the biology department at UCLA acted as scientific consultant on the project. The Eames Office was assisted by the University of California, the Scripps Institution of Oceanography, and the Bureau of Commercial Fisheries, Fishery-Oceanography Center in La Jolla, California.

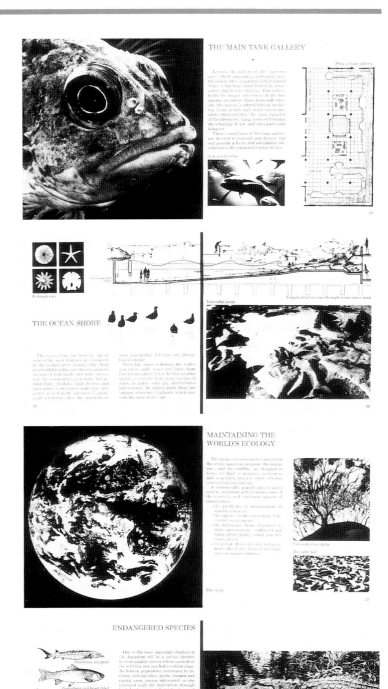

A selection of pages from the aquarium booklet

341

April 6: Edward P. Morgan interviews Charles and Ray on the television program "The Eames Design" for the Public Broadcasting Laboratory, Chicago, Illinois.

Charles receives the Century Club Plaque from the Young Men's Christian Association.

June 10: The Eames Office is awarded the First Federal Award for Good Design for the Aluminum Group chair and second prize for the molded plywood chair, Bonn, West Germany.

June: Charles delivers a talk at the Stedelijk Museum, Amsterdam, Holland.

June 18: Charles lectures at the American Society of Landscape Architects Conference, St. Louis, Missouri.

Charles and staff member Alex Funke photographing the Soft Pad chair

Office staff posing on the foundation for a new building added to the 901 Washington Boulevard space in 1969

Soft Pad Group swivel chair

Staff: 1969
901 Washington Boulevard
Donval Barnard
Henry Beer
Joan Breitman
Judith Bronowski
James Bumgardner
Jehane Burns
Linda Buzzell
Barbara Charles
Danny Clawson
Richard Coker
Darryl Conybeare
Peter Dane
Carl Daniel
Annette Del Zoppo
Richard Donges
Philippa Dunne
Maria Ewing
Honor Field
Glen Fleck
James Fletcher
Richard Foy
Alex Funke
Richard Funkhouser
Susan Gandel
Keith Hall
Ella Hogan
Barbara Janoff
Hap Johnson
Susan Kenagy
Ruth Laug
Carl Magnusson
Myra Maxwell
Parke Meek
William Miner
Virgil Mirano
Missy Morris
Pat Naritomi
David Olney
Theodore Orlan
Sam Passalacqua
Constance Pharr
Mariea Poole
Lita Redman
Karl Rimer
Norbert Rozendal
Kenneth Schuster
Mel Shockner
Robert Staples
Frederick Steadry
Linda Strawn
Michio Sugawara
Bill Tondreau
Randall Walker

Designer Alexander Girard on a visit to the Eames House

1969

Soft Pad Group

Structurally the same as the Aluminum Group chairs produced ten years earlier, the Eames Soft Pad Group of chairs has the added feature of upholstered cushions. A side chair (low back), executive chair (high back), two lounge chairs, and an ottoman make up the Soft Pad Group. They were designed to complement the Eames Lounge Chair (pp. 206–207) and the Chaise (pp. 338–339).

As in the Aluminum Group chairs (pp. 226–229), a fabric sandwich is stretched tautly between the die-cast aluminum side members of the Soft Pad Group and held in place by two spreaders. In the Soft Pad chairs, however, fabric shells are sewn to the stretched membrane. Each shell is provided with a zipper so it can be filled with two-inch-thick urethane foam wrapped in polyester fiber batting. The number of back cushions varies with the height of the chair. Like the Aluminum Group chairs, all the chairs in this group have cast aluminum pedestal bases, either in swivel or tilt-swivel versions with casters.

Herman Miller, Inc., began offering the Soft Pad Group in 1969. The original group was upholstered in black leather and had polished aluminum frames. Today, Herman Miller manufactures the chairs in many different fabrics and leathers. The cast aluminum is also available in a cool tone, a warm tone, or in the eggplant-colored coating developed for the Chaise.

Soft Pad Group side chair with a nonswiveling base

Top: Soft Pad Group swivel chair with side arms. Above: Reclining Soft Pad Group chair

Charles lectures at the College of Creative Studies, University of California, Santa Barbara.

Charles is appointed to the editorial board of the Industrial Designers of America.

Staff: 1969
901 Washington Boulevard
Donval Barnard
Henry Beer
Joan Breitman
Judith Bronowski
James Bumgardner
Jehane Burns
Linda Buzzell
Barbara Charles
Danny Clawson
Richard Coker
Darryl Conybeare
Peter Dane
Carl Daniel
Annette Del Zoppo
Richard Donges
Philippa Dunne
Maria Ewing
Honor Field
Glen Fleck
James Fletcher
Richard Foy
Alex Funke
Richard Funkhouser
Susan Gandel
Keith Hall
Ella Hogan
Barbara Janoff
Hap Johnson
Susan Kenagy
Ruth Laug
Carl Magnusson
Myra Maxwell
Parke Meek
William Miner
Virgil Mirano
Missy Morris
Pat Naritomi
David Olney
Theodore Orlan
Sam Passalacqua
Constance Pharr
Mariea Poole
Lita Redman
Karl Rimer
Norbert Rozendal
Kenneth Schuster
Mel Shockner
Robert Staples
Frederick Steadry
Linda Strawn
Michio Suguwara
Bill Tondreau
Randall Walker

Gerald Fried conducting his score for the film *Image of the City*

1969

Film: *Image of the City*

Image of the City is based on the Eames Office exhibition *Photography & the City* (pp. 330–333), which opened at the Smithsonian Institution in Washington, D.C., in June 1968. The film was sponsored by the Westinghouse Electric Corporation. Both the exhibition and film explored the influence of photography on the shaping of cities and its impact on solutions to urban problems.

Originally, two films were made that were designed to be shown together on separate screens to provide simultaneous layers of information. One film showed supplemental details and close-ups of the images in its companion film. The final version, however, combines the imagery from both of the original films into a single-screen projection.

Image of the City uses both live-action footage and still photography. The first part of the film reviews historic photographs and photographic processes. The second part explores contemporary images and new imaging techniques—radar images, thermograms, computer-generated graphics, spectral multiband images, false-color emulsions, and satellite observations—from which a variety of information about cities can be derived.

The narration was written by Charles with Glen Fleck. The accompanying music was composed by Gerald Fried. The film is not in general circulation. (Running time, *Image of the City*: 15 minutes; color.)

A sequence of frames (reading top to bottom left, top to bottom right) from scenes in *Image of the City*. The frames were photographed from 16mm-film footage

The Eames film *A Computer Glossary* is awarded the bronze medal at the Atlanta International Film Festival, Atlanta, Georgia.

October 13: Charles lectures at an American Institute of Architects conference at Salishan, Oregon.

Right: Staff member William Miner working on the *What Is Design?* exhibition plan for the installation at the Louvre

Staff member Bill Tondreau retouching photographic panels used in the Louvre exhibition

Staff: 1969
901 Washington Boulevard
Donval Barnard
Henry Beer
Joan Breitman
Judith Bronowski
James Bumgardner
Jehane Burns
Linda Buzzell
Barbara Charles
Danny Clawson
Richard Coker
Darryl Conybeare
Peter Dane
Carl Daniel
Annette Del Zoppo
Richard Donges
Philippa Dunne
Maria Ewing
Honor Field
Glen Fleck
James Fletcher
Richard Foy
Alex Funke
Richard Funkhouser
Susan Gandel
Keith Hall
Ella Hogan
Barbara Janoff
Hap Johnson
Susan Kenagy
Ruth Laug
Carl Magnusson
Myra Maxwell
Parke Meek
William Miner
Virgil Mirano
Missy Morris
Pat Naritomi
David Olney
Theodore Orlan
Sam Passalacqua
Constance Pharr
Mariea Poole
Lita Redman
Karl Rimer
Norbert Rozendal
Kenneth Schuster
Mel Shockner
Robert Staples
Frederick Steady
Linda Strawn
Michio Suguwara
Bill Tondreau
Randall Walker

1969

Exhibition: *What Is Design?*

In 1969 five designers were invited to participate in an exhibition, *Qu'cest-ce que le <design>?*, at the Musée des Arts Décoratifs. The five designers, each representing his country—Joe Colombo (Italy), Charles Eames (USA), Fritz Eichler (Germany), Werner Panton (Denmark), and Roger Tallon (France)—submitted work from their offices for the exhibition, which also included their printed responses to a series of questions about the nature of the design process.

The Eames room, entitled *Three Clients*, showed work produced for Herman Miller, Inc., the IBM Corporation, and the governments of the United States and India. Floor-to-ceiling photographic blow-ups of the questions and Charles's answers were included in the room. A version of the three-screen slide show *Excellence* (later entitled *G.E.M.*; p. 319), was projected onto a wall screen in the exhibition area from freestanding units of plexiglass-enclosed projectors. Charles's diagram on the design process (p. 13) was made for this exhibition. A film, *Design Q & A* (p. 388), based on the exhibition's questions and Charles's answers, was produced by the Eames Office in 1972. (The exhibition was always referred to by its translated name in the Eames Office.)

Wall of graphic panels prepared by the Eames Office to show the Eames work

Top: 3-screen slide show in the Eames room. Middle: Exhibition graphic panels from the Eames room. Above: Hinged and wall-mounted *Mathematica* timeline in the Eames room

tops

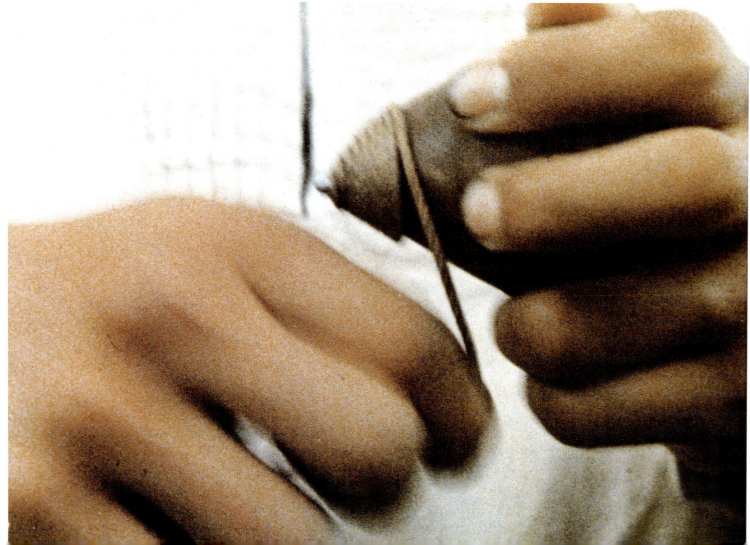

National Fisheries booklet receives a Certificate of Merit at the *Forty-ninth Annual Exhibition of the Art Director's Club of New York*, New York City.

November 18: Charles attends a meeting of the Massachusetts Institute of Technology Arts Commission, Cambridge.

Staff: 1969
901 Washington Boulevard
Donval Barnard
Henry Beer
Joan Breitman
Judith Bronowski
James Bumgardner
Jehane Burns
Linda Buzzell
Barbara Charles
Danny Clawson
Richard Coker
Darryl Conybeare
Peter Dane
Carl Daniel
Annette Del Zoppo
Richard Donges
Philippa Dunne
Maria Ewing
Honor Field
Glen Fleck
James Fletcher
Richard Foy
Alex Funke
Richard Funkhouser
Susan Gandel
Keith Hall
Ella Hogan
Barbara Janoff
Hap Johnson
Susan Kenagy
Ruth Laug
Carl Magnusson
Myra Maxwell
Parke Meek
William Miner
Virgil Mirano
Missy Morris
Pat Naritomi
David Olney
Theodore Orlan
Sam Passalacqua
Constance Pharr
Mariea Poole
Lita Redman
Karl Rimer
Norbert Rozendal
Kenneth Schuster
Mel Shockner
Robert Staples
Frederick Steady
Linda Strawn
Michio Suguwara
Bill Tondreau
Randall Walker

Right: Grant Smith, Glen Fleck, Ray, Pete Seay, Charles, Vince Drayne, Carl Freeborn, Dick Huppertz, and Ted Prendergast from Westinghouse Electric Corporation celebrate Pete Seay's birthday during a meeting of Westinghouse executives and the Eames Office staff

Elmer Bernstein, staff member Glen Fleck, Charles, and Ray at a recording session for the *Tops* soundtrack

1969

Film: *Tops*

Tops was in the planning stage for years. It had its genesis in an earlier film produced for the "Stars of Jazz" television program in 1957 (p. 211). After finishing that first quickly produced effort, Charles decided to make a longer, color version of the film, which he finally began in 1966 and worked on in spare moments between other projects.

Tops is a cinematic celebration of the ancient art and craft of top-making and spinning. One hundred and twenty-three tops spin through the film to the accompaniment of a score by Elmer Bernstein. Using close-up, live-action photography, the film shows tops, old and new, from various countries—China, Japan, India, the United States, France, and England—set in motion in a variety of ways and in a variety of settings. Ad hoc tops—thumbtacks and jacks—appear along with more conventional toy tops. As in the films *Parade* and *Toccata for Toy Trains* (pp. 164–165, 214–217), very small objects share equal space with very large ones, their relative size manipulated by close-up photography. Tops are wound, "brought to life," and "die."

Charles's fascination with spinning tops went back to his childhood; in the film he found a perfect vehicle for demonstrating the beauty of them in motion and for making visual points about the universality of tops, the physics of motion (MIT physics professor Philip Morrison often showed the film to students and colleagues), and the intimate relationship between toys and science. All varieties of them could be found on desktops and work surfaces throughout the Eames Office; Charles and staff members practiced their spinning techniques in preparation for the making of the film. The tops collection was assembled over the years by the Eameses; many of them were gifts from friends and staff members, usually donated with the film in mind (some were borrowed from the Girard and other collections). The actors in the film, as in many other Eames films, included friends, office staff and their children, and (for an instant) an Eames grandchild. Elmer Bernstein wrote and conducted the score. *Tops* has no narration. It is in general circulation. (Running time, *Tops*: 7 minutes, 15 seconds; color.)

Above: A sequence of frames (reading top to bottom left, top to bottom right) from scenes in *Tops*. Opposite: Two frames from the beginning of *Tops*. The frames were photographed from 16mm-film footage

February 25: Charles participates in "Men of Ideas," a lecture series at Carnegie Music Hall, Pittsburgh, Pennsylvania.

Charles at his office desk

Staff: 1970
901 Washington Boulevard
Carla Atwood
Peter Bernstein
Sheila Beste
Joan Breitman
Judith Bronowski
James Bumgardner
Jehane Burns
Linda Buzzell
Ralph Caplan
Barbara Charles
Frank Charon
Darryl Conybeare
Peter Dane
Carl Daniel
Annette Del Zoppo
Joan Divers
Richard Donges
Philippa Dunne
Maria Ewing
Glen Fleck
Richard Foy
Alex Funke
Richard Funkhouser
Susan Gandel
Robert Haggard
Ella Hogan
Jim Horowitz
John Hosken
Hap Johnson
Susan Kenagy
Ruth Laug
William Lipper
Myra Maxwell
Emily Mayeda
William Miner
Nicole Morisset
Debaney Mosher
Pat Naritomi
Gerald Nash
Nancy Ochida
David Olney
Jeannine Oppewall
Theodore Orlan
Sam Passalacqua
Mariea Poole
Lita Redman
Karl Rimer
Max Risselada
Frank Romero
Robert Staples
Frederick Steadry
Michio Suguwara
Bill Tondreau
Randall Walker

A sequence of frames (reading top to bottom left, top to bottom right) from scenes in *Soft Pad*. The frames were photographed from 16mm-film footage

1970

Film: *Soft Pad*

Soft Pad was produced for the Herman Miller Furniture Company to describe the new Eames Soft Pad Group chair system and to explain its design. The film was based on an existing three-screen slide show and was made from still images transferred to film footage and live-action photography shot at the Eames House. Close-ups show details of the construction of the chairs—the leather, stitching, and hardware, and the connections used to join them.

On the occasion of the introduction of a new piece or collection of furniture, the Eames Office often put together a short presentation for Herman Miller management to demonstrate an important design aspect of the new item. Such presentations were often in slide-show form. In the case of *Soft Pad*, the process went a step further, and the slide show was expanded by the addition of live-action footage and transferred to a film that could have wider use as a demonstration tool for the company's sales force to show to clients.

The score, by Buddy Collette, was also used in the *IBM Fair Presentation Film #2* (p. 277). There is no narration. *Soft Pad* is in general circulation. (Running time, *Soft Pad*: 4 minutes; color.)

March 2: Charles presents the Soft Pad Group in a showing in Paris, France.

March 6: Charles presents the Soft Pad Group at the *Vimodrome* exhibition, Milan, Italy.

March 9: Charles is a Ford Foundation consultant at the National Institute of Design, Ahmedabad, India.

Staff: 1970
901 Washington Boulevard
Carla Atwood
Peter Bernstein
Sheila Beste
Joan Breitman
Judith Bronowski
James Bumgardner
Jehane Burns
Linda Buzzell
Ralph Caplan
Barbara Charles
Frank Charon
Darryl Conybeare
Peter Dane
Carl Daniel
Annette Del Zoppo
Joan Divers
Richard Donges
Philippa Dunne
Maria Ewing
Glen Fleck
Richard Foy
Alex Funke
Richard Funkhouser
Susan Gandel
Robert Haggard
Ella Hogan
Jim Horowitz
John Hosken
Hap Johnson
Susan Kenagy
Ruth Laug
William Lipper
Myra Maxwell
Emily Mayeda
William Miner
Nicole Morisset
Michael Mosher
Debaney Murata
Pat Naritomi
Gerald Nash
Nancy Ochida
David Olney
Jeannine Oppewall
Theodore Orlan
Sam Passalacqua
Mariea Poole
Lita Redman
Karl Rimer
Max Risselada
Frank Romero
Robert Staples
Frederick Steadry
Michio Suguwara
Bill Tondreau
Randall Walker

1970

Film: *The Fiberglass Chairs: Something of How They Get the Way They Are*

The Fiberglass Chairs is a cinematic look at the design and production of the Eames fiberglass-reinforced, molded plastic chairs (pp. 342–343). Each step in the production process is shown—from the drawing board to the formation of a clay model, the building of a hand-made prototype, the fiberglass lay-up of the chairs on the assembly line, the casting process, and the finishing and final assembly and packaging of the completed product. Close-up sequences of the movement of people and the machines involved in assembly-line production are choreographed to the music track.

The film was made for Herman Miller, Inc., as another of the films made to demonstrate a piece of Eames furniture to its management and sales staff. Another unspoken but equally important message in *The Fiberglass Chairs* has to do with process and the use of plastic, a much-maligned and misused material, in an honest and forthright way. The film was photographed by staff member Frederick Steadry in Los Angeles at the chair fabricators—Century Plastics and Gerard Metal Craftsmen, Inc. —and at the Herman Miller plant. The music is by Buddy Collette. There is no narration. The film is in general circulation. (Running time, *The Fiberglass Chairs*: 8 minutes, 39 seconds; color.)

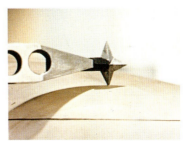

A sequence of frames (reading top to bottom left, top to bottom right) from scenes in *The Fiberglass Chairs*. The frames were photographed from 16mm-film footage

Spring: An Eames filmography and interview with Charles by Paul Shrader are published in *Film Quarterly* magazine.

May 13: Charles is made a Fellow of the American Academy of Arts and Sciences, Boston, Massachusetts.

May: "Algae Removal by Hermit Crabs," an article by Eames staff member Sam Passalacqua, is published in the magazine *Drum and Croaker*. Passalacqua, a designer, maintained the marine animal tanks in the Eames Office throughout the duration of the National Aquarium project (pp. 314–317), and in the process he learned enough about marine life to write an article for a professional journal.

Ray and staff member Myra Maxwell working on a graphic panel

Staff: 1970
901 Washington Boulevard
Carla Atwood
Peter Bernstein
Sheila Beste
Joan Breitman
Judith Bronowski
James Bumgardner
Jehane Burns
Linda Buzzell
Ralph Caplan
Barbara Charles
Frank Charon
Darryl Conybeare
Peter Dane
Carl Daniel
Annette Del Zoppo
Joan Divers
Richard Donges
Philippa Dunne
Maria Ewing
Glen Fleck
Richard Foy
Alex Funke
Richard Funkhouser
Susan Gandel
Robert Haggard
Ella Hogan
Jim Horowitz
John Hosken
Hap Johnson
Susan Kenagy
Ruth Laug
Myra Lipper
Myra Maxwell
Emily Mayeda
William Miner
Nicole Morisset
Michael Mosher
Debaney Murata
Pat Naritomi
Gerald Nash
Nancy Ochida
David Olney
Jeannine Oppewall
Theodore Orlan
Sam Passalacqua
Mariea Poole
Lita Redman
Karl Rimer
Max Risselada
Frank Romero
Robert Staples
Frederick Steadry
Michio Suguwara
Bill Tondreau
Randall Walker

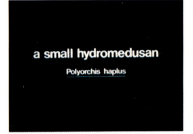

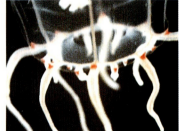

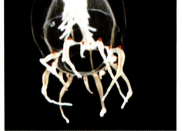

A sequence of frames (reading top to bottom left, top to bottom right) from scenes in *Polyorchis Haplus*. The frames were photographed from 16mm-film footage

1970

Film: *A Small Hydromedusan: Polyorchis Haplus*

Polyorchis Haplus is a short live-action film record of a rare sea creature. Captured by a marine biology student in twelve feet of water in the Pacific Ocean off Zuma Beach, California, it was brought to the Eames Office as part of the developmental study for the National Aquarium project (pp. 314–317, 318, 340–341).

This tiny transparent creature (five-eighths of an inch in size) has only rarely been observed in its natural habitat (its size and the transparency of its form make it difficult to find). It was photographed immediately after it arrived at the office; a macro lens was used to film the close-up footage. The almost full-frame image provides an intimate view of the animal and demonstrates the effect of the creature's symmetrical shape on its movement in the water. The film served as a model for a projected series of films on other sea creatures to be produced as complements to the exhibits planned for the National Aquarium.

Polyorchis Haplus has no narration. Musical accompaniment is a Columbia recording by Glen Gould of the Prelude from Johann Sebastian Bach's Fugue in F Minor. The film is in general circulation. (Running time, *Polyorchis Haplus*: 2 minutes, 35 seconds; color.)

June 1: Charles receives an honorary doctorate of arts from his alma mater, Washington University, St. Louis, Missouri.

June 22: The Eames film *Powers of Ten* is awarded a gold medal at the Atlanta Film Festival, Atlanta, Georgia.

Staff: 1970
901 Washington Boulevard
Carla Atwood
Peter Bernstein
Sheila Beste
Joan Breitman
Judith Bronowski
James Bumgardner
Jehane Burns
Linda Buzzell
Ralph Caplan
Barbara Charon
Frank Charon
Darryl Conybeare
Peter Dane
Carl Daniel
Annette Del Zoppo
Joan Divers
Richard Donges
Philippa Dunne
Maria Ewing
Glen Fleck
Richard Foy
Alex Funke
Richard Funkhouser
Susan Gandel
Robert Haggard
Ella Hogan
Jim Horowitz
John Hosken
Hap Johnson
Susan Kenagy
Ruth Laug
William Lipper
Myra Maxwell
Emily Mayeda
William Miner
Nicole Morisset
Michael Mosher
Debaney Murata
Pat Naritomi
Gerald Nash
Nancy Ochida
David Olney
Jeannine Oppewall
Theodore Oppewall
Sam Passalacqua
Mariea Poole
Lita Redman
Karl Rimer
Max Risselada
Frank Romero
Robert Staples
Frederick Steadry
Michio Suguwara
Bill Tondreau
Randall Walker

1970

Film: *The Black Ships: The Story of Commodore Perry's Expedition to Japan Told with Japanese Pictures of the Time*

The imagery in this film was taken from the nineteenth-century Japanese woodcuts on display in the exhibition *The Japan Expedition 1852–1855 of Commodore Matthew Calbraith Perry*, held at the Smithsonian Institution in Washington, D.C., from October 11 to December 11, 1968, and later at the Union Carbide Building in New York City. The prints record, from the Japanese perspective, Commodore Perry's voyage to Japan in 1853 and the subsequent opening of the country to Western trade.

The Black Ships, in Charles's words, shows "something of the special and rare situations that existed when these two cultures came together…one very sophisticated, one with a highly developed technology." The nineteenth-century prints illustrate what Charles called "the natural exaggeration and distortion that result when a highly traditional civilization records objects and events foreign to its culture."

The film was written by Jehane Burns with Charles. Frederick Steadry, Alex Funke, and Richard Foy were the Eames Office staff members responsible for the production of the film. They were assisted by Smithsonian staff members Karen Loveland, Harold D. Langley, and Roger Pineau. The script includes quotations from Commodore Perry's journals and the memoirs of the U.S. secretary of state who initiated the expedition. The sound track juxtaposes the music from the album "Banjo Kings," an early American fife-and-drum recording from the Smithsonian Institution archives, and traditional Japanese music from tapes provided by the Japanese Embassy. The film is in general circulation. (Running time, *The Black Ships*: 7 minutes, 40 seconds; color.)

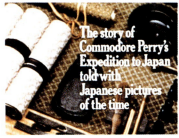 

A sequence of frames (reading top to bottom left, top to bottom right) from scenes in *The Black Ships*. The frames were photographed from 16mm-film footage

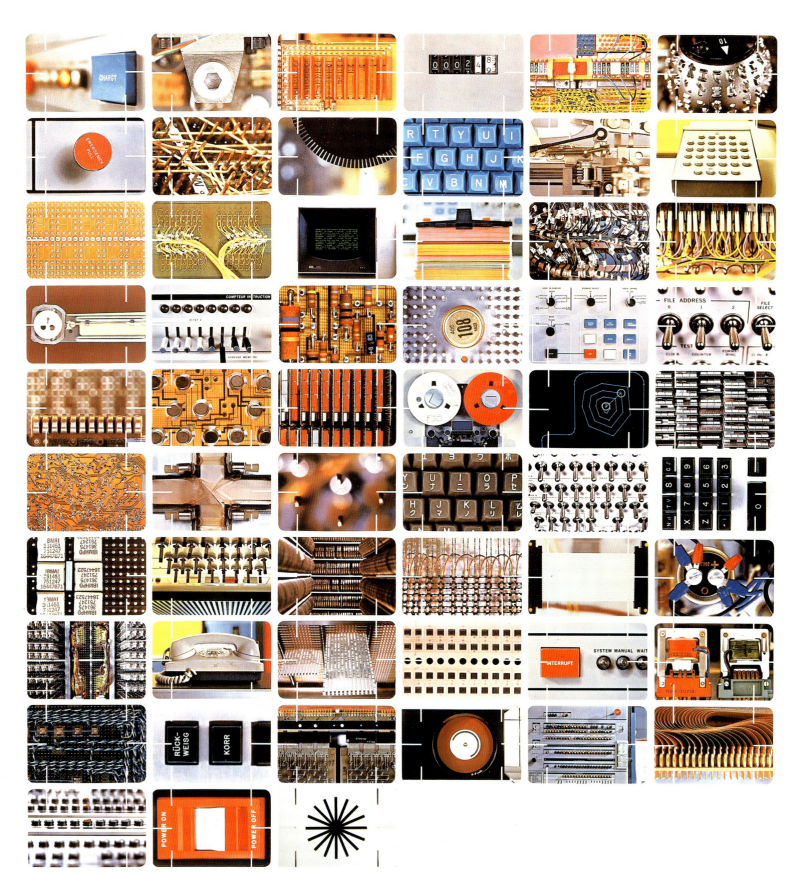

Load button	Data-cell brake assembly	Resistors and capacitors	Running-time usage meter	Voltage-distribution terminal block	Printer element
Power disconnect button	Wire-wrapped pin connections	Disk arm-positioning wheel	Computer-input keyboard	Carriage-return mechanism	Graphic-display controls
Microinstruction selection board	Wiring connected to memory	Alphanumeric display terminal	Cards with punch weight	Relay wiring	Connections to operator lights
Magnetic read/write head	Memory-byte display	Circuit-card mounted resistors	Transistor heat sink	Operator control panel	Magnetic drum connecting switches
Circuit-card contacts	Transistors and circuit connections	Sense amplifiers	Magnetic-tape drive	Computer-drawn dynamic blueprint	Control-circuit modules
Circuit-board connections	Connecting cables	Tips of wiring pins	Keyboard	Magnetic-file control switches	Optical-reader keyboard
Three unloaded circuits	Tape-switching control panel	Computer-tape library	Magnetic core plane	Crossover cable	Capacitor for voltage regulation
Memory-selection transistors	Telephone for computer data	Plastic microprogram cards	Read-only memory	Interrupt button	Two "permissive-make" relays
Sense and inhibit lines	Character-correction keys	Memory-word drive lines	Disk pack and drawer	Operator lights	Read-only memory path
Data and parity display	Power switch	Asterisk motif, reverse side of cards			

July: Charles attends a meeting of the Puerto Rico Advisory Council on Natural Resources.

Charles presents "A Report to President Howard Johnson" to the Massachusetts Institute of Technology 1969–1970 Arts Commission containing his proposals for enlarging and enriching students' experiences in the arts. Charles rejected the practice of requiring students to take "art appreciation" courses; instead, he recommended that students in scientific and technical disciplines be encouraged to develop their communicative abilities by producing "packets of information" about those disciplines (using a wide range of audiovisual techniques) and by teaching a course to an elementary school class for one semester. The need to communicate, would, he reasoned, lead to a recognition of aesthetics as an extension of their own work. The proposal was not acted upon.

Staff: 1970
901 Washington Boulevard
Carla Atwood
Peter Bernstein
Sheila Beste
Joan Breitman
Judith Bronowski
James Bumgardner
Jehane Burns
Linda Buzzell
Ralph Caplan
Barbara Charles
Frank Charon
Darryl Conybeare
Peter Dane
Carl Daniel
Annette Del Zoppo
Joan Divers
Richard Donges
Philippa Dunne
Maria Ewing
Glen Fleck
Richard Foy
Alex Funke
Richard Funkhouser
Susan Gandel
Robert Haggard
Ella Hogan
Jim Horowitz
John Hosken
Hap Johnson
Susan Kenagy
Ruth Laug
William Lipper
Myra Maxwell
Emily Mayeda
William Miner
Nicole Morisset
Michael Mosher
Debaney Murata
Pat Naritomi
Gerald Nash
Nancy Ochida
David Olney
Jeannine Oppewall
Theodore Orlan
Sam Passalacqua
Mariea Poole
Lita Redman
Karl Rimer
Max Risselada
Frank Romero
Robert Staples
Frederick Steadry
Michio Suguwara
Bill Tondreau
Randall Walker

1970

Computer House of Cards

The Computer House of Cards was produced for the IBM Corporation to be given away as a souvenir of the IBM pavilion at the World's Fair in Osaka, Japan.

The inspiration to produce the computer cards came from the work on the film *A Computer Glossary* (p. 325). The diversity and rich imagery of the interior and exterior hardware of the computer were ideally suited to the kind of close-up photography used in the original House of Cards. The Computer House of Cards uses the same playing-card format as the original set (pp. 168–175); each deck of fifty-six computer cards contains an introductory pamphlet explaining, "On these cards are some very close views of the inside and outside of electronic digital computers. Within this world of hardware is a richness and beauty often found when machines are designed to function on the forward edge of technology." The pamphlet also identifies the image on each card—the lights, wiring, circuits, and keyboards of the electronic computer. On the reverse side of each card is the same "asterisk" form (printed in dark blue) used on the back of the original House of Cards. Like the House of Cards, all the cards are slotted for assembly into three-dimensional structures. The 4-by-5-inch transparencies of computer hardware were photographed specifically for the project in the Eames Office or on location at IBM facilities. Taken as a group, the images are a good record of the hardware and the technical terminology of the electronic computer as it was configured in the early 1970s. The cards are also a good example of Charles's practicing what he preached about finding aesthetic pleasure in the inherent character of each discipline. IBM used the cards as gifts for many years. The cards were manufactured by the same company that made the original House of Cards, the West German firm of Otto Maier Verlag.

A House of Cards structure

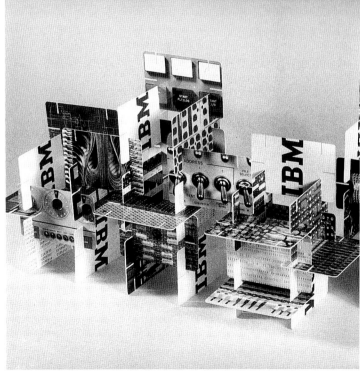

Above: A structure built from the first prototype cards. Opposite: Computer House of Cards

August 29: Charles is made an honorary Fellow of the American Institute of Interior Designers, New York City.

September: Charles attends a meeting of the International Association for Cultural Freedom, Denver, Colorado.

Staff: 1970 / 901 Washington Boulevard / Carla Atwood / Peter Bernstein / Sheila Beste / Joan Breitman / Judith Bronowski / James Bumgardner / Jehane Burns / Linda Buzzell / Ralph Caplan / Barbara Charles / Frank Charon / Darryl Conybeare / Peter Dane / Carl Daniel / Annette Del Zoppo / Joan Divers / Richard Donges / Philippa Dunne / Maria Ewing / Glen Fleck / Richard Foy / Alex Funke / Richard Funkhouser / Susan Gandel / Robert Haggard / Ella Hogan / Jim Horowitz / John Hosken / Hap Johnson / Susan Kenagy / Ruth Laug / William Lipper / Myra Maxwell / Emily Mayeda / William Miner / Nicole Morisset / Michael Mosher / Debaney Murata / Pat Naritomi / Gerald Nash / Nancy Ochida / David Olney / Jeannine Oppewall / Theodore Orlan / Sam Passalacqua / Mariea Poole / Lita Redman / Karl Rimer / Max Risselada / Frank Romero / Robert Staples / Frederick Steadry / Michio Sugawara / Bill Tondreau / Randall Walker

1970

Drafting Chair

The Eames Office first used a fiberglass-reinforced polyester shell for the seat of a drafting chair in the early 1950s, when the molded plastic chairs were introduced (pp. 138–141). The design for a drafting chair was refined over the years until this version was produced in 1970.

The construction of the shell is the same as that of other upholstered plastic shell seats. A sewn vinyl or fabric covering is adhered to a thin urethane foam pad, which in turn is glued to the molded seat and back shells. A charcoal gray or light-tone vinyl edging is sewn to the fabric's outer edges before gluing. The seat is then bolted to an aluminum spider, which is secured to the pedestal base. The central shaft of the base is made of steel with a baked gray hammer-tone finish. It can be adjusted to heights between forty-one and fifty-four inches. Attached to the shaft is a cast aluminum base with a brightly polished finish; a tubular steel footring is the footrest. The stool comes with one-half-inch glides or two-inch casters.

The Eames drafting chairs are still manufactured by Herman Miller, Inc., in an assortment of colors. The fiberglass shell, available in charcoal gray, neutral light, or parchment, comes either without upholstery or upholstered in vinyl or fabric.

Top: Drafting side chair. Above: Drafting armchair

Charles receives a six-year appointment as a member of the National Council of the Arts.

November 12: Charles is made an honorary Fellow of Manchester Polytechnic, Manchester, England.

Staff: 1970
901 Washington Boulevard
Carla Atwood
Peter Bernstein
Sheila Beste
Joan Breitman
Judith Bronowski
James Bumgardner
Jehane Burns
Linda Buzzell
Ralph Caplan
Barbara Charon
Frank Charon
Darryl Conybeare
Peter Dane
Carl Daniel
Annette Del Zoppo
Joan Divers
Richard Donges
Philippa Dunne
Maria Ewing
Glen Fleck
Richard Foy
Alex Funke
Richard Funkhouser
Susan Gandel
Robert Haggard
Ella Hogan
Jim Horowitz
John Hosken
Hap Johnson
Susan Kenagy
Ruth Laug
William Lipper
Myra Maxwell
Emily Mayeda
William Miner
Nicole Morisset
Michael Mosher
Debaney Murata
Pat Naritomi
Gerald Nash
Nancy Ochida
David Olney
Jeannine Oppewall
Theodore Orlan
Sam Passalacqua
Mariea Poole
Lita Redman
Karl Rimer
Max Risselada
Frank Romero
Robert Staples
Frederick Steadry
Michio Suguwara
Bill Tondreau
Randall Walker

1970

Charles Eliot Norton Lectures

In 1970 Charles was appointed the Charles Eliot Norton Professor of Poetry at Harvard University. The Norton chair is traditionally held by an individual who has made a significant contribution to literature, music, or the fine arts. The individual is asked to deliver a series of lectures at Harvard, which are open to the university community. The announced topic of Charles's lectures was "Problems Relating to Visual Communication and the Visual Environment." He delivered six lectures over a six-month period (October 1970 to April 1971), first at the Loeb Drama Center and then at the Harvard Theater, where the lectures were moved to accommodate the large crowds who came to hear Charles speak.

Visual material was an integral part of each lecture. Films, film clips, and slide shows, some produced by the Eames Office over a period of several years and others organized specifically for the lectures, were incorporated into each talk. Eames Office staff built an electronic system for showing and controlling the multiscreen shows, since nothing suitable existed on the market at the time.

In general, the six Norton Lectures were organized around Charles's longtime concerns and preoccupations: his belief in the importance of finding value in the experiences of everyday life, in the need to recognize the difference between choices and constraints, in the importance of discipline, in identifying continuities and discontinuities, and in building connections. He also touched on the usefulness of modeling as a technique to "walk through an experience in order to regroup and try again."

The Norton Lectures were a high point in Charles's use of the slide-show form; in his accompanying comments he summed up his feelings on his preoccupations, which became more intense and concentrated as time went on. It is difficult to reconstruct the lectures; although each talk was organized around a central point, no formal text was written, and the only existing records are incomplete audiotapes and notes made after the lectures were given. To date, the audiotapes, which are of questionable quality, have not been transcribed. In addition, Charles's lecture style of mixing film and slides with anecdotes and the impact of his personality and style of delivery make his lectures almost impossible to impart on the printed page. For this volume, a shorthand notation of the subjects he touched on will be followed by a description of slide shows that were assembled for—or first presented formally in—the Norton Lectures. A list of films shown at each lecture is also included.

Top: Charles delivering a lecture at the Harvard Theater. Middle: The lecture audience in the Loeb Drama Center. Above: People outside the Harvard Theater

December: Charles is awarded the Austrian Gold Medal for Furniture

The Eames Office is awarded the Certificate of Award for the *National Fisheries Center and Aquarium* booklet by the Printing Industries of America

Staff: 1970
901 Washington Boulevard
Carla Atwood
Peter Bernstein
Sheila Beste
Joan Breitman
Judith Bronowski
James Bumgardner
Jehane Burns
Linda Buzzell
Ralph Caplan
Barbara Charles
Frank Charon
Darryl Conybeare
Peter Dane
Carl Daniel
Annette Del Zoppo
Joan Divers
Richard Donges
Philippa Dunne
Maria Ewing
Glen Fleck
Richard Foy
Alex Funke
Richard Funkhouser
Susan Gandel
Robert Haggard
Ella Hogan
Jim Horowitz
John Hosken
Hap Johnson
Susan Kenagy
Ruth Laug
William Lipper
Myra Maxwell
Emily Mayeda
William Miner
Nicole Morisset
Michael Mosher
Debaney Murata
Pat Naritomi
Gerald Nash
Nancy Ochida
David Olney
Jeannine Oppewall
Theodore Orlan
Sam Passalacqua
Mariea Poole
Lita Redman
Karl Rimer
Max Risselada
Frank Romero
Robert Staples
Frederick Steadry
Michio Sugawara
Bill Tondreau
Randall Walker

1970

Charles Eliot Norton Lectures: *Lecture #1*

On October 10, 1970, Charles delivered the first of his six Norton Lectures. He began by talking about the problems of "making choices" and recognizing that the "business of life in general is the primary source of pleasure and aesthetic rewards," rewards that should be arrived at internally, through the "process" of working out problems in a disciplined way. The "process" and "discipline" points were reinforced visually by the films *Powers of Ten* (pp. 336–337), *Tops* (pp. 346–347), a rough, unfinished version of *Banana Leaf* (p. 382), and by the *Circus* slide show, which concluded the lecture.

Charles began using the slide show in 1945 in *Lecture I* as a way of structuring the interplay of visual and verbal information (pp. 50–51). Although some technological refinements were added over the years as equipment became more sophisticated, the form of the shows remained the same. Charles usually began by prefacing his presentation of an announced topic with some introductory remarks about the occasion at which he was speaking and then alternated the slides with his spoken comments (unless a prerecorded track had been produced). Charles did not always follow his prewritten notes or even the announced title for a lecture. Often, something would come up during the course of an event (a question or remark from the audience or a new approach to a subject would occur to him) that changed the direction of the entire lecture.

Circus is a 180-slide, 3-screen (60-pass) slide show accompanied by a sound track featuring circus music and other sounds recorded at a circus. Its central message is that the circus, which seems to be a freewheeling exercise in self-expression, is instead a tightly knit and masterfully disciplined organic accumulation of people, energies, and details. The images and sound (including the narration) were recorded by Charles over a period of several years and assembled in slide-show form for the Norton Lectures. The accompanying music included "Entry of the Gladiators" by Fucik and "Over the Waves" and "Pony Boy" from the circus calliope at the New York World's Fair Continental Circus.

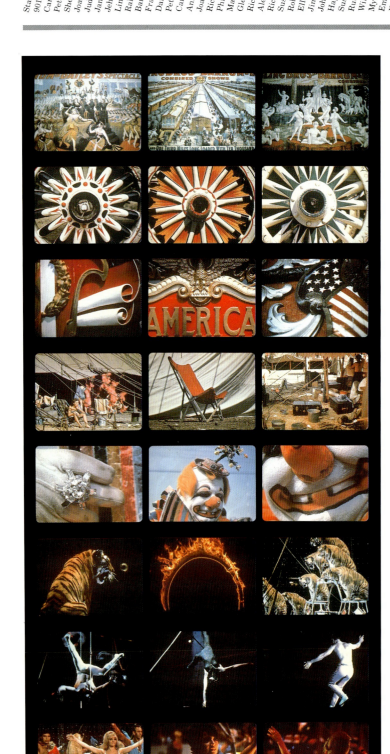

A sequence of 3-image passes (reading top to bottom) selected from the slide show *Circus*.

December 30: Charles lectures to the American Association for the Advancement of Science.

December: Charles is a consultant for a proposed visitor's center at the United Nations, New York City.

Staff: 1970
901 Washington Boulevard
Carla Atwood
Peter Bernstein
Sheila Beste
Joan Breitman
Judith Bronowski
James Bumgardner
Jehane Burns
Linda Buzzell
Ralph Caplan
Barbara Charles
Frank Charon
Darryl Conybeare
Peter Dane
Carl Daniel
Annette Del Zoppo
Joan Divers
Richard Donges
Philippa Dunne
Maria Ewing
Glen Fleck
Richard Foy
Alex Funke
Richard Funkhouser
Susan Gandel
Robert Haggard
Ella Hogan
Jim Horowitz
John Hosken
Hap Johnson
Susan Kenagy
Ruth Laug
William Lipper
Myra Maxwell
Emily Mayeda
William Miner
Nicole Morisset
Michael Mosher
Debaney Murata
Pat Naritomi
Gerald Nash
Nancy Ochida
David Olney
Jeannine Oppewall
Theodore Orlan
Sam Passalacqua
Mariea Poole
Lita Redman
Karl Rimer
Max Risselada
Frank Romero
Robert Staples
Frederick Steadry
Michio Suguwara
Bill Tondreau
Randall Walker

1970

Charles Eliot Norton Lectures: *Lecture #2*

The second lecture in the Norton Lectures was delivered at the Loeb Drama Center on November 2, 1970. After reviewing the main points of the previous lecture, Charles presented his autobiography, which he organized according to pivotal influences on his life (for example, discovering his father's old photographic equipment and teaching himself wet-plate photography before he learned that film had been invented). From his biographical notes he moved into the central points of his lecture, the "realities of changing needs and the necessity to devise visual models for matters of practical concern where linear description isn't enough."

The film *Image of the City* (p. 344) and the *Louvre* slide show were shown as visual evidence that "while it is not possible to predict what the next problems will be, or to prepare specifically for them, it is possible to cultivate a feeling of security about the process of change and the capacity to adapt to it."

The *Louvre* slide show is a 75-image, 3-screen (25-pass) slide show culled from the *Excellence* and *G.E.M.* slide shows produced for IBM and the Smithsonian Institution. (They were revised and renamed *Louvre* for the 1969 *What Is Design?* exhibition; p. 345). Charles used the slides in this context to illustrate the cultivation of enthusiasms and affections, and to encourage a respect for "things" in themselves as an integral part of life and work. The show was accompanied by music originally used for the *ECS* film (p. 266).

The film *Day of the Dead* (pp. 212–213), made in honor of the Mexican religious celebration, and the slide show *Cemeteries* were shown at the conclusion of the lecture as examples of the special, necessary place in our lives for formal ritual.

Cemeteries is a 144-image, 3-screen (48-pass) slide show of photographs of gravestones, markers, and cemetery statuary photographed by Charles in many parts of the world over a period of several years. It was accompanied by music by Elmer Bernstein used originally in the *Dead of the Fifties* film (pp. 244–245).

First four rows: A selection of 3-image passes (reading top to bottom) from the slide show *Louvre*. Rows five through eight: A selection of 3-image passes (reading top to bottom) from the slide show *Cemeteries*

January: Charles becomes a member of the editorial board of *Audience* magazine.

Staff: 1971
901 Washington Boulevard
Jonathan Boorstin
Joan Breitman
Paul Bruhwiler
Jehane Burns
Barbara Charles
Laurence Davis
Richard Donges
Maria Ewing
Glen Fleck
Diane Fuller
Alex Funke
Richard Funkhouser
Richard Gutierrez
Ella Hogan
Hap Johnson
Ellen Kaufman
Ruth Laug
Myra Maxwell
Emily Mayeda
Michael Mosher
Pat Naritomi
Gerald Nash
David Olney
Jeannine Oppewall
Theodore Orlan
Sam Passalacqua
Mariea Poole
Robert Richards
Karl Rimer
Max Risselada
Frank Romero
Douglas Ryan
Kenneth Schuster
Robert Staples
Frederick Steadry
Lynn Stoller
Gene Takeshita
Bill Tondreau
Randall Walker
Dan Zimbaldi
Beth Zimmerman

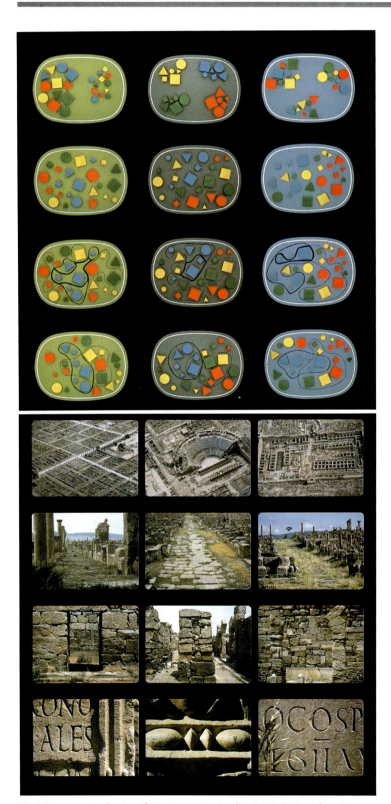

First four rows: A selection of 3-image passes (reading top to bottom) from the slide show *Sets*. Rows five through eight: A selection of 3-image passes (reading top to bottom) from the slide show *Timgad*

1971

Charles Eliot Norton Lectures: *Lecture #3*

In the third lecture, delivered on January 14, 1971, Charles discussed the positive aspects of dealing with constraints in solving problems. *Lecture #3*, in Charles's own words, was "almost parenthetic." He showed a group of films, clips of films, and the slide shows *Sets* and *Timgad*, as examples of what he referred to as "packets" of information. The films he chose were *De Gaulle Sketch* (p. 234), *Symmetry*, from the *Mathematica* peep shows (pp. 260–261), *Introduction to Feedback* (p. 251), *IBM at the Fair* (pp. 304–305), the "dinner party" sequence from *Think* (pp. 284–291), and the *Music of the Fifties* sequence from "The Fabulous Fifties" (pp. 244–245). Charles used each film or segment to demonstrate a single idea and to advocate the production of such "information packets" for teachers to draw upon. Charles also talked about a proposal he submitted to MIT (p. 353) that was directed at aesthetically broadening and enriching students' academic and professional lives.

Sets, a slide show of things that share a common concept, "a little about set theory," was assembled for the Norton Lectures and no longer exists in a continuity as a slide show.

Timgad is a 3-screen, 66-image (22-pass) slide show of images of the ruins of the ancient North African city Timgad. The images run as a visual counterpoint to the sound track, in which the narrators read an exchange of letters concerning civic problems between the Roman emperor Trajan and the philosopher Pliny the Younger, who was appointed governor of Timgad in A.D. 100. Their problems were similar to those we face today: how to fund public works and services. The show was assembled specifically for the Norton Lectures. Pliny's letters are read by Alex Funke and the emperor's by Julian Blaustein.

Staff:1971
901 Washington Boulevard
Jonathan Boorstin
Joan Breitman
Paul Bruhwiler
Jehane Burns
Barbara Charles
Laurence Davis
Richard Donges
Maria Ewing
Glen Fleck
Diane Fuller
Alex Funke
Richard Funkhouser
Ella Hogan
Hap Johnson
Ellen Kaufman
Ruth Laug
Myra Maxwell
Emily Mayeda
Michael Mosher
Pat Naritomi
Gerald Nash
David Olney
Jeannine Oppewall
Theodore Orlan
Sam Passalacqua
Mariea Poole
Robert Richards
Karl Rimer
Max Risselada
Frank Romero
Douglas Ryan
Kenneth Schuster
Robert Staples
Frederick Steadry
Lynn Stoller
Gene Takeshita
Bill Tondreau
Randall Walker
Dan Zimbaldi
Beth Zimmerman

1971

Charles Eliot Norton Lectures: *Lecture #4*

In *Lecture #4*, delivered on March 15, 1971, Charles began by talking about the "pleasures of recognizing inherent form in the solution of problems" and "the importance of learning from primary experiences." The value of structuring information in visual presentations that draw on all of the resources in centers of learning (the central message of *Lecture #3*) was stressed again and related to the university approach to teaching and learning and to getting rid of the "discontinuities."

Along with the films *House of Science* (p. 292), *The Lick Observatory* (p. 334), and *Polyorchis Haplus* (p. 350), two specially assembled slide shows, *Goods* and *Baptistery*, were shown. *Goods* is a 33-image, 3-screen (11-pass) slide show of images of old-fashioned "goods"—kegs of nails, bolts of cloth, cords of wood, coils of rope—shown while Charles talked about the pleasures of recognizing form and the need to learn to draw upon "primary experiences." That led to a discussion of what Charles called the "new covetables," or "concepts and processes which if shared will not diminish in value, will not lead to satiation, and which have to be "wanted" enough to pay the price—the hard work and discipline necessary to arrive at the perception and understanding of the process inherent in the form of the problem." *Goods* was transferred to film in 1982 under the sponsorship of Herman Miller, Inc.

Baptistery is a 57-image, 3-screen (19-pass) slide show of photographs taken by Charles of the Baptistery in Florence, Italy. It was used to illustrate the point that one can "covet without coveting possession," and that "using a camera is one way of eating your cake and having it, too." The accompanying music was from a recording by the New York Brass Ensemble.

First four rows: A selection of 3-image passes (reading top to bottom) from the slide show *Goods*. Rows five through eight: A selection of 3-image passes (reading top to bottom) from the slide show *Baptistery*

Staff: 1971
901 Washington Boulevard
Jonathan Boorstin
Joan Breitman
Paul Bruhwiler
Jehane Burns
Barbara Charles
Laurence Davis
Richard Donges
Maria Ewing
Glen Fleck
Diane Fuller
Alex Funke
Richard Funkhouser
Richard Gutierrez
Ella Hogan
Hap Johnson
Ellen Kaufman
Ruth Laug
Myra Maxwell
Emily Mayeda
Michael Mosher
Pat Naritomi
Gerald Nash
David Olney
Jeannine Oppewall
Theodore Orlan
Sam Passalacqua
Mariea Poole
Robert Richards
Karl Rimer
Max Risselada
Frank Romero
Douglas Ryan
Kenneth Schuster
Robert Staples
Frederick Steadry
Lynn Stoller
Gene Takeshita
Bill Tondreau
Randall Walker
Dan Zimbaldi
Beth Zimmerman

Staff member Robert Staples, designer Lou Danziger, and Charles with a gift from Dorothy Danziger

A selection of 3-image passes (reading from top to bottom) from the slide show *Eero Saarinen*

1971

Charles Eliot Norton Lectures: *Lecture #5*

Lecture #5 was delivered on March 29, 1971. The general subject of the talk, according to Charles, was "work." Examples of work from the Eames Office and from the office of the architect Eero Saarinen were used as visual references. After a recap of the previous lecture, Charles discussed the place of "motive" in work, how to decide what kind of work to do and where to invest your energies. His advice: "Don't take any job with whose objective you do not agree and don't take a job as a stepping-stone to something else....By following these guidelines, you have a chance of bringing your entire experience to the jobs you do and avoiding a lot of misery."

Charles also addressed the need to define the overlapping interests of the designer, the client, and society at large into a mutually shared, flexible, and ever-changing set of criteria that is modified as the designer-client relationship develops (p. 13).

Visual presentations included the *National Fisheries Center and Aquarium* film (p. 318) and the slide shows *Eero Saarinen*, *Tanks*, and *India*. The slide shows were assembled for the lecture. A group of slides called the *Lota* series, images of lotas (an all-purpose vessel used for hundreds of years in India for carrying everything from water to domestic goods) that Charles photographed in India, was also shown.

Eero Saarinen is a 48-image, 3-screen (16-pass) slide show. It begins with slides of Saarinen at work in his office and continues with images of various Saarinen projects. The Saarinen work was used by Charles as a model of how the "systems" approach to work actually functions.

The slide show *Tanks* is a 117-image, 3-screen (39-pass) slide show of images of the marine creatures kept in Eames Office tanks during the developmental work on the National Aquarium project. They were shown to make a point about "process." The accompanying music was "Valse" by Daniel Ouzounoff.

India is a 87-image, 3-screen (29-pass) slide show whose images of people, places, and artifacts were photographed by Charles during several trips he took to India. Shown in this context the images were used to reinforce the "continuity" message of the lecture series. Indian raga music accompanied the slides.

A screening of the *Lota* slide show was the final visual presentation of the fifth lecture. The gradual evolution of the lota was used by Charles on several occasions as an example of the best kind of evolutionary design "process."

A selection of 3-image passes (reading from top to bottom) from the slide show *Tanks*

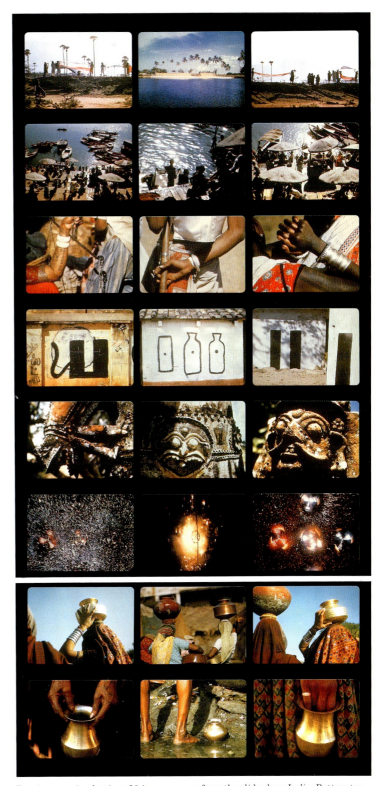

Top six rows: A selection of 3-image passes from the slide show *India*. Bottom two rows: A selection of images from the slide show *Lota*

Staff: 1971
901 Washington Boulevard
Jonathan Boorstin
Joan Breitman
Paul Bruhwiler
Jehane Burns
Barbara Charles
Laurence Davis
Richard Donges
Maria Ewing
Glen Fleck
Diane Fuller
Alex Funke
Richard Funkhouser
Richard Gutierrez
Ella Hogan
Hap Johnson
Ellen Kaufman
Ruth Laug
Myra Maxwell
Emily Mayeda
Michael Mosher
Pat Naritomi
Gerald Nash
David Olney
Jeannine Oppewall
Theodore Orlan
Sam Passalacqua
Mariea Poole
Robert Richards
Karl Rimer
Max Risselada
Frank Romero
Douglas Ryan
Kenneth Schuster
Robert Staples
Frederick Steadry
Lynn Stoller
Gene Takeshita
Bill Tondreau
Randall Walker
Dan Zimbaldi
Beth Zimmerman

Charles and film director Billy Wilder at the Eames Office

1971

Charles Eliot Norton Lectures: *Lecture #6*

On April 26, 1971, Charles delivered the sixth and final lecture in the Norton series. After recapping the previous lecture, he discussed the "environment of the professional process, an environment which does not necessarily show in the final product but which is always there." The slide show *Movie Sets* helped to illustrate the point. *Movie Sets*, which was based on an earlier one-screen show, was revised for the Norton Lectures to a 240-image, 3-screen (80-pass) slide show of photographs of location shots and studio sets from several Billy Wilder films (*Irma La Douce, Sabrina, The Spirit of St. Louis, Ace in the Hole,* and *The Private Life of Sherlock Holmes*). The track includes "wild sound" recorded during the making of the films.

Charles also talked about the importance and usefulness of models of all kinds as tools for the study and investigation of concepts, ideas, and systems and about the potential of the modern electronic computer as a tool for modeling.

In addition to the slide show, the animation prologue from the film *House of Science* (p. 292) and the films *A Computer Glossary* (p. 325), *The Information Machine* (pp. 222–225), and *Toccata for Toy Trains* (pp. 214–215) were shown.

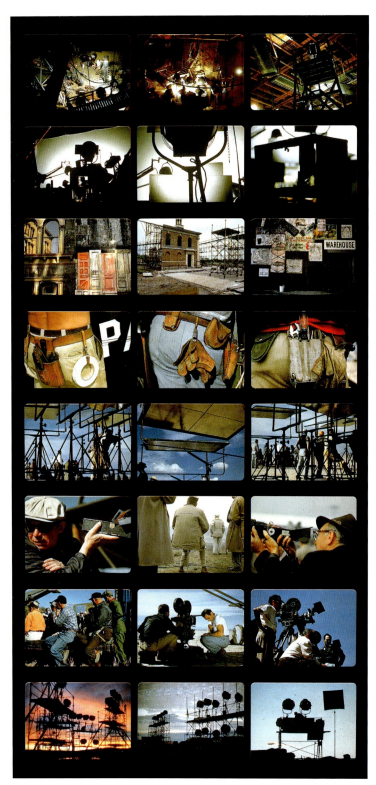

A sequence of 3-image passes (reading top to bottom) from the slide show *Movie Sets*

Charles is made a member of the Alfred Sloan Foundation Steering Committee, New York City.

Staff: 1971
901 Washington Boulevard
Jonathan Boorstin
Joan Breitman
Paul Bruhwiler
Jehane Burns
Barbara Charles
Laurence Davis
Richard Donges
Maria Ewing
Glen Fleck
Diane Fuller
Alex Funke
Richard Funkhouser
Richard Gutierrez
Ella Hogan
Hap Johnson
Ellen Kaufman
Ruth Laug
Myra Maxwell
Emily Mayeda
Michael Mosher
Pat Naritomi
Gerald Nash
David Olney
Jeannine Oppewall
Theodore Orlan
Sam Passalacqua
Mariea Poole
Robert Richards
Karl Rimer
Max Risselada
Frank Romero
Douglas Ryan
Kenneth Schuster
Robert Staples
Frederick Steadry
Lynn Stoller
Gene Takeshita
Bill Tondreau
Randall Walker
Dan Zimbaldi
Beth Zimmerman

1971

Two-Piece Plastic Chair and Two-Piece Secretarial Chair

In 1970 a chair adapted from the plywood dining chair (DCM; pp. 58–61) was produced for Herman Miller, Inc., by the Eames Office, working with Sol Fingerhut at Century Plastics. Fingerhut had perfected a new molding compound that made it possible to produce the chair back and seat of plastic resin with the shock-mount connection molded into the form itself instead of being applied after the forming process. The chair was essentially a "soft" DCM; the fabric and the foam pad were glued together and in turn glued onto the plastic seat and back and edged with vinyl. The chair is made in one height, and the frame is identical to the one used for the DCM. Herman Miller, Inc., still produces the chair.

The Eames two-piece secretarial chair was designed to fill a perceived need for an adjustable padded chair for office use. It was adapted from earlier Eames chairs; its shape was based on the two-piece plastic chair, which in turn was based on the plywood DCM. A molding compound developed for the two-piece plastic chair was used for this chair also. The chair is adjustable in height and has a padded seat and back. Molded polyester seat and back panels support the upholstered pads, which were glued to vacuum-formed rubber pans and then bolted together. A spine of chrome-plated stainless steel, similar to the shape of the brace joining the seat and back of the DCM, connected the seat and back. A stamped-steel spider joined the seat to the cast aluminum four-legged base with casters. The height of the seat, the height of the back rest, and the angle of the back rest could be adjusted by turning cast aluminum handles on the spine. The two-piece secretarial chairs were first sold by Herman Miller, Inc., in 1971; production was discontinued in 1981.

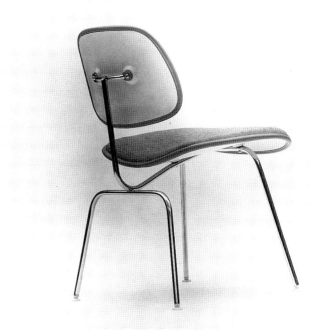

Two-piece plastic chair based on the DCM and used as a model for the two-piece secretarial chair

Profile of the two-piece secretarial chair

Panels from the first two decades represented on the *Computer Perspective* History Wall

1900

Charles speaks at the Art Center School of Design, Pasadena, California.

Staff: 1971
901 Washington Boulevard
Jonathan Boorstin
Joan Breitman
Paul Bruhwiler
Jehane Burns
Barbara Charles
Laurence Davis
Richard Donges
Maria Ewing
Glen Fleck
Diane Fuller
Alex Funke
Richard Funkhouser
Richard Gutierrez
Ella Hogan
Hap Johnson
Ellen Kaufman
Ruth Laug
Myra Maxwell
Emily Mayeda
Michael Mosher
Pat Naritomi
Gerald Nash
David Olney
Jeannine Oppewall
Theodore Orlan
Sam Passalacqua
Mariea Poole
Robert Richards
Karl Rimer
Max Risselada
Frank Romero
Douglas Ryan
Kenneth Schuster
Robert Staples
Frederick Steady
Lynn Stoller
Gene Takeshita
Bill Tondreau
Randall Walker
Dan Zimbaldi
Beth Zimmerman

Charles and IBM's president, Frank Carey, discussing the History Wall

1971

Exhibition: *A Computer Perspective*

A Computer Perspective, an exhibition designed by the Eames Office for the IBM Corporation, was installed in the IBM Corporate Exhibit Center on Madison Avenue and 57th Street in New York City. It opened on February 17, 1971, and closed in mid-1975. The exhibition traced the history, from 1890 to 1950, of the development of the modern electronic computer along three major paths: the growth of logical automata, the development of statistical machines, and the evolution of calculators.

A "History Wall," composed of six eight-foot panels, each representing a decade, documented the key events and inventions of the sixty-year period. Artifacts, documents, and photographs mounted in overlapping layers were displayed in chronological order to illustrate the complex historical and scientific events that contributed to the development of the computer. An overlay of lines and text blocks, laid out on a glass panel installed over the length of the entire wall, provided a viewing guide, explanatory text, and caption material. In addition to the wall, which was the focal point of the exhibition, both vintage and modern machines, including early electric tabulators, punch-card

Visitors viewing the installed History Wall

Panels from the second two decades represented on the History Wall

Charles and Eliot Noyes reviewing the plan for the *Computer Perspective* exhibition

Michael Sullivan and Lynn Stoller, IBM management representatives who were the Eameses' liaisons for *Computer Perspective*

Zeke Seligson, an IBM manager, on a visit to the Eames Office

A section of the glass overlay in front of the History Wall indicating lines of computer development

The Hollerith tabulating machine used in the 1890 U.S. census with the History Wall in the background

Panels from the last two decades of the History Wall

Charles is appointed to the Visiting Committee on the Arts at the Massachusetts Institute of Technology, Cambridge.

Statistical tabulators, one part of the freestanding exhibition elements

Visitors playing the interactive "Twenty Questions" game in the exhibition

Detail of the AV Rack with the History Wall in the background

A view of the *Computer Perspective* exhibition through the window of the IBM Corporate Exhibit Center

Staff members Robert Staples and Alex Funke planning the exhibition's graphic production

Staff members Barbara Charles and David Olney working on the History Wall mock-up

accounting machines, data processors, and modern computers, were arranged on display stands in the adjacent space.

A multiscreen slide show of five hundred images, called the "AV [or Audiovisual] Rack," accompanied the exhibition and highlighted a cross section of the newest computer applications. Visitors could also play an interactive game of "Twenty Questions" with a computer by trying to guess which subject (animal, vegetable, or mineral) the computer had selected.

The exhibition represented two years of research and preparation by the Eames Office. Robert Staples was the staff member responsible for the organization and design of the exhibition, and Barbara Charles compiled the research. Glen Fleck and Ralph Caplan wrote the exhibition text. I. Bernard Cohen and Owen Gingerich of Harvard University served as consultants.

The History Wall in the exhibition *A Computer Perspective* represented a new Eames Office approach to presenting historical material in timeline form. Unlike previously produced timelines, which were essentially two-dimensional in form, the *Computer Perspective* timeline included actual computer artifacts that projected out from the wall interspersed with panels of graphics and documents and other objects and pictorial materials placed at varying distances from the back panel of the wall. As the visitor moved along the wall, the objects appeared and disappeared from view in a constantly shifting display. Complex to mount and to read, the wall, which provided an analog to the multiplicity of technical and social influences that shaped the development of the electronic computer, required a willingness to become involved and a reasonable amount of concentration from the viewer.

The exhibition was the first of several designed by the Eames Office for the IBM Corporate Exhibit Center.

Charles photographing a one-inch scale model of the *Computer Perspective* exhibition

Staff members Bill Tondreau, Richard Steadry, an unidentified staff member, Barbara Charles, and Glen Fleck preparing the model for photography

An early Eames Office scale model of the exhibition space

November 6: The House of Cards (pp. 168–175) receives a certificate of merit from the German Industrial Exhibition.

Right: The Eames Office develops a proposal for an exhibition on information and related material for *The Washington Post*, Washington, D.C. The proposal did not go forward

Staff: 1971
901 Washington Boulevard
Jonathan Boorstin
Joan Breitman
Paul Bruhwiler
Jehane Burns
Barbara Charles
Laurence Davis
Richard Donges
Maria Ewing
Glen Fleck
Diane Fuller
Alex Funke
Richard Funkhouser
Richard Gutierrez
Ella Hogan
Hap Johnson
Ellen Kaufman
Ruth Laug
Myra Maxwell
Emily Mayeda
Michael Mosher
Pat Naritomi
Gerald Nash
David Olney
Jeannine Oppewall
Theodore Orlan
Sam Passalacqua
Mariea Poole
Robert Richards
Karl Rimer
Max Risselada
Frank Romero
Douglas Ryan
Kenneth Schuster
Robert Staples
Frederick Steadry
Lynn Stoller
Gene Takeshita
Bill Tondreau
Randall Walker
Dan Zimbaldi
Beth Zimmerman

1971

Film: *Computer Landscape*

Computer Landscape was made as a complement to the exhibition *A Computer Perspective* (pp. 364–369), which was installed in 1971 at the IBM Corporate Exhibit Center in New York City.

The word "landscape" in the film's title tells the message. Photographed in live-action, the film provides a glimpse into the operation of large-system computers and the people who operate them and shows how a large modern computer room looks. The film features close-ups and details of computers and other data-processing equipment found in computer facilities.

Shown along with the exhibition of historical artifacts, the film demonstrates the vast difference between the capacity to process information in early hand-operated calculators and in the electronic data processors of today and the resulting dramatic increase in the amount of and access to information. The film had limited use in the exhibition; it is not in general circulation. The score for *Computer Landscape* was composed and conducted by Elmer Bernstein. It has no narration. (Running time, *Computer Landscape*: 10 minutes; color.)

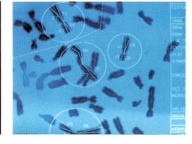

A sequence of frames (reading top to bottom left, top to bottom right) from scenes in *Computer Landscape*. The frames were photographed from 16mm-film footage

December 15: Charles lectures at The Architectural League of New York City.

Staff: 1971
901 Washington Boulevard
Jonathan Boorstin
Joan Breitman
Paul Bruhwiler
Jehane Burns
Barbara Charles
Laurence Davis
Richard Donges
Maria Ewing
Glen Fleck
Diane Fuller
Alex Funke
Richard Funkhouser
Richard Gutierrez
Ella Hogan
Hap Johnson
Ellen Kaufman
Ruth Laug
Myra Maxwell
Emily Mayeda
Michael Mosher
Pat Naritomi
Gerald Nash
David Olney
Jeannine Oppewall
Theodore Orlan
Sam Passalacqua
Mariea Poole
Robert Richards
Karl Rimer
Max Risselada
Frank Romero
Douglas Ryan
Kenneth Schuster
Robert Staples
Frederick Steadry
Lynn Stoller
Gene Takeshita
Bill Tondreau
Randall Walker
Dan Zimbaldi
Beth Zimmerman

Staff member Randall Walker building a molding form

Staff member Karl Rimer laying up the Loose Cushion chair shape

1971

Loose Cushion Armchair

In 1968 the Eames Office began to experiment with incorporating molded polyurethane foam into the design of chairs and sofas. Molded foam had several advantages over cushion foam: contours could be shaped, seat and back pads would be firm and comfortable, and its use would eliminate the need to keep upholstery under tight tension. The Loose Cushion Armchair was introduced by Herman Miller, Inc., in 1971. It was based to some extent on the shape and materials of the 1950 fiberglass armchair (pp. 138–141) but was quite different in proportion and construction. The shaped aluminum base was an adaptation of the Time-Life Chair of 1960 (pp. 248–249).

The Loose Cushion Armchair has a formed-in-place urethane foam filling. This unique process bonds together the chair's fabric or vinyl cover, foam core, and outer shell. The fabric is cut and sewn to size (except for the vinyl, which has no seams) and then vacuum-drawn into a mold. The matching mold is the already-formed polyester seat shell. The molds with the sandwiched fabric are held together by a metal ring clamped to the shell's contour. Urethane foam is injected through a hole left in the seat mold, filling the space between the shell and the fabric and varying in thickness from ¾ inch to 3 inches. A wide band of vinyl binds the edges together, and a loose padded cushion with a welted edge is attached to the contoured seat with Velcro strips.

The Loose Cushion Armchair can be used as a desk, lobby, or conference room chair. Herman Miller still produces the chair in a 30-inch height (with plastic glides) and a 32-inch height (with 2-inch casters), and in dark-tone, neutral light, and parchment-colored shells. The molded upholstery is available in a choice of fabrics and has dark or light vinyl edging.

A tufted-cushion chair and a Loose Cushion Sofa, an expanded two-seater version of the chair, were designed but never produced beyond the prototype. The base of the sofa was similar to the base developed for the Tandem Seating systems (pp. 274–275).

Top: Profile of an early version of the Loose Cushion Sofa and the swivel reclining chair. Above: Swivel chair and sofa

Production model of the swivel reclining Loose Cushion Armchair

Left and right: Ray and Charles wearing printed faces from an illustrated magazine

Staff: 1971
901 Washington Boulevard
Jonathan Boorstin
Joan Breitman
Paul Bruhwiler
Jehane Burns
Barbara Charles
Laurence Davis
Richard Donges
Maria Ewing
Glen Fleck
Diane Fuller
Alex Funke
Richard Funkhouser
Richard Gutierrez
Ella Hogan
Hap Johnson
Ellen Kaufman
Ruth Laug
Myra Maxwell
Emily Mayeda
Michael Mosher
Pat Naritomi
Gerald Nash
David Olney
Jeannine Oppewall
Theodore Orlan
Sam Passalacqua
Mariea Poole
Robert Richards
Karl Rimer
Max Risselada
Frank Romero
Douglas Ryan
Kenneth Schuster
Robert Staples
Frederick Steadry
Lynn Stoller
Gene Takeshita
Bill Tondreau
Randall Walker
Dan Zimbaldi
Beth Zimmerman

1971

Film: *Clown Face*

Clown Face was made for Bill Ballantine, director of the Clown College of Ringling Brothers' Barnum & Bailey Circus. Intended as a record of famous clowns' makeup and as a training film, it is a close-up look at the precise and classical art of applying makeup.

In his book *Clown Alley*, Bill Ballantine recalls that he first met the Eameses in the summer of 1948 when they photographed the backyard activity of the circus during a Los Angeles engagement. The Ballantines and the Eameses kept in touch through the years, and Ballantine acted as a guide (and protector) during Charles's photo sessions at the circus.

Ballantine, who often quoted Charles and showed Eames slides in his clown alley classes, approached Charles to provide him with "a casual couple of hundred feet of film" that he could use in teaching clown makeup. Charles agreed and filming sessions on location at the circus were arranged to coincide with an Oakland, California, performance. Shooting began at eight A.M. and continued through each day, with Charles working around the clowns' participation in the performances. At the time he made the film, Charles was on the board of the Ringling Clown College.

The "casual couple of hundred feet of film" that began as a tutorial on clown makeup became a twenty-minute film that is also an exercise in demonstrating the concept of symmetry, using the symmetry of the human face as its example.

Several famous clowns from the Ringling Brothers' Circus, including Otto Griebling, Frosty Little, and Lou Jacobs, appear in the film applying their own special makeup in "Clown Alley." The circus music playing on the film's sound track was recorded from the performances (it indicated to the clowns what was appearing in the ring and how much time was left until their next appearance). There is no narration. The film is in general circulation. The original version of the film, finished in 1971, was recut to a shorter version in 1972. (Running time, *Clown Face*: 16 minutes; color.)

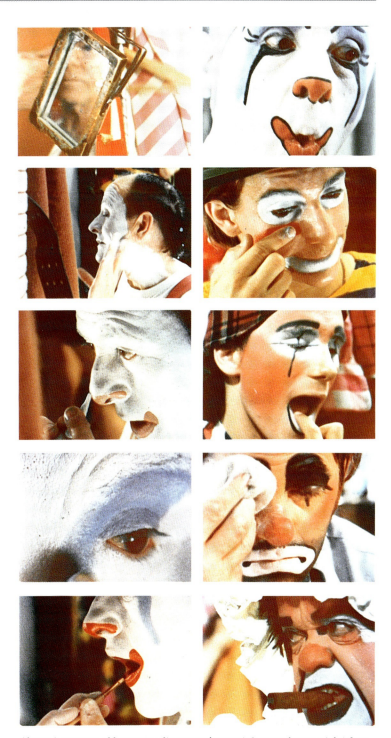

Above: A sequence of frames (reading top to bottom left, top to bottom right) from scenes in *Clown Face*. Opposite: Two frames from the beginning of *Clown Face*. The frames were photographed from 16mm-film footage

January 11: Charles lectures at the IBM Communication Conference, New York City.

Staff: 1972
901 Washington Boulevard
Philip Bedel
Joseph Bishop
Jonathan Boorstin
Joan Breitman
Paul Bruhwiler
Jehane Burns
Richard Donges
Ann Enkoji
Maria Ewing
Glen Fleck
Diane Fuller
Alex Funke
Richard Funkhouser
Margaret Gruen
Ann Helverson
Ella Hogan
Hap Johnson
Ellen Kaufman
Sarah Kuhn
Emily Mayeda
Myron Moskwa
John Neuhart
David Olney
Jeannine Oppewall
Donna Orr
Sam Passalacqua
Mariea Poole
Marny Randall
Robert Richards
Karl Rimer
Michael Ripps
Steve Slocomb
Robert Staples
Michael Uris
Bill Tondreau
Randall Walker
Morris Zaslavsky
Nancy Zaslavsky

Jazz drummer Shelly Manne during the recording session for the *Computer Perspective* sound track

 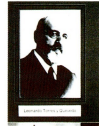 

1972

Film: *Computer Perspective*

The film *Computer Perspective* was based on an existing slide show the Eames Office had made about the exhibition *A Computer Perspective*, produced for the IBM Corporation in 1971. The film is a visual survey of the collection of artifacts, ideas, events, and memorabilia displayed in the exhibition to represent important milestones in the development of the electronic computer. A rapid succession of still images and live-action footage of the exhibition details the decade-by-decade (1890–1950) progression of events in science, technology, history, and business that culminated in the electronic computer.

The script was written by Glen Fleck with Charles and narrated by Gregory Peck and Joan Gardner. The music was composed and conducted by Elmer Bernstein with percussion improvisation by jazz musician Shelley Manne. *Computer Perspective* is not in general circulation. (Running time, *Computer Perspective*: 8 minutes; color.)

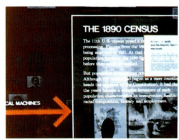 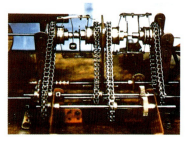

A sequence of frames (reading top to bottom left, top to bottom right) from scenes in *Computer Perspective*. The frames were photographed from 16mm-film footage

Staff: 1972
901 Washington Boulevard
Philip Bedel
Joseph Bishop
Jonathan Boorstin
Joan Breitman
Paul Bruhwiler
Jehane Burns
Richard Donges
Ann Enkoji
Maria Ewing
Glen Fleck
Diane Fuller
Alex Funke
Richard Funkhouser
Margaret Gruen
Ann Helverson
Ella Hogan
Hap Johnson
Ellen Kaufman
Sarah Kuhn
Emily Mayeda
Myron Moskwa
John Neuhart
David Olney
Jeannine Oppewall
Donna Orr
Sam Passalacqua
Mariea Poole
Marry Randall
Robert Richards
Karl Rimer
Michael Ripps
Steve Slocomb
Robert Staples
Michael Uris
Bill Tondreau
Randall Walker
Morris Zaslavsky
Nancy Zaslavsky

Jesse Takamiyama lying on the Eames Chaise

1972

Film: *Sumo Wrestler*

Sumo Wrestler was a "spur-of-the-moment" film made during a chance visit to the Eames Office by a world-class Japanese sumo wrestler, Jesse Takamiyama, and his hairdresser. Introduced to the Eameses by Miyoko Sasaki, an Eames friend and former staff member, the two guests stopped long enough for Charles to record on film the step-by-step preparation of the traditional coiffure Takamiyama wore only while wrestling. Born in Hawaii, Takamiyama was the first foreign sumo wrestler to be honored in Japan.

The involved discipline of preparing and dressing the hair according to a traditional set of rules was as intriguing to Charles as the discipline of a clown applying makeup or of a Viennese baker preparing and serving beautiful pastries according to established and time-honored customs (p. 203). Charles delighted in discovering processes such as the sumo hairdressing routine, processes that reaffirmed his belief in the need to identify, preserve, and learn from the best of traditional forms.

Sumo Wrestler was photographed in color but was left unfinished, and there is no narration or sound track.

A sequence of frames (reading top to bottom left, top to bottom right) from scenes in the unfinished film *Sumo Wrestler*. The frames were photographed from 16mm-film footage

February 8: Nancy Hanks of the National Endowment for the Arts and Charles speak at Scripps College, Claremont, California.

The Eames Office works on a film about the scientific process for *Scientific American* magazine entitled *Complexity*. The film is not completed.

Staff: 1972
901 Washington Boulevard
Philip Bedel
Joseph Bishop
Jonathan Boorstin
Joan Breitman
Paul Bruhwiler
Jehane Burns
Richard Donges
Ann Enkoji
Maria Ewing
Glen Fleck
Diane Fuller
Alex Funke
Richard Funkhouser
Margaret Gruen
Ann Helverson
Ella Hogan
Hap Johnson
Ellen Kaufman
Sarah Kuhn
Emily Mayeda
Myron Moskwa
John Neuhart
David Olney
Jeannine Oppewall
Donna Orr
Sam Passalacqua
Mariea Poole
Marny Randall
Robert Richards
Karl Rimer
Michael Ripps
Steve Slocomb
Robert Staples
Michael Uris
Bill Tondreau
Randall Walker
Morris Zaslavsky
Nancy Zaslavsky

1972

Exhibition: *Wallace J. Eckert: Celestial Mechanic*

The exhibition *Wallace J. Eckert: Celestial Mechanic*, which was first installed in February 1972 in the IBM Corporate Exhibit Center at 590 Madison Avenue in New York City, documented the work of astronomer Wallace Eckert. Working with IBM, Eckert helped introduce computers into the field of astronomy. His contributions to celestial navigation, star mapping, and the study of the complex motions of the moon were detailed in the show. As director of the Nautical Almanac Office in the early 1940s, Eckert produced the first air almanac. He was invited by Thomas Watson, Sr., president of IBM, to join the corporation in 1944, and he became the director of the Watson Scientific Computing Laboratory at Columbia University. In 1954, while at Columbia, Eckert was instrumental in the development of the Naval Ordnance Research Calculator, which was then the most powerful computing machine of its time.

The exhibition was divided into three main areas: "Air Almanac," "Lunar Theory," and "Astronomy." It included a timeline of Eckert's career, photographs and text explaining his work and its place in astronomy, and quotations from his writings. A glass display case held memorabilia and samples of Eckert's research materials. Some of the exhibits were mounted on painted plywood columns with aluminum bases and mirrored Plexiglas plinths. Others were hung in the windows facing Madison Avenue and 57th Street. Gary Harvey and Display Studios, Inc., of Astoria, New York, fabricated the exhibit structures.

Exhibition venues: Museum of Science, Boston, Massachusetts; Burndy Library, Stamford, Connecticut; Krohn Observatory, Cincinnati, Ohio; American Astronomical Society, University of Rochester, Rochester, New York.

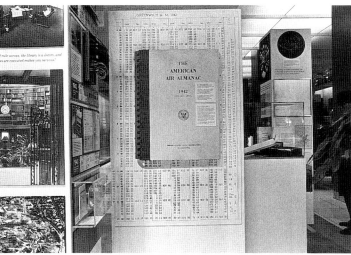

Above: A memorabilia case showing Eckert's personal effects and books. Opposite top: Display pylons from the *Eckert* exhibition seen through the windows at 590 Madison Avenue. Opposite: View of the *Eckert* exhibition in the IBM Corporate Exhibit Center

Top: Detail of the columnar timeline designed by the Eames Office for the exhibition. Above: Display pylon featuring Eckert's air almanac

March 20: Charles speaks to the University of Toronto Alumni Association of the Faculty of Architecture, Toronto, Canada.

April 4: Charles delivers a lecture at the University of Colorado, Boulder.

April 10: Charles speaks at Pratt Institute, Brooklyn, New York.

Staff: 1972
901 Washington Boulevard
Philip Bedel
Joseph Bishop
Jonathan Boorstin
Joan Breitman
Paul Bruthwiler
Jehane Burns
Richard Donges
Ann Enkoji
Maria Ewing
Glen Fleck
Diane Fuller
Alex Funke
Richard Funkhouser
Margaret Gruen
Ann Helverson
Ella Hogan
Hap Johnson
Ellen Kaufman
Sarah Kuhn
Emily Mayeda
Myron Moskwa
John Neuhart
David Olney
Jeannine Oppewall
Donna Orr
Sam Passalacqua
Mariea Poole
Marny Randall
Robert Richards
Karl Rimer
Michael Ripps
Steve Slocomb
Robert Staples
Michael Uris
Bill Tondreau
Randall Walker
Morris Zaslavsky
Nancy Zaslavsky

1972

Exhibition: *Fibonacci: Growth and Form*

After the exhibition *A Computer Perspective* (pp. 364–369), the Eames Office designed a series of small traveling exhibitions on astronomy and mathematics-oriented subjects for the IBM Corporate Exhibit Center in New York City. IBM originally wanted the Eames Office to design exhibitions to celebrate seasonal holidays, but Charles decided to incorporate scientific subject matter that was relevant to each holiday into each exhibition. *Fibonacci: Growth and Form*, which was shown in the spring, was about the mathematical pattern that occurs in growing things.

Leonardo Fibonacci (c.1170–1250), an Italian mathematician, devised a numerical sequence in which each succeeding number is the sum of the two numbers immediately preceding it. The same proportional sequence, which combines additive and geometric properties, was found in the growth patterns of plants. The Eames exhibition explained the Fibonacci sequence and its relationship to the golden section (the nineteenth-century term for an "ideal" geometric proportion).

The exhibition, installed in the street-level display area in the corner of the IBM building at Madison Avenue and 57th Street, consisted of two triforms constructed out of back-to-back rectangular birch plywood panels joined by Y-shaped aluminum connectors. Text, diagrams, and photographs of plants and flowers taken by Charles, Alex Funke, and Bill Tondreau were mounted on the twelve surfaces. Hanging panels with photographs and text were placed in the windows. Clusters of potted flowers and plants were also added to the installation. Jehane Burns wrote the display text; Robert Staples was the staff designer responsible for developing the exhibition. The exhibition was fabricated by Gary Harvey and Display Studios, Inc., of Astoria, New York.

Exhibition venues: Museum of Science, Boston, Massachusetts; Coe College, Ames, Iowa; Burndy Library, Stamford, Connecticut; IBM Data Processing Division Headquarters, White Plains, New York. *Connections: The Work of Charles and Ray Eames*: Wight Art Gallery, University of California, Los Angeles; Humanities Research Center, University of Texas, Austin; Washington University and Laumeier Gallery, St. Louis, Missouri; University of East Anglia, Norwich, England. *Five Small Exhibitions*: University of Cincinnati, Cincinnati, Ohio; University of Arizona, Tucson.

Opposite top: The *Fibonacci* exhibition seen through the windows of the IBM Corporate Exhibit Center. Opposite: View of the *Fibonacci* exhibition

Top: Images of flowers photographed for the *Fibonacci* exhibition by Charles and the Eames Office staff. Above: A detail of an exhibition graphic panel explaining the Fibonacci sequence

April 11: Charles speaks at the Philadelphia Museum of Art, Philadelphia, Pennsylvania.

April 13: Charles is appointed to the Architects' Panel of the National Council on the Arts.

April 14: Charles meets with the USIA Jefferson Committee in Washington, D.C., in a preliminary planning session for the United States bicentennial celebrations.

April 16: Charles lectures at the Dartington Seminar, Devon, England.

Staff: 1972
901 Washington Boulevard
Philip Bedel
Joseph Bishop
Jonathan Boorstin
Joan Breitman
Paul Bruhwiler
Jehane Burns
Richard Donges
Ann Enkoji
Maria Ewing
Glen Fleck
Diane Fuller
Alex Funke
Richard Funkhouser
Margaret Gruen
Ann Helverson
Ella Hogan
Hap Johnson
Ellen Kaufman
Sarah Kuhn
Emily Mayeda
Myron Moskwa
John Neuhart
David Olney
Jeannine Oppewall
Donna Orr
Sam Passalacqua
Mariea Poole
Marry Randall
Robert Richards
Karl Rimer
Michael Ripps
Steve Slocomb
Robert Staples
Michael Uris
Bill Tondreau
Randall Walker
Morris Zaslavsky
Nancy Zaslavsky

A sequence of frames (reading top to bottom left, top to bottom right) from scenes in *Cable*. The frames were photographed from 16mm-film footage

1972

Film: *Cable: The Immediate Future*

Cable, made for the Corporation for Public Broadcasting with a grant from the National Science Foundation, surveys and reports on the background of cable television, its place in the world of television, and its future potential as a communications tool in the workplace, educational institutions, the home, and the community.

Charles turned the management and production of the *Cable* film over to staff member Glen Fleck, a veteran of many Eames Office films. The film was made in the Eames Office and includes live-action footage of people using cable television as a medium for accessing information. Animated sequences explain the history of cable television and how the medium functions. Glen Fleck wrote the narration and directed the film. The narration was read by Casey Casem, Joan Gardner, and John Neuhart. Philip A. Rubin acted as technical adviser. The music is by Buddy Collette. The film is not in general circulation. (Running time, *Cable*: 10 minutes; color.)

April 27: Charles speaks to the Manhattan Beach Association for Gifted Children, Joslyn Center, Manhattan Beach, California.

May 7: Charles receives the Industrial Arts Medal from the American Institute of Architects, Houston, Texas.

May 17: Charles lectures to the Associated Councils of the Arts Conference, Minneapolis, Minnesota.

Staff: 1972
901 Washington Boulevard
Philip Bedel
Joseph Bishop
Jonathan Boorstin
Joan Breitman
Paul Bruhwiler
Jehane Burns
Richard Donges
Ann Enkoji
Maria Ewing
Glen Fleck
Diane Fuller
Alex Funke
Richard Funkhouser
Margaret Gruen
Ann Helverson
Ella Hogan
Hap Johnson
Sarah Kuhn
Ellen Kaufman
Emily Mayeda
Myron Moskwa
John Neuhart
David Olney
Jeannine Oppewall
Donna Orr
Sam Passalacqua
Mariea Poole
Marny Randall
Robert Richards
Karl Rimer
Michael Ripps
Steve Slocomb
Robert Staples
Michael Uris
Bill Tondreau
Randall Walker
Morris Zaslavsky
Nancy Zaslavsky

Raymond Redheffer shooting the stop-motion animation for *Alpha*

1972

Film: *Alpha*

Alpha is the first in a series of three films on mathematics conceived and produced by Raymond Redheffer, professor of mathematics at the University of California, Los Angeles, and mathematics consultant to the *Mathematica* exhibition (pp. 254–259). The film was made in the Eames Office with the design and technical assistance of Eames staff members John Neuhart, Steve Slocomb, Karl Rimer, and Richard Donges. Redheffer, an Eames friend and colleague since *Mathematica*, took seriously Charles's advice to search out the aesthetic character of his discipline. Charles made staff and equipment available to Redheffer to try out his ideas in a series of films.

Alpha is a stop-motion, animated sequence, photographed by Redheffer, that begins with an algebraic expression, elaborates on it (until the screen is filled with symbols and numbers), and then reduces it back to its original form. The film has no narration and was designed to run as a continuous loop (forward or backward) that could be augmented with the explanation of a classroom teacher. The sequence was produced by photographing cut-out characters and symbols against a glass plane; the symbols were moved step-by-step through the action. The music track was assembled from jazz recordings.

The short film was designed to be a commercial for the IBM Corporation to present on a network television broadcast. Although never shown on television, the film is in general circulation and was added to the IBM Corporation Film Library to be made available to schools and interested institutions. (Running time, *Alpha*: 1 minute, 16 seconds; color.)

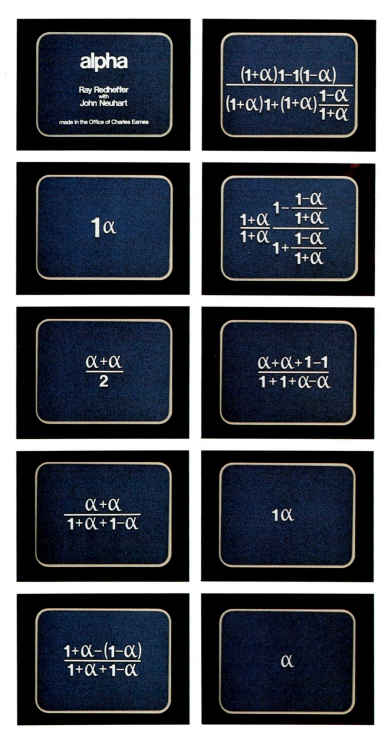

A sequence of frames (reading top to bottom left, top to bottom right) from scenes in *Alpha*. The frames were photographed from 16mm-film footage

May 25: Charles delivers the commencement address at the School of Medicine, University of Pittsburgh, Pittsburgh, Pennsylvania.

Staff: 1972
901 Washington Boulevard
Philip Bedel
Joseph Bishop
Jonathan Boorstin
Joan Breitman
Paul Bruhwiler
Jehane Burns
Richard Donges
Ann Enkoji
Maria Ewing
Glen Fleck
Diane Fuller
Alex Funke
Richard Funkhouser
Margaret Gruen
Ann Helverson
Ella Hogan
Hap Johnson
Ellen Kaufman
Sarah Kuhn
Emily Mayeda
Myron Moskwa
John Neuhart
David Olney
Jeannine Oppewall
Donna Orr
Sam Passalacqua
Mariea Poole
Marny Randall
Robert Richards
Karl Rimer
Michael Ripps
Steve Slocomb
Robert Staples
Michael Uris
Bill Tondreau
Randall Walker
Morris Zaslavsky
Nancy Zaslavsky

1972

Film: *Banana Leaf: Something About Transformations and Rediscovery*

Banana Leaf is a parable, photographed in live action, about the use of eating utensils in India. The film is a social commentary about the significance and status people attach to their artifacts. Charles had told the story of the banana leaf in a lecture to the American Association for the Advancement of Science in December 1971:

> The very poor man [in India] eats his meal off a banana leaf. A little higher in the scale is a low-fired earthenware dish, a *tali*. Then a glazed *tali*; then brass, then bell bronze, or polished marble, which are both very handsome—then to show you can do better than that, you get into things that are rather questionable: silver plate, solid silver—presumably even gold. But there are some superior men—with not only means but understanding, and probably some spiritual training as well—who will go a step further, and eat off a banana leaf.

The film begins with a peasant eating his meal from a banana leaf and progresses up the social ladder, showing more and more precious eating utensils used by people of higher and higher castes. It ends with a member of the highest caste, a priest, who, like the peasant, is seen eating from a banana leaf.

Banana Leaf is an unfinished, unreleased film that was transferred to video; it was written and narrated by Charles. It was begun as a *Mathematica* exhibition peep show (pp. 260–261) to demonstrate the concept of relative values. (Running time, *Banana Leaf*: 1 minute, 32 seconds; color.)

A sequence of frames (reading top to bottom left, top to bottom right) from scenes in *Banana Leaf*. The frames were photographed from 16mm-film footage

382

Charles is appointed a visiting lecturer at the School of Architecture and Urban Planning, University of California, Los Angeles.

Staff: 1972
901 Washington Boulevard
Philip Bedel
Joseph Bishop
Jonathan Boorstin
Joan Breitman
Paul Bruhwiler
Jehane Burns
Richard Donges
Ann Enkoji
Maria Ewing
Glen Fleck
Diane Fuller
Alex Funke
Richard Funkhouser
Margaret Gruen
Ann Helverson
Ella Hogan
Hap Johnson
Ellen Kaufman
Sarah Kuhn
Emily Mayeda
Myron Moskwa
John Neuhart
David Olney
Jeannine Oppewall
Donna Orr
Sam Passalacqua
Mariea Poole
Marny Randall
Robert Richards
Karl Rimer
Michael Ripps
Steve Slocomb
Robert Staples
Michael Uris
Bill Tondreau
Randall Walker
Morris Zaslavsky
Nancy Zaslavsky

Ray with an SX-70 camera

Eames, Llisa, Aristides, and Lucia Demetrios on a visit to the Eames Office

1972

Film: *SX-70*

In 1972 the Polaroid Corporation commissioned the Eames Office to produce a film introducing the new and revolutionary SX-70 instant-photography camera, which had been developed by Edwin Land. The film documents the invention of the system, demonstrates several potential uses for the camera, and shows how the camera operates. It was first shown at a Polaroid stockholders' meeting and used subsequently within Polaroid as a sales tool.

The film was produced from live-action footage and some animated segments. The script was written with Glen Fleck and included a concluding statement by MIT physicist Philip Morrison, a longtime friend of Edwin Land. The music was composed and conducted by Elmer Bernstein.

SX-70 was the first of four films made for Polaroid by the Eames Office (pp. 434, 442, 443). The film won a Bronze Plaque at the Columbus International Film Festival in 1975. It is in general circulation. (Running time, *SX-70*: 11 minutes; color.)

A sequence of frames (reading top to bottom left, top to bottom right) from scenes in *SX-70*. The frames were photographed from 16mm-film footage

Staff: 1972
901 Washington Boulevard
Philip Bedel
Joseph Bishop
Jonathan Boorstin
Joan Bretiman
Paul Bruhwiler
Jehane Burns
Richard Donges
Ann Enkoji
Maria Ewing
Glen Fleck
Diane Fuller
Alex Funke
Richard Funkhouser
Margaret Gruen
Ann Helverson
Ella Hogan
Hap Johnson
Ellen Kaufman
Sarah Kuhn
Emily Mayeda
Myron Moskwa
John Neuhart
David Olney
Jeannine Oppewall
Donna Orr
Sam Passalacqua
Mariea Poole
Marny Randall
Robert Richards
Karl Rimer
Michael Ripps
Steve Slocomb
Robert Staples
Michael Uris
Bill Tondreau
Randall Walker
Morris Zaslavsky
Nancy Zaslavsky

Owen Gingerich, professor of astronomy and the history of science at Harvard, staff member Jeannine Oppewall, and Charles reviewing *Copernicus* exhibition plans

1972

Exhibition: *Copernicus*

Copernicus, the third science-related exhibition produced by the Eames Office for the IBM Corporate Exhibit Center in New York City, celebrated the five-hundredth anniversary of the astronomer's birth. Nicholaus Copernicus, considered the founder of modern astronomy, developed the theory that the sun was at the center of the universe and traveled in an orbit that affected the motion of other heavenly bodies, including the orbit of the earth. The exhibition provided an overview of Copernicus's life, his work in astronomy, and the relationship of his theories to those of earlier and later astronomers and physicists.

The exhibition was mounted on a rectangular structure of glass and laminate panels attached to an overhead Unistrut grid. Mounted photographs, diagrams, and text were attached directly to the glass- and Formica-clad plywood display walls. Plexiglas artifacts cases were affixed to the panel supports. Each vertical glass or Formica unit dealt with a specific aspect of Copernicus's life. The titles of each subject unit —"Copernicus at School," "Medieval Curriculum," "Astronomy and the Theologians," "Ancient Cosmologies," "Celestial Physicists—Kepler, Galileo, and Newton," and "The Age of Exploration"—appeared at the top of the vertical panels.

Copernicus's heliocentric theory (detailed in his book *De Revolutionibus*) challenged the geocentric world models of Aristotle and Ptolemy that had been the basis of astronomical calculations for centuries. Exhibition panels compared the two concepts, and a working mechanical model showed how each system accounts for the same

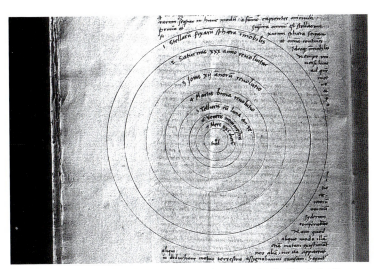

Above: A photographic detail from Copernicus's manuscript *De Revolutionibus*. Opposite top: *Copernicus* exhibition looking through the windows of the IBM Corporate Exhibit Center. Opposite: Graphic panel at the entrance to the exhibition showing a star map from the sixteenth century

Views of the vertical panels of photographs and text in the *Copernicus* exhibition that were devoted to different periods in Copernicus's life

I. Bernard Cohen, professor of the history of science at Harvard University, and Charles reviewing exhibition text

Staff member Richard Donges working on a model that was used in the *Copernicus* exhibition for demonstrating geocentric and heliocentric theories

Staff member Emily Mayeda preparing the puppets for the *Copernicus* exhibition Christmas display of Polish toys and objects

Staff member Sam Passalacqua preparing the Polish paper cutouts for the *Copernicus* exhibition Christmas display

celestial phenomena. The installation also included a timeline presenting Copernicus's biography in relation to historic events from 1460 to 1650. Exhibition visitors were given an illustrated pamphlet that summarized the exhibition and incorporated a foldout of the timeline.

Charles traveled to Europe and took most of the photographs used in the exhibition at Jagiellonian University, Kraców and Frombork Cathedral in Poland, where Copernicus lived and worked most of his life, and at the Uppsala University Library in Sweden, where his books, treatises, and manuscripts were taken as war booty during the Thirty Years War. Owen Gingerich, professor of astronomy and the history of science and I. Bernard Cohen, professor of the history of science (both from Harvard University), served as consultants on the project. Jehane Burns and Jeannine Oppewall researched and wrote the exhibition text. Robert Staples and Richard Donges developed the exhibition structures and the working models. Gary Harvey and Display Studios, Inc., of Astoria, New York, fabricated the exhibition panels.

For the December 1972 opening, the windows of the IBM Corporate Exhibition Center on Madison Avenue were filled with objects used in Polish Christmas celebrations. Breads in the shape of animals and fish, puppets collected by the Eameses and Alexander Girard, peasant's paper cutouts, a Polish pie, an elaborate six-foot model cathedral made of tinfoil (the winning entry in a Kraków competition where Charles purchased it), and a Christmas creche were part of the Christmas show.

Exhibition venues: California Museum of Science and Industry, Los Angeles; Pacific Science Center, Seattle, Washington; San Diego Hall of Science, San Diego, California; Lawrence Hall of Science, Berkeley, California; Adler Planetarium, Chicago, Illinois; National Air and Space Administration Bicentennial, Washington, D.C.; Exposition on Science and Technology, Cape Kennedy, Florida; Ontario Science Centre, Toronto, Canada; Exploratorium, San Francisco, California. *Connections: The Work of Charles and Ray Eames*: Wight Art Gallery, University of California, Los Angeles; Humanities Research Center, University of Texas, Austin; Washington University and Laumeier Gallery, St. Louis, Missouri. *Five Small Exhibitions*: University of Cincinnati, Cincinnati, Ohio; University of Arizona, Tucson.

Opposite: Close-up photographs of Polish toys and objects used in the Christmas display in the *Copernicus* exhibition. The Christmas material was shown in the IBM Corporate Exhibit Center only; it did not travel with the exhibition

Top, middle, and above: Views through the IBM Corporate Exhibit Center windows of the Polish Christmas cathedral, creche, and puppets

November 30: Charles attends an Alfred Sloan Memorial Foundation meeting, New York City.

Staff: 1972
901 Washington Boulevard
Philip Bedel
Joseph Bishop
Jonathan Boorstin
Joan Breitman
Paul Bruhwiler
Jehane Burns
Richard Donges
Ann Enkoji
Maria Ewing
Glen Fleck
Diane Fuller
Alex Funke
Richard Funkhouser
Margaret Gruen
Ann Helverson
Ella Hogan
Hap Johnson
Ellen Kaufman
Sarah Kuhn
Emily Mayeda
Myron Moskwa
John Neuhart
David Olney
Jeannine Oppewall
Donna Orr
Sam Passalacqua
Mariea Poole
Marty Randall
Robert Richards
Karl Rimer
Michael Ripps
Steve Slocomb
Robert Staples
Michael Uris
Bill Tondreau
Randall Walker
Morris Zaslavsky
Nancy Zaslavsky

1972

Film: *Design Q & A*

Design Q & A is a slide film (slides transferred to film footage) about Charles's philosophy of design and the work of the Eames Office. The images—furniture, toys, exhibitions, films, and graphics executed by the Eames Office—are shown in counterpoint to the voice track, in which Charles answers questions posed to him about the design process. The questions, asked by Madame L'Amic of the Musée des Arts Decoratifs in Paris, and answered individually by five designers, were the basis of the exhibition *What Is Design?* (p. 345) held at the Louvre in 1969.

Madame L'Amic's questions and Charles's answers are part of the introduction to this book (pp. 13–15). Charles's answers are an excellent synthesis of his thinking on matters of design and the design process. They define the Eames philosophy and sum up his thirty years of experience as a designer.

Production of the film was sponsored by Herman Miller, Inc. The film's opening and closing guitar music was composed and performed by Laurindo Almeida. The film is in general circulation. (Running time, *Design Q & A*: 5 minutes; color.)

A sequence of frames (reading top to bottom left, top to bottom right) from scenes in *Design Q & A*. The frames were photographed from 16mm-film footage

January 11: Charles delivers a talk at an IBM Corporation communications conference.

Staff: 1973
901 Washington Boulevard
Donald Amundson
Beth Belof
Lonnie Browning
Jehane Burns
Richard Donges
Ann Enkoji
Maria Ewing
Glen Fleck
Alex Funke
Richard Funkhouser
Margaret Gruen
Ann Helverson
Hap Johnson
Harold Lind
Emily Mayeda
Myron Moskwa
John Neuhart
David Olney
Jeannine Oppewall
Donna Orr
Sam Passalacqua
Mariea Poole
Marny Randall
Robert Richards
Karl Rimer
Michael Ripps
Steve Slocomb
Robert Staples
Michael Uris
Randall Walker
Morris Zaslavsky
Nancy Zaslavsky

Musician Laurindo Almeida and Charles at the recording session for *Exponents*

1973

Film: *Exponents: A Study in Generalization*

Exponents is the second in a series of three films on mathematics (pp. 381, 398) developed and animated by Raymond Redheffer and produced in the Eames Office with the technical assistance of staff members Michael Ripps, Steve Slocomb, and Karl Rimer. Charles continued to support Redheffer's efforts because he believed that the films were excellent examples of multidisciplinary thinking.

The film's animation begins by showing the behavior of specific exponents and concludes with the general laws all exponential expressions obey. Algebraic equivalencies are animated and presented visually in simple terms by the manipulation of formulaic expressions. Like its predecessor, *Alpha*, the animated sequences were filmed using only cutout characters and symbols moved against a glass plane that was positioned under the animation camera and photographed frame-by-frame by Redheffer. The film is designed to be a lively and exuberant presentation of the "architecture of algebra," achieved without the use of narration.

The music for *Exponents*, composed and performed by Laurindo Almeida, accompanies the animated sequences. *Exponents* is in general circulation. The film won awards in 1975 from the New York Animation Festival, the Columbus International Film Festival, and the Committee for International Non-Theatrical Events. (Running time, *Exponents*: 3 minutes, 6 seconds; color.)

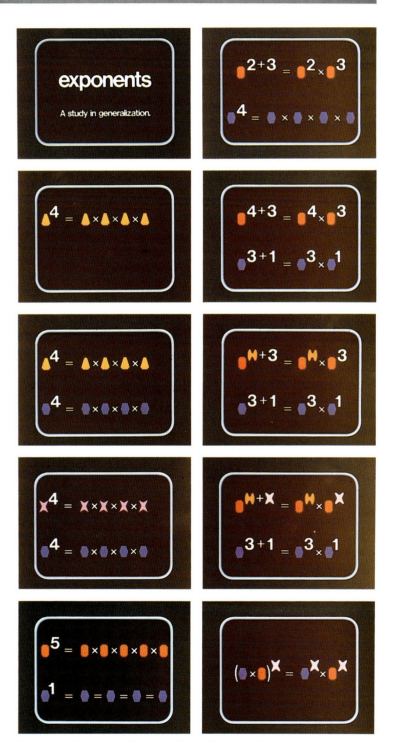

A sequence of frames (reading top to bottom left, top to bottom right) from scenes in *Exponents*. The frames were photographed from 16mm-film footage

Top: A view of the one-inch-scale model of the *Franklin and Jefferson* exhibition built in the Eames Office. Above: A detail of the one-inch-scale model

January 30–February 5: Charles attends the National Science Foundation Conference on Bicentennial Science Planning, University of Arizona, Tempe.

February 8: Charles attends the First Federal Design Assembly press briefing, National Endowment for the Arts, Washington, D.C.

Staff: 1973
901 Washington Boulevard
Donald Amundson
Beth Belof
Lonnie Browning
Jehane Burns
Richard Donges
Ann Enkoji
Maria Ewing
Glen Fleck
Alex Funke
Richard Funkhouser
Margaret Gruen
Ann Helverson
Hap Johnson
Harold Lind
Emily Mayeda
Myron Moskwa
John Neuhart
David Olney
Jeannine Oppewall
Donna Orr
Sam Passalacqua
Mariea Poole
Marny Randall
Robert Richards
Karl Rimer
Michael Ripps
Steve Slocomb
Robert Staples
Michael Uris
Randall Walker
Morris Zaslavsky
Nancy Zaslavsky

1973

Film: *Franklin and Jefferson: Authors of Independence and Architects of the American Experiment*

The Eames Office was commissioned by the United States Information Agency (USIA) to design a traveling exhibition on the life of Thomas Jefferson as part of the American Revolution bicentennial celebrations in 1976. In researching the project, however, it became apparent that a more interesting exhibition could be told by contrasting the life of Thomas Jefferson with his older contemporary, Benjamin Franklin. By comparing the philosophies of two of the primary figures of the American Revolution (the intellectual Jefferson with the pragmatic Franklin), the point of view of each man, it was hoped, would be brought into sharper focus. The study film *Franklin and Jefferson* was produced to present the proposal to the client and to provide a cinematic trip through the proposed exhibition. The film was later used by the USIA to provide information to the embassies and museums that were scheduled to show it during the bicentennial celebrations.

Animation, live-action footage, slides and still photography transferred to film were incorporated into the film outline of the exhibition. The film includes views of the exhibition study model, a timeline of significant historical events of the period, and photographs of Franklin's and Jefferson's writings, personal belongings, and the places where they lived and worked.

Franklin and Jefferson was written by Jehane Burns with Charles. Research and assistance on script development was done by Jeannine Oppewall. The film was narrated by Nina Foch and Philip Bourneuf. The music track included eighteenth-century music from a Smithsonian recording, Mozart's "Brunette" and "Sonata for Piano," and "Bunker Hill" by Andrew Law. Music for the introduction to the film featured the Vienna Philharmonic Wind Group performing "Divertimento" and Menuetto No.3 in E-flat Major. (Running time: *Franklin and Jefferson*: 13 minutes, 4 seconds; color.)

A sequence of frames (reading top to bottom left, top to bottom right) from scenes in *Franklin and Jefferson*. The frames were photographed from 16mm-film footage

Babbage's Analytical Engine

There had been a single, clear glimpse of the computer idea when Charles Babbage designed an "Analytical Engine" about a hundred years before the first modern computer appeared.

His machine was never built, but it combined the essential parts of the computer idea. His machine would calculate, it would process statistics, and it would automatically guide its own actions based on the answers it was producing.

Prologue

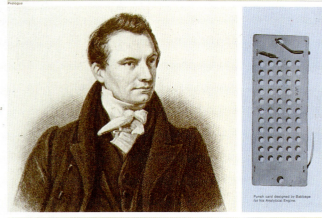

Punch card designed by Babbage for his Analytical Engine.

Perhaps it is because Charles Babbage's work belongs more to our time than to his own that it remains of special interest. While he is recognized today largely for his work on calculating machines, he made other enduring contributions as well. His pushiest effort to secure government subsidies helped set an important precedent, and his book, On the Economy of Machinery and Manufacturers, laid the groundwork for what we know today as operations research.

As a child in Somerset, Babbage's health was poor, and his education at home encouraged such interest and freedom in the field of mathematics that later, at Trinity College, his tutors were a disappointment. As undergraduates, Babbage, John Herschel, and George Peacock founded The Analytical Society, promising each other to "do their best to leave the world wiser than they found it."

Drawn to intellectual societies, Babbage was involved in the founding of the Royal Astronomical Society. Among his friends were Thomas Carlyle, Charles Darwin, Charles Dickens, Pierre Simon de Laplace, Sir Marc Isambard Brunel, Sir George Everest, and the Countess of Lovelace (Lord Byron's daughter), who, through her understanding of mathematics, machines, and the Babbage theories, has been able to pass on some of the most intelligible accounts of Babbage's work.

Babbage's ideas were so advanced and his standards so high that most efforts to realize his plans during his own lifetime were bound to be unsuccessful. Because of this, many view his life as a series of disappointments, missing the magnitude of his productivity and the breadth of his vision.

**Calculating Machines
Statistical Machines
Logical Machines**

It was the bringing together of these three lines of machine development, in the middle of the twentieth century, that made possible an entirely new kind of machine—the electronic digital computer.

Prologue

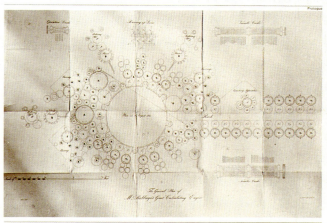

While working on a "special-purpose" calculator in 1823—his Difference Engine—Babbage started the design for a massive device which, if built, would have been the first general purpose machine: the Analytical Engine. Capable of doing any mathematical operation, it would follow the instructions programmed into it by its operators, and even go on to make decisions about which instructions to follow next, based on the results of its own work.

The Analytical Engine's design contained a great many features we now associate with the modern computer. Both information and instructions were entered on punch cards, and stored in a memory (which Babbage called the "store"). Following instructions on the operation cards, a processing unit (the "mill") performed operations on the information and returned the results to the "store." The final results were to be printed out, or automatically set in type.

The Analytical Engine was conceived to be on a grand scale. Powered by steam, it would store a thousand fifty-digit numbers in its memory. When the machine needed additional values for the calculation in progress, it was to signal its operators by ringing a bell.

1890

Punch Cards for Commerce

Masses of government census data had been quickly and automatically processed by Hollerith machines. Now, large industries began applying the machines to their own data-handling problems. Chief among those industries were railroads, insurance companies, and public utilities.

1900 Statistical Machines

Herman Hollerith

Filing section of the Metropolitan Life Insurance Company's home office

To accommodate more information for business use, Hollerith increased the size of his punch cards. He chose the size of the dollar bill then in use, and this became a standard.

The amount of information the card could carry was increased in the late 1920s by changing the size and spacing of the holes, without changing the size of the card itself.

As each company extended the use of punch card accounting to new departments, cards were ordered with special layouts and colors.

View taken at the Tabulating Machine Company's factory in Washington, D.C. around the turn of the century.

Big Business and Small Facts

Herman Hollerith developed an electric adding mechanism and incorporated it into his tabulating equipment. This made it feasible for railroads to use punch card machines for their waybill statistics—what was shipped, who shipped it, who received it, how much it weighed, the shipping charges, and routes taken.

Insurance companies, with actuarial statistics to correlate and mortality predictions to make, were quick to see the advantages of machine tabulation.

Public utilities had similar problems: keeping track of very large numbers of very small amounts.

Statistical Machines 1900

Telephone companies had large numbers of transactions to be recorded and billed.

With an electrical integrator, the Hollerith machines could add as well as count.

Railroad freight departments required "a veritable army of clerks."

Staff: 1973
901 Washington Boulevard
Donald Amundson
Beth Belof
Lonnie Burns
Jehane Burns
Richard Donges
Ann Enkoji
Maria Ewing
Glen Fleck
Alex Funke
Richard Funkhouser
Margaret Gruen
Ann Helverson
Hap Johnson
Harold Lind
Emily Mayeda
John Moskwa
David Olney
Jeannine Oppewall
Donna Orr
Sam Passacaqua
Mariea Poole
Marry Randall
Robert Richards
Karl Rimer
Michael Ripps
Steve Slocomb
Robert Staples
Michael Uris
Randall Walker
Morris Zaslavsky
Nancy Zaslavsky

1973

Book: *A Computer Perspective*

The book *A Computer Perspective* is based on the exhibition of the same name designed for the IBM Corporation in 1971 (pp. 364–369). Like the exhibition, the book is a pictorial essay on the origins and development of the computer from 1890 to 1950. The text and images are drawn from the History Wall panels used in the exhibition, which displayed pictorial material on the ideas, events, and individuals relevant to the history of the computer, as well as artifacts from each decade.

Three categories of innovation are outlined in the book: logical automata, statistical machines, and calculating machines. The material is organized by decade, but it is not simply a chronology of devices or ideas. Rather, elements of the intellectual and socioeconomic environment of each period are included to demonstrate that many historical forces contributed to the development of the modern computer. This approach, also used in the exhibition, makes the book useful both to the general reader and to the specialist.

Swiss designer Paul Bruhwiler, working for the Eames Office as a free-lance designer, designed the book layout based on the organization of the exhibition; Glen Fleck was the editor. The developmental work was sponsored by the IBM Corporation. I. Bernard Cohen, professor of the history of science at Harvard University, acted as consultant and wrote the book's introduction. Harvard University Press published the 174-page volume, which is now out of print. The book was included in the American Institute of Graphic Artists' list of the outstanding "Fifty Books of the Year" in 1973.

Above: Four double-page spreads from *A Computer Perspective* about computer systems from the early twentieth century

Opposite: Three double-page spreads from *A Computer Perspective* about inventors Charles Babbage and Herman Hollerith

Left: Consultants and IBM managers who assisted on the *Movable Feasts* exhibition lunching at the Eames House (left to right): I. Bernard Cohen, Patricia Arfman of IBM, Charles, Frances Cohen, Michael Sullivan of IBM, and Owen Gingerich

Staff: 1973
901 Washington Boulevard
Donald Amundson
Beth Belof
Lonnie Browning
Jehane Burns
Richard Donges
Ann Enkoji
Maria Ewing
Glen Fleck
Alex Funke
Richard Funkhouser
Margaret Gruen
Hap Helverson
Ann Helverson
Harold Lind
Emily Mayeda
John Moskwa
David Neuhart
Jeannine Oppewall
Donna Orr
Sam Passalacqua
Mariea Poole
Marry Randall
Robert Richards
Karl Rimer
Michael Ripps
Steve Slocomb
Robert Staples
Michael Uris
Randall Walker
Morris Zaslavsky
Nancy Zaslavsky

1973

Exhibition: *Movable Feasts and Changing Calendars*

As part of the Copernican Year—and to celebrate the Easter season—the Eames Office designed a small exhibition for the IBM Corporate Exhibit Center in New York City about "the movable feast, the astronomy that goes with it, and something about calendars in general." The exhibition was installed in the street-level gallery of IBM's Madison Avenue building.

"A movable feast," according to the text for the exhibition, "is an annual observance that does not fall on the same date each year. Every cultural group has its calendar and its feasts, both movable and fixed; nearly all of them go back to celebrations of seasonal happenings." Beginning with primitive societies, the exhibition explores how people have used astronomy to organize their yearly calendars: "the recording of seasonal and astronomical reoccurrences is the beginning of written history. There was a calendar before there was an alphabet." The three types of calendars—lunar, lunisolar, and solar—were also displayed.

Above: The title panel for the exhibition. Opposite top: A view of the exhibition looking through the windows of the IBM Corporate Exhibit Center. Opposite: A view of the exhibition

EVENTS LEADING UP TO OUR CALENDAR

The calendar we use today is directly descended from the Roman calendar, reorganized by Julius Caesar, with borrowings from the astronomical knowledge of Alexandria.

The Roman Calendar before Julius Caesar

The Egyptian Calendar

The Julian Reform 708 A.U.C./46 B.C.

Caesar Augustus 746 A.U.C./8 B.C.

How Did The Week Get Here?

The Council of Nicaea 325 A.D.

New Pressures for Reform

The Gregorian Rule 1582 A.D.

The Eleven-day Adjustment 1752 A.D.

B.C. and A.D.

Present Considerations

An exhibition graphic panel representing the historical development of the Western calendar

Right: Cover of the catalog from the retrospective exhibition *The Furniture of Charles Eames*. The exhibition of furniture from the collections of The Museum of Modern Art opened at the museum on April 16

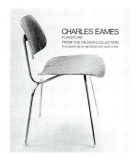

Robert Blaich of Herman Miller, Inc., on a visit to the Eames Office

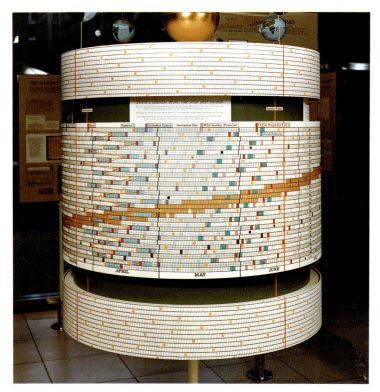

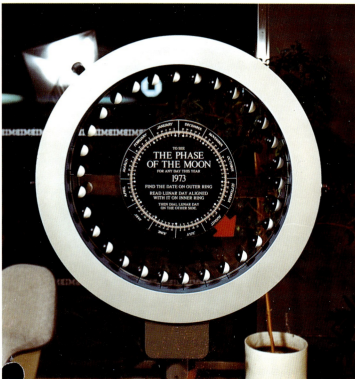

Top: The calendar drum. Above: An interactive device from the exhibition that demonstrated the phases of the moon

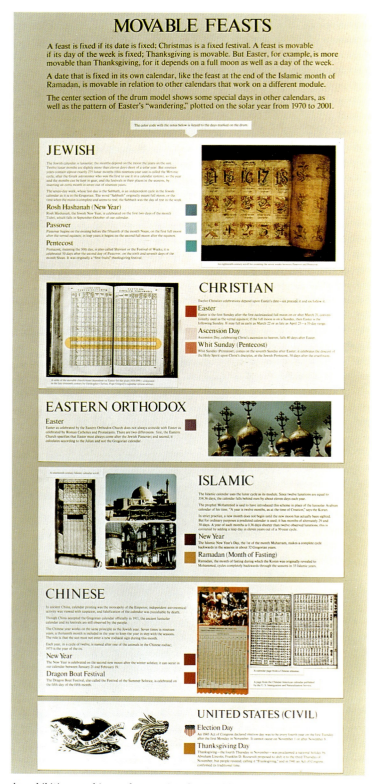

An exhibition graphic panel comparing the movable feasts of various cultures and religions

396

April 23: Charles presents the slide show *Copernicus* to the National Academy of Sciences, Washington, D.C.

Staff member Jehane Burns writing the text for the *Calendars* exhibition

Staff member Jeannine Oppewall working on research for the *Calendars* exhibition

Staff member Harold Lind working on graphics for the *Calendars* exhibition

---

Explanatory text and photographs and drawings of historical figures and events, of people performing rites and observing special days, and of objects used in seasonal celebrations were mounted on laminate-faced, double-sided graphic panels supported on single- and double-pole supports. The panels were edged with gold-colored mirror strips on which a leaf pattern was silk-screened. Photographs were hung in the windows. As in other Eames installations, potted seasonal flowers—daffodils, ranunculuses, freesias, lilies, daisies, and tulips—were grouped around the installation and in the exhibit center windows as an additional reminder of the season.

A large drum made in the Eames Office demonstrated how calendar years and feast days are determined. The drum was divided into horizontal strips, each of which represented one solar year, with the succession of days and full moons marked. The drum charted certain seasonal celebrations—Christian Easter, Orthodox Easter, Passover, Rosh Hashanah, Ramadan, Islamic New Year, winter and summer soltices, vernal and autumnal equinoxes, Thanksgiving and leap-year day—and showed how their dates change from year to year. A large interactive device allowed visitors to find the phase of the moon and its position in the sky on any day and hour of the lunar months in 1973, the year of the exhibition.

Two paper orreries (with pins to mark the paths of the planets through the year) were produced by Philip Morrison, professor of physics at MIT, and his wife, Phylis, and were distributed by IBM in conjunction with the Copernican Year exhibitions.

I. Bernard Cohen and Owen Gingerich of Harvard University were consultants on the project to the Eames Office. Albert and Donna Wilson also assisted in the preparation of the exhibition. Jehane Burns and Jeannine Oppewall researched and wrote the exhibition text. Robert Staples and Richard Donges developed the structures. Gary Harvey and Display Studios, Inc., of Astoria, New York, fabricated the exhibition.

Exhibition venues: IBM Corporation Americas and Far East Headquarters, Tarrytown, New York. *Connections: The Work of Charles and Ray Eames*: Wight Art Gallery, University of California, Los Angeles; Humanities Research Center, University of Texas, Austin; Washington University and Laumeier Gallery, St. Louis, Missouri. *Five Small Exhibitions*: University of Cincinnati, Cincinnati, Ohio; University of Arizona, Tucson.

An exhibition graphic panel explaining the effects of the changes of the seasons

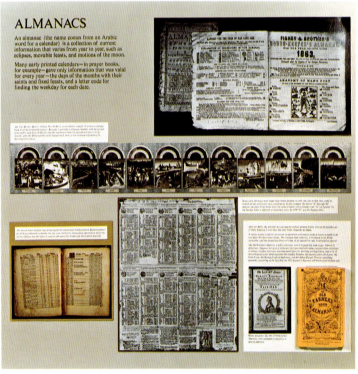

An exhibition graphic panel showing a variety of almanacs

Charles receives the "Diploma di Collaborazione" from the *Triennale di Milano*, Milan, Italy.

Staff: 1973
901 Washington Boulevard
Donald Amundson
Beth Belof
Lonnie Browning
Jehane Burns
Richard Donges
Ann Enkoji
Maria Ewing
Glen Fleck
Alex Funke
Richard Funkhouser
Margaret Gruen
Ann Helverson
Hap Johnson
Harold Lind
Emily Mayeda
Myron Moskwa
John Neuhart
David Olney
Jeannine Oppewall
Donna Orr
Sam Passalacqua
Mariea Poole
Marny Randall
Robert Richards
Karl Rimer
Michael Ripps
Steve Slocomb
Robert Staples
Michael Uris
Randall Walker
Morris Zaslavsky
Nancy Zaslavsky

A photographic composite of Charles and Ray manipulating spinning, illuminated yo-yos given to them by Jane Cahill of IBM

1973

Film: *Two Laws of Algebra: Distributive and Associative*

Two Laws of Algebra is the third in the three-film series (pp. 381, 389) conceived and developed by mathematician Raymond Redheffer and produced with the technical assistance of Eames staff members Steve Slocomb and Michael Ripps. The success of the first two films led Redheffer to adapt his techniques to another area in mathematics that could be treated in the same fashion. Charles was a willing participant and, as before, made Eames Office facilities available to Redheffer.

The film is an animated demonstration of the distributive and associative processes in algebra. It employs the same production techniques used in the first two films (*Alpha* and *Exponents*): stop-motion animation of cutout characters and symbols. There is no narration; the accompanying music was composed and performed by Laurindo Almeida. *Two Laws of Algebra* is in general circulation and is included in the IBM Corporation Film Library. (Running time, *Two Laws of Algebra*: 4 minutes; color.)

A sequence of frames (reading top to bottom left, top to bottom right) from scenes in *Two Laws of Algebra*. The frames were photographed from 16mm-film footage

October 17: The Eames film *SX-70* (p. 383) receives the Special Jury Award at the Seventeenth Annual San Francisco International Film Festival, San Francisco, California.

Right: Museum director William McCann, Charles and IBM manager Michael Sullivan at the opening of the *Copernicus* exhibition (pp. 384–387) at the California Museum of Science and Industry, Los Angeles

Staff: 1973
901 Washington Boulevard
Donald Amundson
Beth Belof
Lonnie Browning
Jehane Burns
Richard Donges
Ann Enkoji
Maria Ewing
Glen Fleck
Alex Funke
Richard Funkhouser
Margaret Gruen
Ann Helverson
Hap Johnson
Harold Lind
Emily Mayeda
Myron Moskwa
John Neuhart
David Olney
Jeannine Oppewall
Donna Orr
Sam Passalacqua
Mariea Poole
Marny Randall
Robert Richards
Karl Rimer
Michael Ripps
Steve Slocomb
Robert Staples
Michael Uris
Randall Walker
Morris Zaslavsky
Nancy Zaslavsky

1973

Film: *Copernicus*

The film *Copernicus* was made from a 3-screen slide show originally assembled for an international symposium celebrating the five-hundredth anniversary of Copernicus's birth. The symposium was organized by the Smithsonian Institution and held at the American Academy of Sciences on April 23, 1973.

The film, for which the slides were transferred to film, was made for the Smithsonian and was sponsored by the IBM Corporation. Images of the places in which Copernicus lived and worked, as well as of his artifacts, books, and original manuscripts, are accompanied by a narrative about the scientific context in which Copernicus came to understand and formulate his heliocentric theory of the universe.

The musical score, composed and conducted by Elmer Bernstein, is in the spirit of fifteenth-century music. The narration, written with Jehane Burns and read by John Ragin, quotes Copernicus's writings and those of his peers. The film is in general circulation. (Running time, *Copernicus*: 9 minutes, 30 seconds; color.)

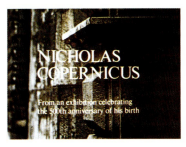 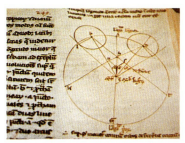

A sequence of frames (reading top to bottom left, top to bottom right) from scenes in *Copernicus*. The frames were photographed from 16mm-film footage

Staff: 1973
901 Washington Boulevard
Donald Amundson
Beth Belof
Lonnie Browning
Jehane Burns
Richard Donges
Ann Enkoji
Maria Ewing
Glen Fleck
Alex Funke
Richard Funkhouser
Margaret Gruen
Ann Helverson
Hap Johnson
Harold Lind
Emily Mayeda
Myron Moskwa
John Neuhart
David Olney
Jeannine Oppewall
Donna Orr
Sam Passalacqua
Mariea Poole
Marny Randall
Robert Richards
Karl Rimer
Michael Ripps
Steve Slocomb
Robert Staples
Michael Uris
Randall Walker
Morris Zaslavsky
Nancy Zaslavsky

1973

Exhibition: *On the Shoulders of Giants*

On the Shoulders of Giants presented the work of five men who advanced the science of astronomy in the period between Copernicus and Newton: Tycho Brahe (1546–1601), Johannes Kepler (1571–1630), René Descartes (1596–1650), Galileo Galilei (1564–1642), and William Gilbert (1540–1603). The title of the exhibition was taken from a quotation by Sir Isaac Newton: "If I have seen further, it is by standing on the shoulders of giants." Produced for the IBM Corporate Exhibit Center in New York City as part of the program of science exhibitions designed by the Eames Office, this installation, like those that preceded it, coincided with a holiday season, the pre-Christmas month of Advent.

The installation was mounted on seven freestanding display units, each consisting of three vertical glass or opaque panels joined together to form an isosceles triangle. Each transparent unit presented the work of one scientist. Text, photographs, and other illustrative material were mounted on both sides of the glass panels. The two opaque display triangles were set up as supplements to the units on Kepler and Galileo. A large, introductory graphic panel provided a map of the exhibition, showing how the scientists' work intersected and how each had responded to Copernicus's proposition "that the earth was not fixed at the center of a heavenly system." The graphic panels were produced in the Eames Office, and the exhibition units were fabricated by Robert Shultz and Associates in San Gabriel, California.

The observations and laws developed by the five scientists during the late sixteenth and early seventeenth centuries eventually led to Newton's work in calculus and his development of the principles of gravitation. In addition to the exhibition, a puppet show entitled *Two Stones* was presented on videotape. Three puppet characters—Salviacci, representing Galileo's point of view; Simpliccio, an Aristotelian; Segredo, Salviacci's companion—engaged in a dialogue concerning falling bodies. When the *Newton* exhibition opened in the IBM Corporate Exhibit Center on December 20, 1973, *On the Shoulders of Giants* was kept in the space to serve as its "prologue."

I. Bernard Cohen, professor of the history of science at Harvard University, was the exhibition consultant. Text for the exhibition was written by Jehane Burns. Richard Donges was responsible for developing the structures.

Top and above: Visitors viewing freestanding display units on Tycho Brahe and William Gilbert. Opposite top: Entry to the exhibition. Opposite: Visitors to the exhibition

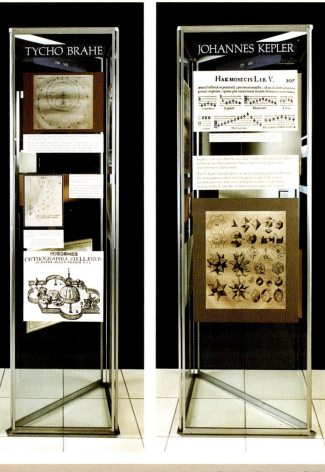
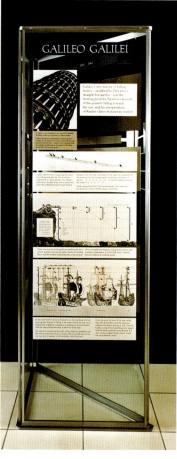

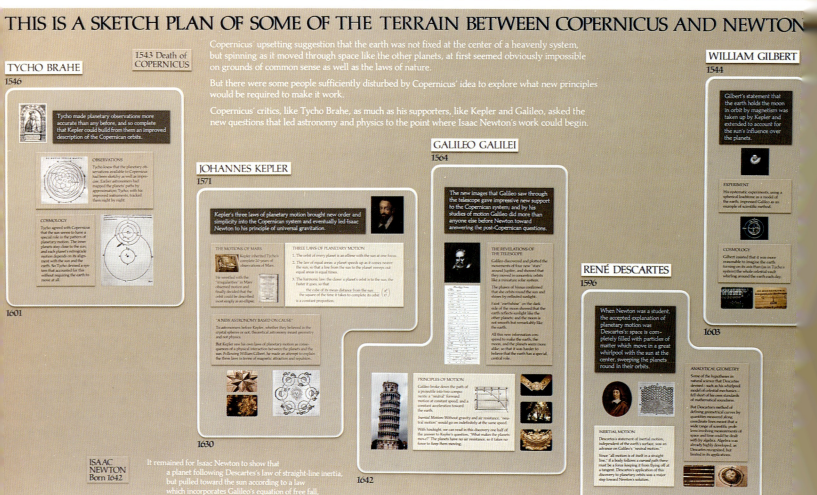

Top: The title face of each of the freestanding units on the five astronomers.
Above: A timeline of their work explaining the relationships between the scientists

Left: Scholar Alexander Pogo with Jeannine Oppewall at the California Institute of Technology Library, which provided material for the *On the Shoulders of Giants* exhibition

Exhibition venues: National Air and Space Administration Bicentennial Exposition on Science and Technology, Cape Kennedy, Florida; IBM Data Processing Division Headquarters, White Plains, New York. *Connections: The Work of Charles and Ray Eames*: Washington University and Laumeier Gallery, St. Louis, Missouri. *Five Small Exhibitions*: University of Cincinnati, Cincinnati, Ohio; University of Arizona, Tucson.

A scene from the puppet show based on Galileo's dialogues

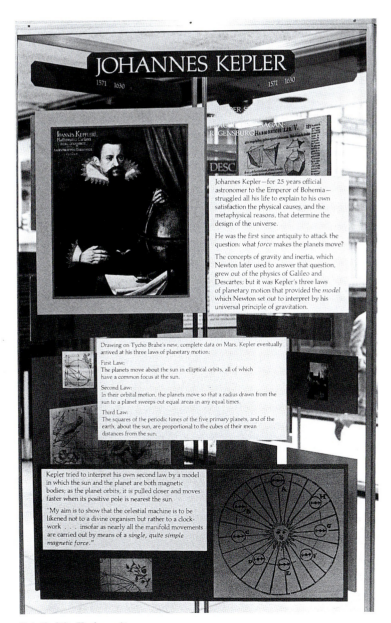

Detail of the Kepler unit

Views of the exhibition in the IBM Corporate Exhibit Center

Staff: 1973
901 Washington Boulevard
Donald Amundson
Beth Belof
Lonnie Browning
Jehane Burns
Richard Donges
Ann Enkoji
Maria Ewing
Glen Fleck
Alex Funke
Richard Funkhouser
Margaret Gruen
Ann Helverson
Hap Johnson
Harold Lind
Emily Mayeda
Myron Moskwa
John Neuhart
David Olney
Jeannine Oppewall
Donna Orr
Sam Passalacqua
Mariea Poole
Marry Randall
Robert Randall
Karl Rimer
Michael Ripps
Steve Slocomb
Robert Staples
Michael Uris
Randall Walker
Morris Zaslavsky
Nancy Zaslavsky

I. Bernard Cohen and staff member Jehane Burns conferring on *Newton* exhibition copy

1973

Exhibition: *Isaac Newton: Physics for a Moving Earth*

On December 20, 1973, *Isaac Newton: Physics for a Moving Earth* opened at the IBM Corporate Exhibit Center on Madison Avenue and 57th Street in New York City. The show presented Newton's achievements in astronomy and mathematics and completed a year of Eames-IBM exhibitions on scientific subjects (pp. 378–379, 384–387, 394–397, 400–403). As background to Newton's story, the Eames exhibitions *Copernicus* and *On the Shoulders of Giants* were shown at the same time. A display of objects from early English Christmas celebrations was added to the exhibition to celebrate Newton's birth on Christmas Day, 1692.

The *Newton* exhibition consisted of four two-sided display units, each with six rectangular panels (three to a side and aligned horizontally). The dark red laminated panels were attached to steel poles and mounted on pedestal bases. Each side of the three panels was organized around a period of Newton's life: "Newton's Youth," "Early Studies at Cambridge," "The Plague Years," "Woolsthorpe," "Trinity: The Middle Years," and the "Royal Society." Two additional sections, "Proof of the Ellipse" and "The *Principia*," covered specific scientific achievements. The upper panels displayed large color photographs of places or things relating to the subjects described in the text below. Several large photographic panels were suspended from the gallery's ceiling. The photographs were shot on location by Charles in England and in Italy.

Newton was a traveling exhibition designed to be disassembled for shipping. All text and photographic materials were mounted onto the prefabricated wood and steel display structures in the Eames Office before shipment to New York City. Jehane Burns wrote the exhibition text and I. Bernard Cohen served as the consultant on the project. A foldout brochure on Newton's contributions to astronomy and physics, with a prologue on some of the men whose work carried the disciplines forward between the eras of Copernicus and Newton, was given to visitors. A timeline of the years 1550 to 1725, presenting a synopsis of the achievements of Newton, his predecessors, and his contemporaries, accompanied the exhibition. A second foldout publication, *A Sampler of Isaac Newton's Innovations in Mathematics*, was prepared for IBM with the assistance of Raymond Redheffer. The

Opposite top: View of the *Newton* exhibition through the IBM Corporate Exhibit Center windows. Opposite: View of the *Newton* exhibition

Above: Views of the *Newton* exhibition showing a section of the Christmas display, the freestanding exhibition units, and a glimpse of the Christmas display behind the *Newton* display stands

Top, middle, and above, left and right: A selection of graphic and text panels from the exhibition showing aspects of Newton's life

Staff member David Olney mocking up a graphic panel

Ray and staff member Richard Donges checking panel layout

Parke Meek assembling a Christmas wreath for the *Newton* exhibition

exhibition structures were designed by Richard Donges and fabricated by Robert Shultz and Associates in San Gabriel, California.

In honor of Newton's birth and the opening of the *Newton* exhibition, the Eames Office, with the assistance of Alexander Girard, designed a display of artifacts and images drawn from English Christmas celebrations of the seventeenth and eighteenth centuries. The Christmases of that period were twelve-day feasts in which, according to the exhibition text, "Christian celebration had come to amicable terms with the much more ancient local ceremonies." Seven red pedestals were installed just behind the glass windows of the IBM Corporate Exhibit Center. Each square, rectangular, and circular pedestal held an artifact relating to Christmas celebrations—a wassail bowl, plum pudding, Christmas pie, a Christmas box, a wren box, and objects associated with the "Lord of Misrule" (one chosen to direct the sports and revels of an English family during the Christmas holidays). The objects were explained by graphic elements mounted around the sides of the pedestals.

The Christmas exhibit included a large Plexiglas case with musical instruments from the seventeenth and eighteenth centuries—trumpets, oboes, and violins. Several graphic panels described other customs of the period. Stage sets and costumes reproduced after original sketches by Inigo Jones, the seventeenth-century English court architect, were shown as examples of the elaborate machinery and stage settings designed for allegorical "masque" performances that celebrated the monarchy. Potted orange trees, evergreens, and garlands lined the exhibition, mirroring the English tradition of decking churches "with all manner of green during the Christmas season."

Exhibition venues: Exploratorium, San Francisco, California; Huntington Beach Public Library, Huntington Beach, California; California Museum of Science and Industry, Los Angeles; Pacific Science Center, Seattle, Washington; Ontario Science Center, Toronto, Canada; San Diego Hall of Science, San Diego, California. *Connections: The Work of Charles and Ray Eames*: Wight Art Gallery, University of California, Los Angeles; Humanities Research Center, University of Texas, Austin; Washington University and Laumeier Gallery, St. Louis, Missouri. *Five Small Exhibitions*: University of Cincinnati, Cincinnati, Ohio; University of Arizona, Tucson.

Top: The Inigo Jones setting for a masque. Middle: A view of the *Newton* exhibition Christmas display. Above: Details of *Newton* exhibition Christmas display elements

January 14: Charles lectures at California State Polytechnic University, Pomona.

Right: Walter McQuade and architects Benjamin and Jane Thompson with Charles at the Eames Office

Mildred Friedman and Dean Swanson of the Walker Art Center at the Eames Office

Staff: 1974
901 Washington Boulevard
Donald Amundson
Beth Belof
Lonnie Browning
Jehane Burns
Samuel Carson
Brigitte Delorme
Barbara Diamond
Richard Donges
John Downes
Ann Enkoji
Maria Ewing
John Fitzmaurice
Carlton Flamer
Helen Frazier
Alex Funke
Richard Funkhouser
Michael Glickman
Thomas Gregory
William Gubin
Alain Huin
Hap Johnson
Michael Jordan
Susan Lieberman
Harold Lind
Emily Mayeda
John Neuhart
Joe Nicholson
Jacek Nieko
David Olney
Jeannine Oppewall
Donna Orr
Sam Passalacqua
Mariea Poole
Marny Randall
Michael Ripps
Michael Russell
Ted Schliesman
Steve Slocomb
Alexandra Snyder
Robert Staples
Margaret Starr
Craig Stearns
Melody Sternoff
Greg Thomas
Bill Tondreau
Michael Uris
Randall Walker
Jack Wells
Morris Zaslavsky
Nancy Zaslavsky

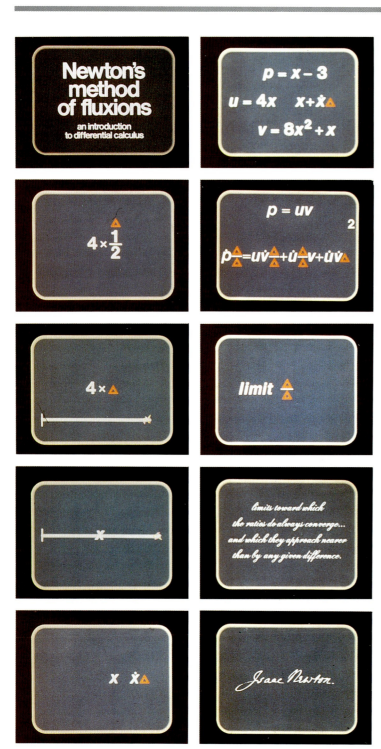

A sequence of frames (reading top to bottom left, top to bottom right) from scenes in *Newton's Method*. The frames were photographed from 16mm-film footage

1974

Film: *Newton's Method*

Made in conjunction with the *Newton* exhibition (pp. 404–407), *Newton's Method* was a film produced by the Eames Office and transferred to videotape to be shown in a room adjacent to the exhibition. The film describes Newton's inventions, including differential calculus and the mathematical questions relative to it. It also illustrates the classical relationship between gravity and the logarithm of falling bodies.

The film uses the same animation production techniques employed in the earlier films *Alpha*, *Exponents*, and *Two Laws of Algebra*. The narration was written by Raymond Redheffer and read by Alex Funke; the accompanying lute music was performed by Morris Mizrahi. The film is in general circulation. (Running time: *Newton's Method*: 3 minutes, 25 seconds; color.)

February 7: Charles speaks at the School of Art, Yale University, New Haven, Connecticut.

The exhibition, *Excellence in Design: Charles Eames Furniture*, opens at the Grand Rapids Art Museum, Grand Rapids, Michigan.

Staff: 1974
901 Washington Boulevard
Donald Amundson
Beth Belof
Lonnie Browning
Jehane Burns
Samuel Carson
Brigitte Delorme
Barbara Diamond
Richard Donges
John Downes
Ann Enkoji
Maria Ewing
John Fitzmaurice
Carlton Flamer
Helen Frazier
Alex Funke
Richard Funkhouser
Michael Glickman
Thomas Gregory
William Gubin
Alain Huin
Hap Johnson
Michael Jurdan
Susan Lieberman
Harold Lind
Emily Mayeda
John Neuhart
Joe Nicholson
Jacek Nieko
David Olney
Jeannine Oppewall
Donna Orr
Sam Passalacqua
Mariea Poole
Marny Randall
Michael Ripps
Michael Russell
Ted Schliesman
Steve Slocomb
Alexandra Snyder
Robert Staples
Margaret Starr
Craig Stearns
Melody Sternoff
Greg Thomas
Bill Tondreau
Michael Uris
Randall Walker
Jack Wells
Morris Zaslavsky
Nancy Zaslavsky

Charles and staff member Richard Donges discussing the *Franklin and Jefferson* exhibition project with Jack Masey of the USIA

1974

Film: *Kepler's Laws*

Like *Alpha* (p. 381), *Kepler's Laws* is a short film made to demonstrate a single mathematical concept. This film uses animated graphic symbols and a constant time frame to diagram and explain the laws of planetary motion devised by the sixteenth-century astronomer Johannes Kepler. It was produced to accompany the exhibition *On the Shoulders of Giants* (pp. 400–403).

Staff member Alex Funke developed the storyboard and the mechanical animation techniques. The film has no narration and is accompanied by "Little Suite," guitar and lute music written by Vincenzo Galilei, Galileo Galilei's father, and performed by Laurindo Almeida. (Running time, *Kepler's Laws*: 2 minutes, 48 seconds; color.)

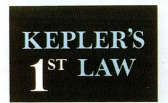
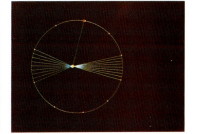
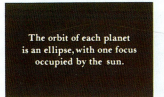

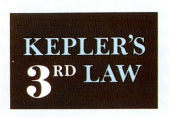
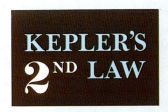
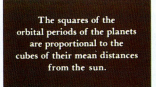

A sequence of frames (reading top to bottom left, top to bottom right) from scenes in *Kepler's Laws*. The frames were photographed from 16mm-film footage

Right: Charles and Ray with the Eames Office staff who worked on the Newton cards: Alexandra Snyder, Donald Amundson, Harold Lind, Nancy Zaslavsky, Hap Johnson, Jehane Burns, Richard Donges, John Neuhart, Bill Tondreau, Sam Passalacqua, and Lonnie Browning

Staff: 1974
901 Washington Boulevard
Donald Amundson
Beth Belof
Lonnie Browning
Jehane Burns
Samuel Carson
Brigitte Delorme
Barbara Diamond
Richard Donges
John Downes
Ann Enkoji
Maria Ewing
John Fitzmaurice
Carlton Flamer
Helen Frazier
Alex Funke
Richard Funkhouser
Michael Glickman
Thomas Gregory
William Gubin
Alain Huin
Hap Johnson
Michael Jurdan
Susan Lieberman
Harold Lind
Emily Mayeda
Joe Nicholson
Jacek Nieko
David Olney
Jeannine Oppewall
Donna Orr
Sam Passalacqua
Mariea Poole
Marty Randall
Michael Ripps
Michael Russell
Ted Schliesman
Steve Slocomb
Alexandra Snyder
Robert Staples
Margaret Starr
Craig Stearns
Melody Sternoff
Greg Thomas
Bill Tondreau
Michael Uris
Randall Walker
Jack Wells
Morris Zaslavsky
Nancy Zaslavsky

1974

Newton Cards

A special edition of twelve decks of twenty-six cards was produced by the Eames Office for the IBM Corporation to present to American Nobel-prize laureates in the sciences at a dinner given by IBM in 1974. The images printed on the playing cards were selected from photographs taken by Charles on location in England at Sir Isaac Newton's home and at Cambridge University for the *Newton* exhibition (pp.404–407). The images included views of Trinity College, Cambridge, where Newton served as a fellow for more than thirty years, and reproductions of pages from his treatises on motion, gravity, and differential calculus.

The cards were produced in the Eames Office; each set of color photographs was printed by staff member Bill Tondreau and mounted on one side of card stock. The reverse side of each card was covered with marbled paper. The cards were edged in gold leaf, and a gift box with the recipient's name on the cover was made for each deck. A bound facsimile edition of Newton's *Principia* accompanied the cards.

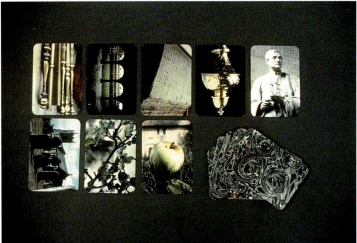

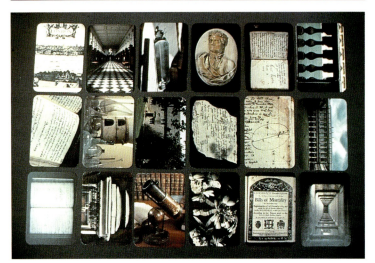

Top: Newton cards package. Middle and above: Newton deck of cards

Staff: 1974
901 Washington Boulevard
Donald Amundson
Beth Belof
Lonnie Browning
Jehane Burns
Samuel Carson
Brigitte Delorme
Barbara Diamond
Richard Donges
John Downes
Ann Enkoji
Maria Ewing
John Fitzmaurice
Carlton Flamer
Helen Frazier
Alex Funke
Richard Funkhouser
Michael Glickman
Thomas Gregory
William Gubin
Alain Huin
Hap Johnson
Michael Jurdan
Susan Lieberman
Harold Lind
Emily Mayeda
Joe Neuhart
John Nicholson
Jacek Nieko
David Olney
Jeannine Oppewall
Donna Orr
Sam Passalacqua
Mariea Poole
Marry Randall
Michael Ripps
Michael Russell
Ted Schlesman
Steve Slocomb
Alexandra Snyder
Robert Staples
Margaret Starr
Craig Stearns
Melody Sternoff
Greg Thomas
Bill Tondreau
Michael Uris
Randall Walker
Jack Wells
Morris Zaslavsky
Nancy Zaslavsky

Perry Miller Adato of WNET Television and Ray in a planning session for Adato's "An Eames Celebration," aired on public television stations

1974

Film: *Callot*

Charles was invited to deliver the prestigious Penrose Memorial Lecture to the American Philosophical Society in Philadelphia on March 18, 1974. Returning to one of his favorite themes, he delivered a lecture entitled "The Disciplines of the Circus." The film *Callot* was made to accompany the lecture. The film's images were drawn from the stylized rituals and gestures of commedia dell' arte characters as depicted in small (three-inch-by-four-inch) engravings by the seventeenth-century French printmaker Jacques Callot. *Callot* is a tour de force of filmmaking; it was filmed directly from original engravings, which were photographed on a camera stand under high magnification and often in fields only one-half inch wide. *Callot* was photographed in black and white and printed on color stock to achieve a rich, saturated color tint.

The three-screen *Circus* slide show (p. 356) assembled for the Norton Lectures from images of the circus photographed by Charles since the 1940s was also shown at the Philadelphia lecture. *Callot* has no narration. The music is "English Fantasy" by John Dowland, performed by Julian Bream on RCA Records. *Callot* is in general circulation. (Running time, *Callot*: 2 minutes, 45 seconds; color.)

A sequence of frames (reading top to bottom left, top to bottom right) from scenes in *Callot*. The frames were photographed from 16mm-film footage

April 28: Charles lectures to the American Academy of Arts and Sciences, Washington, D.C.

May 8: Charles lectures to students of the Department of Agriculture, College of Environmental Design, and Department of Architecture at the University of California, Berkeley.

May 15: Charles delivers a lecture at the Massachusetts Institute of Technology, Cambridge.

September 28: Charles lectures to the Alliance of California Arts Councils.

October 17: Charles lectures to the Association of Architects, American Institute of Architects, New York City.

November 15: Charles talks to students at the Art Center College of Design, Pasadena, California.

November 15: Charles receives the Distinguished Service Citation from the American Institute of Architects, California Council, Los Angeles.

Staff member Michael Glickman working on the plan for the *Philosophical Gardens* exhibition

Staff: 1974
901 Washington Boulevard
Donald Amundson
Beth Belof
Lonnie Browning
Jehane Burns
Samuel Carson
Brigitte Delorme
Barbara Diamond
Richard Donges
John Downes
Ann Enkoji
Maria Ewing
John Fitzmaurice
Carlton Flamer
Helen Frazier
Alex Funke
Richard Funkhouser
Michael Glickman
Thomas Gregory
William Gubin
Alain Huin
Hap Johnson
Susan Jordan
Harold Lieberman
Emily Lind
Joe Mayeda
Jacek Nicholson
David Nieko
Jeannine Olney
Donna Oppewall
Sam Orr
Mariea Passalacqua
Marny Poole
Michael Randall
Ted Ripps
Steve Russell
Alexandra Schliesman
Robert Slocomb
Margaret Snyder
Craig Staples
Melody Stearns
Greg Sternoff
Bill Thomas
Michael Tondreau
Randall Uris
Jack Walker
Morris Wells
Nancy Zaslavsky
Zaslavsky

1974

Exhibition: *Philosophical Gardens*

The exhibition *Philosophical Gardens* opened in the spring of 1974 in the IBM Corporate Exhibit Center in New York City. The last in the series of small science exhibitions designed for IBM by the Eames Office to celebrate the Copernican Year (pp. 384–387, 394–397, 400–403, 404–407), *Philosophical Gardens* was organized around two issues that emerged in the field of plant study in seventeenth-century England following the Newtonian revolution: mathematical reasoning and the methodical collection of data. The work of the Reverend Stephen Hales (1677–1761), a naturalist who believed in Newton's theories and who systematically investigated plant growth and nourishment, and that of Robert Hooke (1635–1702), whose published engravings of organisms seen through the microscope opened up new possibilities for studying plant physiology, were featured in the exhibition.

Hales was the first naturalist to apply "number, weight, and measure" to the study of the ways in which plants take in and disperse nutrients from the soil and from the air. His work set the standard for future experimentation in plant physiology. Hooke predicted that new instruments would enable people to investigate directly the structure and workings of living things. The major experiments of Hales were re-created in detail in the Eames Office so that they could be photographed for the exhibition.

The primary exhibit structure was a wooden gazebo with latticework panels. Photographs and text copy were mounted directly onto the prefabricated structure and onto additional latticework units used as title panels. Designed for traveling, the display units were assembled in the Eames Office and shipped to New York City and to later exhibition sites. A specimen table with binocular microscopes and seedlings growing under bell jars was added to allow visitors to view live plants and explore their structure. An abundance of potted spring flowers was placed around the base of the gazebo. Michael Glickman was responsible for developing the exhibition, and Jehane Burns wrote the exhibition text. The structures were fabricated by Ernie Meadows of Santa Monica, California.

Exhibition venues: Field Museum, Chicago, Illinois; IBM Building, Chicago, Illinois. *Connections: The Work of Charles and Ray Eames*: Wight Art Gallery, University of California, Los Angeles; Humanities Research Center, University of Texas, Austin; Washington University and Laumeier Gallery, St. Louis, Missouri; University of East Anglia, Norwich, England.

A freestanding exhibition panel

Above: A specimen table with growing plants and binocular microscopes.
Opposite: A view of the exhibition's gazebo structure with Madison Avenue in the background

February 3: "An Eames Celebration," produced by Perry Miller Adato, airs on public television stations.

February 1975: *Fortune* magazine publishes an article by Walter McQuade about the work of the Eames Office

March 12: Charles lectures at the American Club of Paris, Paris, France.

March 25: Charles delivers a talk at Washington University, St. Louis, Missouri.

April: Charles and Ray receive the Elsie de Wolfe Award from the Society of Interior Designers, New York City.

April: Charles and Eliot Noyes collaborate on "Design and Creativity," a presentation for the American Iron and Steel Institute, Atlanta, Georgia.

Staff member Michael Ripps filming The Metropolitan Museum of Art proposal film

Staff: 1975
901 Washington Boulevard
Karen Altman, Donald Amundson, Tim Anderson, Alexander Bounds, Lonnie Browning, Paul Bruhwiler, Jehane Burns, Stan Croner, Barbara Diamond, Richard Donges, Hamilton Driggs, Ann Enkoji, Maria Ewing, John Fitzmaurice, Alex Funke, Etsu Garfias, John Gilchrist, Alain Huin, Hap Johnson, Mark Keiserman, James Kennedy, Ruth Kennedy, Harold Lind, Emily Mayeda, David Meckel, John Neuhart, David Olney, Jeannine Oppewall, Sam Passalacqua, Dick Petrie, Mariea Poole, Michael Ripps, Michael Russell, Steve Slocomb, Jane Spiller, Robert Staples, Margaret Starr, Melody Sternoff, Birgitta Thornton, David Travers, Randall Walker, Jack Wells, Michael Wiener, Nancy Zaslavsky

1975

Film: *Metropolitan Overview*

Charles was approached by Thomas Hoving, director of The Metropolitan Museum of Art in New York City, to design a central guide to its collections that would also serve as an information center for the museum-going public. It was Hoving's objective to make the museum's vast resources and collections more accessible by providing an information-retrieval system that would link the collections in a new and innovative way. Such a system would make use of videodisc and computer technologies. A wing extending into Central Park was to be added to the museum to house the information center.

The Eames Office plan for the ground floor of the new wing of the museum included an "Information Hall," an expanded "Junior Museum," and redesigning the foyer. The Information Hall was divided into two long aisles with two apses at one end and opening onto the foyer at the other end. In one of the aisles a three-dimensional walk-through timeline of the museum's treasures was organized by historical period and place of origin. The museum's collections were introduced to visitors by photographic images and by actual examples from the collections. The other aisle contained information on the history of the museum—the civic and private supporters who contributed to the museum's growth and the individuals who shaped its collections. A special-purpose information area included a computer-retrieval system where visitors could call up information from the catalog of the permanent collections, and glass kiosks were provided for viewing a menu of videotapes. A small theater for showing short films and an open-seating area for lectures or informal conversations were at the end of the hall.

The proposals were presented in a "study" film that included live-action footage, animation, and still photography of a one-inch scale model of the proposed exhibition area in the museum built by the Eames Office. Live-action views of the museum and its visitors and reproductions of historical material and works of art from the museum's collections were included. The film was produced with the cooperation of the educational and curatorial staff of the museum. Charles wrote the script with Jehane Burns. Elmer Bernstein composed the music. The proposal was not implemented; a grant from Walter Annenberg, which was to have funded the proposal, was withdrawn after the city and the museum became involved in a dispute over the new addition. The film is not in general circulation. (Running time, *Metropolitan Overview*: 9 minutes; color.)

Opposite top: Aerial view of museum with the new wing shown at the bottom
Opposite: ¼-inch scale model of the ground floor of the proposed new addition

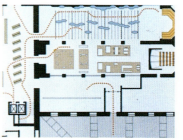

A sequence of frames (reading top to bottom left, top to bottom right) from scenes in *Metropolitan Overview*. The frames were photographed from 16mm-film footage

June 25: Charles delivers a lecture on "Media, Museums, and the Design Process" at the Association of Museums Seventieth Annual Conference, New York City.

June 27: Ray becomes a member of the Education Panel of the American Council of the Arts, New York City.

October 1: Charles and Raymond Redheffer are awarded the Bronze Praxinoscope for the film *Exponents* (p. 389) by the New York International Animation Festival, New York City.

Charles with Jane Cahill and Charles Hollister of the IBM Corporation at the Paris opening of the *Franklin and Jefferson* exhibition

Staff: 1975
901 Washington Boulevard
Karen Altman
Donald Amundson
Tim Anderson
Alexander Bounds
Lonnie Browning
Paul Bruhwiler
Jehane Burns
Stan Croner
Barbara Diamond
Richard Donges
Hamilton Driggs
Ann Enkoji
Maria Ewing
John Fitzmaurice
Alex Funke
Etsu Garfias
John Gilchrist
Alain Huin
Hap Johnson
Mark Keiserman
James Kennedy
Ruth Kennedy
Harold Lind
Emily Mayeda
David Meckel
John Neuhart
David Olney
Jeannine Oppewall
Sam Passalacqua
Dick Petrie
Mariea Poole
Michael Ripps
Michael Russell
Steve Slocomb
Jane Spiller
Robert Staples
Margaret Starr
Melody Sternoff
Birgitta Thornton
David Travers
Randall Walker
Jack Wells
Michael Wiener
Nancy Zaslavsky

1975–1977

Exhibition: *The World of Franklin and Jefferson*

The World of Franklin and Jefferson was an exhibition produced for the American Revolution Bicentennial Administration as part of the bicentennial celebrations. The Eames Office designed the traveling exhibition with the cooperation of The Metropolitan Museum of Art, New York City, and through a grant from the IBM Corporation. During 1975 the exhibition toured Europe under the supervision of the United States Information Agency. The inaugural installation of the exhibition opened in the Grand Palais in Paris on January 11, 1975. The show then traveled to the National Museum of Poland, Warsaw, and the British Museum, London. The exhibition began its United States tour at The Metropolitan Museum of Art, opening in March 1976. It was later installed at the Art Institute of Chicago and at the Los Angeles County Museum of Art. It ended its tour in Mexico City at the National Museum of Anthropology in June 1977.

The World of Franklin and Jefferson was divided into four sections, each distinguished by subject and design treatment. The first section, "Friends and Acquaintances," introduced the friends, colleagues, and adversaries of the two men and provided background material on the influences that shaped their thinking and actions. Photographs and text blocks (with quotations) were mounted on the four sides of the "monoliths"— freestanding structures of stacked, laminate-faced plywood boxes of various sizes. Each monolith was finished with a detailed walnut base. Plexiglas cases housed related artifacts set on surfaces of paper, wood, marble, or velvet. Among the artifacts were eighteenth-century Paul Revere silver, Wedgwood ceramics, toys, books, games, and scientific and musical instruments.

The second part of the installation, "Contrast and Continuity," presented biographies of Franklin and Jefferson, comparing the two men and stressing their commitment to the independence movement. Two-sided structures of horizontal panels attached to steel poles were mounted on pedestal bases similar to the units used in the *Newton* exhibition (pp. 404–407). Each three-paneled side displayed information on a single aspect of the two men's lives—"Franklin, Printer," "Franklin and Colonial Unity," "Young Jefferson," and "Jefferson in '76," among others.

The story behind the three major documents of American independence—the Declaration of Independence,

Opposite top: View of the installation of the *Franklin and Jefferson* exhibition in Paris showing the Georgian-style doorway. Opposite: Opening night of the Paris installation

Views of the Paris installation. Top: "Friends and Acquaintances" area. Middle: "Contrast and Continuity" area. Above: "Jefferson and the West" area

Right: A view of the exhibition *Women in Astronomy*, designed and produced in the Eames Office by Michael Glickman. The exhibition was sponsored by IBM in recognition of International Women's Year

National Museum of Poland staff examining the House of Cards (pp. 168–175), a gift from the Eames Office

Staff member Michael Russell installing the *Franklin and Jefferson* exhibition

Views of the *Franklin and Jefferson* exhibition in Warsaw. Top: "Three Documents" area. Middle: Georgian-style doorway. Above: "Contrast and Continuity" area

the Constitution, and the Bill of Rights, and Franklin's and Jefferson's roles in their execution was the subject of "Three Documents," the third section of the exhibition. A history of the events leading up to the writing of these documents, including details about the drafting of each, were laid out on display structures like those in the second section. Full-size color reproductions of the three documents were mounted on one side of freestanding walls.

The fourth area of the show, "Jefferson and the West," was devoted to Jefferson's interest in America's westward expansion. The U-shaped configuration of the reverse sides of the document walls contained text and photographs describing Jefferson's fascination with the West, its native inhabitants, and his support of the Louisiana Purchase Act. Numerous artifacts were shown in this section, including a stuffed American bison, examples of Native American cultures from the Heye Foundation and the Southwest Museum, paintings by George Catlin from the Museum of Natural History in New York City, and William Clark's original field notebook, all set against a wall-sized painted sky backdrop. A large map charted the route of the Lewis and Clark expedition.

In addition to the four main exhibition areas, the installation included a timeline detailing the events of Franklin's and Jefferson's lives, wall-mounted graphic panels with supplementary images and information, and overhead cloth banners of quotations from the writings and speeches of the two men. Two panoplies of flags, weapons, and musical instruments from the Revolutionary War hung on the walls. New paintings, sculpture, costumes, and artifacts from the eighteenth century were added to each installation. Objects selected from the collections of each of the museums on the tour were added to the exhibition and gave each installation special character. In

Three details of artifacts displayed in the Warsaw installation

November 10: Charles gives a lecture to the members of the Royal Society of Arts, National Film Theater, London, England.

November 11: Charles speaks at the British Film Institute, London, England.

November 12: Charles lectures at the Architectural Association, London, England.

November: Charles speaks at the Royal College of Art, London, England.

November: Charles speaks to the Benjamin Franklin Fellows, London, England.

November 25: Charles makes a presentation at the opening of the exhibition *The Design Process at Herman Miller* (which features the work of the Eameses, George Nelson, Alexander Girard, and Bill Probst) at the Walker Art Center, Minneapolis, Minnesota. Right: Cover of the catalog for the Walker Art Center exhibition

Charles and staff members Jehane Burns and Jeannine Oppewall talking with Harold Skramstad during a visit to the Eames Office

Paris, a press used by Franklin was added to the show; in Warsaw, a medal given to Tadeusz Kòsciuszko by the Society of the Cincinnati was exhibited; in London, an eighteenth-century glass harmonica invented by Franklin was shown; in Mexico City, contemporary portraits, furniture, pottery, large silver ingots and dies of medals made in Mexico were added. Assistance in gathering local artifacts for the European showings was given by Helene Baltrusaitis in Paris, Michael Lipchinsky in Warsaw, Margaret Hall in London, and Mildred Constantine in Mexico City. In the United States, a Franklin printing press and a Franklin stove from The Metropolitan Museum of Art's collections were added along with an orrery loaned by Bern Dibner, a spinning wheel, paintings, furniture, and other decorative arts of the period. Where the exhibit space permitted, a full-scale replica of an eighteenth-century Georgian-style American doorway flanked by low balustrades acted as a monumental archway leading to a section dealing with the Founding Father's documents.

A four-paneled souvenir timeline, a twenty-eight-page catalog, and a poster designed by Paul Bruhwiler accompanied the European tour of the exhibition. The first versions of these publications were produced for the show's European audiences and were printed in French, Polish, and English. The cover of the catalog and the poster featured a portion of the American Revolutionary flag from Bennington, Vermont. In the timeline, text and illustrations recounted highlights of Benjamin Franklin's and Thomas Jefferson's lives and their relationship to the historical events of their day.

For the exhibition's return to the United States, a new poster, souvenir timeline, and catalog were produced. The central image changed from the Bennington flag to a line

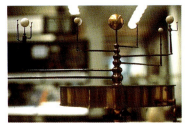

Four details of artifacts displayed in the London installation

Views of the London installation. Top: the artifacts display. Middle: "Friends and Acquaintances" area. Above: Wall panoply in the "Contrast and Continuity" area

419

Eames Office secretary Ann Enkoji

Staff member Donald Amundson working on devices for the *Franklin and Jefferson* exhibition

Staff member Randall Walker working on *Franklin and Jefferson* exhibition drawings

Charles and Ray presented with gold watches in recognition of their thirty years of service as consultants to Herman Miller, Inc.

View of the New York City installation

SX-70, *Alpha*, and *Exponents* receive an award at the Columbus International Film Festival, Columbus, Indiana.

Jerome Weisner and Charles deliver a talk, "An Evening with Franklin and Jefferson," at the Los Angeles County Museum of Art, Los Angeles, California.

Charles's sister, Adele Franks, on a visit to the Eames Office

Charles wearing his Benjamin Franklin-style glasses

Parke Meek and Ray at the opening of *Franklin and Jefferson* in Los Angeles

Top: Eighteenth-century objects from New York collections. Middle: A view of the timeline through a display of eighteenth-century artifacts. Above: Four details of artifacts displayed in the exhibition

Views of the New York City installation. Top: "Friends and Acquaintances" monoliths. Middle: The exhibition timeline. Above: Eighteenth-century paintings and costumes

Staff member Michael Wiener working on *Franklin and Jefferson* exhibition graphics

Staff member Lonnie Browning working on *Franklin and Jefferson* exhibition photography

Top: View of the entrance to the Mexico City installation. Middle: The artifacts display area. Above: Four details of artifacts displayed in the Mexico City installation

conversion composite of Franklin's and Jefferson's portraits. The foldout timeline was significantly expanded in size and content. The catalog was reprinted as a seventy-eight-page book (p. 426). A thirty-two-page catalog was printed for Mexico City.

The World of Franklin and Jefferson was specially adapted to each gallery space; a new study model was made for each exhibit area. All of the display elements were constructed to be knocked down for shipment, and the show was refurbished between each installation. The Eameses and members of the office staff—Richard Donges, Jehane Burns, Jeannine Oppewall, and Michael Russell—supervised the successive installations. In each space, the floors were carpeted, the walls painted white, and a grid of overhead track lighting was installed. All the blocks of text copy, ceiling banners, and captions were translated into the language of the host country. Brigitte Delorme translated the French, Jacek Niecko the Polish, and Francisco Perea the Spanish.

Work on the exhibition began in 1972. Major contributors on the Eames staff included Jehane Burns, Jeannine Oppewall, Richard Donges, Michael Russell, and Barbara Diamond. All color photographs, with the exception of mural blow-ups, were printed in the office by Bill Tondreau.

The World of Franklin and Jefferson was by far the most complex exhibition ever designed by the Eames Office, and it was the last major project undertaken before Charles's death in August 1978. The number of elements in it, the complexity of the research and writing, the location photography, and the complicated travel arrangements and schedule combined to make the production of this exhibition a major achievement. The exhibition presented a historic subject with great energy and richness—the imagery, gathered on location and from documents from the Revolutionary War, was extraordinarily rich and diverse, and the amount of information contained in the show was enormous—the wealth of detail and text was much more than could be absorbed in one visit.

The IBM Corporation arranged the public relations for the exhibition tour and sponsored various events around the exhibition.

Exhibition venues: Grand Palais, Paris, France (January 11–March 10, 1975); National Museum, Warsaw, Poland (May 18–July 9, 1975); British Museum, London, England (September 17–November 16, 1975); The Metropolitan Museum of Art, New York City (March 5–May 2, 1976); The Art Institute of Chicago, Chicago, Illinois (July 4–September 1, 1976); Los Angeles County Museum of Art, Los Angeles, California (November 2, 1976–January 2, 1977); National Museum of Anthropology, Mexico City, Mexico (April 15–June 15, 1977).

Eames Office is awarded the Federal Design Council Award of Excellence for the *Franklin and Jefferson* exhibition.

Staff member Paul Bruhwiler working on *Franklin and Jefferson* exhibition graphics

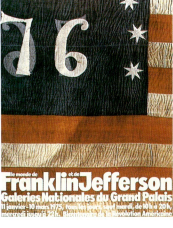
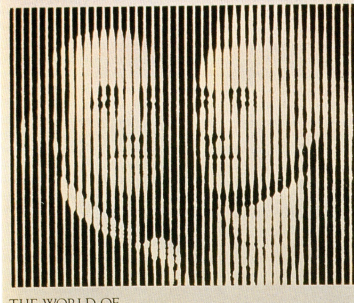
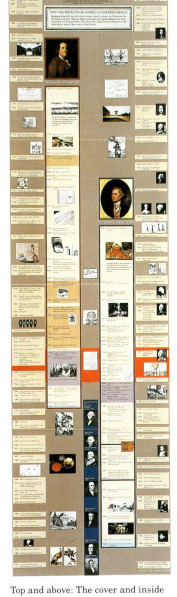
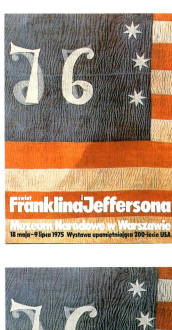
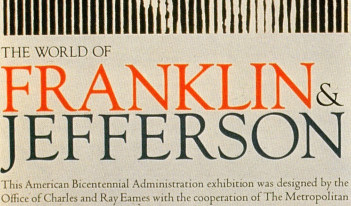

Top: Front and back covers of the Paris exhibition catalog designed by the Eames Office. Above: The exhibition poster designed for the Los Angeles installation

Top and above: The cover and inside of the European timeline

Top, middle, and above: Posters designed for the installations in Paris, Warsaw, and London

423

Charles and writer Barbara Diamond

Staff member Jehane Burns working on exhibition text

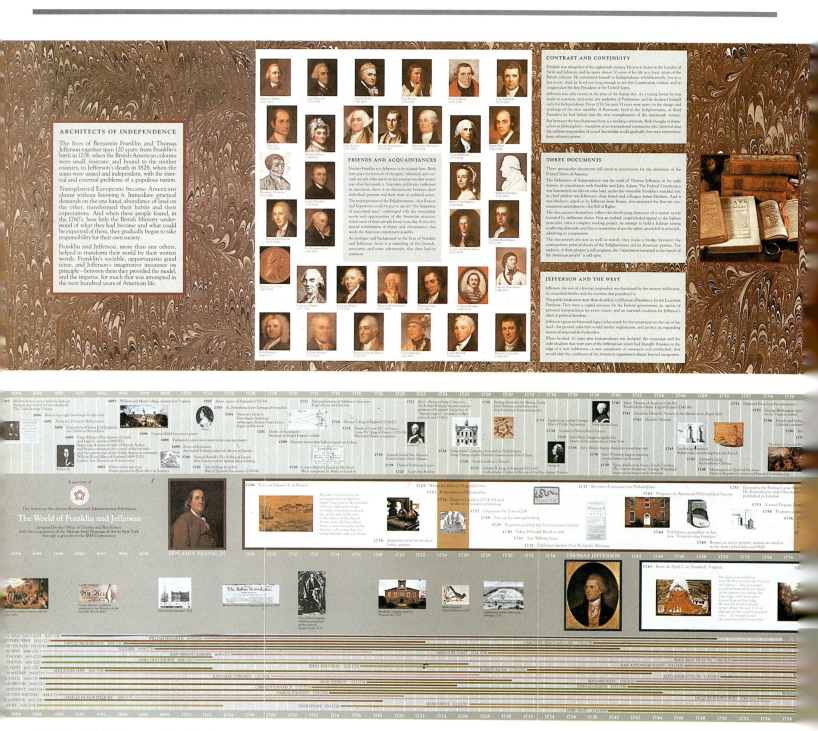
Top, left and right: The cover of the *Franklin and Jefferson* timeline designed by the Eames Office and given to exhibition visitors in New York, Chicago, and Los Angeles. Above, left and right: The inside panels of the timeline

Charles and staff member Etsu Garfias in the office slide room

Bill Lacy, a colleague of Charles's on the National Endowment, working on a special project on time management in the Eames Office

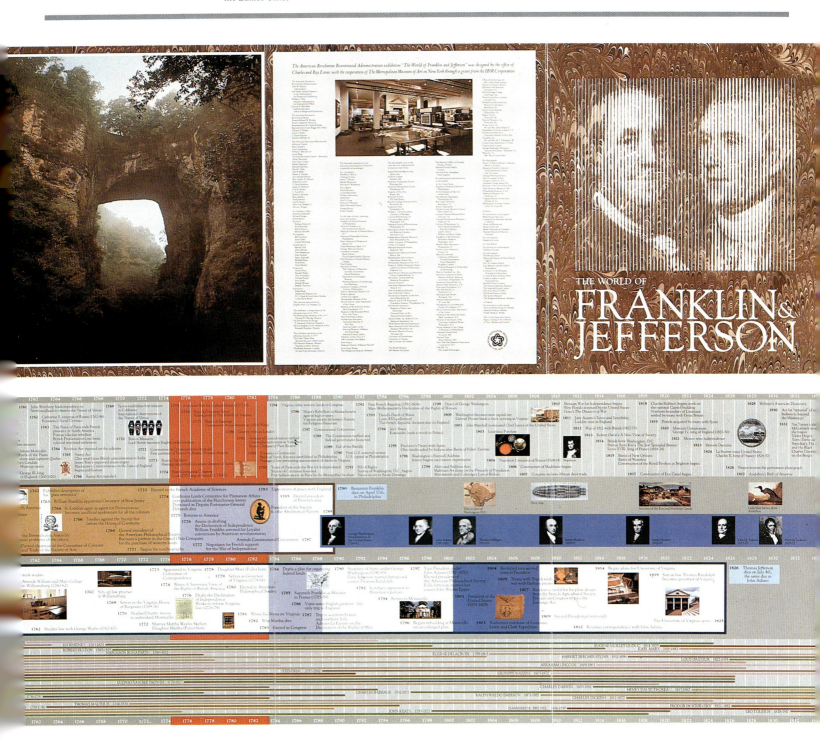

January 27: Charles receives an honorary doctorate of laws from the University of Southern California, Los Angeles.

Staff: 1976
901 Washington Boulevard
Donald Amundson
Jehane Burns
Stan Croner
Richard Donges
Philippa Dunne
Robert Eber
Marilyn Eisenberg
Maria Ewing
John Fitzmaurice
Alex Funke
Etsu Garfias
John Gilchrist
Hap Johnson
James Kennedy
Ruth Kennedy
Pamela Knight
Emily Mayeda
David Meckel
John Neuhart
David Olney
Jeannine Oppewall
Sam Passalacqua
Francisco Perea
Michael Ripps
Ron Rozzelle
Michael Russell
Jane Spiller
Margaret Starr
Birgitta Thornton
David Travers
Randall Walker
Michael Wiener
John Williams

Staff members David Meckel and Ron Rozzelle working on the layout and production of *The World of Franklin and Jefferson* exhibition book

A selection of double-spreads from the book

1976

Book: *The World of Franklin and Jefferson*

The book *The World of Franklin and Jefferson* was produced to accompany the exhibition of the same name (pp. 416–425). Like the exhibition, the book was designed by the Eames Office with the cooperation of The Metropolitan Museum of Art in New York City and through a grant from the IBM Corporation.

The subject matter of the book mirrors that of the exhibition, focusing on the lives of two of the most influential architects of American independence. The book also is divided into four sections: "Friends and Acquaintances," "Contrast and Continuity," "Three Documents," and "Jefferson and the West." The European version was designed by Paul Bruhwiler and the American edition by Dick Petrie.

The text, which was written by Jehane Burns and Barbara Diamond and researched by Jeannine Oppewall, is illustrated with images used in the exhibition, including photographs of artifacts and places, portraits, and paintings and illustrations from the Revolutionary War era. The seventy-eight-page book was published in both hardcover and softcover editions and was printed in full color by George Rice and Sons in Los Angeles. It is out of print.

February 19: Charles delivers the National Science Foundation Lecture at the American Association for the Advancement of Science meeting, Boston, Massachusetts.

Right: Boyce Nemec, an acoustical engineer and lighting expert, on a visit to the Eames Office. Nemec was a consultant to the Eames Office on The House of Science and the New York World's Fair

A card made by the Eames Office for Michael J. Sullivan, celebrating his twenty-fifth anniversary with IBM

Staff: 1976
901 Washington Boulevard
Donald Amundson
Jehane Burns
Stan Croner
Richard Donges
Philippa Dunne
Robert Eber
Marilyn Eisenberg
Maria Ewing
John Fitzmaurice
Alex Funke
Etsu Garfias
John Gilchrist
Hap Johnson
Michael Jones
James Kennedy
Ruth Kennedy
Pamela Knight
Emily Mayeda
David Meckel
John Neuhart
David Olney
Jeannine Oppewall
Sam Passalacqua
Francisco Perea
Michael Ripps
Ron Rozzelle
Michael Russell
Jane Spiller
Margaret Starr
Birgitta Thornton
Bill Tondreau
David Travers
Randall Walker
Michael Wiener
John Williams

1976

Film: *The World of Franklin and Jefferson: The Opening of an Exhibition (Paris Opening)*

This film documents the opening of *The World of Franklin and Jefferson* exhibition at the Grand Palais in Paris in 1975. It captures the hectic final moments of preparation before the opening and the reactions of the first visitors to the exhibition.

The film was made to celebrate the first opening in the three-year run of *The World of Franklin and Jefferson* exhibition and to permanently record some of its essence and the first-night excitement. Work on the exhibition had been intensive since 1972, and the opening of the Paris installation was the culmination of years of research and labor. In the film's prologue, a sequence of slides (transferred to film) shows the installation in progress. The film continues with live-action footage of the French public viewing the exhibition. The narration was written by Charles with Jehane Burns and read by Nina Foch and Philip Bourneuf. The accompanying music, a Quartet for Oboe, Clarinet, Horn, and Bassoon in E-flat Major, by Karl Stamitz, was performed by members of the Berlin Philharmonic. The film is not in general circulation. (Running time, *The World of Franklin and Jefferson: The Opening of an Exhibition*: 7 minutes, 33 seconds; color.)

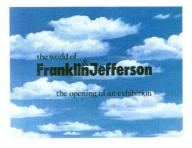

A sequence of frames (reading top to bottom left, top to bottom right) from scenes in *The World of Franklin and Jefferson: The Opening of an Exhibition*. The frames were photographed from 16mm-film footage

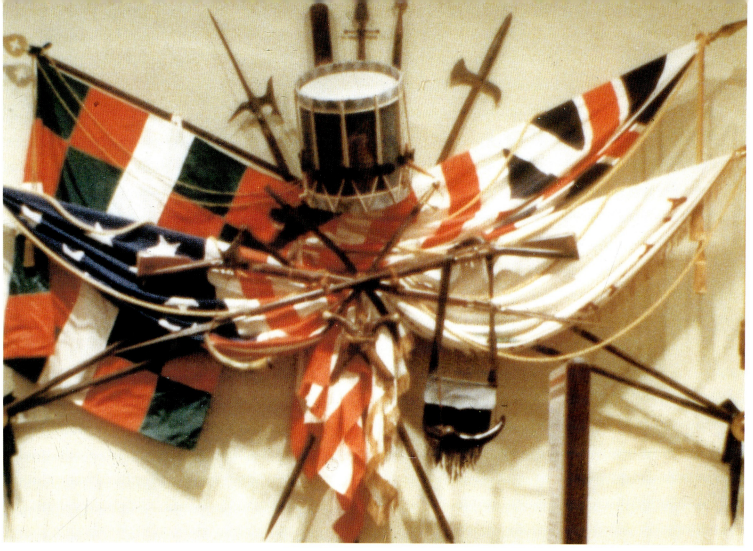

The film *Powers of Ten* is awarded first prize at the Montreal Psychics Film Exposition, Montreal, Canada.

Staff: 1976
901 Washington Boulevard
Donald Amundson
Jehane Burns
Stan Croner
Richard Donges
Philippa Dunne
Robert Eber
Marilyn Eisenberg
Maria Ewing
John Fitzmaurice
Alex Funke
Etsu Garfias
John Gilchrist
Hap Johnson
Michael Jones
James Kennedy
Ruth Kennedy
Pamela Knight
Emily Mayeda
David Meckel
John Neuhart
David Olney
Jeannine Oppewall
Sam Passalacqua
Francisco Perea
Michael Ripps
Ron Rozzelle
Michael Russell
Jane Spiller
Margaret Starr
Birgitta Thornton
Bill Tondreau
David Travers
Randall Walker
Michael Wiener
John Williams

Eames Office secretaries Etsu Garfias and Philippa Dunne

1976

Film: *The World of Franklin and Jefferson*

In this film the material from *The World of Franklin and Jefferson* exhibition was adapted to a cinematic presentation organized along the exhibition's guidelines. Using live-action footage and film shot from stills and slides, the film shows artifacts from the lives of both men, where they lived and worked, and close-ups of the three important documents of American independence they helped draft. A dual timeline on the lives of Franklin and Jefferson traces their lives and the events of the time.

The film, one of the longest ever made by the Eames Office, was made for the American Revolution Bicentennial Administration and was sponsored by the IBM Corporation. The script was written by Jehane Burns with Charles and narrated by Orson Welles and Nina Foch. The music is by Elmer Bernstein. The film is in general circulation. (Running time, *The World of Franklin and Jefferson*: 28 minutes, 20 seconds; color.)

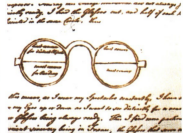

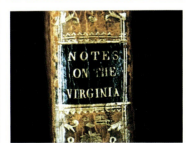
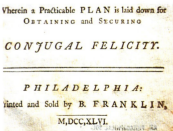

Above: A sequence of frames (reading top to bottom left, top to bottom right) from scenes in *The World of Franklin and Jefferson*. Opposite: Two images from the beginning of *The World of Franklin and Jefferson*. The frames were photographed from 16mm-film footage

429

March: Charles and Ray receive the Outstanding Service Award from the United States Information Agency for the exhibition *The World of Franklin and Jefferson.*

March 3: Charles speaks to The Architectural League, New York City.

March 23 and 30 and April 6: Charles lectures at The Metropolitan Museum of Art, New York City.

Staff: 1976
901 Washington Boulevard
Donald Amundson
Jehane Burns
Stan Croner
Richard Donges
Philippa Dunne
Robert Eber
Marilyn Eisenberg
Maria Ewing
John Fitzmaurice
Alex Funke
Etsu Garfias
John Gilchrist
Hap Johnson
Michael Jones
James Kennedy
Ruth Kennedy
Pamela Knight
Emily Mayeda
David Meckel
John Neuhart
David Olney
Jeannine Oppewall
Sam Passalacqua
Francisco Perea
Michael Ripps
Ron Rozzelle
Michael Russell
Jane Spiller
Margaret Starr
Birgitta Thornton
Bill Tondreau
David Travers
Randall Walker
Michael Wiener
John Williams

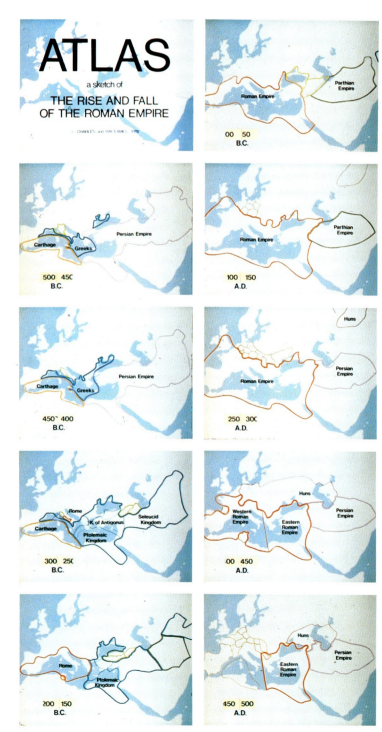

A sequence of frames (reading top to bottom left, top to bottom right) from scenes in *Atlas*. The frames were photographed from 16mm-film footage

1976

Film: *Atlas: A Sketch of the Rise and Fall of the Roman Empire*

Atlas, in Charles's words in the film's original introduction, is a "little sketch which gives in a very short amount of time an idea of what the rise and fall of the Roman Empire really looked like." The film begins in 500 B.C. with a map of political boundaries in Europe and the Near East. As a time clock at the bottom of the screen steadily marks off the years—eight years to a second—the boundaries on the map change, at first moving outward to show the Roman Empire's growth, including the conquests of Alexander the Great. The map then shrinks back as the power of the Romans declined. The film ends at the invasion of the Huns and the sack of Rome in A.D. 476.

The making of the film was inspired by Charles's fondness for the Penguin historical atlases, which contain maps of ancient, medieval, and modern times. The film was assembled quickly and coincided with the United States bicentennial celebrations. Tom Horton, director of University Relations at the IBM Corporation, on seeing the film, remarked that 1976 was also the two-hundredth anniversary of Edward Gibbon's book *Decline and Fall of the Roman Empire*. When the film was first shown at the American Association of the Arts in Boston, Charles introduced it as "In celebration of the two-hundredth anniversary of," paused, and continued, "the publication of the first volume of Gibbon's *Decline and Fall of the Roman Empire*."

The narration was written by Charles and Jehane Burns and spoken live in the film's first showing. A later version had a recorded narration by Alex Funke, with music by David Spears.

The film was essentially an experiment in the visual and organic depiction of the passage of time, a technique that Charles felt could be applied in films about many other events and in many scientific disciplines. The film was not finished in a polished form and is not in general circulation. (Running time, *Atlas*: 2 minutes, 30 seconds; color.)

April 13: Charles and Ray are given honorary memberships in the American Institute of Architects, Southern California Chapter, Los Angeles.

April 19: Charles lectures to the Missouri State Historical Society, St. Louis.

April 22: Charles talks at the American Society of Interior Designers Student Honor Awards Evening, Riviera Country Club, Pacific Palisades, California.

Architect A. Quincy Jones and Elaine Sewell Jones with Ray at the opening of the *Images of Early America* exhibition

Staff: 1976
901 Washington Boulevard
Donald Amundson
Jehane Burns
Stan Croner
Richard Donges
Philippa Dunne
Robert Eber
Marilyn Eisenberg
Maria Ewing
John Fitzmaurice
Alex Funke
Etsu Garfias
John Gilchrist
Hap Johnson
Michael Jones
James Kennedy
Ruth Kennedy
Pamela Knight
Emily Mayeda
David Meckel
John Neuhart
David Olney
Jeannine Oppewall
Sam Passalacqua
Francisco Perea
Michael Ripps
Ron Rozzelle
Michael Russell
Jane Spiller
Margaret Starr
Birgitta Thornton
Bill Tondreau
David Travers
Randall Walker
Michael Wiener
John Williams

1976

Exhibition and Book: *Images of Early America*

The exhibition *Images of Early America* was designed and produced for Herman Miller, Inc., as part of its celebration of the United States bicentennial. A companion book by the same title was published after the exhibition. The small exhibition of photographs was installed in the lobby of the Herman Miller showroom in Los Angeles in 1976. The book, a collection of many of the photographs in the exhibition, was published by Herman Miller and distributed as a bicentennial gift to staff and customers.

The photographs were shot while the Eames Office was at work on *The World of Franklin and Jefferson* exhibition and the *Look of America* film at various locations along the eastern seaboard of the United States (in states that were part of the original thirteen colonies). The images—exterior and interior views of existing structures dating from the eighteenth and nineteenth centuries—include government buildings, homes and mansions, churches, college buildings, and farms. The images range from panoramic views to close-up architectural details.

The photographs were taken by Charles and staff members Bill Tondreau and Alex Funke. One image is printed per page in the book and is accompanied by a caption identifying the subject and location. The limited edition, forty-seven-page book was printed in full color by Graphic Press in Los Angeles, California.

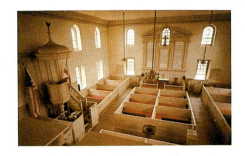

Cover of the booklet *Images of Early America*: Pohick Church, Fairfax County, Virginia

Views of the exhibition installed in the Herman Miller showroom in Los Angeles

Quaker meetinghouse in Old Sturbridge Village, Massachusetts

Dwight Barnard House in Deerfield, Massachusetts

Stone wall and meetinghouse in Sudbury, Massachusetts

Woods at Carter's Grove, near Williamsburg, Virginia

Handrail in Charleston, South Carolina

The U.S.S. *Constitution* in Boston, Massachusetts

A selection of photographs from *Images of Early America*

Right: Eames Office group portrait. Front row, left to right; Bill Tondreau, Etsu Garfias, Jeannine Oppewall, Emily Mayeda, Ray, John Fitzmaurice. Middle row, left to right: David Olney, Hap Johnson, Lonnie Browning, Sam Passalacqua, Jane Spiller, Jehane Burns. Back row, left to right:, Donald Amundson, Randall Walker, Michael Russell, Charles, Richard Donges, Michael Jones, David Meckel, Ron Rozzelle, and Alex Funke

Kitchen garden at Mount Vernon, Virginia

The Natural Bridge in Virginia

Interior, Lemon Hill, Fairmount Park, Philadelphia, Pennsylvania

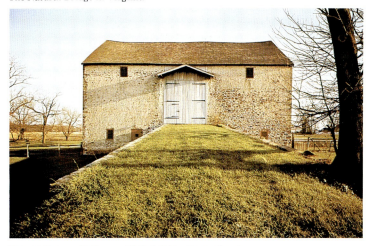

Barn at Graeme Park, near Philadelphia, Pennsylvania

Carter's Grove Plantation House, near Williamsburg, Virginia

Cooperage in Old Sturbridge Village, Massachusetts

June 25: Charles lectures on "Media, Museums, and the Design Process" at the Association of American Museums' Seventieth Annual Conference.

Staff: 1976
901 Washington Boulevard
Donald Amundson
Jehane Burns
Stan Croner
Richard Donges
Philippa Dunne
Robert Eber
Marilyn Eisenberg
Maria Ewing
John Fitzmaurice
Alex Funke
Etsu Garfias
John Gilchrist
Hap Johnson
James Jones
Ruth Kennedy
Pamela Knight
Emily Mayeda
David Meckel
John Neuhart
David Olney
Jeannine Oppewall
Sam Passabacqua
Francisco Perea
Michael Ripps
Ron Rozzelle
Michael Russell
Jane Spiller
Margaret Starr
Birgitta Thornton
Bill Tondreau
David Travers
Randall Walker
Michael Wiener
John Williams

Ted Voss of Polaroid Camera Corporation on a visit to the Eames Office

Charles on the film set for *Something about Photography*

A sequence of frames (reading top to bottom left, top to bottom right) from scenes in *Something about Photography*. The frames were photographed from 16mm-film footage

1976

Film: *Something about Photography*

In a conversation between Charles and Edwin Land, the inventor of the Polaroid cameras, Land mentioned that he wanted the pictures taken with the new Polaroid SX-70 system to be the best possible, not just "snapshots." He asked Charles to make a film to demonstrate the simplest and most basic rules of picture taking that would also demonstrate that "instant photography" could be used in personally meaningful and unique ways. Although Land did not require that Polaroid cameras be used in the film, Charles, an advocate of instant photography, decided to use the SX-70 as the basis of *Something about Photography*. Scheduled to be shown at a stockholders' meeting in the spring of 1976, the film explains the operation and use of the SX-70 camera and makes a personal statement— something about photography—about the photographic process.

In the film Charles expresses his own philosophy of picture taking, emphasizing the advantages of immediacy in the use of instant photography. He used cameras throughout his life to make visual notes about the world around him, as well as for images used in Eames exhibitions and films and to record the work of the Eames Office. In 1976, while preparations for the exhibition *Connections: The Work of Charles and Ray Eames* were under way, he estimated that there were close to 300,000 photographic images in the Eames Office files dating from the early 1940s. He considered the camera to be an indispensable tool—a way to have your cake and eat it, too. In the film's narration he stresses again that the picture-taker need only look at the people and the everyday events and things he cares deeply about to find the most meaningful subjects for photographs.

The script was written with Jehane Burns and narrated by John Neuhart and Charles. The musical accompaniment was composed and conducted by Donald Specht. It is in general circulation. (Running time, *Something about Photography*: 8 minutes, 32 seconds; color.)

July 25: The Eames House (pp. 106–121) is among 260 buildings listed in the *American Institute of Architects Journal* as the "Proudest Achievements of American Architecture."

August 6: Charles lectures to the Friends of the Library, University of California, Los Angeles.

November 9: Charles delivers a lecture to the American Academy of Arts and Sciences, Boston, Massachusetts.

November 23: Charles lectures to the Pasadena Chapter of the Southern California Chapter of the American Institute of Architects.

December: Charles lectures at the Annenberg School of Communications, University of Southern California, Los Angeles.

Staff: 1976
901 Washington Boulevard
Donald Amundson
Jehane Burns
Stan Croner
Richard Donges
Philippa Dunne
Robert Eber
Marilyn Eisenberg
Maria Ewing
John Fitzmaurice
Alex Funke
Etsu Garfias
John Gilchrist
Hap Johnson
Michael Jones
James Kennedy
Ruth Kennedy
Pamela Knight
Emily Mayeda
David Meckel
John Neuhart
David Olney
Jeannine Oppewall
Sam Passalacqua
Francisco Perea
Michael Ripps
Ron Rozzelle
Michael Russell
Jane Spiller
Margaret Starr
Birgitta Thornton
Bill Tondreau
David Travers
Randall Walker
Michael Wiener
John Williams

Right: Hugh De Pree (left) and Glen Walters (far right), chairman and president, respectively, of Herman Miller, Inc., with Charles and Ray during an office visit

1976

Slide Show: *Tall Ships*

Tall Ships is a 108-image, 3-screen (36-pass) slide show. The images were photographed during the tall ships procession into New York City's harbor on July 4, 1976, in honor of the American Revolution bicentennial. Charles and staff member Richard Donges, who were installing *The World of Franklin and Jefferson* exhibition in Chicago, went to New York City and photographed from on board a ship hired for the event by the IBM Corporation.

The "Blue Danube" and "Radetsky March" accompanied the slide show.

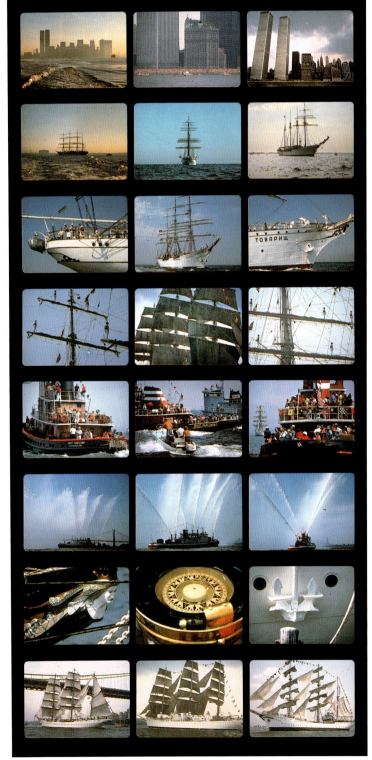

A sequence of 3-image passes (reading top to bottom) from the slide show *Tall Ships*

December 7, 1976–February 7, 1977: An exhibition about the Eames Office, *Connections: The Work of Charles and Ray Eames*, conceived, organized, and designed by John and Marilyn Neuhart, is held at the Wight Art Gallery, University of California, Los Angeles. The retrospective exhibition was shown at three locations in the United States and at seven in Great Britain and Europe. Right: Cover of the *Connections* exhibition catalog

Above: A view of the *Connections* exhibition. Right: Charles and Ray at the *Connections* exhibition with Ray's childhood friends and her brother. Top row, left to right: Lewis Pierce, Barney Reese, Charles, and Howard Reese. Bottom row, left to right: Marion Pierce, Ray, Ryland and Maurice Kaiser

Staff: 1976
901 Washington Boulevard
Donald Amundson
Jehane Burns
Stan Croner
Richard Donges
Philippa Dunne
Robert Eber
Marilyn Eisenberg
Maria Ewing
John Fitzmaurice
Alex Funke
Etsu Garfias
John Gilchrist
Hap Johnson
Michael Jones
James Kennedy
Ruth Kennedy
Pamela Knight
Emily Mayeda
David Meckel
John Neuhart
David Olney
Jeannine Oppewall
Sam Passalacqua
Francisco Perea
Michael Ripps
Ron Rozzelle
Michael Russell
Jane Spiller
Margaret Starr
Birgitta Thornton
Bill Tondreau
David Travers
Randall Walker
Michael Wiener
John Williams

1976

Film: *The Look of America*

The film *The Look of America* was produced for Charles Montgomery, director of the Yale University Art Gallery (and a former director of Winterthur in Delaware). While assembling an exhibition for Yale on the history of the Revolutionary War that was scheduled to open at the Victoria and Albert Museum in London, Montgomery approached Charles about the possibility of providing a film that could be used to complement the artifacts in his exhibition.

Using both live-action footage and film shot from stills and slides, *The Look of America* traces the social, religious, and economic development of America from its first years of colonization to the beginnings of industrialization. It shows the land, architecture, and artifacts of the times and relates the history of urban and rural communities. According to the film's narration, "The impetus of technological invention would carry Americans into a new wilderness of commerce and production."

The Look of America was sponsored by Yale University and the National Endowment for the Humanities. The film was written by Jehane Burns with Charles and narrated by Norman Lloyd. Jeannine Oppewall researched the verbal and visual content and assisted in developing the script. The music was composed and conducted by Elmer Bernstein. It is in general circulation. (Running time, *The Look of America*: 26 minutes, 25 seconds; color.)

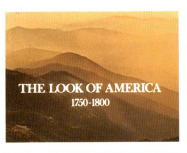

A sequence of frames (reading top to bottom left, top to bottom right) from scenes in *The Look of America*: The frames were photographed from 16mm-film footage

January 1: Charles is appointed Regents' Professor for the winter quarter at the University of California, Los Angeles.

February 10: Ray is named Woman of the Year by the California Museum of Science and Industry Muses, Los Angeles.

March 7: The exhibition, *The Design Process at Herman Miller*, organized by the Walker Art Center in Minneapolis opens at Winnipeg Art Museum, Winnipeg, Canada.

March: Charles delivers the Doubleday Lecture at the Smithsonian Institution, Washington, D.C.

March 8: Charles lectures at the University of Manitoba, Manitoba, Canada.

Right: Charles and Ray with Marilyn and John Neuhart on the last day of the exhibition *Connections: The Work of Charles and Ray Eames*, Wight Art Gallery, University of California, Los Angeles

Staff: 1977
901 Washington Boulevard
Donald Amundson, Lucia Dewey Atwood, Tina Beebe, Dennis Bishop, Jon Boorstin, Jehane Burns, Dennis Carmichael, Susan Chevalier, Tom Conlon, Jim Czajka, Richard Donges, Jessie Duffy, Clark Dugger, Sumiko Eguchi, Olivia Emery, Maria Ewing, John Fitzmaurice, Alex Funke, Etsu Garfias, Myron Guran, James Hoekama, James Hong, Reed Hutchinson, Stan Ishikawa, Hap Johnson, Michael Jones, Susan Kingsbury, Janet Kroll, Jeremy Lepard, Ruby Little, Gary Lund, Emily Mayeda, David Meckel, Parke Meek, Michael Murphy, John Neuhart, David Olney, Jeannine Oppewall, Sam Passalacqua, Thomas Patch, Gayle Pearson, Deborah Rice, Ron Rozzelle, Michael Russell, Eric Saarinen, Sheila Selden, Steve Slocomb, Doreen Small, Jane Spiller, Margaret Starr, Bill Tondreau, Michael Underhill, Max Underwood, Frederick Usher, Wendy Vanguard, Randall Walker, Michael Wiener, Eddie Williams, Susan Winslow, Ted Wu

1977

Film: *Daumier: Paris and the Spectator*

Daumier explores the world of nineteenth-century Paris using illustrations and caricatures of the time, particularly the graphic work of Honoré Daumier. Adapted and narrated by art historian Judith Wechsler from a lecture she gave at MIT, the film reveals the spectacles and sights of Paris street life, its theaters and salons, and the continuing parade of its spectators. In addition to Daumier, the film includes illustrations by Gustave Doré, Paul Gavarni, Jean Ignace Grandville, Marc Monnier, Travies, Amédée Cham, Pigal, and Vernet.

Charles felt that Wechsler's approach to the subject—demonstrating the relationship of art to daily life—was worthy of a film, and he attempted to capture the spirit of her classroom lecture in *Daumier*. Wechsler appears in the film and is the narrator. *Daumier* is a combination of live-action footage and stills shot from original drawings and photographs. The music was composed and conducted by Elmer Bernstein. *Daumier* is in general circulation. (Running time, *Daumier*: 18 minutes; color.)

A sequence of frames (reading top to bottom left, top to bottom right) from scenes in the film *Daumier: Paris and the Spectator*. The frames were photographed from 16mm-film footage

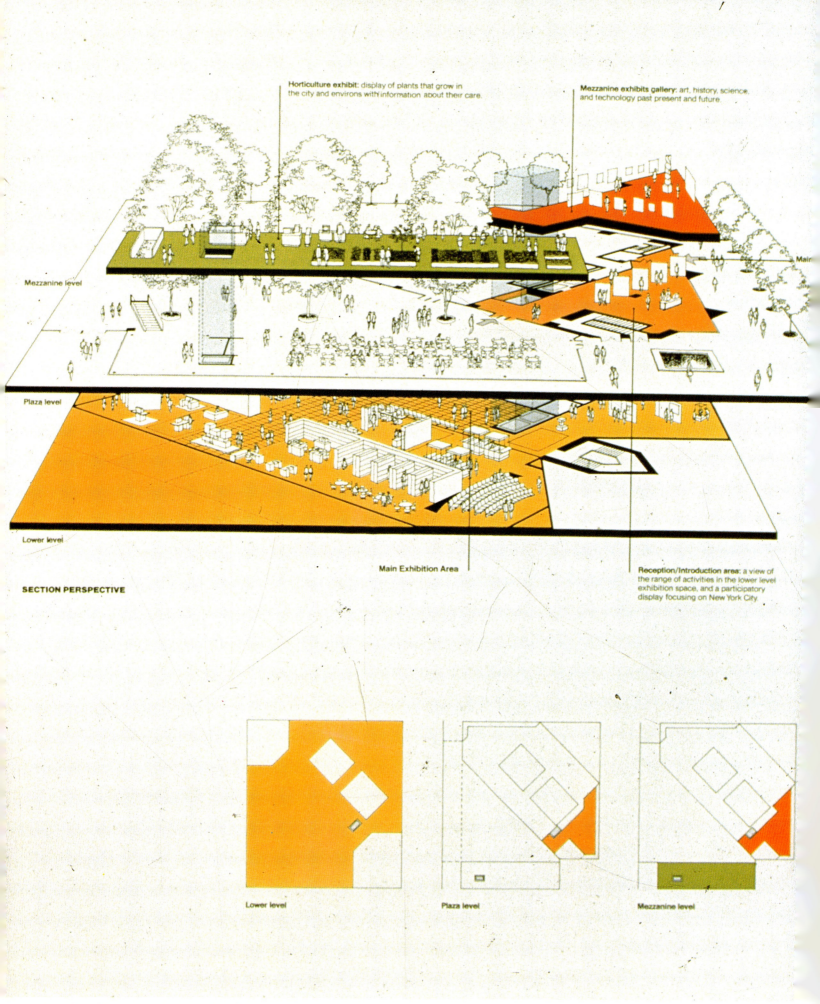

Above: Plan of the lower level, street level, and mezzanine areas

April 19: Charles gives a lecture to the Sloan Luncheon Group, New York City.

April 21: Charles lectures at the Center for the Arts, Wesleyan University, Middletown, Connecticut.

Charles lectures at the Exhibit Seminar, Yale University, New Haven, Connecticut.

May 17: Charles lectures in the Artist-in-Residence Program, Greenwich High School, Greenwich, Connecticut.

May 18: Charles is made a member of the American Academy and Institute of Arts and Letters.

May 20: Charles receives an honorary appointment to the National University of Peru, Lima.

Right: David Olney, Michael Sullivan of IBM, Ted Wu, Michael Russell, and Charles reviewing plans for the IBM proposal

Staff: 1977
901 Washington Boulevard
Donald Amundson
Lucia Dewey Atwood
Tina Beebe
Dennis Bishop
Jon Boorstin
Jehane Burns
Dennis Carmichael
Susan Chevalier
Tom Conlon
Jim Czajka
Jessie Duffy
Richard Donges
Clark Dugger
Sumiko Eguchi
Olivia Emery
Maria Ewing
John Fitzmaurice
Alex Funke
Etsu Garfias
Myron Guran
James Hoekema
James Hong
Reed Hutchinson
Stan Ishikawa
Hap Johnson
Michael Jones
Susan Kingsbury
Janet Kroll
Jeremy Lepard
Ruby Little
Gary Lund
Emily Mayeda
David Meckel
Parke Meek
Michael Murphy
John Neuhart
David Olney
Jeannine Oppewall
Sam Passalacqua
Thomas Patch
Gayle Pearson
Deborah Rice
Ron Rozzelle
Michael Russell
Eric Saarinen
Sheila Selden
Steve Slocomb
Doreen Small
Jane Spiller
Margaret Starr
Bill Tondreau
Michael Underhill
Max Underwood
Frederick Usher
Randall Walker
Wendy Vanguard
Michael Wiener
Eddie Williams
Susan Winslow
Ted Wu

1977

IBM 590 Corporate Exhibit Center Proposal

The IBM 590 Proposal was the first version of a plan designed by the Eames Office for a proposed exhibition space in the IBM Corporation's new regional headquarters (designed by Edward Larrabee Barnes) at 590 Madison Avenue in New York City. The proposal described the division of the 15,000 square feet of space into three levels: plaza level, lower level, and mezzanine. Many of the ideas first proposed for the *IBM Museum Proposal* film (pp. 328–329) were incorporated into this later plan.

The plan for the IBM gallery space, located on the ground and lower floors of the new building, was aimed at making the IBM center "a gathering point and reflector for the company's best thinking." It was to be open to the public and was designed to help people find out more about computers. It included a show of "antique" calculators and a center devoted to computer concepts (the ideas on which computers are based and the terms specific to computing). The 1971 *A Computer Perspective* exhibition (pp. 364–369) was to be reinstalled and a new edition of the *Mathematica* exhibition (pp. 254–259) introduced to the New York City area. A section of the center was set aside as an "information-access" area, where visitors could have hands-on experience trying out computer programs and applications and investigating the "latest and best" innovations in the world of computing. Other spaces were designated for seminar rooms, special exhibits galleries, a theater, and a library. The plaza-level reception area included an introduction to the exhibit center, an interactive visitor-participation program, featuring information about New York City, and a glass-enclosed public garden.

The plan for this information center was the last in a series of Eames Office proposals advocating centers for the dispersal of information made over the years to various clients, beginning with the Jefferson Memorial in 1947 (pp. 84–85). None of these proposals, each of which was complex in concept, execution, and maintenance, was realized by the Eames Office.

The elements of the proposal were incorporated into a completed plan for the exhibition center detailed in the 1979 Eames Office film *A Report on the IBM Exhibition Center* (p. 450).

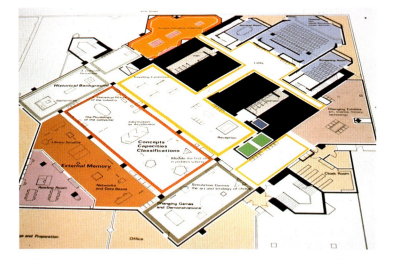

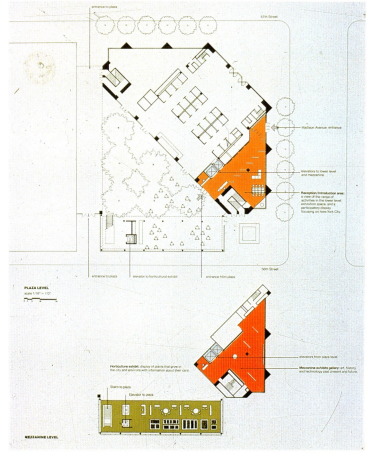

Top: Plan view of the exhibition level of the IBM Corporate Exhibit Center. Above: Plan view of the reception and introduction areas of the IBM Corporate Exhibit Center

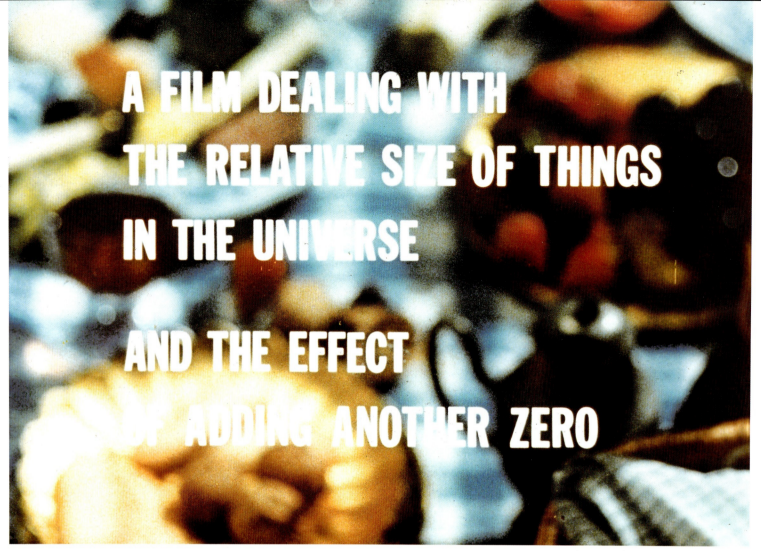

May 27: Charles delivers the commencement address and receives an honorary doctorate of fine arts in industrial design from the Art Center College of Design, Pasadena, California. Ray receives an honorary doctorate of fine arts in communication design.

June 11: Charles receives an honorary doctorate of humanities from Michigan State University, East Lansing.

July 19: Charles talks at the American Academy in Rome, Italy.

The Look of America receives the Silver Plaque from the Thirteenth Chicago International Film Festival, Chicago, Illinois; and the Golden Eagle Award from the Council on Non-Theatrical Events.

Charles and Ray receive the J.W. Robinson and Max Factor Excellence of Design Award, Municipal Art Gallery, Los Angeles, California.

Charles and Ray are made members of the Alliance Graphique Internationale.

Right: Physicist Philip Morrison at the Eames Office recording the narration for *Powers of Ten*

Staff: 1977
901 Washington Boulevard
Donald Amundson
Lucia Dewey Atwood
Tina Beebe
Dennis Bishop
Jon Boorstin
Jehane Burns
Susan Chevalier
Dennis Carmichael
Tom Conlon
Jim Czajka
Richard Donges
Jessie Duffy
Clark Dugger
Sumiko Eguchi
Olivia Emery
Maria Ewing
John Fitzmaurice
Alex Funke
Elsu Garfias
Myron Guran
James Hoekema
James Hong
Reed Hutchinson
Stan Ishikawa
Hap Johnson
Michael Jones
Susan Kingsbury
Janet Kroll
Jeremy Lepard
Ruby Little
Gary Lund
Emily Mayeda
David Meckel
Parke Meek
Michael Murphy
John Neuhart
David Olney
Jeannine Oppewall
Sam Passalacqua
Thomas Patch
Gayle Pearson
Deborah Rice
Ron Rozzelle
Michael Russell
Eric Saarinen
Sheila Selden
Steve Slocomb
Doreen Small
Jane Spiller
Margaret Starr
Bill Tondreau
Michael Underhill
Max Underwood
Frederick Usher
Wendy Vanguard
Randall Walker
Michael Wiener
Eddie Williams
Susan Winslow
Ted Wu

1977

Film: *Powers of Ten: A Film Dealing with the Relative Size of Things in the Universe, and the Effect of Adding Another Zero*

Powers of Ten is an updated, finished version of the study film produced in 1968 (pp. 336–337). In the ten years between the two versions, many advances in theory and research had occurred. The new version adds two powers of ten—a hundredfold increase—to each end of the journey into the universe and to the return trip into the microstructure of a carbon atom in the human body. The site of the journey's start was changed from a Florida golf course to a park bordering Lake Michigan in Chicago, to allow the journey to approach the disk of the galaxy approximately at right angles. By adding a zero to each jump, the film is able to explore the universe, ending at ten to the power of twenty-five. The journey back to earth and into the microscopic world ends at ten to the minus-sixteenth power. The same restrictions set in the first film applied to the second version—the line of travel is always perpendicular to the hand of the sleeping man and eleven seconds elapse between each power shift.

The concept was expanded from the first film with the assistance of Philip Morrison, professor of physics at MIT, who also narrated the film, and other authorities in astrophysics, cellular biology, genetic chemistry, and particle physics. A book (*Powers of Ten*) based on the film journey was produced in 1982 by Phylis and Philip Morrison for the *Scientific American Library* series. Ray provided material from the Eames Office for the book.

Music for the film was composed and conducted by Elmer Bernstein. It is in general circulation. (Running time, *Powers of Ten*: 9 minutes; color.)

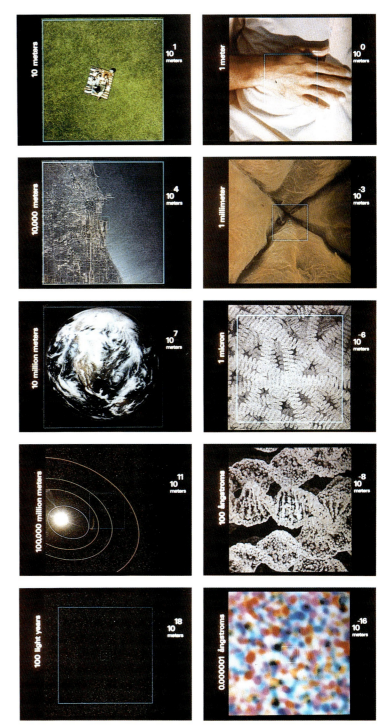

Above: A sequence of frames (reading top to bottom left, top to bottom right) from scenes in the film *Powers of Ten*. Opposite: Two frames from the beginning of *Powers of Ten*. The frames were photographed from 16mm-film footage

September 11: Charles receives the key to the city of St. Louis and the Gateway Arch of St. Louis Trophy from Mayor John H. Poelker.

September 12–October 23: The exhibition, *Connections: The Work of Charles and Ray Eames* opens in the Art Gallery, Steinberg Hall, and in the gallery at Laumeier Park, St. Louis, Missouri.

October 18: Charles and Ray receive the Medalist Award from the American Institute of Graphic Arts, New York City.

October 19: Charles speaks to the Massachusetts Institute of Technology Contributions Council, Cambridge.

November 3: Charles lectures to the Regional Meeting of the Associated Collegiate Schools of Architecture, University of Southern California, Los Angeles.

Right: Charles sitting on the steps of his childhood home in St. Louis, Missouri

Staff: 1977
901 Washington Boulevard
Donald Amundson
Lucia Dewey Atwood
Tina Beebe
Dennis Bishop
Jon Boorstin
Jehane Burns
Susan Carmichael
Dennis Carmichael
Tom Conlon
Jim Czajka
Richard Donges
Jessie Duffy
Clark Dugger
Sumiko Eguchi
Olivia Emery
Maria Ewing
John Fitzmaurice
Alex Funke
Etsu Garfias
Myron Guran
James Hoekema
James Hong
Reed Hutchinson
Stan Ishikawa
Hap Johnson
Michael Jones
Susan Kingsbury
Janet Kroll
Jeremy Lepard
Ruby Little
Gary Lund
Emily Mayeda
David Meckel
Parke Meek
Michael Murphy
John Neuhart
David Olney
Jeannine Oppewall
Sam Passacaqua
Thomas Patch
Gayle Pearson
Deborah Rice
Ron Rozzelle
Michael Russell
Eric Saarinen
Sheila Selden
Steve Slocomb
Doreen Small
Jane Spiller
Margaret Starr
Bill Tondreau
Michael Underhill
Max Underwood
Frederick Usher
Wendy Vanguard
Randall Walker
Michael Wiener
Eddie Williams
Susan Winslow
Ted Wu

1977

Film: *Polavision*

Polavision was produced for the Polaroid Corporation to demonstrate the features of their new instant-movie camera system—Polavision. The film begins with an introduction to the system and continues with examples demonstrating some of the ways the instant-movie camera could be employed by amateur photographers shooting the immediate source material of everyday life. Although the length of the system's two-and-a-half-minute film cassette posed something of a challenge, Charles and the Eames Office staff were enthusiastic about the camera. Six short vignettes, each the length of the Polaroid film cassette, illustrate the point. The film emphasizes the importance of planning and composition in the photographic process and includes how-to-do-it demonstrations of stop-motion photography and animation.

The film includes both live-action photography and film shot from stills and slides. The six vignettes—"Macbeth," "Kites," "The Trunk in the Attic," "The Chase," "Llisa Draws a Letter," and "Bicycles"—were shot in the Eames Office and on location. "Macbeth" depicts children interpreting the Shakespearean play. "Kites" is the story of making and flying a kite. "The Trunk in the Attic" records the discovery of forgotten stored belongings. In "The Chase," a girl chases her brother, who has stolen her diary. "Llisa Draws a Letter" is about a young girl who opens a gift package and draws a thank-you letter. "Bicycles" is a panoramic view of people riding their bicycles.

Andrew Duggan narrated the *Polavision* script, which was written by Charles and Jehane Burns. Music for the film was composed and conducted by Elmer Bernstein. The film is not in general circulation. (Running time, *Polavision*: 15 minutes; color.)

The vignettes were incorporated in 1978 into two separate films. "Bicycles," "Masks" (formerly called "The Trunk in the Attic"), and "The Chase" were included in the first and "Llisa Draws a Letter," "Kites," and "Macbeth" in the second. The music for "Masks" and "The Chase" was written by Elmer Bernstein (used earlier in the *House* film). The score for "Bicycles" was written and conducted by Bob Zwirn. This condensed version of *Polavision* is in general circulation. (Running time, each film: 7 minutes, 30 seconds; color.)

A sequence of frames (reading top to bottom left, top to bottom right) from scenes in *Polavision*. The frames were photographed from 16mm-film footage

January 12: Ray attends a meeting of the American Academy in Rome's plenary session, Rome, Italy.

February 15: Ray is on the jury for the Boston Art Directors' Club's Silver Anniversary Awards in Visual Communication, Boston, Massachusetts.

February 16: Ray attends a meeting of the National Institute of Education, Washington, D.C.

Staff: 1978
901 Washington Boulevard
Donald Amundson, Lucia Dewey Atwood, Tina Beebe, Burt Berenson, Lonnie Browning, Jehane Burns, Ken Cheng, Richard D'Amore, Christopher Dill, Paul Dixon, Sylvia Domney, Richard Donges, Clark Dugger, Sumiko Eguchi, John Fitzmaurice, Kathe Flynn, Alex Funke, Etsu Garfias, Karen Good, Marcy Goodwin, James Hoekema, Paul Howard, Robert Hunt, Frank Huttinger, Stan Ishikawa, Chris Jenkins, Hap Johnson, Michael Jones, David Lafferty, Howard Lathrop, Dan McLaughlin, Emily Mayeda, John Neuhart, David Olney, Sam Passalacqua, Gayle Pearson, Ched Reeder, Audrey Roberts, Tom Rossiter, Keith Rouse, Ron Rozzelle, Pamela Rubin, Michael Russell, Jane Spiller, Margaret Starr, Bayard Storey, Jr., Hatsuko Tanabe, Bill Tondreau, Randall Walker, Michael Wiener, Bill Wietsma, Eddie Williams

1978

Film: *Sonar One-Step*

Sonar One-Step was made by the Eames Office for the Polaroid Corporation and was first shown in May 1978 at a stockholders' meeting. The film was produced to explain and demonstrate the operation of a new Polaroid camera with an automatic sonar-based focusing system. It examines the technology and provides some background on the system's development. It was shot in the Eames Office and on location, using live-action photography and animation.

The script for the film was written with Jehane Burns and Alex Funke and was narrated by Marvin Miller. The score is by Donald Specht. The film is not in general circulation. (Running time, *Sonar One-Step*: 8 minutes; color.)

A selection of frames (reading top to bottom left, top to bottom right) from scenes in *Sonar One-Step*. The frames were photographed from 16mm-film footage

March 21: Ray is a member of the Rockefeller Panel at the Eighteenth Annual National Art Association Convention, Houston, Texas.

April 3: Charles and Ray receive honorary doctorates from the University of Cincinnati, Cincinnati, Ohio.

Staff member James Hoekema planning the *Art Game*

Staff: 1978
901 Washington Boulevard
Donald Amundson
Lucia Dewey Atwood
Tina Beebe
Burt Berenson
Lonnie Browning
Jehane Burns
Ken Cheng
Richard D'Amore
Christopher Dill
Paul Dixon
Sylvia Domney
Richard Donges
Clark Dugger
Sumiko Eguchi
John Fitzmaurice
Kathe Flynn
Alex Funke
Etsu Garfias
Karen Good
Marcy Goodwin
James Hoekema
Paul Howard
Robert Hunt
Frank Huttinger
Stan Ishikawa
Chris Jenkins
Hap Johnson
Michael Jones
David Lafferty
Howard Lathrop
Dan McLaughlin
Emily Mayeda
John Neuhart
David Olney
Sam Passalacqua
Gayle Pearson
Ched Reeder
Audrey Roberts
Tom Rossiter
Keith Rouse
Ron Rozzelle
Pamela Rubin
Michael Russell
Jane Spiller
Margaret Starr
Bayard Storey Jr.
Hatsuko Tanabe
Bill Tondreau
Randall Walker
Michael Wiener
Bill Wietsma
Eddie Williams

1978

Film: *Art Game*

The Eames Office was commissioned by the IBM Corporation to produce two videodisc programs to explore the potential of videodisc technology. The first of these, *Art Game*, is an interactive videodisc program designed to demonstrate the use of the interactive videodisc in conjunction with the personal computer. A two-minute sample film made in 1977 was later incorporated into a twelve-minute film completed in June 1978, six months before the commercial introduction of videodisc technology. The film described the program for IBM.

Art Game includes a two-minute introduction and a five-minute section on six Impressionist and Post-Impressionist painters. Eight hundred still frames, representing one hundred paintings and detail views of each, were photographed for the program. The "game" was designed to help viewers develop visual analysis skills by learning to distinguish the styles of six painters in a common school. A "player," after viewing the introductory segments, could select one painter to "study." As each painting appeared in random order, viewers decided whether or not it was done by the painter in question. Before deciding, the player could view a detail or compare the painter with others already correctly identified. After deciding, players received a brief comment explaining how each painting related to the painter's overall approach. The commentary was in two forms, on-screen text and voice-over narration. Although simulated using a personal computer (another new tool) and professional video equipment, *Art Game* was not made available for public use.

Art Game film segments and painting commentaries were written by James Hoekema (who also designed the interactions) and Jehane Burns. The film was narrated by Bill Hunt and Nellie Bellflower. Accompanying music by Eric Satie was arranged by Elmer Bernstein. The film exists in three forms: one with printed text, one with voice-over narration, and one with both. The film is not in general circulation. (Running time, *Art Game*: 12 minutes; color.)

A sequence of frames (reading top to bottom left, top to bottom right) from scenes in *Art Game*. The frames were photographed from 16mm-film footage

444

May 19: Charles delivers a commencement address at the New Mexico Institute of Mining and Technology, Socorro.

May 21: The Eames House (pp. 106–121) receives the Twenty-Five-Year Award from the American Institute of Architects, New York City.

May 28: Charles receives an honorary doctorate of human letters from Bucknell University, Lewisburg, Pennsylvania.

June 11–14: Charles speaks on "Making Connections" at the Twenty-Eighth International Design Conference, Aspen, Colorado.

The film *Powers of Ten* (pp. 440–441) is awarded the Gold Medal for Scientific Research from the Greater Miami International Film Festival, Miami, Florida.

Film producer Jon Boorstin directing a scene from *Merlin*

Staff: 1978
901 Washington Boulevard
Donald Amundson
Lucia Dewey Atwood
Tina Beebe
Burt Berenson
Lonnie Browning
Jehane Burns
Ken Cheng
Richard D'Amore
Christopher Dill
Paul Dixon
Sylvia Donney
Richard Donges
Clark Dugger
Sumiko Eguchi
John Fitzmaurice
Kathe Flynn
Alex Funke
Etsu Garfias
Karen Good
Marcy Goodwin
James Hoekema
Paul Howard
Robert Hunt
Frank Huttinger
Stan Ishikawa
Chris Jenkins
Hap Johnson
Michael Jones
David Lafferty
Howard Lathrop
Dan McLaughlin
Emily Mayeda
John Neuhart
David Olney
Sam Passacqua
Gayle Pearson
Ched Reeder
Audrey Roberts
Tom Rossiter
Keith Rouse
Ron Rozzelle
Pamela Rubin
Michael Russell
Jane Spiller
Margaret Starr
Bayard Storey, Jr.
Hatsuko Tanabe
Bill Tondreau
Randall Walker
Michael Wiener
Bill Wietsma
Eddie Williams

1978

Film: *Merlin and the Time Mobile*

Merlin and the Time Mobile was the second film simulation of a proposed interactive videodisc game program produced by the Eames Office for the IBM Corporation. At the beginning of the program, a player is given a choice of visiting one of several locations from different historical periods: Camelot, Giza, or the Forbidden City. A series of life-threatening situations confronts the player at the chosen location, and to survive, the player selects from a list of available options, moving quickly through time and space (via videodisc technology) to avoid penalties. In the film simulation of the program, Camelot is the chosen location and Merlin is the main character. The videodisc was never produced commercially.

The film was shot by Eric Saarinen. The narration was written by Jon Boorstin and performed by actors Richard Johnson, Bill Adler, and Jeff Corey. The music is an electronic composition by Bill Tondreau. The film is not in general circulation. (Running time, *Merlin and the Time Mobile*: 2 minutes, 45 seconds; color.)

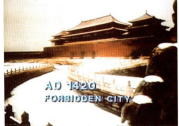

A sequence of frames (reading top to bottom left, top to bottom right) from scenes in *Merlin and the Time Mobile*. The frames were photographed from 16mm-film footage

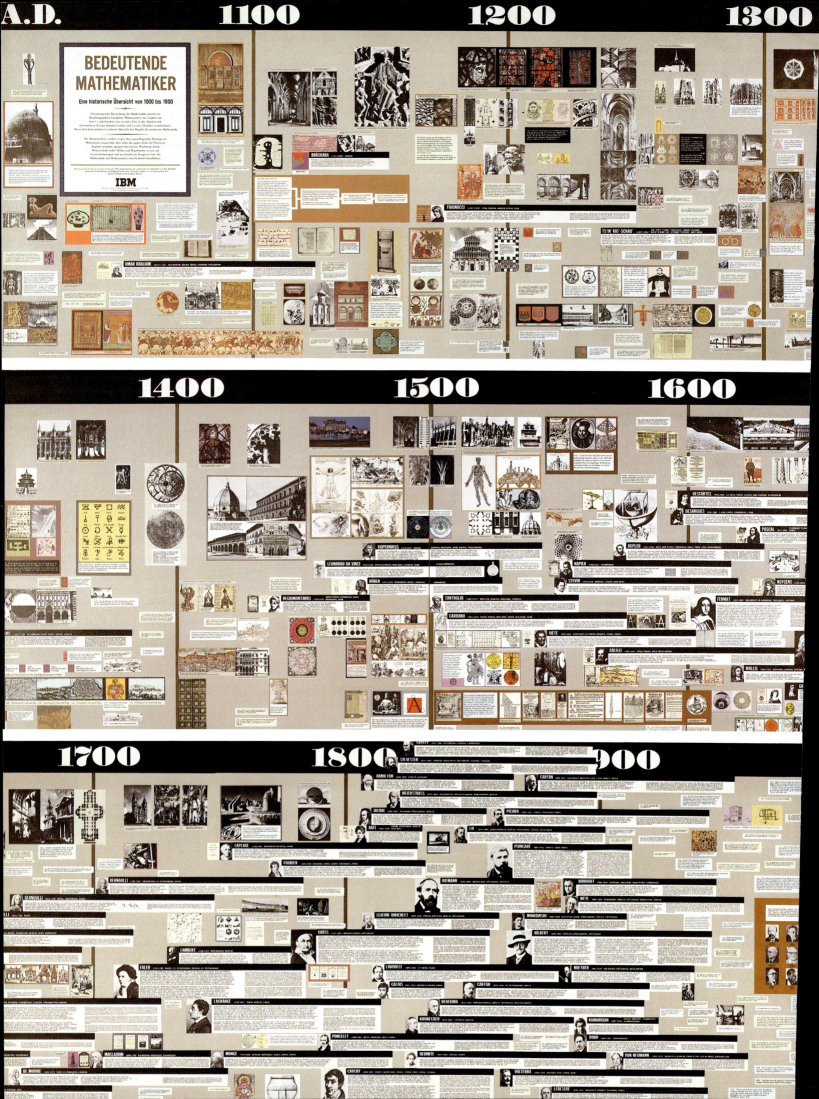

July 24: Ray participates in the Japan Society CULCON Symposium, Tokyo, Japan.

July 7: The film *Powers of Ten* (pp. 440–441) receives a Diploma of Participation and the Silver Medal from the XVII Festival Internazionale Del Film Di Fantascienza, Trieste, Italy.

Powers of Ten receives the Red Ribbon Award from the American Film Festival, New York City.

Ray and staff member Tina Beebe working on the German *Mathematica* timeline

Staff: 1978
901 Washington Boulevard
Donald Amundson
Lucia Dewey Atwood
Tina Beebe
Burt Berenson
Lonnie Browning
Jehane Burns
Ken Cheng
Richard D'Amore
Christopher Dill
Paul Dixon
Sylvia Domney
Richard Donges
Clark Dugger
Sumiko Eguchi
John Fitzmaurice
Kathe Flynn
Alex Funke
Etsu Garfias
Karen Good
Marcy Goodwin
James Hoekema
Paul Howard
Robert Hunt
Frank Huttinger
Stan Ishikawa
Chris Jenkins
Hap Johnson
Michael Jones
David Lafferty
Howard Lathrop
Dan McLaughlin
Emily Mayeda
John Neuhart
David Olney
Sam Passalacqua
Gayle Pearson
Ched Reeder
Audrey Roberts
Tom Rossiter
Keith Rouse
Ron Rozzelle
Pamela Rubin
Michael Russell
Jane Spiller
Margaret Starr
Bayard Storey, Jr.
Hatsuko Tanabe
Bill Tondreau
Randall Walker
Michael Wiener
Bill Wietsma
Eddie Williams

1978

German *Mathematica* Timeline

The German version of the *Mathematica* timeline was produced for the German branch of the IBM Corporation. The title of the timeline was changed from "Men of Modern Mathematics" to "Significant Mathematicians" (*Bedeutende Mathematiker*), and the text was translated into German. Biographies of two German mathematicians —Friedrich Riesz and Stefan Banach— were added to the chronology. The lower section dealing with general world history was augmented and brought up to date (some corrections also were made in dates assigned to early events). The end of the timeline had the most extensive additions, outlining the discoveries and advances in mathematics after the publication of the original English version in 1966. A few minor modifications in the layout were made to accommodate the longer length of the German text blocks.

Raymond Redheffer, professor of mathematics at UCLA and author of the original timeline, wrote the new biographies and acted as consultant on the project. The publication was produced and printed in the United States and distributed by IBM Germany. Tina Beebe was responsible for the complex production work and supervised the printing of the timeline.

BEDEUTENDE MATHEMATIKER

Eine historische Übersicht von 1000 bis 1900

Chronologische Darstellung der Mathematik anhand von Kurzbiographien berühmter Mathematiker. Sie beginnt mit dem 11. Jahrhundert, also zu einer Zeit, in der Algebra und Geometrie in Europa bekannt wurden und zu einer Disziplin verschmolzen. Diese Zeit kennzeichnet in vielerlei Hinsicht den Beginn der modernen Mathematik.

Die Mathematiker wurden wegen ihrer grundlegenden Beiträge zur Mathematik ausgewählt. Ihre Zahl, die gegen Ende der Übersicht deutlich zunimmt, spiegelt das enorme Wachstum dieser Wissenschaft wider. Bilder und Begleittexte weisen auf Geistesströmungen und geschichtliche Ereignisse hin, die Mathematik und Mathematiker entscheidend beeinflußten.

Produziert durch Charles und Ray Eames für IBM. Biographien und mathematischer Begleittext von Ray Redheffer. Deutsche Überarbeitung von Wolfgang Walter und Alexander Stephan in Zusammenarbeit mit Heddy Redheffer und Irmgard Walter.

IBM

© Copyright International Business Machines Corporation, Armonk, N.Y. 1966
© Copyright IBM Deutschland GmbH 1978

Timeline title block

Porträt	Name	Lebenszeit	Geburtsort	Wirkungsstätten	Sterbeort
	BOOLE	1815-1864	LINCOLN;	DONCASTER, WADDINGTON, CORK,	BALLINTEMPLE/CORK

ZU ARM, UM EINE SCHULE ZU BESUCHEN, LERNTE GEORGE BOOLE ALS AUTODIDAKT FÜNF SPRACHEN. MATHEMATIKUNTERRICHT ERHIELT ER VON SEINEM VATER. MIT 16 UNTERSTÜTZTE ER ALS ELEMENTARLEHRER SEINE ELTERN, MIT 20 BESASS ER SEINE EIGENE SCHULE. UNZUFRIEDEN MIT DEN VORGESCHRIEBENEN TEXTEN, BEGANN ER SEINE PRIVATEN STUDIEN DER MEISTER LAGRANGE UND LAPLACE.

Ohne die Verdienste von Leibniz und de Morgan zu schmälern, markiert Booles 82seitige Abhandlung „The Mathematical Analysis of Logic" den Anfang der Booleschen Algebra. Boole wandte seine Algebra auf Mengen und Aussagen an; ihr Gebrauch in den Grundlagen der Mathematik und in der Schaltkreistheorie stand damals noch aus.—Der Satz von Boole über quadratische Formen ist das erste allgemeine Ergebnis der Invariantentheorie.

Lebensbeschreibung — **Mathematische Leistungen**

Above: Panel from the printed timeline displaying biographical information on the mathematician George Boole. Opposite: The printed timeline (divided into three sections for inclusion in this volume)

The film *Powers of Ten* (pp. 440–441) is awarded the Golden Eagle from the Council on International Non-Theatrical Film and the Bronze Cindy from the Information Film Producers of America.

Staff: 1978
901 Washington Boulevard
Donald Amundson
Lucia Dewey Atwood
Tina Beebe
Burt Berenson
Lonnie Browning
Jehane Burns
Ken Cheng
Richard D'Amore
Paul Dixon
Christopher Dill
Sylvia Domney
Richard Donges
Clark Dugger
Sumiko Eguchi
John Fitzmaurice
Alex Flynn
Etsu Garfias
Karen Good
Marcy Goodwi
James Hoeken
Paul Howard
Robert Hunt
Frank Huttinger
Stan Ishikawa
Chris Jenkins
Hap Johnson
Michael Jones
David Lafferty
Howard Lathrop
Emily Mayeda
Dan McLaughlin
John Neuhart
David Olney
Sam Passalacqua
Gayle Pearson
Ched Reeder
Audrey Roberts
Tom Rossiter
Keith Rouse
Ron Rozzelle
Pamela Rubin
Michael Russell
Jane Spiller
Margaret Starr
Bayard Storey, Jr.
Hatsuko Tanabe
Bill Tondreau
Randall Walker
Michael Wiener
Bill Wietsma
Eddie Williams

Ray, Charles, and Elmer Bernstein at a recording session for the film *Cézanne*

A sequence of frames (reading top to bottom left, top to bottom right) from scenes in *Cézanne: The Late Work*. The frames were photographed from 16mm-film footage

1978

Film: *Cézanne: The Late Work, With Quotations from His Letters and Reminiscences*

Cézanne was compiled from 35mm slides photographed by Charles and his office staff in 1977 at an exhibition of the late work of Paul Cézanne, which was organized by The Museum of Modern Art in New York City and the Reunion des Musées Nationaux in Paris. The exhibition was supported by the IBM Corporation and the National Endowment for the Humanities. The film was sponsored by IBM.

Charles and Ray, impressed by the exhibition, wanted to make a film as an enduring record of the show. Because of low light levels in the galleries, they could only photograph still images. The slides were then transferred to film using a new computer-managed motion-control system devised by staff member Bill Tondreau that allowed a motion-picture camera to pan smoothly across or zoom in on a 35mm slide. In the film, the camera moves across details of paintings and Cézanne's studio, providing an intimate, close-up view of the artist's work.

Cézanne's own words, taken from his letters, provide the narration, which was read by Lew Ayres in the English version of the film. The French version was read by Christian Marquand. Art historian Judith Wechsler advised on the storyboard and with Jehane Burns edited the narration. The music was composed and conducted by Elmer Bernstein. The film is not in general circulation. (Running time, *Cézanne: The Late Work*: 10 minutes; color.)

August 21: Charles dies in St. Louis, Missouri, while on a consulting trip for a new project at the Missouri Botanical Gardens.

October 9: The exhibition *Connections: The Work of Charles and Ray Eames* opens at the Sainsbury Centre for Visual Arts, University of East Anglia, Norwich, England.

October 9: Charles is posthumously awarded a citation for distinguished contributions to the visual arts from the National Association of Schools of Art.

November 1: Architect and engineer Konrad Wachsman delivers a talk entitled "Charles Eames" in honor of Charles at the School of Architecture, University of Southern California, Los Angeles.

November 8: The Rt. Honorable Anthony Wedgwood Benn (a friend of Charles) delivers "A Tribute to Charles Eames" at the U.S. Embassy, London, England.

Hugh De Pree and Ray at the Eames Office during a visit of Herman Miller, Inc., licensees

Staff: 1978
901 Washington Boulevard
Donald Amundson
Lucia Dewey Atwood
Tina Beebe
Burt Berenson
Lonnie Browning
Jehane Burns
Ken Cheng
Richard D'Amore
Christopher Dill
Paul Dixon
Sylvia Donney
Richard Donges
Clark Dugger
Sumiko Eguchi
John Fitzmaurice
Kathe Flynn
Alex Funke
Etsu Garfias
Karen Good
Marcy Goodwin
James Hoekema
Paul Howard
Robert Hunt
Frank Huttinger
Stan Ishikawa
Chris Jenkins
Hap Johnson
Michael Jones
David Lafferty
Howard Lathrop
Dan McLaughlin
Emily Mayeda
John Neuhart
David Olney
Sam Passalacqua
Gayle Pearson
Ched Reeder
Audrey Roberts
Tom Rossiter
Keith Rouse
Ron Rozzelle
Pamela Rubin
Michael Russell
Jane Spiller
Margaret Starr
Bayard Storey, Jr.
Hatsuko Tanabe
Bill Tondreau
Randall Walker
Michael Wiener
William Wietsma
Eddie Williams

1978

Film: *Degas in the Metropolitan*

Degas was produced for The Metropolitan Museum of Art in New York City to be a permanent record of a major exhibition. The film was compiled from 35mm transparencies. The images, photographed by Charles, Judith Wechsler, and staff members Jehane Burns and Bill Tondreau at the 1978 exhibition of Degas's works at the Metropolitan, are of his paintings, sculpture, and drawings. To transfer the slide images to film, the Eames Office used the computer-managed, motion-control system employed for the *Cézanne* film (p. 448).

The script was written with Jehane Burns and the curator of the exhibition, Charles Moffett of the Metropolitan. Moffett also was the narrator. The music is by Eric Satie and Frédéric Chopin, played by pianist Zita Carno under the direction of Elmer Bernstein. The film is not in general circulation. (Running time, *Degas in the Metropolitan*: 10 minutes; color.)

A sequence of frames (reading top to bottom left, top to bottom right) from scenes in *Degas in the Metropolitan*. The frames were photographed from 16mm-film footage

February 15: Ray is on the jury of "Design Twenty-Five" of the Boston Art Directors' Club's Silver Anniversary Awards in Visual Communication, Boston, Massachusetts.

June 12: Ray receives the Gold Medal Award for both Charles and herself from the Royal Institute of British Architects, London, England.

Right: Eames Office portrait of staff members and friends. First row, left to right: Sylvia Kennedy, Emily Mayeda, Ray, Jill Mitchell, Sylvia Domney, Marcy Goodwin. Second row, left to right: John Neuhart, Sam Passalacqua, John Fitzmaurice, Howard Lathrop, Marilyn Neuhart, Kent Smith, Jehane Burns, Clark Dugger, Karen Good, Richard Knarr. Back row, left to right: James Hoekema, Nina Elston, Randall Walker, Richard Donges, Michael Jones

Staff: 1979
901 Washington Boulevard
Donald Amundson
Lucia Dewey Atwood
Tina Beebe
Bruce Block
Lonnie Browning
Jehane Burns
Ed Conners
Sylvia Domney
Richard Donges
Clark Dugger
Nina Elston
Karen Fielding
John Fitzmaurice
Kathe Flynn
Alex Funke
Etsu Garfias
Karen Good
Marcy Goodwin
Charlie Gurd
James Hoekema
Lynn Horiuchi
Paul Howard
Frank Huttinger
Hap Johnson
Michael Jones
Bob Kahn
Joel Katz
Richard Kroll
Howard Lathrop
Emily Mayeda
Jill Mitchell
John Neuhart
Jeff Newmaster
David Olney
Sam Passalacqua
Audrey Roberts
Kent Smith
Sonia Socher
Randall Walker
Michael Wiener
Bill Wietsma
Eddie Williams
Buzz Yudell

1979

Film: *A Report on the IBM Exhibition Center*

A Report on the IBM Exhibition Center is the last of the Eames "study" films produced to outline or present a project concept for client review. The film presents the proposals designed by the Eames Office for the utilization of the public spaces in the new IBM Corporation building at 590 Madison Avenue in New York City. It is a more detailed look at the division of space and the type and scope of the proposed exhibition plan first proposed by the Eames Office in 1977, which envisaged the IBM center as "a gathering point and a reflector for the company's best thinking." The completed film was presented to IBM in 1979 after Charles's death, but the proposal was not implemented.

The film incorporated live-action footage of the model, animation, and film shot from stills and slides. A section on "Inventions," proposing a traveling exhibition of that title, was added to the end of the film. The script for the film was written by Jehane Burns and James Hoekema and was narrated by Art Balinger and Sandy Kenyon. The music was composed and conducted by Elmer Bernstein. The film is not in general circulation. (Running time, *A Report on the IBM Exhibition Center*: 11 minutes, 40 seconds; color.)

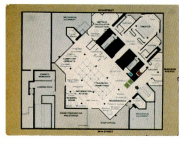

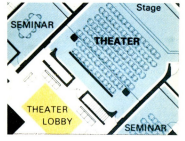

A sequence of frames (reading top to bottom left, top to bottom right) from scenes in *A Report on the IBM Exhibition Center*. The frames were photographed from 16mm-film footage

1984

Eames Teak and Leather Sofa

The last piece of furniture produced in the Eames Office was a sofa with arms. A version was completed in model form in 1967 but was then set aside. The office returned to the idea in the mid-1970s, and work on a wood and leather three-seat sofa was begun in 1976 under Charles's direction.

The first prototypes and tooling were developed in cooperation with the Vitra organization. (Vitra, the Herman Miller affiliate in Switzerland headed by Willy Fehlbaum and subsequently by his son Rolf, had a long-standing professional relationship and friendship with the Eameses.) The sofa was completed in the Eames Office after Charles's death. It went into production in 1984 at the Herman Miller, Inc., factory in Italy.

A variation on the 1954 Sofa Compact (pp. 190–191) and the 1964 3473 three-piece sofa (pp. 282–283), the teak and leather sofa was designed to complement the Soft Pad Group (pp. 342–343) and the Chaise (pp. 338–339). Arms were added to the three-piece form (after Charles's death), and, unlike the earlier Sofa Compact, the seat and back panels are made of teak or walnut. A fabric-reinforced rubber webbing serves as the support for the padded seat cushions, which snap directly onto the frame. The individual back pads are key-slotted to the wooden back. Two identical die-cast aluminum members serve as integral base/back brace units. The arm castings are also symmetrical and have padded rests. All of the aluminum parts are brightly polished. Richard Donges, Randall Walker, and Michael Wiener were responsible for the developmental work.

Herman Miller manufactures two- and three-seat versions of the sofa. It is available in various colored leathers and in a range of fabrics. In keeping with the Soft Pad Group it was designed to complement, the aluminum parts have a cool-tone, warm-tone, or eggplant gloss finish.

Top: Front view of the production model teak and leather sofa. Middle: Three-quarter view. Above: Profile view

Selected readings:

Books:

Banham, Rayner. *Los Angeles: The Architecture of Four Ecologies*. New York: Harper & Row, 1971.

Caplan, Ralph. *By Design*. New York: St. Martin's Press, 1982.

——. *The Design of Herman Miller: Pioneered by Eames, Girard, Nelson, Propst, Rohde*. New York: Whitney Library of Design, 1976.

Carpenter, Edward. *Industrial Design 25th Annual Design in Review* (Introduction: "A Tribute to Charles Eames"). New York: Whitney Library of Design, 1979.

Clark, Robert J., De Long, David, et al. *Design in America: The Cranbrook Vision 1925–1950*. New York: Harry N. Abrams, Inc., in association with The Detroit Institute of Arts, Detroit, and The Metropolitan Museum of Art, New York, 1987.

De Pree, Hugh. *Business as Unusual*. Zeeland, Michigan: Herman Miller, Inc., 1986.

Drexler, Arthur. *Charles Eames: Furniture from the Design Collection*. New York: The Museum of Modern Art, 1973.

Emery, Marc. *Furniture by Architects: 500 International Masterpieces of Twentieth-Century Design*. New York: Harry N. Abrams, Inc., 1983.

Gandy, Charles D., and Zimmerman-Stidium, Susan. *Contemporary Classics: Furniture of the Masters*. New York: McGraw Hill Book Co., 1981.

Gebhard, David, and Winter, Robert. *A Guide to Architecture in Southern California*. Los Angeles: Los Angeles County Museum of Art, 1965.

Gebhard, David, and Nevins, Deborah. *200 Years of American Architectural Drawing*. New York: Watson-Guptill, 1977.

Gill, Brendan. *The Dream Come True: Great Houses of Los Angeles*. New York: Lippincott & Crowell, 1980.

Girard, A. H., and Laurie, W. D., Jr., eds. *An Exhibition for Modern Living*. Detroit: The Detroit Institute of Arts, 1949.

Greenberg, Cara. *Mid-Century Modern*. New York: Harmony Books, 1984.

Harris, Frank, and Bonenberger, Weston, eds. *A Guide to Contemporary Architecture in Southern California*. Los Angeles: Watling & Company, 1951.

Holland, Laurence B., ed. *Who Designs America?* Princeton Studies in American Civilization no. 6. Garden City, New York: Doubleday Anchor, 1966.

Kaufmann, Edgar, Jr. *Prize Designs for Modern Furniture*. New York: The Museum of Modern Art, 1950.

Larrabee, Eric, and Vignelli, Massimo. *Knoll Design*. New York: Harry N. Abrams, Inc., 1981.

McCoy, Esther. *Case Study Houses 1945–1962*. Los Angeles: Hennessey & Ingalls, Inc., 1977.

Morrison, Philip, and Morrison, Phylis, and the Office of Charles and Ray Eames. *Powers of Ten: About the Relative Size of Things in the Universe*. Scientific American Library vol. I. San Francisco: W. H. Freeman and Company, 1982.

Nelson, George. *Problems of Design*. New York: Whitney Publications, 1957.

Neuhart, John, and Neuhart, Marilyn. *Connections: The Work of Charles and Ray Eames*. (Essay by Ralph Caplan.) Los Angeles: UCLA Art Council, 1976.

Noyes, Eliot. *Organic Design in Home Furniture*. New York: The Museum of Modern Art, 1941.

Office of Charles and Ray Eames. *Images of Early America*. Zeeland, Michigan: Herman Miller, Inc., 1976.

——. *National Fisheries and Aquarium: A Report on the Program and Progress of the National Fisheries Center and Aquarium*. Washington, D.C.: United States Department of the Interior, 1969.

——. *The World of Franklin and Jefferson*. Los Angeles: Eames Office, 1976.

——. Fleck, Glen, ed. *A Computer Perspective*. Cambridge, Massachusetts: Harvard University Press, 1973.

Ostergard, Derek E., ed. *Bent Wood and Metal Furniture: 1850–1946*. Seattle: University of Washington Press, 1987.

Page, Marian. *Furniture Designed by Architects*. New York: Whitney Library of Design, 1980.

Phillips, Lisa, ed. *High Styles: Twentieth-Century American Design*. New York: Summit Books and the Whitney Museum of American Art, 1985.

Pile, John F. *Modern Furniture*. New York: John Wiley & Sons, Inc., 1979.

Periodicals:

"An Eames Celebration." *Architecture SA*, Summer 1980: 33–37.

Auerbach, Alfred. "An Exhibition of Home Furnishing Selected by MOMA." *Arts & Architecture*, 1960: 20–27.

———. "Charles Eames: Reminiscences." *Interior Design*, October 1978: 236–237.

Baroni, Daniele. "Charles Eames and the Methodology of Design." *Ottagono*, June 1981: 8–85.

"Building Toy." *Life*, July 16, 1951: 57–58.

"Casa Estudio en California." Arquidectura, June 1952: 153–156.

"Case Study House by Eames and Saarinen." *Arts & Architecture*, July 1950: 26–39.

"Case Study House for 1949: The Finished House." *Arts & Architecture*, December 1949.

"Case Study House for 1949: The Interior." *Arts & Architecture*, April 1949.

"Case Study House for 1949: The Plan." *Arts & Architecture*, May 1949.

"Case Study House for 1949: The Steel Frame." *Arts & Architecture*, February 1949.

"Case Study House for 1949: Under Construction." *Arts & Architecture*, January 1949.

"Castle Cabana of John Entenza." *Interiors*, December 1950: 92–99.

"Chairs by Charles Eames." *Arts & Architecture*, October 1950: 31.

"Charles and Ray Eames Receive First International Industrial Design Award." *Industrial Design*, December 1960.

"Charles Eames." *Domus*, May 1963.

"Charles Eames, Creator in Plywood." *Interiors*, June 1946.

"Charles Eames' Forward Looking Furniture." *Magazine of Art*, May 1946: 179–181.

"Dallo Studio di Eames." Domus, May 1963: 26–40.

Danilov, Victor. "Mathematica: Exhibition at the Museum of Science and Industry, Chicago." *Museum* (UNESCO), vol. 26, no. 2: 86–98.

"Design for Use." *Arts & Architecture*, September 1944: 21–25, 38.

"Designer's Home of His Own." *Life*, September 11, 1950.

Diehl, Digby. "Q & A Charles Eames." *Los Angeles Times West Magazine*, October 7, 1972.

"Dormitory in a Nutshell: ECS." *Interiors*, November 1961.

"Eames Chairs of Molded Metal Mesh." *Interiors*, April 1952: 106–109.

Eames, Charles. "A Prediction: Less Self Expression for the Designer." *Print*, January–February 1960: 77–79.

———. "City Hall." *Architectural Forum*, May 1943: 72, 88–90.

———. "City Hall." *Arts & Architecture*, June 1943: 22–23.

———. "Design Today." *California Arts & Architecture*, September 1941: 18–19.

———. "Organic Design." *California Arts & Architecture*, December 1941: 16–17.

———. "What Is a House?" *Arts & Architecture*, July 1944.

Eames, Charles, and Entenza, John. "Case Study House #8 and #9." *Arts & Architecture*, January 1945.

"Furniture Show Room." *Arts & Architecture*, October 1949: 26–29.

Gingerich, Owen. "A Conversation with Charles Eames." *The American Scholar*, Summer 1977: 326–337.

Goldstein, Barbara; Lee, Charles; and Polygoides, Stephanos. "The Eames House." *Arts & Architecture*, February 1983: 20–25.

Gueft, Olga. "For Alcoa's Forecast Program, Eames Creates a Sun Machine that Accomplishes Nothing." *Interiors*, 1958: 123, 182–183.

———. "Good Design Exhibit." *Interiors*, 1950: 85–97.

———. "The Low Cost Furniture Exhibit." *Interiors*, March 1950.

"Il Teatro Sospeso di Charles Eames." Domus, March 1965: 25–27.

"Interior Design Data: Tandem Seating." *Progressive Architecture*, November 1962: 140–144.

Johnson, Josephine. "Charles Eames." *Portfolio*, Spring 1950.

Kaufmann, Edgar, Jr. "Charles Eames and Chests." *Art News*, May 1950: 36–40.

———. "For Modern Living—An Exhibition." *Arts & Architecture*, November 1949.

Kenmochi, Isamu. "The Works of Charles and Ray Eames." *Graphic Design*, October 1965: 39–46.

Lacy, Bill N. "Warehouse Full of Ideas." *Horizon*, September 1980.

"Life in a Chinese Kite." *Architectural Forum*, September 1950: 90–96.

McCullogh, Jane Fiske. "Some Thoughts About Eames." *Zodiac*, June 1961: 122–125.

McQuade, Walter. "Charles Eames Isn't Resting on His Chair." *Fortune*, February 1975: 96–105, 144–145.

Miller, Judith Ransom. "Mathematica." *Industrial Design*, May 1961: 38–43.

"Negli Aeroporti, Il Nuovo Divano di Eames." Domus, February 1963.

"Nehru and India: A Walk Through History." *Interiors*, March 1965: 146–151.

"Nelson, Eames, Girard, Probst: The Design Process at Herman Miller." *Design Quarterly*, nos. 98–99, 1975.

Noyes, Eliot. "Charles Eames: Development in Design and Manufacture of Furniture in America." *Arts & Architecture*, September 1946: 26–44.

"Nuovo Eames." Domus, January 1970: 23–27.

"Organic Design: Winning Furniture Designs by Saarinen and Eames from the Museum of Modern Art Competition." *Arts & Architecture*, December 1941: 16–17.

"Residence: Santa Monica, California." *Architectural Forum*, September 1950: 90–96.

Schrader, Paul, ed. "Poetry of Ideas: The Films of Charles Eames." *Film Quarterly*, Spring 1970: 2–19.

"Science Film by Charles Eames." *Arts & Architecture*, July 1962.

Scott W., and Eames, C. "A New Emergency Splint of Plyformed Wood." *U.S. Naval Bulletin*, vol. XLI, no. 5, September 1943: 1423–1428.

"Showroom: Los Angeles, California." *Progressive Architecture*, August 1950: 47–50.

Smithson, Alison, and Smithson, Peter. "An Eames Celebration." *Architectural Design*, September 1966: 432–442.

"Steel on the Meadow." *Interiors*, November 1950: 108–115.

"Steel Shelf with a View." *Architectural Forum*, September 1950: 97–99.

Talmey, Aline. "Eames." *Vogue*, August 8, 1959.

"The Exploring Eye: Eames Sun Mill." *Architectural Review*, February 1959: 105–107.

"Three Chairs: Three Records of the Design Process." *Interiors*, April 1958: 118–122.

"Twirling Toy Run by Sun." *Life*, March 24, 1958: 22–23.

"Useful Objects." *Everyday Art Quarterly*. Walker Art Center, Winter 1950–1951.

Furniture designed by the Office of Charles and Ray Eames is available through Herman Miller, Inc., Zeeland, Michigan. Eames furniture is also manufactured and marketed by Vitra International, Ltd., Basel, Switzerland, and through Herman Miller licensees in a number of countries in Europe and the Far East.

Where practical (or available), measurements for Eames furniture have been provided in the text. Measurements for several lines of furniture that include variations too numerous to list (among them the plastic chairs, the wire chairs, the Aluminum Group, the La Fonda and Time-Life chairs, the Soft Pad group, the segmented tables, and others) have not been included in the text.

Eames films in general circulation are available through Pyramid Films, Santa Monica, California. A selection of films is available on videodisc from Pioneer Laserdisc Corporation of Japan, Santa Monica, California. Eames films will appear on video cassette in the fall of 1989.

Photography credits

Unless otherwise noted, all photographs and drawings in this volume are the property of the Eames Office or the Library of Congress. Eames Office photographs include the work of Charles and Ray Eames and the following staff members: Herbert Matter, Jay Connor, Don Albinson, Parke Meek, Deborah Sussman, Robert Staples, Gordon Ashby, Glen Fleck, Annette Del Zoppo, Theodore Orlan, Alex Funke, Hap Johnson, Jehane Burns, Bill Tondreau, Frederick Steadry, Charles Brittin, Lonnie Browning, Richard Donges, and John Neuhart.

Credits for all other photographs appear below. Photographs by John and Marilyn Neuhart are listed as JMN. For those photographs commissioned by John and Marilyn Neuhart for this volume, the name of the photographer is followed by the initials JMN.

Page 2: Bill Tondreau (JMN; commissioned for the exhibition *Connections: The Work of Charles and Ray Eames*, UCLA, 1976). Page 5: Middle and right: JMN. Page 9: JMN. Page 10: Left: JMN. Page 14: Paul Bruhwiler. Page 21: Top right, middle, and bottom: JMN. Page 23: Top left: Library of Congress. Page 25: Left: The Museum of Modern Art; row three, left: Benjamin Baldwin. Page 31: Top left, middle: *Arts & Architecture* magazine; rows two, three and four: *Arts & Architecture* magazine. Page 33: Top left: JMN. Page 34: Top left: JMN. Page 36: *Arts & Architecture* magazine. Page 37: Top: *Arts & Architecture* magazine; rows two and three: *Architectural Forum* magazine. Page 38: *Arts & Architecture* magazine. Page 39: Top left, rows two through four: *Arts & Architecture* magazine. Top left: *Arts & Architecture* magazine. Page 44: *Arts & Architecture* magazine. Page 45: Top left, rows two through four: *Arts & Architecture* magazine. Page 46: *Arts & Architecture* magazine. Page 47: *Arts & Architecture* magazine. Page 48: *Arts & Architecture* magazine. Page 49: Top right, rows three and four: *Arts & Architecture* magazine. Page 73: Top left and right: *Arts & Architecture* magazine. Page 99: Top left and right: Condé Nast Publications. Page 124: Bottom: The Detroit Institute of Arts. Page 125: Top middle and right, second row: The Detroit Institute of Arts. Page 127: Top: *Portfolio* magazine. Page 141: Top left; row three, left; row four, left: *Everyday Art Quarterly*. Page 176: Don Garber. Page 177: Row five: Don Garber. Page 189: Rows three through five, left and right: Don Albinson. Page 205: Rows two through four: JMN. Page 220: JMN. Page 221: Top middle: Bernard Gardner; rows three and four: JMN. Page 224: JMN. Page 228: Marvin Rand. Page 229: Top left; row two, right: Marvin Rand. Page 233: Top: National Institute of Design, Ahmedabad, India. Page 241: Top right: Elaine Sewell Jones; rows two through seven, right: JMN. Page 244: Top: Don Albinson. Page 247: Top left: Maki. Page 256: Top right: John Bryson. Page 259: Top right: John Bryson. Page 276: Top: JMN. Page 309: Top: *Architectural Design* magazine. Page 395: Row two, left and right: IBM Corporation. Page 396: Top left: The Museum of Modern Art; rows two and three, left and right: IBM Corporation. Page 397: Rows two and three: IBM Corporation. Page 400: Top: IBM Corporation. Page 402: IBM Corporation. Page 412: IBM Corporation. Page 413: Rows two and three: IBM Corporation. Pages 432-433: Herman Miller, Inc. Page 434: Top right: Michael Ripps. Page 435: Top: Bill Tondreau (JMN). Page 436: Middle: Bill Tondreau (JMN).

Photographs by Andrew Neuhart (for John and Marilyn Neuhart) appear on the following pages: Page 5 (left), 30, 31 (top left and middle; rows two, three, four), 36, 37 (top), 38, 39, 41 (top left), 44, 45 (top left, rows two through four), 46, 47, 48, 49 (top right, rows three and four), 53 (top), 72 (bottom), 73 (top left and right), 74 (bottom), 78, 86 (row one), 86 (row three), 87 (row three), 88, 89 (rows two and three), 99 (top left and right), 106 (rows one and two), 107 (rows two through four), 124, 125 (top middle and right, row two), 127 (top), 141 (top left; row three, left; row four, left), 149 (rows two and three), 171, 172, 173, 174, 177 (rows two through four), 180, 184 (row two, right), 209 (top), 218, 222, 225, 255 (rows two and three), 293 (row four), 310, 311 (rows two and three), 322-323, 352, 354, 363 (bottom), 383 (top left), 392-393, 396 (top left), 423 (rows two and three), 426 (rows two through five), 432-433 (rows two through four), 436 (top left), 446, 447, (rows two and three).

Photographs made from 16mm-film footage of Eames films are the property of John and Marilyn Neuhart. The majority of films was photographed by Bill Tondreau for the *Connections* exhibition. Additional films were photographed for this volume by John Neuhart.

	fields as high as 10^8 gauss). White dwarfs have relatively low rotational velocities.
Widmanstätten pattern	structure in iron meteorites, revealed by etching with a mild acid, in which large plates of octahedrally arranged kamacite enclose small fields of taenite.
Wolf-Rayet star	one of a class of very luminous, very hot (with surface temperatures as high as 5×10^4 K) stars whose spectra have broad emission lines (mainly He I and He II), which are presumed to originate from material continually ejected from the star at very high (about 2000 km/s) velocities by stellar winds. They may be the exposed helium cores of stars that were at one time on the H-burning main sequence. Some Wolf-Rayet spectra show dominantly emission lines from ions of C (WC stars); others show dominantly emission lines from the ions of N (WN stars).
xenolith	fragment in a rock of meteorite foreign to its host.
XRF	acronym for X-ray fluorescence analysis. An analytical technique for determining major and minor elements in meteorites.
zodiacal light	a faint glow that extends away from the Sun in the ecliptic plane of the sky, visible to the naked eye in the western sky shortly after sunset or in the eastern sky shortly before sunrise. Its spectrum indicates that it is sunlight scattered by interplanetary dust. The zodiacal light contributes about a third of the total light in the sky on a moonless night.

Acknowledgments

ACKNOWLEDGMENTS

The editors acknowledge the support of National Aeronautics and Space Administration Grant NAGW-1147 and the University of Arizona for the preparation of this book. The following authors wish to acknowledge specific funds involved in supporting the preparation of their chapters.

Anders, E.: NASA Grant NAG 9-52
Boss, A. P.: NASA Grant NAGW-398 *and* NSF Grant AST-8515644
Barber, D.: NERC Grant GR3/5349
Bradley, J. P.: NASA Grant NAS 9-17749
Brett, R.: NASA Contract T-1202P
Cassen, P.: NSF Grant AST 8513644 *and* NASA Grant NAGW 398
Chapman, C. R.: NASA Contract NASW-4266
Clayton, D. D.: NASA Grant NAG 9-100 BASIC
Cronin, J. R.: NASA Grant NSG 7255
Cruikshank, D. P.: NASA Grant NGL 12 001 057
Fegley, B.: NASA Grants NAG 9-108 *and* NAGW-821
Hewins, R. H.: NASA Grant NAG 9-35
Hohenberg, C. M.: NASA Grant NAG 9-7
Hunten, D. M.: NSF Grant AST 85-14520
Kallemeyn, G. W.: NSF Grant EAR 84-08167
Kerridge, J.F.: NASA Grants NAG 9-27 *and* NAGW 347
King, E. A.: NASA Grant NAGW 178
Larimer, J. W.: NSF Grant DDP 8415061 *and* NASA Grants NAG9-48, NAG9-79, NSG 7040
Lee, T.: Grant from National Science Council of the Republic of China NSC 76-0202-M001-16
Levy, E. H.: NASA Grant NSG 7419
Lipschutz, M. E.: NSF Grant DPP 8415061 *and* NASA Grant NAG 9-48
MacPherson, G. J.: NASA Grant NAG 9-230
Marti, K.: NASA Grant NAG 9-41
McSween, H. Y., Jr.: NASA Grant NAG 9-58
Newsom, H. E.: NASA Grant NAG 9-30
Palme, H.: NSF Grant DPP 8415061 *and* NASA Grants NAG 9-48, NAG 9-79
Pizzarello, S.: NASA Grant NSG 7255
Podosek, F. A.: NASA Grant NAG 9-55 *and* The McDonnell Center for the Space Sciences
Reedy, R. C.: NASA Order Number T-294M
Rubin, A. E.: NSF Grant EAR 84-08167 *and* NASA Grant NAG 9-40
Sears, D. W. G.: NASA Grant NAG 9-81, NSF Grant INT 8612744 *and* SERC Grant 9RE 16864
Scott, E. R. D.: NASA Grant NAG 9-30
Steele, I. M.: NASA Grant NAG 9-47
Swindle, T. D.: NASA Grant NAG 9-240
Thiemens, M. H.: NASA Grant NAG 9-83 *and* Camille and Henry Dreyfus Teacher-Scholar Grant
Walker, R. M.: NASA Grant NAG 9-55
Wasson, J. T.: NSF Grant EAR 84-08167 *and* NASA Grant NAG 9-40
Weidenschilling, S. J.: NASA Contract NASW 3214
Wetherill, G. W.: NASA Grants NSG 7437 *and* NAGW 398
Wood, J. A.: NASA Grant NAG 9-28

Woolum, D. S.: NASA Grant NAG 9-57
Zinner, E.: NASA Grant NAG 9-55 *and* NSF Grant EAR 84-15168

The editors also wish to acknowledge the help provided by the following people:

R. H. Becker, J. F. Bell, D. C. Black, W. V. Boynton, D. E. Brownlee, D. S. Burnett, S. M. Cisowski, R. N. Clayton, D. W. Collinson, K. Denomy, D. J. DePaolo, M. J. Drake, O. Eugster, F. P. Fanale, J. L. Gooding, J. Halbout, W. K. Hartmann, F. Hörz, G. R. Huss, I. D. Hutcheon, R. Hutchison, J. H. Jones, S. W. Kieffer, D. Lal, J. C. Laul, G. E. Lofgren, G. W. Lugmair, I. D. R. Mackinnon, U. B. Marvin, D. S. McKay, J. W. Morgan, S. Niemeyer, L. E. Nyquist, J. Oró, D. A. Papanastassiou, C. Patterson, P. Pellas, M. Prinz, E. Rambaldi, J. H. Reynolds, S. M. Richardson, T. Schemenauer, E. Stolper, H. E. Suess, V. L. Trimble, J. C. G. Walker, P. H. Warren, S. E. Woosley.

Index

INDEX*

Accretion disks, 314
   See also Solar nebula
Accretion process, 74, 388, 1150
   gravitational, 362–367
   planetary, 514–515
"Accretional megaregoliths," 156, 159
Accretionary breccias, 170, 171, 184, 194, 195
Achondrites, 4, 9F, 12, 76, 151, 222
   age data, 271–272
   basaltic, 42, 80–96, 265–268
   enstatite, 57, 468
   O-fugacity data, 504
   origins, 36, 44, 56
   Pb isotope data, 263T
   shock effects, 174–175T, 186, 187T, 188, 196
   See also Aubrites; HED meteorites; Ureilites
Acid-soluble/-insoluble phases, 963, 964–966
Adiabat, 167
Adsorption, 556–557
AEM, 865
^{107}Ag, 1100
Agglomeration, 146, 1153–1154
   accretionary agglomerates, 147–148
   See also Regolithic breccias
Agglutinates, 148, 159, 183
^{26}Al, 74–75, 93, 1047–1048, 1101–1103, 1107–1108, 1109
   life of, 1121, 1122, 1123, 1124–1125
Al normalization, 427
"Al-rich chondrules," 755
Alcohols, 814
Aliphatic compounds, 825–827, 1175–1176
Alkali elements, 379, 444–446, 447, 453
Alkanes, 843–844
Allende meteorite. See Meteorites, individual
Alpha emitters, 250
Alpha-phase
   See Kamacite
"Ambipolar diffusion," 558

Amines and amides, 834
Amino acids, 821–824, 844–846, 1175
Amoeboid olivine aggregates (AOAs), 406, 763F, 764, 765, 770
Amoeboid olivine inclusions (AOIs), 406
Anders and Ebihara table of element abundances, 7T–8T
Angular-momentum transfer, 308, 312, 315, 316, 333
Anhysteretic remanent magnetization (ARM), 609, 610
Antarctic meteorites, 50, 51, 89, 481, 482F, 1157, 1159
Apollo-Amor objects, 37, 42, 52, 1157
Apollo Missions, 36, 144, 145, 547, 1139, 1160
Apollo objects, 43, 49, 56, 58
Aqueous alteration, 22, 26F, 115–116, 1150
   chronology of, 287, 292, 294
   future work, 1156, 1160
   in CI chondrites, 127–128, 135–137, 138F, 139–140
   in CM chondrites, 120–121, 122F, 124–125, 135–137, 138F, 139, 140
   in CV and CO chondrites, 118–120, 135
   in matrix, 721–722, 737F
   location in solar system, 131–134
   minerals produced, 116, 117T, 118T
Ar, 554–555
   See also Noble gases
^{40}Ar-^{36}Ar ratio, 554–555, 577
^{40}Ar-^{39}Ar dating, 277–278, 279F, 280–281, 282–285, 294, 295, 545, 1157
Aromatic hydrocarbons, 827–829, 846
As, 446
Asteroids, 43, 44, 46, 56, 57, 58, 160
   achondritic composition, 524
   albedos, 54, 55T, 850
   Angelina 64, 524
   as origin of meteorites, 36–37
   asteroid belt, 364–366, 371
   breccias, 146
   Chiron, 586

---

*See also Contents

Asteroids (*continued*)
  classification, 53T, 54T
  Flora group, 44, 49, 58
  future work, 1156–1158
  heating processes, 74–76
  Hektor, 851
  Hungaria 434, 524
  ice on, 134
  IDPs and, 886–887, 889
  Nysa 44, 524
  organic matter in, 850–851
  origin of, 59–63
  properties, 314
  Psyche 16, 56
  size distribution, 50
  Trojan asteroids, 58
  Vesta, 45, 53, 57, 58, 524, 531, 1156
  See also Planetesimals; Meteorites, general
Astrometric photography, 38
Atmophile elements, 376, 377
Atmospheric ablation spherules, 622
Au, 446, 448, 449
Aubrites, 12, 79, 96–97, 188, 231, 449, 450, 542, 910, 1134, 1157
Aurorae, 226
Authigenic phases, 295, 296
  See also Aqueous alteration

Basalt formation, 75, 80, 84F, 85–86, 87F, 88, 1150
  See also HED meteorites; Achondrites
Basaltic-gabbroic rocks, 174–175T
Beta emitters, 250
B^{2}FH models for element nucleosynthesis, 999–1003
Big Bang, 969, 1024–1026, 1116, 1119
Birefringence, 172
Boltzmann's constant, 578
Brecciation, 12, 22, 26, 27T, 103, 159–161, 171
  compaction ages, 289, 290
    authigenic phases, 295, 296
    fission-track methods, 290–293
    radiometric ages, 295
  monomict breccias, 151, 176
  polymict breccias, 151, 166, 176, 194, 196
  primitive breccias, 147, 148T
  shock metamorphism, 169–172
  See also Regolith breccias; Shock effects
Brownian motion of grains, 318–319, 320

C
  C burning, 1041T, 1042F
  circumstellar C, 934, 939–941, 948T, 949–951
  fractionation, 974, 975F
  grains, 985–986
  insoluble, 836, 837F, 838
  isotopic composition, 842–846, 848, 948T, 967–968
  macromolecular, 847–849
  See also Nucleosynthesis
C/O ratio of nebular gas, 380
Ca
  fractionation, 103T, 402, 404
  isotope anomalies, 1076F, 1077, 1081F, 1087
  nucleosynthesis, 1048–1049
^{41}Ca, 1093
CAIs, 17–18, 157, 343, 455, 489, 674, 1082, 1150
  classification, 753–755
  cooling rates, 411, 412
  future work, 1166, 1170
  in CM chondrites
    chemistry, 775
    isotopic traits, 776
    texture, 771, 772F, 773, 774F, 775
  in CO3 chondrites
    chemistry, 770–771
    isotopic traits, 771
    texture, 768, 769F, 770
  in CV3 chondrites
    chemistry, 764, 765T, 766
    classification, 755, 756F, 757F, 758F, 759
    isotopic traits, 766, 767F, 768
    texture, 759–761, 762F, 763–764
  in ordinary and enstatite chondrites, 777–780
  isotopic exchange in, 912F
  lithophile elements in, 400, 401F, 402
  oxidizing conditions, 498–499
  processes affecting
    condensation of amorphous solids, 787
    liquid condensation, 785–786
    melting, 792–795
    metamorphism, 792
    secondary alteration, 795–796
    vapor-solid condensation, 781–785
    volatilization, 788–791
  radiochronology, 250–252
  refractory elements in, 386
  relict grains, 796–798
  siderophile elements in, 422, 423, 424F
  spinel-pyroxene inclusions, 773
  See also Refractory inclusions
Callisto, 530
Carbonaceous chondrite average value (AVCC), 536, 548, 550, 554
Carbonaceous chondrite fission (CCF), 1099–1100
Carbonaceous chondrites, 6, 9, 16, 17, 224T
  aqueous alteration of, 118–128
  authigenic phases, 213
  elemental abundances in, 513, 514F

elemental variations in, 390, 392
irradiation records, 236, 237
moderately volatile elements in, 437F, 438, 442F, 443F, 444F, 445F, 446F
noble gases in, 540–542, 569, 570, 929, 934, 942
non-Antarctic, 470F, 471
NRM, 608–609, 1154
organic matter in, 819–820, 851–852
 aliphatic hydrocarbons, 825–827
 amino acids, 821, 822F, 823–824, 844–846
 aromatic hydrocarbons, 827–829, 846
 carboxylic acids, 829–831, 842, 843F
 future work, 1175–1177
 insoluble carbon, 836–838, 961
 macromolecular C, 847–849, 977
 nitrogen heterocycles, 831–833
 origin of, 838–839, 840F, 841
 other organic matter, 834, 835T
paleomagnetic intensity, 610
See also Elements, general; Matrix of chondrites
Carbonates, 127, 139–140
Carbonyl compounds, 834
Carboxylic acids, 829–830, 842, 843F
Cataclastic breccias, 146–147, 148T
Cathodoluminescence, 815
Ceres, 349, 365, 366
Chalcogenide trends, 468
Chalcophile elements, 94, 376, 377, 447
Chassigny. *See* SNC meteorites
Chemical equilibrium, 384–385
Chondrites
 abundances of siderophiles, 421, 422F, 423F, 424–425
 classification, 15T, 16–21, 1155–1156
 elemental abundance patterns, 21F, 387F, 398F, 399F, 400F, 422F
 Fe in, 418–419F, 420F, 421
 fractionation
  elemental, 385–386, 387F, 388
  interpretation of patterns, 402, 403F, 404, 405F, 406, 407F, 408
  patterns, 397, 398F, 399F, 400F
  intergroup redox variations, 492, 493F, 494, 495F
 secondary properties, 22, 25, 26, 27
See also Carbonaceous chondrites; Enstatite chondrites; Meteorites, individual; Ordinary chondrites
Chondrules, 4, 9, 136, 336, 343, 387, 457
 chemical composition, 638, 639F, 640F, 1153
 crystallization, 631, 632, 642–643, 644F, 645
 defined, 619–623
 distribution to types, 626, 627T

experimental studies
 BO chondrules, 667F, 668T, 670–671, 672T
 PO chondrules, 663, 664F, 665–666, 668T, 669F
 pyroxene-rich, 672–674
 significance of, 674–675
 techniques in, 660–661, 662F, 663
formation, 1150
 conclusions regarding, 710
 conditions for, 681T, 682T
 energy for, 683–684, 697–700, 705–706
 environment for, 684, 685F, 686–687
 impact, 702–704
 in dusty solar nebula, 692–694
 infall, 701–702
 lightning, 706–708
 magnetic flares, 708–709
 models for, 689–692
 precursor components, 645, 646T, 647, 687–689
 future work, 1166, 1169–1171
 GOP chondrules, 625, 626
 isotopic exchange, 914–915F
 isotopic properties, 647, 648F, 649–650
 magnetic fields, 637
 matrix in, 731, 732F
 melting system, 641–642, 643F
 mineralogy, 628F, 629F, 630–631
 porphyritic and nonporphyritic, 625–626
 relict grains, 632–634
 size and shape, 635–636
 surface festures, 651–654
 texture, 623, 624F
See also Grains; Rims
Chromatography, 833
Circumstellar material, 948T, 949–951, 1066
See also Isotope effects; Nucleosynthesis
Clasts, 83, 103, 719, 722, 725, 734
 eucritic, 152F
 impact melt, 183, 184, 193
 in Allende, 156–157
 in fission-track dating, 293–294, 295
 in HEDs, 85, 86
 in howardites, 154F
 in Semarkona, 130
 in stony meteorites, 149T
 occurrence of, 150, 151
Clathrate hydrates, 574–575
Cloud rotation rates, 308–309
Clumping, 693, 889
^{247}Cm, 1103
CNO ices, 62
Co/Mg ratio, 90–91, 92F
Coagulation of particles, 317–318, 320, 349
 differential settling, 357–358

Coagulation (continued)
mechanisms, 354, 355F, 356–357
thermal, 356–357
time scales for, 368F
turbulence, 358–359
Cohenite, 598
Collision, 354–355
collisional growth of particles, 360–362
Collision-induced shock metamorphism, 169–171
Collisional efficiency, 361
Comet plasma tails, 206
Cometary origins of chondrites, 43, 52, 55–56, 134
Cometesimals. See Planetesimals
Comets, 36–37, 316
cometary fragments, 38, 39–40
composition, 530
Encke, 43
Halley, 575, 849, 851, 877, 879F, 885–886
IDPs and, 884–885, 887, 888
Kohoutek, 877, 878F, 879F, 884–885
nuclei, 574–575
organic matter in, 851
Schwassmann-Wachmann I, 586
Comminution, 741
Compaction ages. See Brecciation
"Compound" chondrules, 651, 687
Concordia diagrams, 255F
Condensation, 1153
in chondrule formation, 692
nebular condensation, 740–741
of Mg-silicates and S, 377–378
of some elements, 382T
See also individual elements
Cooling rates, 107, 108, 109, 112, 278–281, 293, 346, 385, 1157
Core formation, 89–96
Cores, 512, 1150
"Cosmic abundances," 6, 999F, 1005
Cosmic rays. See Galactic cosmic rays; Solar cosmic rays
Cosmochemistry, 331, 375–376, 377
Coulomb barrier, 216, 1000
Cr, 524
isotope anomalies, 1078, 1080F, 1082F, 1087
Cratering, 651–654, 687
Curie temperature, 597, 598, 607

D, 583–584
ion-molecule reactions, 969, 970T, 971F
D/H ratios
anomalies, 882–883
carriers, 963, 964F, 965F, 966
fractionation, 973, 974

in IDPs, 882–883, 967
in meteorites, 959, 960, 961T–962T
"Dark-zoned" chondrules, 626
Decay systems. See Radiometric dating
Degassing, 285
Deimos, 145
Dendritic solidification, 77
Depletion, 106
of moderately volatile elements, 441–442, 453–455
See also under individual bodies and element classifications
Diamond, 939, 940, 948T, 950, 986, 1179
Dicarboxylic acids, 830, 846–847
Diffusion rates, 385
Diogenites, 12, 76
See also HED meteorites
Disequilibrium condensation, 740
Disequilibrium shock effects, 181
Doppler shifts, 308
Drag. See Gas drag
Dust. See Interplanetary dust particles (IDPs)
Dust/gas ratio, 320–322, 323F, 354
Dwarf stars, 1022, 1023, 1024F

Earth
atmosphere, 579, 580, 581–583
density, 417, 517
element ratios, 518, 519F, 520F, 521, 523, 524, 570
extinct radionuclides, 1095, 1110, 1111
IDPs in, 863
magnetosphere, 705–706
Mn content of mantle, 452
noble gases, 528, 566
O-isotopes, 910–911
Earth-crossing orbits, 38, 41, 42, 57, 283–284
Electromagnetic induction, 75
Electron spin resonance, 490
Elements, general
abundance smoothness, 1008
abundances, 5F, 7T–8T
cosmochemical classification, 377F, 378–379, 380
highly labile, 16F, 20, 462–464, 466–469, 1166
in Antarctic meteorites, 481, 482F
in Cumberland Falls inclusion, 482, 483F
in carbonaceous chondrites, 470–471
in enstatite chondrites, 472–473
in ordinary chondrites, 474, 475T, 476–480
significance, 484–485
moderately volatile, 437–438, 448T
condensation temperatures, 438, 439T, 440

fractionation, 456–458
geochemical classification, 441–442
  in carbonaceous chondrites, 442–446
  in enstatite chondrites, 448–449
  in ordinary chondrites, 447–448
  in ungrouped meteorites, 449–450
  patterns of, 454, 455
  planetary aspect of, 450, 451F, 452F, 453
  significance, 453–455
  solar abundances, 1006F, 1007F, 1009F
  sources of information regarding, 381–388
  See also Fractionation process; Nucleosynthesis *and individual elements and classification of elements*
Energy dispersive spectroscopy (EDS), 862, 865
Enstatite chondrites, 6, 9, 16, 17, 1157
  elemental variations, 390, 392
  noble gases, 569–570
  non-Antarctic, 472, 473F
  O-fugacity data, 504
  paleomagnetic intensity, 611
Epsilon-phase, 189
Equilibrium condensation, 81, 103, 769, 780–781, 782
  calculations, 466–467
  theory, 515–516
Equilibrium shock effects, 180–181
Equilibrium thermodynamics, 331
Eu anomalies, 79, 88, 779
Eucrites, 12, 15, 57, 75, 76
  depletion factors, 84T
  element ratios, 524
  O isotopes, 911
  origin and composition, 80, 81T, 82F, 83–84, 88
  parent body, 452
  See also HED meteorites
Europa, 530
"Explosive burning," 1040
Extinct-nuclide dating, 256
  See also Radionuclides, extinct

Fall-times of meteorites, 40, 41T, 42
Fe
  as key element, 379
  chemistry, 383–384
  condensation of, 381
  Fe abundance peak, 1004, 1075
  fractionation, 427–429
  oxidation, 16, 18F, 19F, 20
  See also Siderophile elements
Fe/Si ratios, 413, 417, 419
Fireballs, 36, 38, 39
Fischer-Tropsch type (FTT) process, 839, 841, 844, 845, 846, 847, 972, 1176
Fission-track methods, 291–294

Fluffy Type A inclusions. *See* Inclusions
"Fluid-drop chondrules," 635
Fossil-grain theory, 1130
Fractionation processes, 376, 1153, 1167
  in basalt formation, 80–81, 83–89
  in chondrites, 385–388, 405–413, 431, 433
  in eucrite formation, 80, 81
  in processing atmospheric volatiles, 568–572
  isotopic, 901
  Mg/Si, 411, 413
  of moderately volatile elements, 451–452
  on Moon, 573, 574
  See also under individual bodies and element classifications
Fragmental breccias, 116, 118T
Framboids, 128, 129F
Free-decay interval, 1116
Freeze-thaw disaggregation, 774
Fremdlinge, 18, 489, 749, 750F, 751, 1151, 1173
FU Orionis phase, 309, 323
FUN inclusions. *See* Refractory inclusions
Fused-bead method, 391

Galactic cosmic rays, 205, 225, 226, 233, 291
  defined, 208T, 209–210
  elemental abundances and isotopic ratios, 212
  energy spectrum, 217
  VH nuclei, 213, 224, 226, 230
Galaxies
  chemical evolution of, 1026, 1027F, 1028–1031
  disk galaxies, 1027F
  elements in, 1024–1026
  M81 (spiral), 1023, 1025F
  Milky Way, 1022, 1024, 1026
Gamma phase. *See* Taenite
Gamma-ray astronomy, 1058, 1059
Gamma-ray-emitting radionuclides, 226
Ganymede, 530
Gas accretion, 317–318
Gas drag, 321, 356, 368
  effect on planetesimals, 362, 363
  in meteorite formation, 330, 331
Gas-dust equilibrium, 381
Gas-retention ages, 277–278, 281
Ge, 14, 453
Gegenschein, 884
Glass, 148, 159, 176
  glassy spherules, 622, 623
"Goldreich-Ward planetesimals," 352
Grains
  future work, 1173–1174, 1186
  grain settling, 314

Grains (*continued*)
  growth/destruction, 317–319, 320, 324
  in solar nebula, 1153
  metal phase, 816–817
  mineral grains in chondrites, 808, 809, 810F, 811F, 812
  presolar
    C grains, 948T, 949–951, 985–986
    destruction and interstellar mixing, 986–988
    future work, 988–989
    single pyroxene, 815–816
    See also Relict grains
Granulitic breccias, 147, 148T
Graphite, 503–504, 985–986

H
  isotopic components in meteorites, 966–967, 968
  See also D/H ratios
Halogens, 379, 444, 446
HAP phase, 119
Hayashi stage, 75
HDO, 568
He
  isotopic pattern, 546–547
  See also Noble gases
HED meteorites
  basalts and core formation in parent body, 80, 89–91, 92F, 94–96
  breccias, 153, 160
  depletion factors, 92F, 93F, 94
  magnetic minerals in, 601
  shock effects in, 186, 188
Herbig-Haro objects, 693
Heterogeneous-accretion model, 516
Hexahedrites, 12–13
Hibonite, 752, 764F, 771–772, 774–775, 782
Homogeneous-accretion model, 516
"Hot nebula" problem, 780–781
Howardites, 12, 15, 57
  basalts in, 85F, 86
  See also HED meteorites
HRTEM imaging, 118, 121
Hugoniot curve, 167, 168F, 191, 192F
Hydrocryogenic alteration, 132–133
Hydrodynamic escape, 577–580, 581–583
Hydroxyacids, 844–846
Hydroxycarboxylic acids, 831
Hysteresis parameters of meteorites, 599, 600F, 601

^{129}I, 1105
  excess, 1127, 1130
  in planets, 1110, 1111
  isotopic variations, 1129–1130
  life, 1120, 1121, 1122, 1123

I-Xe dating system, 1127, 1128F
  correlation with chemical properties, 1134, 1135F
  correlations with other chronometers, 1131–1132
  future work, 1181, 1182
  location of ^{129}Xe excess, 1136–1138
  resetting system, 1138–1139
  shock effects, 1139–1140
  significance of, 1140–1144
  ^{129}Xe/^{132}Xe ratios and, 1132, 1133F, 1134
Iapetus, 849, 1151
Ice in atmosphere formation, 585–586
Igneous processes, 75, 691, 1158–1159
  See also Basalt formation; HED meteorites; Meteorites, general
Impact, 50, 51, 151
  cratering, 170, 171
  in chondrule formation, 689–691
  melting, 74
  velocities, 193T, 194F, 195F
  See also Brecciation; Shock effects
Impact-melt breccias, 117, 118T, 170, 183
Impedance-match method, 191
Inclusions, 9, 157, 621, 729, 1153
  A16-S3, 788, 789
  ALVIN, 789–790
  Blue Angel, 772, 774, 784, 792, 796
  C1, 1064, 1065, 1071F, 1072–1074, 1076–1078, 1076F, 1078F, 1079F, 1080F, 1082
  corundum-bearing, 775
  dark inclusions, 729, 735
  EGG-3, 1065, 1078F, 1079F, 1131
  EK 1-4-1, 1064, 1065, 1071F, 1072–1074, 1074F, 1076–1083, 1076F, 1078F, 1079, 1087, 1131
  Fluffy Type A, 723, 760–761, 784
  GR-1, 790
  HAL, 779, 1076–1077, 1076F, 1082
  MUM-I, 773–774, 777
  OSCAR, 770, 771
  RNZ, 770, 771
  troilite, 744
  USNM 1623-5, 789
  WA, 1102F, 1108
  See also CAIs; Refractory inclusions
Incompatible trace elements, 83, 84
Induction heating of asteroids, 75, 97
Infall rates, 335, 338–339, 1027–1028
Instrumental neutron activation analysis (INAA), 391
Intergranular melting, 176, 192
Intergroup redox variations, 492–494, 495F
Interplanetary dust particles (IDPs), 861–862
  anhydrous, 889, 890
  aqueous alteration and, 130F, 131, 140

astrophysical objects and, 877, 878, 879F, 880, 881F
crystal growth, 871F, 872
D excesses in, 882–884, 967
future work, 1164, 1177–1178, 1182–1183
isotopic measurements, 882–884
luminescence spectra of, 875, 880
mineralogical properties, 868, 869F, 870
optical properties, 873F, 874F, 875, 876F
origin of, 863, 864F, 884–886
physical properties of, 865, 865F, 867F
solar-flare tracks and, 887, 888F
Interstellar cloud material, 969–979, 970T, 971F, 975F, 1179–1180
Interstellar medium (ISM), 1029, 1033, 1057–1058, 1059
See also Nucleosynthesis
Interstellar molecules
as origin of D-rich material, 976, 977F, 978–979
ion-molecule reactions, 969, 971
synthesis of deuterated molecules, 972–974
See also D; Grains
Io, 580
Ions
ion-molecule reactions, 969–974, 976
IRAS dust bands, 884, 886
Irradiation records, 229
future work, 1160–1162
in early solar-system chronology, 230–235
models for meteorite parent-body formation, 230–236
See also Particles, energetic
Isochron diagrams, 253, 254F
Isotope-dilution mass-spectroscopy method, 392
Isotope effects
defined, 901–902
O reservoirs and exchange, 912–914, 915F, 916
of bulk meteorites, 908, 909, 910F, 913
Isotopic anomalies, 1059, 1063, 1064T, 1065
heavy elements
r-, s-, and p- processes, 1069, 1070F, 1071F, 1072–1074
interpreting data, 1066–1069
theoretical enhancement factors, 1083, 1084T, 1084, 1085F
See also Refractory inclusions *and individual elements*

Jupiter, 57, 60, 61F, 63, 64, 283, 365, 529–530, 582–583, 969

K-Ar dating, 249, 260, 278, 294, 1135, 1136

Kamacite, 11F, 12, 13, 77, 189–191, 421, 596
magnetic trends, 599, 601
Keplerian velocity, 330, 331, 334
Kerogen, 836–838, 961, 964, 966, 1176–1177
Kirkwood gap, 9, 10
Kr, 1097
isotopic patterns, 552F, 553T, 554, 936F, 944–945
See also Noble gases
KREEP, 89

LAP phase, 119
Lightning, 706–708
"Limiting" flux, 578–579
Lithification process, 159–161, 176, 183, 184
Lithophile elements, 15, 16, 376, 377
refractory, 395–396
CAI patterns, 400–402, 409, 410F
future work, 410–411, 412T, 413, 1163–1164
in chondrites, 397–400, 402–408
Low-mass/high mass stars, 305–306
"Low-temperature age plateaux," 281

Magma-ocean fractionation, 80–81, 86
Magnetic flaring, 708–709
Magnetic induction, 133
Magnetic properties of meteorites, 595, 599–601, 1167
magnetic minerals in, 596T, 597–599
paleointensity, 609–611
significance of paleomagnetism, 612
See also Natural remanent magnetization
Magnetite, 128, 598
Mars, 60, 63
as source of SNC meteorites, 36, 566, 568, 572–573
atmosphere, 576–577, 579, 580, 581
density, 517
ejecta, 286, 287
element ratios, 521, 523, 570
extinct radionuclides, 1110, 1111
gases, 528, 529, 566
satellites, 145
Mars-crossing orbits, 42
Maskelynite, 166, 182
Matrix of chondrites, 9, 387, 620–621, 1153
defined, 718, 719
chemical composition
in carbonaceous chondrites, 733F, 734T
in ordinary chondrites, 730T, 731F, 732F
future work, 1171–1172
metamorphism and alteration, 736–738

Matrix of chondrites (*continued*)
    mineralogy and petrology, 720, 721*T*
        in carbonaceous chondrites, 725–726, 727*T*, 728*T*, 729*T*, 730
        in ordinary chondrites, 722*F*, 723*F*, 724*F*, 725, 726*F*
    O isotope data, 735*F*, 736
    origin of material, 738–739, 740*T*, 741–742
    secondary processes, 742
Maunder Minimum, 226
Megaregolith, 171
Megaregolith model for gas-rich meteorite formation, 239
Melt pockets, 176, 181–182
Melting system, open and closed, 641–642, 643
Mercury (planet), 145, 417, 517, 529
Mesosiderites, 12, 15, 58, 196, 504
Metal-silicate fractionation, 51–52, 418, 427*F*, 428–429, 431–432
Metamorphism, 22–23, 239, 1150
    See also Thermal metamorphism of chondrites
Meteorites, general
    asteroidal origins, 36–37, 56–58
        evidence linking with S-asteroids, 44–45
        mechanisms for delivery to Earth, 41–44
        orbits, 38, 39*F*, 40–41
        resolutions to spectrophotometric paradox, 49–52, 55–56
        spectrophotometric paradox defined, 45–46*F*, 47*F*, 48
    calculating fO$_2$ in, 490*T*, 491*F*
    classification of, 3, 4*T*, 6, 29
    gas-rich, 157–158, 232*T*, 236–239, 1162
        irradiation records in, 231–236
        model for parent-body formation, 236–239
    irons, 6, 13*F*, 14, 452, 493–494, 504
        energetic-particle events, 226–227
        exposure ages, 207*F*, 222
        IAB irons, 12, 76, 78
        igneous activity, 76–80
        shock effects, 188–191
        siderophiles in, 425, 426*F*
    porous/nonporous, 173, 176, 180
    presolar components, 948*T*, 949–952
    primitive material in, 715–717
    reduced meteorites, 445
    relationship to planets, 450–453, 518*F*, 530–531
    specimens of, 10*F*, 11*F*
    stony-irons, 6, 9, 12, 48
        breccias, 146, 147*T*, 148–149*T*
        ungrouped, 449–450
    See also individual meteorite classifications

Meteorites, individual
    Abee, 472, 473, 598
    Acapulco, 78, 449, 450*F*, 494
    Al Rais, 964, 968
    ALHA 76009, 607
    ALHA 77081, 78, 449, 492
    ALHA 77257, 609
    ALHA 77260, 605
    ALHA 77278, 492
    ALHA 77307, 811
    ALHA 78113, 449, 450
    Allegan, 647
    Allende, 21, 464, 465*T*, 610
        age of, 260, 261*F*, 262–263
        anomalies in, 1064–1065
        CAIs. *See* Inclusions
        chondrules, 647, 649, 738
        fluid alteration in, 1138–1139
        I-Xe age, 1136, 1143
        importance of, 799, 820, 1172
        inclusions, 119, 156*F*, 157, 160, 161, 271, 272, 396, 400, 752, 753, 760–761, 763, 766, 793
        isotope effects, 877–878, 880
        matrix, 162*F*, 726, 1131
        Ne in, 546
        noble gas in, 541
        NRM in, 607, 608–609
        O isotopes, 900*F*
        REE in inclusions, 755, 758
    AMP group, 911
    Angra Dos Reis (ADOR), 12, 78–79, 97, 263, 264*T*, 265, 272, 291, 1101
        sea 10
    Anlong, 494
    Arapahoe, 1143
    Arch, 445, 499
    Bald Mountain, 605
    Bali, 793
    Barwell, 284
    Bencubbin, 12, 78, 947
    Beréba, 266
    Bishunpur, 129, 719, 722, 815, 960, 963, 965
    Bjurböle, 607, 635, 647, 649, 1129, 1131, 1142
    Bouvante, 85, 86, 88
    Brachina, 56, 78
    Bruderheim, 283, 647
    Cangas de Onis, 150*F*
    Canyon Diablo, 252, 255, 260, 262, 266
    Chainpur
        chondrules, 635, 645, 647, 649
        D/H ratios, 959, 960
        matrix, 722, 1131, 1141–1142
        rims, 720–721
    Changde, 494

Changxing, 494
Cochabamba, 125
Cold Bokkeveld, 121, 125, 126F, 824, 1138
Colony, 770
Crescent, 824
Cumberland Falls, 188, 449, 450, 482, 483F
Dhajala, 494, 651, 777, 778, 779
Dimmitt, 936
Djermaia, 224
Dyalpur, 554
EETA 79001, 286, 539, 572, 573
Efremovka, 445, 752, 753, 763, 1110F, 1125
Enon, 449
Enshi, 494
Essebi, 499, 752
Fayetteville, 292, 547
Felix, 491
Goalpara, 609
Grant, 220
Grosnaja, 499, 726, 753
Guareña, 279, 1158
Homestead, 268
Ibitira, 84, 267
Indarch, 472
Isna, 770
Ivuna, 127, 959
Jilin, 217
Jodzie, 153–154, 155F
Jonzac, 272
Juvinas, 266, 267
Kaba, 726
Kaidun, 964, 968
Kakangari, 78, 494, 720
Kapoeta, 86, 88, 153F, 233, 295
Kelly, 151
Kernouve, 1143
Khohar, 467, 724
Knyahinya, 268
Krymka, 129, 130, 724, 737, 936, 965
Lancé, 118, 119, 770, 771
Leoville, 445, 492, 499, 760–761, 767, 916
Lodran, 12, 78
Lunan, 494
Marjalahti, 91
Mazapil, 36
Menow, 1143
Mezö-Madaras, 269, 279, 636
Mighei, 124F, 139F, 824
Mokoia, 119F, 726, 738, 763, 959
Mount Morris, 449, 494
Mundrabilla, 1143
Murchison, 125, 133, 362, 444, 1172
    aliphatic hydrocarbons, 826, 827
    amino-acid content, 821, 822F, 823–824, 845–846
    aromatic hydrocarbons in, 827–829
    carboxylic acids in, 829–831, 842, 843F
    dicarboxylic acids in, 846–847
    grains, 809, 810, 811, 816
    I-Xe age, 1142, 1143–1144
    importance of, 820–821
    isotope patterns, 776, 914
    matrix, 123F, 775
    Ne in, 546, 931, 933
    other organic matter, 834, 838, 843–844, 848
    Xe-S in, 942F, 946
Murray, 126F, 445, 776, 824, 933, 959
    chondrules, 635, 645
    organic matter in, 829, 834
Nadiabondi, 1143
Nawapali, 121, 125
Netschaëvo, 494
Nogoya, 123F, 125, 138, 139, 824
Nuevo Laredo, 85, 260, 266, 267–268
Olivenza, 605–606
Orgueil, 271, 287, 295, 824, 838, 959
    aqueous alteration, 134, 140
    I-Xe age, 1136, 1142, 1143
    Ne in, 930–931
    sulfates in, 127, 128F
Ornans, 499, 645, 769, 770, 1172
Parnallee, 649
Peace River, 283, 284F
Pesyanoe, 231, 535, 537
Piancaldoli, 636, 654
Pontlyfni, 449, 494
Qingzhen, 472, 645, 778
Renazzo, 636, 934, 961, 964F, 965, 968
St. Mesmin, 224, 293, 484
St. Séverin, 1157
Santa Cruz, 824
Semarkona, 129, 491, 659, 1139
    chondrules, 130, 429–430, 636, 642, 644F, 645, 649
    D in, 960, 963, 964, 965
    inclusions, 777, 778F
    matrix, 723, 724, 725, 737, 1159
Sharps, 724, 725
Shaw, 280
Sioux City, 266
South Oman, 540, 555
Stannern, 84, 85, 86, 88, 266, 272
Staroe Pesyanoe. *See* Pesyanoe
Sepuhee, 480
Suwahib (Buwah), 494
Tennasilm, 257
Tierra Blanca, 449
Tieschitz, 129, 130, 636–637, 724, 725

Meteorites (*continued*)
  Toluca, 1157
  Verkhne Dnieprovsk, 191
  Vigarano, 118, 443, 445, 726, 738, 1143–1144
    inclusions, 752, 753, 760–761, 767, 784–785, 789
  Weatherford, 78, 947
  Weston, 223, 233, 293
  Willaroy, 494
  Winona, 12, 78, 449, 494
  Xingyang, 494
  Y-7308, 86, 87, 272
  Y-74450, 85, 88
  Y-75011, 267
  Y-790003, 968–969
  Y-790112, 968–969
  Y-82042, 457
  Ybbitz, 779
^{26}Mg, 1101, 1102F, 1103, 1108–1109, 1110F
"Microchondrules," 636
Microcraters, 148, 159
Microdistribution studies, 466
Micrometeorites. *See* Interplanetary dust particles (IDPs)
Microtwins, 190
Midinfrared spectra of IDPs, 873–875
Milky Way. *See* Galaxies
Miller-Urey (MU) synthesis, 839, 841, 845, 1175, 1176
Minimum-mass nebula, 316
Mixing diagrams, 402, 403F, 404, 405F
Mn, 524
^{53}Mn, 1104
Molecular clouds, 305, 311
Mo, 91F
Monte Carlo techniques, 221
Moon, 63, 273, 529, 1167
  atmosphere, 573–574
  breccias, 148–149, 159, 547, 548
  density, 417
  elements in, 452, 524
  extinct radionuclides, 1095, 1110, 1112
  impact history, 282
  O isotopes, 910, 911
  regoliths, 144, 145
MORP fireballs, 39
Multiple zone mixing (MZM), 1085, 1087
Murchison meteorite. *See* Meteorites, individual
"Mysterite," 480

N
  anomaly, 947, 949
  isotope patterns, 907, 968, 1161, 1162
Na/Mg ratios, 437
Nakhlites. *See* SNC meteorites

Natural remanent magnetization (NRM), 595, 601, 602F, 603F, 604F, 605, 611
  carriers of, 598, 599, 608–609
  heating and shock effects, 606–607
  heterogeneous magnetization, 607
Nd, 252, 1071F, 1072–1073, 1101
Ne
  isotope patterns, 543, 544F, 545–546, 930F, 932F
  planetary Ne, 938T
  solar Ne, 537T, 544F, 545, 548T
  spallation-produced ^{21}Ne, 230F, 233–235, 239
Ne-E, 929, 930F, 931F, 932F, 933–934, 1106–1107
Neptune, 316
Neumann bands, 189
Neutron activation analysis (NAA), 391
Neutron capture
  processes involving, 1000, 1001F, 1004, 1010
  p-process, 1003
  r-process, 1002–1003
  s-process, 1001–1002F, 1010
Neutron decay, 1000–1003
Neutron-rich equilibria, 1047
Ni fractionation, 13, 14, 427–429
Nitrogen heterocycles, 831–833
Noble gases, 157, 158, 1161
  components of, 928–929
  shock effects, 184–185
  trapped in meteorites, 535–536
    Ar, 554–555
    future work, 560–561
    He, 546–547
    Kr, 552–554
    location of, 540, 541F, 542–543
    Ne isotope patterns, 543–546
    planetary pattern, 527, 538F, 539, 556–558, 559F, 560
    solar/subsolar patterns, 527, 536, 537T, 540, 542–543
    Xe, 547–551
Novae, 1057–1058
Nucleocosmochronology, 1114–1116, 1117T
  future work, 1181–1183
  long-lived radionuclides, 1117–1119
  short-lived radionuclides, 1119–1121
  significance of, 1124–1125
  very short-lived radionuclides, 1121–1124
  See also I-Xe dating system; ^{26}Al
Nucleosynthesis, 342, 908, 939, 995–996, 1056
  early theories, 1000–1004
  future work, 1180–1181
  heavy element
    r-process, 1014F, 1015–1017, 1150
    s-process, 1011–1012, 1013F

nuclide abundances, 1004–1008, 1010
production histories, 1115F
shell nucleosynthesis in massive stars,
    1039, 1040F
  C and Ne burning, 1040–1043
  O burning, 1043–1046
  problem nuclei, 1047–1049
stellar
  closed-box model, 1032
  double-shell-asymptotic-giant-branch-
    burning, 1051–1052, 1053F, 1054–
    1056
  early, 1021–1023
  in Big Bang, 1024–1026
  infall rate, 1033–1035
  novae, 1057–1058
  related to degenerate cores, 1049, 1051
  significance, 1058–1059
  sources, 1050T–1051T
  thermonuclear evolution, 1036, 1037F,
    1038–1039
  Type I Supernovae, 1056–1057
Suess abundance rules, 997–999
See also Galaxies; Isotopic anomalies; Radionuclides, extinct
Nuclides
  abundance regularities, 997–998, 999F
  cosmogenic, 218T
  See also Nucleosynthesis; Radionuclides, extinct
"Nuevo Laredo trend," 83

O
  ^{16}O anomalies, 411, 526, 527F, 918–919
  as volatile element, 380
  in galaxies, 1023–1024
  O burning, 1043, 1044, 1045F, 1046F
  O yield in ISM, 1025F, 1038–1039
  See also Nucleosynthesis
O fugacity, 107, 440, 460
  in carbonaceous chondrites, 499T, 500F
  in chondrule formation, 684–685
  methods for measuring, 490–492
  silicate-dust enrichments, 343, 344, 501,
    502T
O isotope effects, 20–21, 133, 902–904,
    905F, 906, 908
  fractionation, 913–914
  in planet composition, 526, 527F
  magnitude of effect, 909, 910–911
  See also Matrix of chondrites; Solar nebula
Occam's razor, 233
Octahedrites, 13
Olivine, 1153, 1161–1162
  condensation, 382–383
  during metamorphism, 103
  fayalitic, 497, 498, 501, 507
  grains, 809–812, 813F, 814, 815

  in chondrite matrix, 723–724, 725, 726,
    727T, 739, 740T, 741
  in chondrules, 625–626
  olivine-rich rocks, 177–178T
Onion-shell models, 108, 109F, 294
Oort cloud, 37, 316, 324, 574
Opaque minerals, 729T
Orbital decay, 356, 369
Orbits of meteorites, 38, 39F, 40–41
Ordinary chondrites, 6, 9, 16, 135
  elemental variations, 390, 392
  metamorphism, 103–107, 104F, 105F,
    110–111
  mineralogy, 19, 20F
  moderately volatile elements, 447–448
  noble gases, 542
  non-Antarctic equilibrated, 476, 477F,
    478, 479F, 480F, 481
  non-Antarctic unequilibrated, 474, 475,
    476F
  O-fugacity data, 505
  paleomagnetic intensity, 610
  shock facies, 28T
  subtypes, 25T, 26
  volatile elements, 474–480
  See also Elements, general; Matrix of
    chondrites
Organic matter. See Carbonaceous chondrites
    and other individual bodies
Orion nebula, 880
Outgassing-age distribution, 281, 285
Oxidation states
  future work, 1166–1167
  indications in chondrites, 492–495
  parent-body processes, 502, 502F, 504–
    505, 506F
  significance of, 506–508
  solar-nebular processes, 495–498, 501–502

P-T conditions, 76, 115, 418
P-T-X-H_2O conditions, 116
Pallasites, 12, 15, 56, 58
Parthenope, 49
Particle-track radiography, 466
Particles. See Interplanetary dust particles
    (IDPs); Particles, energetic; Planetesimals
Particles, energetic
  classes, 208T
  environment
    nature of, 207–213
    of early solar system, 228–230
    time variations in, 225–228
  modes and products of interaction
    determining exposure ages, 221–225
    direct implantation, 213
    energy loss and lattice damage, 213–
      217, 214F

Particles (*continued*)
  nuclear reactions, 216–221, 218*T*
Pb-Pb ages, 262, 267, 271*T*, 281, 1157
^{107}Pd, 1100*F*, 1107
Pd condensation temperature, 440*T*
Perihelia of meteorites, 38, 39, 40*F*, 43
Petrographic types of meteorites, 23*T*–24*T*
Phase-equilibria methods, 491
Phobos, 145
Phoebe, 586
Photolysis, 976–977
Photometric photography, 38
Phyllosilicates, 107, 115, 121, 729
Pigeonite, 86
Pioneer Venus Mission, 566
Plane-front solidification, 77
Planetesimals, 316
  Al-rich, 109
  chondrule formation and, 691–692
  formation of, 348–349, 350*T*, 351
    collisional growth and radial migration, 61*F*, 360–362
    conclusions regarding, 367–369
    gravitational accretion, 362–367
    settling and coagulation, 351–352, 353*F*, 354, 355*F*, 356, 357–358
    thermal coagulation, 356–357
    turbulent coagulation, 358–359
  icy material, 574–575, 585–587
  impact of, 74
  in core composition, 513
  in planet composition, 524, 526
Planets
  atmosphere, 1168–1169
    hydrodynamic escape, 577–580
    impact mechanism, 576–577
    inner planets, 566, 567*T*, 568
    role of meteorites, 568–569, 570*F*, 571*F*, 572
    small bodies, 573–575
  chondritic meteorites and, 530–531
  chondrule formation and, 689–692
  composition, 1167
    cometary influx, 526
    major elements, 518–519
    meteoritic analogy, 512–513
    models for, 513–517
    noble gases, 527, 528*F*, 529, 567*T*, 570*F*, 571*F*
    O isotope data, 526, 527*F*
    refractory-element ratios, 519*F*, 520*F*, 521*F*, 522*F*, 523–524
    siderophile trace elements, 525–526
  density of inner planets, 517*T*, 518*F*
  differentiated, 441, 453
  extinct radionuclides in, 1110–1111

outer-planet satellites, 529–530
See also individual planets
Platelets, 128, 871, 889
Poorly characterized phases (PCPs), 121–122, 598, 599
POP spherules, 674
Post-accretionary thermal processing, 108–109, 467–468, 469*T*, 484–485
Poynting-Robertson drag, 887
PP spherules, 673
PR*, 91
Prairie Network fireball data, 51
Prior's Rules, 418–419, 492
Progressive shock metamorphism, 179*T*, 180
Protoplanets, 515
See also Planetesimals
Protostars, 308, 309, 310
Protostellar collapse
  axisymmetric models, 311–312, 314, 315
  spherically symmetric models, 310–311
  three-dimensional models, 312–313
Protostellar wind, 309
Proto-Sun, 314–315, 322–324, 330–331
^{244}Pu, 291, 292, 1094–1095, 1097–1099, 1100, 1101, 1102, 1113, 1114, 1157
Pu fission tracks, 291, 293
Pu/U fractionation, 291–293, 294
Pyroxene, 17, 18, 103, 172, 173, 293, 1153, 1161–1162
See also Chondrules
Pyrrhotite, 118*T*, 598

Q component, 539, 541–542, 571, 572, 1168
Q-Ne, 546
Q-type planetary noble gases, 556, 558

Radial migration, 360–362, 369, 1153
Radiative acceleration, 321
Radiative transfer calculations, 322, 324
Radioactive decay, 901, 1001*F*, 1002, 1003, 1094, 1095, 1115, 1121
Radioactive isotopes, 74–75
Radiochemical neutron activation (RNAA), 391
Radiometric dating, 249, 260–261, 295
  decay constants, 250*T*, 251
  methods for, 253–257
  normalization conventions, 251–252
  primordial ratios, 253*T*
Radionuclides, 107, 250*T*
See also ^{129}I and other individual radionuclides
Radionuclides, extinct
  "cosmic chemical memory," 1109*F*
  defined, 1093–1095
  evidence for, 1095, 1096*T*, 1097–1104
  future work, 1181–1182

INDEX

"live" in early solar system, 1105–1110, 1150
planetary occurrences, 1110–1111
See also Nucleocosmochronology
Raman microprobe technique, 875, 876F, 877, 882F
Rankins-Hugoniot equation, 169
Rare Earth Elements (REEs), 79, 408F, 779, 1153
  Group II CAI patterns, 410F, 756F
  in inclusions, 755, 758, 775, 783, 786
  in rims, 790–791
  patterns, 401, 409, 410F, 413, 756F
Rb-Sr dating system, 259, 260, 261, 267, 287, 295, 1137, 1157, 1162, 1165
Reaction rates, 385
Recrystallized matrix, 722
Red giants, 1022–1023, 1057
Reflectance spectrum, 46F, 47F
Refractory elements, 378
See also Lithophile elements
Refractory inclusions, 746–747, 754T
  Cr anomalies, 1078, 1080, 1087
  defined, 747
  FUN, 396, 411, 766, 791, 904, 1181
  C1, 1069
  EK 1-4-1, 1069–1073, 1076–1079
  HAL, 1076, 1077
  history for, 913F, 914
  future work, 1172–1173
  in CV3 chondrites, 759
  isotope anomalies in, 1065, 1069, 1070F, 1071F, 1072–1073, 1076–1077
  primary phases, 748, 749F, 750–751
  rim sequences, 751F, 752–753
  secondary phases, 753
Refractory metal nuggets, 749–751
Refractory spherules, 777
Regolith model for gas-rich meteorites, 236, 237
Regolithic breccias, 144–145, 194, 1160
  asteroidal regolith formation, 51, 52, 134, 159–160, 161F
  characteristics of, 150, 151F, 153–154, 156–157
  classification of, 146–149
  compaction ages, 289, 290, 296–297
  exposure ages, 236
  problem areas, 161–162
  trace elements in, 480, 484
Relict grains, 632–634, 796, 797, 798F, 1154
  relict olivine, 812–815
Remote-sensing techniques, 44–45
Resonance mechanism, 41, 42
Ribbons, 871
Rims, 719
  composition, 722, 729, 731, 732
  in matrix, 740, 741
  of chondrules, 652–654, 687
  of inclusions, 251F, 752–753, 774
  formation, 789–790
  Wark-Lovering rims, 790
  textures, 736
R_o, 1129, 1130, 1131, 1134–1136
See also ^{129}I
Rods, 871
Rotation, 321
RP chondrules, 672
"Rubble-pile" parent body, 108, 109F
Runaway growth, 366–367

Saponite, 119
Satellites, organic matter in, 849–850
Saturn, 529–530, 849, 969
Scanning electron microscope (SEM), 154, 156, 862, 865
Schreibersite, 598
Secondary-collision products, 43
Secondary processes, 71, 72F
See also individual processes
Sedimentation, 320–321
Semarkona meteorite. See Meteorites, individual
Serpentine, 127, 870, 871
"Sharp isochronism," 1128, 1129
Shergottites. See SNC meteorites
Shock effects, 22, 26, 27, 28T, 133
  brecciation, 169, 170F, 171–172
  chemical and physical effects, 184–185
  impact velocities and colliding bodies, 191–196
  in achondrites, 186–188
  in chondrite groups, 180–184
  pressure and temperature, 172–173F, 176, 180
  in irons, 188–189, 190F, 191
  physics of, 166–168
Shock heating, 167, 172–180, 281–286, 314, 468, 476–477
Shock lithification, 146, 160, 184
Shock metamorphism, 170
Shock veins, 181, 182F
Shock velocity, 167
Si
  burning, 1047, 1048
  isotopes, 916, 920
  normalization, 447–448
Siderophile elements, 15, 16, 376, 377, 378–379
  content variations in chondrites, 431, 432F
  depletion, 89, 90, 455, 457–458
  future work, 433–434, 1164–1165
  in iron meteorites, 425–426
  interpretation of patterns, 426, 427F, 428F, 429

Siderophile elements (*continued*)
  moderately volatile, 430–431
  overall abundance in chondrites, 418–420, 421–425
  refractory, 417–418, 422F, 423, 429–430
Sm, 1066, 1067F, 1068–1069
^{146}Sm, 1101, 1107, 1120–1121
Sm-Nd decay system, 249, 250, 251, 264, 265, 267, 287
Small-body model for gas-rich meteorite formation, 238–239
Smectite, 119, 120F, 129
SNC meteorites, 12, 36, 78, 524, 911
  chronology of, 286–287
  noble gases in, 566, 568, 572–573
Sobotkite, 119
Solar cosmic rays, 225–226, 233
Solar energetic particles, 211, 212, 1161
Solar flares, 157–158, 159, 209, 228, 996
Solar-flare particles, 206, 225
Solar-flare protons, 225
Solar-flare tracks, 145, 158, 233, 887, 888F
  VH ion tracks, 232
Solar nebula, 1151, 1152, 1153, 1167
  accretion disk model, 335–336, 337F, 338–339
    nebular gas pressure, 343, 344T
    other aspects of, 344–345
    recent models, 339–343
    viscous accretion disks, 332, 333F, 334–335
  Cameron & Pine 1973 model, 331–332
  Cameron's 1962 model, 330–331, 332
  equilibrium condensation, 780–781
  future work, 1178–1179
  isotopic variation in, 899–900
    causes, 901–904, 905F, 906–908
    reservoirs, 916–919
    significance of study, 919–920
  magnetic field in, 612, 1154
  primitive, 313–314, 315F, 316
  solid components, 1152
  temperature and pressure history, 1151
  thermal processing, 346
  time scales for evolution, 1150
Solar system, 1162–1163
  age of, 259–260, 265–267, 268, 269F, 1162
    significance of evidence, 270–273
  formation
    dust-to-gas ratios in, 320–322
    moderately volatile elements in, 455–456
    See also Solar nebula
  heating in, 74–76
  impact history, 282–283
  See also Protostellar collapse
Solar wind, 75, 159, 227, 230, 235, 516, 996
  as source of Ne, 545
  defined, 208
  implantation, 145, 158
  importance of records, 231
  particles, 206, 210
Solid-electrolyte-electrochemical method, 490
Spallation, 546, 901, 969, 1004, 1161
  importance of records, 233–235
  See also Particles, energetic
Spherulites, 128
"Spinach," 121, 123F, 137
Spinel, 18, 752, 755, 761, 762F, 782, 933, 950–951, 1179
Spiral density waves, 62, 315, 316
Sr ratios, 253, 267, 268, 271T, 294–295, 1165
Standard mean ocean water (SMOW), 20, 22F, 568, 978
Stars
  AGB stars, 1051, 1053F, 1054–1055
  disk stars, 1022, 1023
  formation, 710
  Population II, 1022, 1024
  solar-type, 305–306, 308–310
  See also Galaxies; Nucleosynthesis; Protostellar collapse
Stellar luminosity, 306, 309, 311
Stellar winds, 228, 235, 323–324
  See also Solar wind
STEM analysis, 865
Stepped-heating technique, 277, 278, 283F, 929
Stochastic effect, 44, 50
Stoichiometry, 399
Stokes drag law, 360
Strecker-cyanohydrin mechanism, 845
Suess abundance rules, 997–999
Sun, 4, 210, 456
  as source of energetic particles, 207–209
  bulk composition, 996–999
  energy efficiency, 705
  sunlight, 45
SUNOCONs, 1043, 1044, 1048
Sunspots, 226
Super-refractory material, 409–410
Supernovae, 1056–1057

T-Tauri stage, 75, 133, 228, 229, 233–236, 1160, 1161
T-Tauri stars, 76, 228, 309, 310, 311
T-Tauri wind, 349, 612
Taenite phase, 12, 13, 77, 189, 421, 597
Taurus-Auriga cloud complex, 306, 308, 309, 310
Taurus molecular cloud complex, 306, 307F
Tektites, 622
Teller-Redlich product rule, 902

TEM analysis, 118, 868
Tertiary processes, 72F
Tetrataenite, 597–598
  as NRM carrier, 608
  magnetic trend, 599, 601
Th, 1097, 1099
Th-Pb decay system, 249
Thermal gradients, 334
Thermal metamorphism, 278–281, 378
  future work, 1156, 1159–1160
  heat sources, 107–108
  in unequilibrated chondrites, 110–112
  parent-body structures, 108, 109F
  temperature and pressure during, 105–107
  textual evidence for, 103, 104F, 105F
  volatile elements in, 109–110, 463–464, 467–468, 476–480
Thermochemical calculations, 381–385
  variables in, 386–387
Thermodynamic calculations, 496
Thermoluminescence, 25–26, 110, 111F, 115, 184–185, 1156
Thermomagnetic analysis, 596, 597F
Thermonuclear synthesis. *See* Nucleosynthesis
Thermoremanent magnetization (TRM), 598, 607, 609
Ti isotope anomalies, 411, 916–917, 920, 1049, 1077, 1078F, 1079F, 1081F, 1082F, 1087, 1154
Titan, 585–586
Titanomagnetite, 598–599, 601
Tochilinite phase, 122, 123F, 124, 125F, 137–139
Total pressure, 384–385
Trace elements, 76
  distribution, 281
  highly volatile, 463, 464, 465T
  in chondrules, 638–639
  in inclusions, 782–783
  moderately volatile, 439–444, 446–450
  shock effects and, 184–185
  siderophile, 422–426, 429–431, 525F, 526
Transmission electron microscopy. *See* TEM analysis
Turbulence, 313, 321, 334, 338
  particle-settling and, 352, 353F, 354
  turbulent coagulation, 358–359

^{235}U, 1103
^{238}U, 291, 1097
U fission tracks, 291
U-Pb decay systems, 249, 250, 251, 253–254, 256, 260, 267
"Ultrarefractory component," 783
Ultraviolet flux, 349, 516
Ultraviolet luminosity, 228

Unequilibrated chondrites, 103, 107
"Unfrozen water," 132
Uranus, 529–530
Ureilites, 12, 79–80, 96–97, 188, 540, 911
Urey-Craig diagram, 419F

V, 524
V-Cr-Mn depletions, 524, 526, 530
Velocity of particles, 351F
Venera Missions, 566
Venus
  atmosphere, 580, 582, 583
  density, 517
  element ratios, 521, 583–584, 969
  noble gases in, 529, 542, 566, 584–587
Viking spacecraft, 572, 573
Viscous accretion disks. *See* Solar nebula
Viscous remanent magnetization (VRM), 602, 605
Visual radiants, 40
"Volatile-loss" process, 471
Vugs, 182, 1152

W 33A infrared object, 880, 881F
Water
  ice, 115, 133
  liquid, 133
  vapor, 131
Wet-chemistry method, 391
White dwarfs, 1056–1058
Widmanstätten structure, 13
Wollastonite needles, 783–784, 789, 1152

X component, 539, 542
X-ray fluorescence analysis, 391
Xe, 528, 539
  abundance, 569–570
  in planets, 581–582
  isotope patterns, 936F, 942F, 943F, 1096F, 1097, 1098F, 1139–1140, 1141T, 1142, 1143T
  See also I-Xe dating; Noble gases
^{129}Xe, 1105, 1107
  See also I-Xe dating
Xe-HL, 1168
  carriers of, 937, 939
  discovery and isolation, 934, 935F, 936F
  origin, 940, 941F
Xe/Kr ratios, 569, 570F
Xe-S
  components and carriers, 945F, 946–947
  discovery and origin, 941, 942, 943F, 944F
Xenoliths, 136, 150, 760, 793, 1153

Z elements, 997
Zodiacal light, 884